Mathematical Modeling and Simulation in Mechanics and Dynamic Systems, 3rd Edition

Mathematical Modeling and Simulation in Mechanics and Dynamic Systems, 3rd Edition

Guest Editors

Maria Luminița Scutaru
Catalin I. Pruncu
Luciano Lamberti

MDPI

Basel • Beijing • Wuhan • Barcelona • Belgrade • Novi Sad • Cluj • Manchester

Guest Editors
Maria Luminița Scutaru
Department of Mechanical Engineering
Transilvania University of Brașov
Brașov
Romania

Catalin I. Pruncu
Departimento di Meccanica, Matematica e Management
Politecnico di Bari
Bari
Italy

Luciano Lamberti
Dipartimento di Meccanica, Matematica e Management
Politecnico di Bari
Bari
Italy

Editorial Office
MDPI AG
Grosspeteranlage 5
4052 Basel, Switzerland

This is a reprint of the Special Issue, published open access by the journal *Mathematics* (ISSN 2227-7390), freely accessible at: https://www.mdpi.com/journal/mathematics/special_issues/Math_Model_Simul_Mech_Dyn_Syst_3.

For citation purposes, cite each article independently as indicated on the article page online and as indicated below:

Lastname, A.A.; Lastname, B.B. Article Title. *Journal Name* **Year**, *Volume Number*, Page Range.

ISBN 978-3-7258-7518-4 (Hbk)
ISBN 978-3-7258-7519-1 (PDF)
https://doi.org/10.3390/books978-3-7258-7519-1

Contents

About the Editors

Maria Luminiţa Scutaru

Maria Luminiţa Scutaru is Professor at the Transilvania University of Brasov, Romania. Her research interests include mathematical modeling, simulation of dynamic systems, applied mechanics, and control theory. She has published extensively in reputable journals and has participated in numerous international research projects in applied mathematics and engineering.

Catalin I. Pruncu

Catalin I. Pruncu is a Visiting Research Fellow at Brunel University London (UK) and a Senior Visiting Research Fellow at Politecnico di Bari (Italy). He previously served as an Associate Lecturer within the School of Engineering and the Built Environment at Buckinghamshire New University (BNU). With more than a decade of research experience across academia and industry, including IMI Truflo Marine Ltd., BAE Systems, Rolls Royce, and C2 Technology, Dr. Pruncu has also held research appointments at the University of Birmingham, Imperial College London, and the University of Strathclyde. His expertise spans numerical methods, machine learning (ML), the mechanical behaviour of materials, EBSD analysis, and advanced manufacturing processes.

Luciano Lamberti

Luciano Lamberti is currently a Full Professor at the Dipartimento di Meccanica, Matematica e Management, Politecnico di Bari, Bari, Italy. From 1998 to 1999, he was a Researcher at the University of Florida. In 2001, he served as a Research Associate at the Illinois Institute of Technology. His main interest is mathematical optimization and mechanics of materials.

Preface

Mathematical modeling and simulation play a crucial role in understanding, predicting, and controlling complex phenomena in mechanics and dynamic systems. Over the past decades, the development of computational methods and numerical algorithms has allowed researchers to tackle problems that were previously intractable. The present reprint contains the articles accepted for publication in the Special Issue "Mathematical Modeling and Simulation in Mechanics and Dynamic Systems, 3rd Edition" of the MDPI *Mathematics* journal. These contributions illustrate state-of-the-art research in modeling, simulation, and analysis of dynamic and mechanical systems, covering topics such as nonlinear dynamics, control systems, computational mechanics, numerical methods, multibody simulations, and applications in engineering and physics.

The collected papers demonstrate both theoretical developments and practical applications, providing insights into methods for simulating and understanding complex phenomena in mechanical and dynamic systems.

As Guest Editors of this Special Issue, we are grateful to the authors for their high-quality contributions, to the reviewers for their constructive feedback, and to the MDPI administrative staff for their support in bringing this project to completion. Special thanks are due to the Managing Editor of the Special Issue, Dr. Syna Mu, for his excellent collaboration and assistance.

Maria Luminiţa Scutaru, Catalin I. Pruncu, and Luciano Lamberti
Guest Editors

mathematics MDPI

Article

An Isogeometric Over-Deterministic Method (IG-ODM) to Determine Elastic Stress Intensity Factor (SIF) and T-Stress

Khadija Yakoubi [1,*], Ahmed Elkhalfi [1,*], Hassane Moustabchir [2], Abdeslam El Akkad [1,3], Maria Luminita Scutaru [4,*] and Sorin Vlase [4,5]

1 Faculty of Science and Technology, Sidi Mohamed Ben Abdellah University, Fez 30000, Morocco; abdeslam@usmba.ac.ma
2 Laboratory of Systems Engineering and Applications (LISA), Sidi Mohamed Ben Abdellah University, Fez 30000, Morocco; hmoustabchir@hotmail.com
3 Département de Mathématiques, Centre Regional des Métiers d'Education et de Formation de Fès Meknès (CRMEF Fès-Meknès), Rue de Koweit 49, Ville Nouvelle, Fez 30050, Morocco
4 Department of Mechanical Engineering, Faculty of Mechanical Engineering, Transylvania University of Brasov, B-dul Eroilor 29, 500036 Brasov, Romania; svlase@unitbv.ro
5 Technical Sciences Academy of Romania, B-dul Dacia 26, 030167 Bucharest, Romania
* Correspondence: khadija.yakoubi@usmba.ac.ma (K.Y.); ahmed.elkhalfi@usmba.ac.ma (A.E.); lscutaru@unitbv.ro (M.L.S.)

Abstract: In order to examine the significance of Stress Intensity Factor and T-stress (K-T parameters) in modeling pressure-cracked structures, we propose a novel method known as the Isogeometric Over-Deterministic Method IG-ODM. IG-ODM utilizes the computation of stress and displacement fields through Extended Isogeometric Analysis to improve the geometry and enhance the crack. Subsequently, these results are incorporated into the Williams expression, resulting in a set of deterministic equations that can be solved using a common solving method; this particular combination has never been attempted before. IG-ODM enables the computation of stress intensity factor SIF, T-stress, and higher-order parameters in the Williams expansion. To validate the effectiveness of this method, we conducted tests on a single-edge uniaxial-stress-cracked plate and a central uniaxial-stress-cracked plate. The results showed an error ranging from 0.06% to 2%. The obtained results demonstrate accuracy and satisfaction when compared to existing findings.

Keywords: T-stress; X-IGA; over-deterministic method; IG-ODM; abaqus; MATLAB; NURBS

MSC: 82C27; 65K15

1. Introduction

Asymptotic analysis is an approach which consists of giving an asymptotic development using the defect parameters and the links with the stress/strain field around the crack. According to Cotterell [1], the first term of Williams expansion is the stress intensity factor SIF, determining crack initiation, the next is the T-stress controlling the stability of the crack direction, and the third verifies the stability of the crack propagation.

Several studies have demonstrated that T-stress has a major impact on crack behavior. Nejati et al. [2] investigated the link between T-stress and material properties. Matvienko [3] discussed the influence of T-stress in fracture mechanics. Ayatollahi and Zakiri [4] studied the effect of T-stress on fringe patterns around the crack tip in mode II using the theory of photoelasticity. Jayadevan [4] demonstrated that when the T-stress is negative, the plastic zone appears like butterfly wings. When there is a positive T-stress, these wings will reverse towards the back of the fracture. Ayatollahi and Hashmi [5] demonstrated the remarkable effect of composite patching on T-stress. Sherry et al. [6] described various methods, such as the Eshelby J-integral method, weight function technique, interaction integral method, stress substitution method, and stress difference methods, for determining T-stress. T-stress affects the plastic zone [7] and propagation direction [8]. A negative T-stress stabilizes the fracture path, which means that a minor disruption in the crack path is soon attenuated, whereas a positive T-stress emphasizes deviations, and crack initiation angle [9]. Miao et al. [10] evaluated the role of T-stress on crack initiation and crack bottom plasticity through 3D finite element analysis of three specimens: CCP, CTS, and FPB. Yakoubi et al. [10] studied the utility of the K-T approach in modeling pressure fractured structures.

In the literature, there are several methods to determine the crack parameters, specifically T-stress. These include Stress Different Methods (SDM) introduced by Yang et al. [11], which eliminate errors by considering the variation of numerical values near the crack point. Maleski et al. developed the Extrapolation method, and Wang et al. calculated the stress by the superposition method; in the case of a sample with a fracture loaded with the nominal mode T is a superposition of the T-stress for two situations: the first is a stress T for a cracked specimen loaded with a pressure $\sigma(x)$ on its lips, while the second is a stress T in an uncracked specimen under a nominal load. Hou et al [12] developed the Esheby integral approach for estimating the T-stress, which takes advantage of the path-independent J-integral's characteristics. The over-deterministic method (ODM) [13] is another approach used to determine crack parameters, including SIF, T-stress, and higher-order parameters in the Williams expansion. ODM has demonstrated efficacy in several studies [14,15].

The SIF and T-stress are crucial in the research of cracking in linear elasticity. Singular stress entities are frequently used to represent the area around the crack tip. SIF is used to assess their resistance. The parameter T is the non-singular stress that characterizes the local stress field near the fracture tip. T-stress has the role of enriching the parameter K (SIF) and the model in the elastic stress zone. The majority of approaches only consider SIF extraction and pay little attention to T-stress and higher-order terms. The transverse constraint, or T-stress, acts parallel to the crack's propagation.

Isogeometric analysis (IGA) is a computer approach for simulating physical processes in engineering and mathematics. IGA is an approach that integrates finite element analysis (FEA) with classical NURBS-based CAD design tools. It has shown promising results in various fields, including vibration analysis [16,17], composites, and optimization problems [18]. Farshid Fathi et al. [19] presented geometrically nonlinear extended iso-geometric analysis (X-IGA) for cohesive fracture. Wenbin Hou et al. [20] coupled X-IGA and B++ spline to study crack behavior in 2D elasticity solids. X-IGA combines isogeometric analysis with the extended finite element method (X-FEM), utilizing IGA for accurate geometry representation and X-FEM for crack enrichment. The dynamic fracture behavior of stationary fractures in isotropic/orthotropic medium under impact stress was studied by Yadav et al. [21] using the X-IGA approach. Ghorashi et al. [20] demonstrated that X-IGA outperforms X-FEM in terms of accuracy, requiring significantly fewer elements to achieve an error of less than 0.1.

The objective of this study is to compute the K-T parameters in a simple and efficient method; IG-ODM employs Extended Isogeometric Analysis to calculate stress and displacement distributions, thereby refining the geometry and augmenting crack behavior. These outcomes are then integrated into the Williams expression, yielding a series of deterministic equations solvable through a conventional method. This unique combination represents an unprecedented endeavor in this field.

The article is organized as follows: Section 2 discusses X-IGA and iso-geometric over-deterministic method. Section 3 presents the numerical application, result, and discussion. Finally, the conclusion is provided in the subsequent section.

2. Models and Method

2.1. Extended Iso-Geometric Analysis (IGA)

IGA use Non-Uniform Rational B-Splines (NURBS) as a discretization method for analysis. The IGA can produce correct results even with large meshes, whereas the finite element technique (FEM) requires refining. B-splines are defined from a knot vector. A knot vector is a set of increasing reals defined in the parameter space.

$$\Xi = \{\xi_1, \xi_2, \ldots, \xi_{n+p+1}\}\ ;\ \xi_i < \xi_{i+1} \tag{1}$$

where $\xi_i \in$ R is the ith knot, $i = 1, 2, \ldots, n + p + 1$, p is the polynomial order, and n is the number of basis functions. The B-spline basis functions are defined by the following:

For $p = 0$,

$$N_{i,0} = \begin{Bmatrix} 1 & \xi_i \leq \xi < \xi_{i+1} \\ 0 & otherwise \end{Bmatrix} \tag{2}$$

For $p = 1, 2, \ldots,$

$$N_{i,p}(\xi) = \frac{\xi - \xi_i}{\xi_{i+p} - \xi_i} N_{i,p-1} + \frac{\xi_{i+p+1} - \xi}{\xi_{i+p+1} - \xi_{i+1}} N(\xi)_{i+1,p-1} \tag{3}$$

The properties of B-spline basis function are as follows:

- Partition of unity: $\sum_{i=1}^{n} N_{i,p}(\xi) = 1$;
- The continuity of the basic functions is C^{p-1}, where p is the polynomial degree and m is the multiplicity of the knot;
- The support of $N_{i,p}$ is included in $[\xi_i, \xi_{i+p+1}]$;
- The first derivative of a B-spline basis function.

$$\frac{d}{d\xi} N_{i,p}(\xi) = \frac{p}{\xi_{i+p} - \xi_i} N_{i,p-1}(\xi) - \frac{p}{\xi_{i+p+1} - \xi_{i+1}} N_{i+1,p-1}(\xi) \tag{4}$$

NURBS are built from B-spline functions by assigning a weight to each control point. NURBS are still the dominating engineering design technology. T-splines are recent technical generalizations based on NURBS that can be somewhat unstructured. T-splines are a NURBS superset, and their local refinement features enable solving the gap/overlap problems of intersecting NURBS surfaces more easily.

$$R_i^p(\xi) = \frac{N_{i,p}(\xi) w_i}{\sum_{i=1}^{n} N_{i,p}(\xi) w_i} \tag{5}$$

where $N_{i,p}(\xi)$ is the i^{me} B-Spline function of degree p; w_i : weight. The basic function and the control points Bi are combined linearly to create the B-spline curve:

$$C(\xi) = \sum_{i=1}^{n} N_{i,p} Bi \tag{6}$$

There are three types of refinement in iso-geometric analysis:

1. Knot insertion is the h-refinement; this refinement changes the basic functions $N_{i,p}$ defined on a node vector, to a new basis $\check{N}_{i,p}$:

$$\sum_{i}^{n} N_{i,p}.P_i = \sum_{i}^{n+1} \check{N}_{i,p} P_i \tag{7}$$

2. Degree elevation entails raising the polynomial order of the basic functions, and well nodes are added to the edge. The added values are values that already exist in the initial node vector, they are the p-refinement.
3. k-refinement involves refinement steps h and p [22,23], and increases continuity as well as polynomial order.

Extended Isogeometric analysis X-IGA is a coupling between the extended finite element method X-FEM [23] and the IGA. The IGA aims to present the exact geometry, and X-FEM to model the crack by enrichment. X-IGA extends the capabilities of IGA by providing precise analysis of complicated structural phenomena such as fracture propagation and deformation, which are critical in materials science and engineering.

The level set technique is used for enrichment, which identifies the position of the crack and the crack tip in order to enrich it with the necessary function. Sethian and Osher [23] proposed the level set method as a numerical method for tracking the evolution of interfaces and shapes. The LSM is a great complement to the X-FEM because it informs you where and how to enrich:

$$u(\xi) = \sum_{i}^{n} Ri(\xi)u_i + \sum_{j}^{n_{cf}} Rj(\xi)[H(\xi) - H(\xi_j)]a_j + \sum_{k}^{n_{ct}} Rk(\xi) \sum_{\alpha=1}^{4} [\psi_\alpha(\xi) - \psi_\alpha(\xi)]b_{\alpha k} \tag{8}$$

where Ri is the basis function; n_{cf} is the number of nodes enriched by the Heaviside function; n_{ct} is the number of nodes enriched by the functions of enrichments in the crack tip; ψ_α: the functions of enrichments in the crack tip and H is the Heaviside function,

$$H(\xi) = \begin{Bmatrix} +1 \ \varphi(\xi) > 0 \\ 0 \ \varphi(\xi) = 0 \\ -1 \ \varphi(\xi) < 0 \end{Bmatrix},$$

$u_i, a_j, b_{\alpha k}$ represent the classical, discontinuous, and singular degrees of freedom, respectively.

2.2. *Iso-Geometric Over-Deterministic Method*

IG-ODM is based on the calculation of displacement and stress around the crack point (Figure 1).

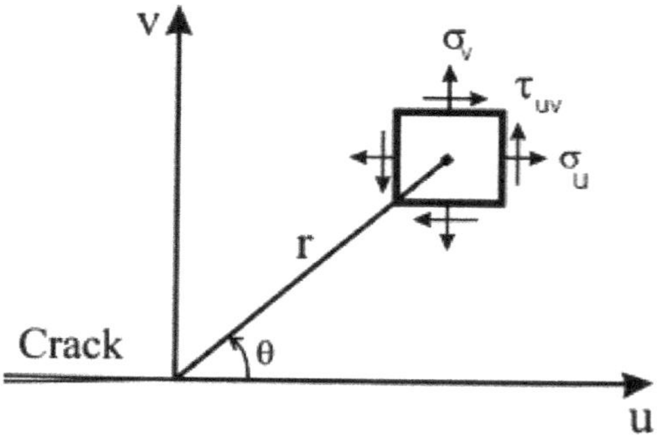

Figure 1. Stresses in a Cartesian reference frame.

These results are then introduced into the Williams expression [24], yielding a set of over-deterministic equations. The least squares method [13] is used to solve these equations and obtain the crack parameters. In our study, we utilize the X-IGA numerical technique to obtain a more precise displacement field. By improving the precision of the displacement field, we can achieve more accurate parameter computation using the ODM technique in Figure 2.

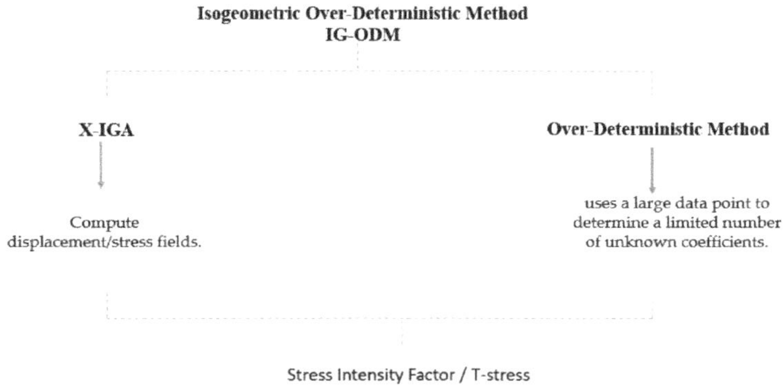

Figure 2. Diagram of the proposed IG-ODM method.

The displacement field at the crack tip:

$$\begin{aligned} u &= \sum_{n=0}^{N} \tfrac{A_n}{2\mu} r^{n/2} \times \left\{k + \tfrac{n}{2} + (-1)^n \cos\tfrac{n}{2}\theta - \tfrac{n}{2}\cos\left(\tfrac{n}{2} - 2\right)\theta\right\} \\ &\quad + \sum_{n=0}^{M} \tfrac{B_n}{2\mu} r^{n/2} \times \left\{-k - \tfrac{n}{2} + (-1)^n \sin\tfrac{n}{2}\theta - \tfrac{n}{2}\sin\left(\tfrac{n}{2} - 2\right)\theta\right\} \\ v &= \sum_{n=0}^{N} \tfrac{A_n}{2\mu} r^{n/2} \times \left\{k - \tfrac{n}{2} - (-1)^n \sin\tfrac{n}{2}\theta - \tfrac{n}{2}\sin\left(\tfrac{n}{2} - 2\right)\theta\right\} \\ &\quad + \sum_{n=0}^{M} \tfrac{B_n}{2\mu} r^{n/2} \times \left\{k - \tfrac{n}{2} + (-1)^n \cos\tfrac{n}{2}\theta - \tfrac{n}{2}\cos\left(\tfrac{n}{2} - 2\right)\theta\right\} \end{aligned} \tag{9}$$

u and v are the displacement in x and y directions, $\mu = \frac{E}{2}(1+\vartheta)$ is the shear modulus, and k the Kolosov constant.

Equation (6) can be written as

$$u = \sum_{n}^{N} A_n f_n^1(r,\theta) + \sum_{n}^{M} B_n f_n^2(r,\theta);\ \ v = \sum_{n}^{N} A_n g_n^1(r,\theta) + \sum_{n}^{M} B_n g_n^2(r,\theta) \tag{10}$$

$f_n^1(r,\theta)$, $f_n^2(r,\theta)$, $g_n^1(r,\theta)$ and $g(r,\theta)$ are functions of coordinates r and θ; A_n and B_n are related to the crack parameters, SIF K_1 and K_2, T-stress and the higher order parameters.

$$K1 = \sqrt{2\pi}A_1\ ,\ T = 4A_2. \tag{11}$$

The set of equations can be represented as follows, if there are k nodes near the crack:

$$[U]_{2L} = [C]_{2L(N+M+2)}[X]_{(N+M+2)}. \tag{12}$$

The terms An and Bn are associated with the mode I and mode II components of deformation, respectively. For n = 0, the displacement components can be written as

$$u_0 = f_0 A_0 = \frac{\kappa+1}{2\mu}A_0;\ v_0 = g_0 B_0 = \frac{\kappa+1}{2\mu}B_0. \tag{13}$$

Equation (12) is the rigid body translation of the crack tip that is independent of the position of the points. κ is the Kolosov constant, and μ is the shear modulus.

The term B2 refers to the crack's rigid body rotation with regard to the crack tip.

$$u = \frac{\kappa+1}{2\mu}B_2 r sin\theta;\ v = \frac{\kappa+1}{2\mu}B_2 cos\theta \tag{14}$$

The amplitude of the crack's rigid body rotation is equal to the angle formed by the initial direction of the fracture and the bisector of crack faces following structural deformation. $[U]$ contains the nodal displacement calculated by extended iso-geometric analysis X-IGA, so

$$u(\xi) = \sum_{i}^{n} R_i(\xi)u_i + \sum_{j}^{n_{cf}} R_j(\xi)\left[H(\xi) - H(\xi_j)\right]a_j + \sum_{k}^{n_{ct}} R_k(\xi)\sum_{\alpha=1}^{4}[\psi_\alpha(\xi) - \psi_\alpha(\xi)]b_{\alpha k} \quad (15)$$

The second term in the equation represents the enrichment of the discontinuity, and the third to model the crack tip, and the NURBS basic function R_i are presented by Equations (3) and (4). $[C]$ includes the values of functions $f(r,\theta)$ and $g(r,\theta)$ at the nodal position.

$$f(n,r,\theta) = \frac{n}{2}r^{\frac{n}{2}-1}\left[\left(2+\frac{n}{2}+(-1)^n\cos\left(\frac{n}{2}-1\right)\theta - \left(\frac{n}{2}-1\right)\cos\left(\frac{n}{2}-3\right)\theta\right] \quad (16)$$

$$g(n,r,\theta) = \frac{n}{2}r^{\frac{n}{2}-1}\left[\left(2-\frac{n}{2}-(-1)^n\cos\left(\frac{n}{2}-1\right)\theta + \left(\frac{n}{2}-1\right)\cos\left(\frac{n}{2}-3\right)\theta\right] \quad (17)$$

$[X]$ includes the coefficients of the Williams expansion, unknown parameters, SIF, T-stress and higher-order terms:

$$[C]^T[U] = [C]^T[C][X];\ [X] = \left([C]^T[C]\right)^{-1}[C]^T[U]. \quad (18)$$

The least-squares approach is used to calculate the unknown parameters.

3. Results

In order to investigate the crack parameters in pure mode I using IG-ODM, we conducted tests on two geometries: the SECT and the CCT, as shown in Figure 3. The geometric dimensions used in the test were $h = w = 4$, $a = 1$ and $\sigma = 1$ MPa [13]. For the calculations, we selected the Young's modulus (E) as 1000 MPa and the Poisson's ratio (v) as 0.3.

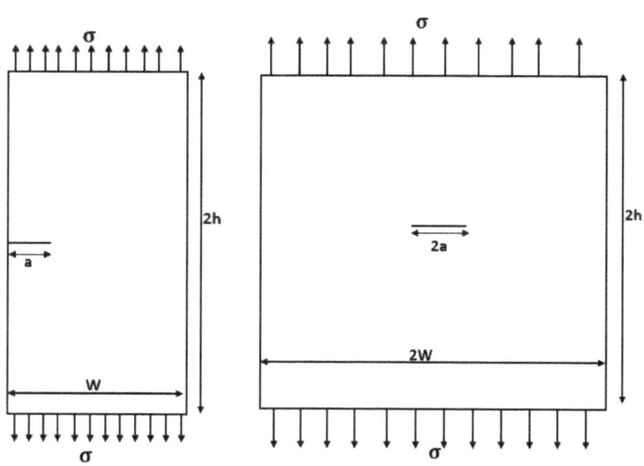

Figure 3. SECT and CCT.

In the case of the CCT specimen, we employed 1600 control points, 1444 nodes, and a polynomial order of p = q = 3. For the SECT specimens, we used 1200 nodes and 1352 control points (Figure 4). the type of crack is sharp. The X-IGA method was utilized to compute the displacement fields, while the ODM (over-deterministic method) was employed to calculate the higher-order parameters in the Williams series.

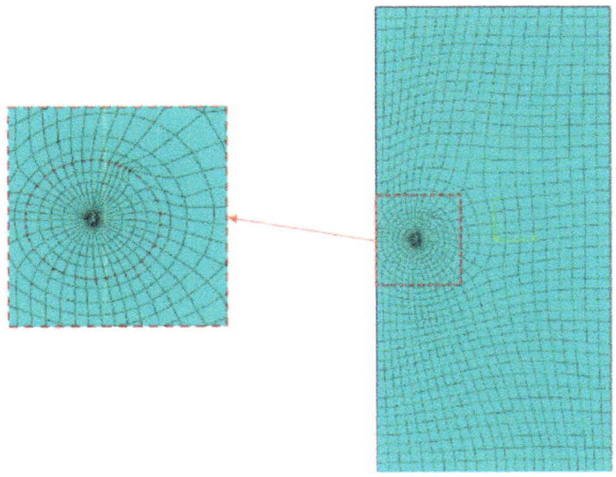

Figure 4. Meshes of SECT and CCT specimen.

The input parameters (the polynomial order, control points, and node vectors) are the initial phase in the MATLAB 2020 software computing approach for the X-IGA implementation. Secondly, the crack data are introduced. For determining the crack position and enrichment points, we employed the level set approach. Then, the boundary conditions, nodal force vector, and stiffness matrix are determined.

After obtaining the displacement and stress fields using X-IGA, we select a ring around the crack tip (as shown in Figure 4). The selected ring satisfies the condition $a/4 < r < a/2$, where a is the crack length. In order to ensure the solvability of the system, the number of equations must be greater than twice the number of unknowns, following the inequality $2k \geq 2(N + M + 2)$ [14], where K is the number of nodes used to compute SIF and T-stress; and N and M are the numbers of terms used in the Williams expression for mode 1 and 2, respectively.

We have selected 52 nodes to calculate the SIF and T-stress, denoted as K = 52. In our calculation, we consider N = 10 terms in the Williams series for Mode I crack analysis. A MATLAB algorithm is used to compute the unknown parameters, employing the least-squares method [25].

Tables 1 and 2 present the SIF K1 and T-stress for the Mode I crack under static loading. To evaluate the accuracy of the proposed method, we calculate the error using the formula: $\frac{K_{IG-ODM}-Ki}{Ki} \times \mathbf{100}$. The distribution of stress intensity factor by X-IGA et X-FEM at the crack tip as a function of crack size for the CCT and SECT specimen, as illustrated in Figures 5 and 6.

Table 1. SIF and T-stress for CCT specimens.

	K1 [MPa$\sqrt{m}$,]	Error = $\frac{K_{IG-ODM}-Ki}{Ki} \times 100$	T-Stress [MPa]	Error = $\frac{T_{IG-ODM}-Ti}{Ti} \times 100$
IG-ODM	1.8884	---	−1.1037	---
Ref. [13]	1.9252	1.911%	−1.1044	0.06%
Ref. [26]	1.923	1.799%	−1.1116	0.64%

Table 2. SIF and T-stress for SECT specimens.

	K1 [MPa$\sqrt{m}$,]	Error = $\frac{K_{IG-ODM}-Ki}{Ki} \times 100$	T-Stress [MPa]	Error = $\frac{T_{IG-ODM}-Ti}{Ti} \times 100$
IG-ODM	2.6631		−0.6129	---
Abaqus Contour Integral	2.657	0.2%	−0.6008	2%
Ref. [13]	2.6560	0.267%	−0.6028	1.6%

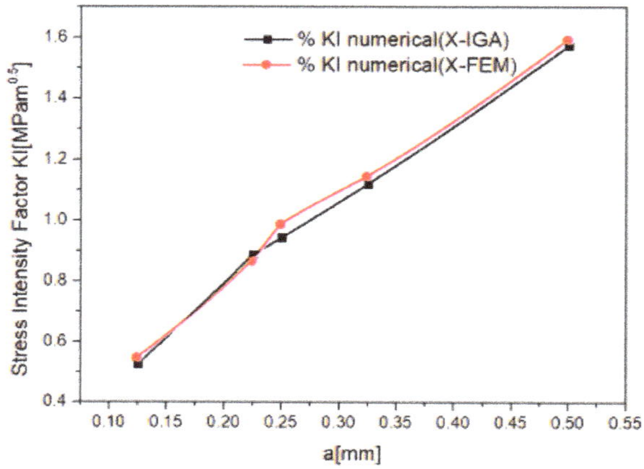

Figure 5. Distribution of stress intensity factor by X-IGA et X-FEM at the crack tip as a function of crack size for CCT specimen.

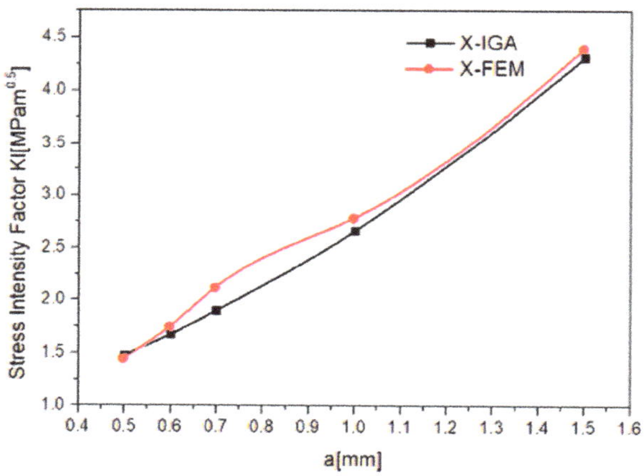

Figure 6. Distribution of stress intensity factor by X-IGA et X-FEM at the crack tip as a function of crack size for SECT specimen.

For the CCT specimen, the IG-ODM yields a SIF of 1.888MPa$\sqrt{m}$, with an inaccuracy of 1.911% compared to reference [13] and 1.799% compared to reference [26]. The T-stress obtained is −1.1037 MPa, with an error of less than 0.64% (Table 1). These results demonstrate that the proposed method exhibits errors ranging from 0.06% to 2% when compared to other research studies.

Table 2 compares the SIF and T-stress results obtained by IG-ODM for SECT specimens to those obtained by previous studies. The error is less than 0.26 percent for SIF and less than 2 percent for T-stress.

In Figure 5, which pertains to the CCT geometry, the SIF obtained from the X-IGA method shows an upward trend as the crack size (a) increases. This indicates that larger cracks result in higher stress intensity at the crack tip.

Similarly, Figure 6 presents the SIF variation for the SECT geometry. Here as well, the SIF obtained from the X-IGA method exhibits a rising pattern with increasing crack size (a). This implies that larger cracks lead to higher stress intensity in the SECT specimen.

Figure 7 represents the variation of T-stress by stress different method using X-IGA and X-FEM as a function of the size of the crack *a*; the absolute value of T decreases with the increase in a.

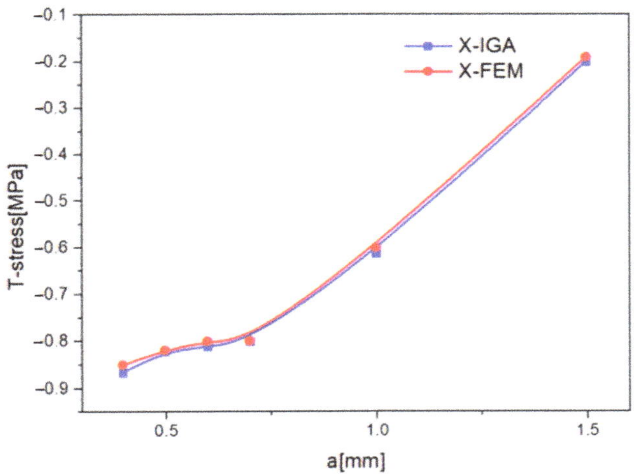

Figure 7. T-stress calculated by stress different method SDM for SECT specimens.

4. Discussion and Conclusions

The paper discusses the fracture parameters SIF (stress intensity factor) and T-stress using a novel IG-ODM (Isogeometric Over-Deterministic Method) approach.

Most approaches concentrate primarily on SIF extraction, with little focus devoted to T-stress and higher-order terms. The objective of this work is to more precisely determine SIF and T-stress using the IG-ODM approach, and evaluate its accuracy compared to other methods. The approach involves computing the displacement and stress around the crack using extended isogeometric analysis X-IGA, incorporating the results into the Williams expression, and obtaining crack parameters through the least-squares method.

Computing fracture parameters provides valuable insights into the crack, its propagation, and the stability of its path. Ensuring the accuracy of these computations is crucial, and X-IGA has proven to be effective in various studies. For instance, Yin et al. [27] used the X-IGA to study static crack problems in the two-dimensional model, achieving an error of $e_{K1} = 0.1406\%$ for an edge-crack plate with 656 control points, and obtained excellent results for K1 for the center crack. Additionally, a comparison between X-IGA and X-FEM demonstrated that X-IGA is more accurate than X-FEM with fewer elements and less computation time [28]. El Fakkoussi et al. [29] emphasized the importance and accuracy of X-IGA compared to FEM and X-FEM in computing SIF at the point of an external crack in an arc under internal pressure. Ghorashi et al. [20] demonstrated that X-IGA provides computation times twice as fast as X-FEM. Even with a large mesh, the X-IGA approach is more accurate than the finite element method [10], so the number of elements is chosen according to calculation time, in order to reduce costs.

Leveraging these advantages, the paper aimed to achieve greater precision in computing the displacement field using X-IGA, followed by the application of ODM (Over-Deterministic Method), which has also proven to be effective in computing the coefficients of the Williams series. Accurate results were obtained, demonstrating that IG-ODM is an efficient method for computing crack characteristics such as SIF and T-stress. We selected the distance of the ring from the fracture tip to verify $a/4 < r < a/2$, because of the relatively substantial numerical errors that exist in nodes extremely near the crack tip.

The ODM approach, based on the stress field, was originally proposed by Cheng Hou et al. [12] for the computation of SIF and T-stress; they achieved accurate results for SECT (K_1 = 2.6525 MPa$\sqrt{m}$, T = −0.5984 MPa) and CCT (K_1 = 1.9252 MPa$\sqrt{m}$, T = −1.1044 MPa), with an error of less than 1.124% compared to other research. YufeiLi et KanZheng [14] also examined the SIF and T-stress using ODM based on the displacement field, employing the nodal findings of X-FEM analysis. The effectiveness of the FEODM (Finite Element Over-Deterministic Method) was demonstrated in the work of R. Ayatollahi et al. [30]. The benefit of the IG-ODM approach we have described compared to other ways employing ODM; the geometry and the crack are precisely represented [31–33] using the X-IGA method.

The observed negative T-value implies a stable fracture propagation direction, while a positive T-value indicates an unstable direction, as discussed by Cotterell et al. [34]. Another study [35–41] showed that a negative T-value reduced the crack initiation angle while a positive T value raises it.

The IG-ODM has yielded significant and accurate results, which can be attributed to the accuracy of X-IGA extended isogeometric analysis as compared to the finite element approach (FEM), as well as the efficacy of the over-deterministic ODM approach, which calculates a limited number of unknown coefficients from a large number of data points [42]. In this work, a coupling of the X-IGA method with the over-deterministic method (ODM) are proposed to calculate the T-stress and the SIF at the crack tip for mode I. This work aims to take advantage of the benefits of X-IGA and ODM. IG-ODM is based on the calculation of stress and displacement fields by X-IGA to better present the geometry and enrich the crack, thereby introducing the results into the Williams iv expression, from which a set of deterministic equations is obtained whose solution is obtained by the least-squares method.

- The T-stress is introduced to enrich SIF, in a better presentation of the crack.
- The SIF and T-stress are determined using IG-ODM, which is an efficient method for computing fracture parameters.
- The IG-ODM approach proves to be more efficient when the displacement field is accurately determined, utilizing a more precise numerical method such as X-IGA.
- IGA, as a technology, allows for interaction with CAD systems, leading to improved solution accuracy and reduced computational costs.
- In order to obtain accurate results using IG-ODM, it is essential that the number of crack parameters exceeds the number of nodal displacements determined by X-IGA.
- Because of the relatively significant numerical errors that exist in nodes that are very near to the fracture tip, it is better to obtain the essential data from nodes that are further away from the crack tip, and it is preferable to select nodes from a particular ring.

The studied subject allows for further development and obtaining new results in the field. We expect to develop a new project where the authors will employ IG-ODM to investigate cracking problems in complex geometries, demonstrating its potential for accurate analysis and understanding in such scenarios.

Author Contributions: Conceptualization, K.Y., A.E., H.M., A.E.A., M.L.S. and S.V.; methodology, K.Y., A.E., H.M. and A.E.A.; validation, K.Y., A.E., H.M., A.E.A., M.L.S. and S.V.; formal analysis, K.Y., A.E., H.M. and A.E.A.; investigation, K.Y., A.E., H.M. and A.E.A.; writing—original draft preparation, K.Y., A.E., H.M. and A.E.A.; writing—review and editing, K.Y., A.E., H.M., A.E.A., M.L.S. and S.V.; supervision, K.Y., A.E., H.M., A.E.A., M.L.S. and S.V. All authors have read and agreed to the published version of the manuscript.

Funding: The APC was funded by Transilvania University of Brasov.

Data Availability Statement: Not applicable.

Conflicts of Interest: The authors declare no conflict of interest.

References

1. Cotterell, B. Notes on the paths and stability of cracks. *Int. J. Fract.* **1966**, *2*, 526–533. [CrossRef]
2. Nejati, M.; Ghouli, S.; Ayatollahi, M.R. Crack tip asymptotic fields in anisotropic planes: Importance of higher order terms. *Appl. Math. Model.* **2021**, *91*, 837–862. [CrossRef]

3. Matvienko, Y.G. The effect of crack-tip constraint in some problems of fracture mechanics. *Eng. Fail. Anal.* **2020**, *110*, 104413. [CrossRef]
4. Jayadevan, K.R.; Narasimhan, R.; Ramamurthy, T.S.; Dattaguru, B. Effect of T-stress and loading rate on crack initiation in rate sensitive plastic materials. *Int. J. Solids Struct.* **2002**, *39*, 1757–1775. [CrossRef]
5. Ayatollahi, M.R.; Hashemi, R. Computation of stress intensity factors (KI, KII) and T-stress for cracks reinforced by composite patching. *Compos. Struct.* **2007**, *78*, 602–609. [CrossRef]
6. Sherry, A.H.; France, C.C.; Goldthorpe, M.R. Compendium of t-stress solutions for two and three dimensional cracked geometries. *Fatigue Fract. Eng. Mater. Struct.* **1995**, *18*, 141–155. [CrossRef]
7. Shahani, A.R.; Tabatabaei, S.A. Effect of T-stress on the fracture of a four point bend specimen. *Mater. Des.* **2009**, *30*, 2630–2635. [CrossRef]
8. Fayed, A.S. Numerical Analysis of Crack Initiation Direction in Quasi-brittle Materials: Effect of T-Stress. *Arab. J. Sci. Eng.* **2019**, *44*, 7667–7676. [CrossRef]
9. Miao, X.T.; Zhou, C.Y.; Lv, F.; He, X.H. Three-dimensional finite element analyses of T-stress for different experimental specimens. *Theor. Appl. Fract. Mech.* **2017**, *91*, 116–125. [CrossRef]
10. Yakoubi, K.; Montassir, S.; Moustabchir, H.; Elkhalfi, A.; Pruncu, C.I.; Arbaoui, J.; Umar Farooq, M. An Extended Finite Element Method (XFEM) Study on the Elastic T-Stress Evaluations for a Notch in a Pipe Steel Exposed to Internal Pressure. *Mathematics* **2021**, *9*, 507. [CrossRef]
11. Yang, B.; Ravi-Chandar, K. Evaluation of elastic T-stress by the stress difference method. *Eng. Fract. Mech.* **1999**, *64*, 589–605. [CrossRef]
12. Hou, C.; Wang, Z.; Jin, X.; Ji, X.; Fan, X. Determination of SIFs and T-stress using an over-deterministic method based on stress fields: Static and dynamic. *Eng. Fract. Mech.* **2021**, *242*, 107455. [CrossRef]
13. Ayatollahi, M.R.; Nejati, M. An over-deterministic method for calculation of coefficients of crack tip asymptotic field from finite element analysis: Calculating coefficients of crack tip asymptotic field from FE analysis. *Fatigue Fract. Eng. Mater. Struct.* **2011**, *34*, 159–176. [CrossRef]
14. Li, Y.; Zheng, K. Crack tip asymptotic field coefficients analyses based on extended finite element method using over-deterministic displacement field fitting method. *Theor. Appl. Fract. Mech.* **2021**, *113*, 102971. [CrossRef]
15. Cuong-Le, T.; Nguyen, K.D.; Nguyen-Trong, N.; Khatir, S.; Nguyen-Xuan, H.; Abdel-Wahab, M. A three-dimensional solution for free vibration and buckling of annular plate, conical, cylinder and cylindrical shell of FG porous-cellular materials using IGA. *Compos. Struct.* **2021**, *259*, 113216. [CrossRef]
16. Shafei, E.; Faroughi, S.; Rabczuk, T. Nonlinear transient vibration of viscoelastic plates: A NURBS-based isogeometric HSDT approach. *Comput. Math. Appl.* **2021**, *84*, 1–15. [CrossRef]
17. Hinz, J.; Jaeschke, A.; Möller, M.; Vuik, C. The role of PDE-based parameterization techniques in gradient-based IGA shape optimization applications. *Comput. Methods Appl. Mech. Eng.* **2021**, *378*, 113685. [CrossRef]
18. Hou, W.; Jiang, K.; Zhu, X.; Shen, Y.; Hu, P. Extended isogeometric analysis using B++ splines for strong discontinuous problems. *Comput. Methods Appl. Mech. Eng.* **2021**, *381*, 113779. [CrossRef]
19. Fathi, F.; de Borst, R. Geometrically nonlinear extended isogeometric analysis for cohesive fracture with applications to delamination in composites. *Finite Elem. Anal. Des.* **2021**, *191*, 103527. [CrossRef]
20. Ghorashi, G.; Valizadeh, N.; Mohammadi, S. Extended isogeometric analysis for simulation of stationary and propagating cracks. *Int. J. Numer. Methods Eng.* **2012**, *89*, 1069–1101. [CrossRef]
21. Yadav, A.; Godara, R.K.; Bhardwaj, G. A review on XIGA method for computational fracture mechanics applications. *Eng. Fract. Mech.* **2020**, *230*, 107001. [CrossRef]
22. Nguyen, V.P.; Bordas, S.P.A.; Rabczuk, T. Isogeometric analysis: An overview and computer implementation aspects. *Math. Comput. Simul.* **2015**, *117*, 89–116. [CrossRef]
23. Montassir, S.; Yakoubi, K.; Moustabchir, H.; Elkhalfi, A.; Rajak, D.K.; Pruncu, C.I. Analysis of Crack Behaviour in Pipeline System Using FAD Diagram Based on Numerical Simulation under XFEM. *Appl. Sci.* **2020**, *10*, 6129. [CrossRef]
24. Williams, M.L. On the Stress Distribution at the Base of a Stationary Crack. (10 June 2021)ASME. *J. Appl. Mech.* **1957**, *24*, 109–114. [CrossRef]
25. Sanford, R.J. Application of the least-squares method to photoelastic analysis: Two global methods for determining certain key parameters from full-field fringe patterns based on the method of least squares are presented. *Exp. Mech.* **1980**, *20*, 192–197. [CrossRef]
26. Xiao, Q.Z.; Karihaloo, B.L.; Liu, X.Y. Direct determination of SIF and higher order terms of mixed mode cracks by a hybrid crack element. *Int. J. Fract.* **2004**, *125*, 207–225. [CrossRef]
27. Bui, Q.; Zheng, X.; Gu, S. Static and dynamic fracture analysis in elastic solids using a multiscale extended isogeometric analysis. *Eng. Fract. Mech.* **2019**, *207*, 109–130. [CrossRef]
28. Nguyen-Thanh, N.; Valizadeh, N.; Nguyen, M.N.; Nguyen-Xuan, H.; Zhuang, X.; Areias, P.; Zih, Y.; Bazilevsg, L.; De Lorenzisa, T.; Rabczuk, T. An extended isogeometric thin shell analysis based on Kirchhoff–Love theory. *Comput. Methods Appl. Mech. Eng.* **2015**, *284*, 265–291. [CrossRef]
29. El Fakkoussi, S.; Moustabchir, H.; Elkhalfi, A.; Pruncu, C.I. Application of the Extended Isogeometric Analysis (X-IGA) to Evaluate a Pipeline Structure Containing an External Crack. *J. Eng.* **2018**, *2018*, 4125765. [CrossRef]

30. Ayatollahi, M.R.; Nejati, M.; Ghouli, S. The finite element over-deterministic method to calculate the coefficients of crack tip asymptotic fields in anisotropic planes. *Eng. Fract. Mech.* **2020**, *231*, 106982. [CrossRef]
31. Lai, W.; Yu, T.; Bui, T.Q.; Wang, Z.; Curiel-Sosa, J.L.; Das, R.; Hirose, S. 3-D elasto-plastic large deformations: IGA simulation by Bézier extraction of NURBS. *Adv. Eng. Softw.* **2017**, *108*, 68–82. [CrossRef]
32. Montassir, S.; Moustabchir, H.; Elkhalfi, A.; Scutaru, M.L.; Vlase, S. Fracture Modelling of a Cracked Pressurized Cylindrical Structure by Using Extended Iso-Geometric Analysis (X-IGA). *Mathematics* **2021**, *9*, 2990. [CrossRef]
33. Kapoor, H.; Kapania, R.K. Geometrically nonlinear NURBS isogeometric finite element analysis of laminated composite plates. *Compos. Struct.* **2012**, *94*, 3434–3447. [CrossRef]
34. Cotterell, A. Slightly curved or kinked cracks. *Int. J. Fract.* **1980**, *16*, 155–169. [CrossRef]
35. Codarcea-Munteanu, L.; Marin, M.; Vlase, S. The study of vibrations in the context of porous micropolar media thermoelasticity and the absence of energy dissipation. *J. Comput. Appl. Mech.* **2023**, *54*, 437–454. [CrossRef]
36. Kim, J.-H.; Paulino, G.H. T-stress, mixed-mode stress intensity factors, and crack initiation angles in functionally graded materials: A unified approach using the interaction integral method. *Comput. Methods Appl. Mech. Eng.* **2003**, *192*, 1463–1494. [CrossRef]
37. Shah, P.D.; Tan, C.L.; Wang, X. T-stress solutions for two-dimensional crack problems in anisotropic elasticity using the boundary element method. *Fatigue Fract. Eng. Mater. Struct.* **2006**, *29*, 343–356. [CrossRef]
38. Sladek, J.; Sladek, V. Evaluation of the Elastic T-stress in Three-dimensional Crack Problems Using an Integral Formula. *Int. J. Fract.* **2000**, *101*, 47–52. [CrossRef]
39. Wang, X. Elastic T-stress solutions for semi-elliptical surface cracks in finite thickness plates. *Eng. Fract. Mech.* **2003**, *70*, 731–756. [CrossRef]
40. Koubaiti, O.; Elkhalfi, A.; El-Mekkaoui, J.; Mastorakis, N. Solving the problem of constraints due to Dirichlet boundary conditions in the context of the mini element method. *Int. J. Mech.* **2020**, *14*, 12–22.
41. El Ouadefli, L.; El Moutea, O.; El Akkad, A.; Elkhalfi, A.; Vlase, S.; Scutaru, M.L. Mixed Isogeometric Analysis of the Brinkman Equation. *Mathematics* **2023**, *11*, 2750. [CrossRef]
42. El Ouadefli, L.A.; El Akkad, S.A.; El Moutea, O.; Moustabchir, H.; Elkhalfi, A.; Scutaru, L.M.; Muntean, R. Numerical simulation for Brinkman system with varied permeability tensor. *Mathematics* **2022**, *10*, 3242. [CrossRef]

mathematics

MDPI

Article

Gibbs–Appell Equations in Finite Element Analysis of Mechanical Systems with Elements Having Micro-Structure and Voids

Sorin Vlase [1,2,*], Marin Marin [3,4] and Calin Itu [1]

1 Department of Mechanical Engineering, Transilvania University of Brașov, 500530 Brașov, Romania
2 Technical Sciences Academy of Romania, 030167 Bucharest, Romania
3 Department of Mathematics and Computer Science, Transilvania University of Brașov, 500091 Brașov, Romania
4 Academy of Romanian Scientists, 050045 Bucharest, Romania
* Correspondence: svlase@unitbv.ro

Abstract: In this paper, the authors propose the application of the Gibbs–Appell equations to obtain the equations of motion in the case of a mechanical system that has elements with a micro-polar structure, containing voids. Voids can appear as a result of the processing or manufacturing of the parts, or can be intentionally introduced. This research involves a model of the considered solid material containing voids. To determine the dynamic behavior of such a system, the Gibbs–Appell (GA) method is used to obtain the evolution equations, as an alternative to Lagrange's classical description. The proposed method can be applied to any mechanical system consisting of materials with a micro-polar structure and voids. The study of such systems is interesting because the literature shows that even a reduce number of small voids can produce significant variations in physical behavior. The proposed method requires a smaller number of mathematical operations. To apply this method, the acceleration energy is calculated, which is then used to derive the equations. The method comes with advantages in the application to multibody systems having the mentioned properties and, in particular, in the study of robots and manipulators. Using the GA method, it is necessary to do a fewer differentiation operations than applying the Lagrange's equations. This leads to a reduced amount of computation for obtaining the evolution equations.

Keywords: FEM; MBS; analytical dynamics; micropolar; voids; micropolar media; Gibbs–Appell; energy of accelerations

MSC: 65N30; 65N15; 65G99; 76D07; 76D99

1. Introduction

Recent years have led to an impressive development of the materials used in various fields of engineering. Such materials have appeared in aviation, the automotive industry, the naval industry, in the construction of robots and manipulators, in medicine, etc. However, these materials may contain voids accidentally created during manufacturing, in certain situations, may significantly alter the properties of the materials. Sometimes, these voids can be introduced intentionally or appear controlled, if a certain technological process is used. This has caused the interest of researchers in this type of materials [1].

Because to the difficulty in developing appropriate models, most studies are experimental. Tests have been carried out to ascertain how the mechanical properties change when voids appear [2–4]. Theoretical approaches are still at an unsatisfactory level, due to the numerous parameters that must be taken into account [5–7]. For this reason, it has been emphasized that there is a need to develop numerical procedures to solve these problems [8]. A first attempt to develop models using appropriate numerical methods is made in [9–11].

In the manufacturing process of some materials, especially composite materials, voids may appear, which are generally undesirable phenomena. These voids are generally filled with air. However, they may be filled with other gases, depending on the manufacturing process used. For manufacturers, the appearance of voids which are unexpected is an undesirable thing; a defect. These voids will have an influence on the physical properties of the respective material. Their existence can lead to the decrease in some important mechanical properties for the user and in the worst cases can cause the destruction of the material or the manufactured part. A void that appears can cause the initiation of cracks and ultimately reduce the life span.

It is also possible that other substances with a negative final influence on the material appear in these voids. The appearance of voids can also influence the isotropy of the material. In the study of composite and polymeric materials in general, voids negatively influence behavior. Therefore, it is necessary to develop suitable models with numerical solution capabilities for the study of polymeric materials used in engineering applications. There are many reasons for the appearance of voids and they relate to the manufacturing process, the wear of the machines, and the training of the personnel involved in the manufacture of the material. One example, the case of adhesive bonding, is presented in [12]. Another example, where voids can significantly influence material properties in the case of a polymer thin film, is presented in [13]. There are also a few cases in which the existence of voids in materials can be beneficial. Such examples are presented in specific applications [14,15].

Over time, as a result of the engineering requirements regarding the study of these materials, models that can predict their mechanical behavior have been developed and researched [16–19]. The cases solved so far are very simple. The development of complex models is necessary, and in this context the use of FEM could represent a main direction of analysis. The problem with voids is that, even in small concentrations, their existence will cause large variations in mechanical and physical properties [20–26]. The first studies in the field by Cowin and Goodman [27] resulted in the creation of the granular theory. Applications immediately appeared in various fields, first of all in the research of soils and rocks, and then of human bones [28].

In general, voids appear in materials that also exhibit microstructure (MS) properties, especially polymeric composite materials [29–32]. Thus, a theoretical support has been provided for the analysis of these materials. Unfortunately, a theoretical support is not enough for the analysis of practical engineering cases. This difference is mainly determined by the complexity of the equations that arise. Approximation methods and numerical methods are needed to solve some real-world applications. In this context, the FEM proves to be the main tool that makes the analysis of these structures possible [33].

The wealth of developed finite elements and well-verified procedures within FEMs make this method one that can successfully address such materials [34–38]. For composite, bi- or multiphase materials, useful results are presented in [39–42]. In this paper, the FEM is used for the dynamic analysis of such bodies. Basic notions for the application of FEM to hollow micropolar bodies are proposed in [43,44], and some developments are made in [45,46].

This paper aims to provide a model for determining the elastic behavior of a solid body with voids and micro-structure, using a formalism provided by Analytical Mechanics. For this, the FEM is used together with an analytical method to establish the equations of motion. The main difficulty is the complexity of the analytical formulas. To facilitate the analysis, the authors propose the use of another method (as an alternative to Lagrange's Equations (LE), the Gibbs–Appell (GA) equations, introducing the rarely used notion of acceleration energy.

In most engineering applications, the analysis method for writing the equations of motion in the FEM is represented by Lagrange's formalism. After performing this operation, using classic assembly methods, applying the boundary conditions, and introducing forces and moments corresponding to the studied problem, the system of equations that describe the movement of the system is finally obtained. The choice of a suitable finite element for modeling the studied mechanical system will determine the shape functions used; based on these, after the integrations, the coefficients of the motion equations will be obtained. The hypothesis of small deformations is considered to be valid. A number of papers have addressed the subject of the motion of systems with elastic elements using one-dimensional finite elements [47–53], and also more sophisticated finite elements [54–56].

LEs are usually preferred to determine the evolution equations for an element [57–60]. Recent works have begun to use and reconsider other methods of Analytical Mechanics in the analysis of such systems. GA equations will be the authors' choice as an alternative solution to LE to study the mechanics of a material with micro-structure and voids, having a general motion. Using this method has several advantages. So, the number of operations used to determine the system of differential equations (and, consequently, the time and cost of designing using these materials) can decrease.

The GA equations represent a method for solving non-holonomic systems that presents some advantages over the other methods offered by Analytical Mechanics. The method was proposed in 1879 [61] by Gibbs and rediscovered by Appell in 1899. The notion introduced for the application of the method is that of the energy of accelerations. The method essentially is an application of Gauss's principle of minimum constraint. The obtained results are equivalent to the results obtained by applying other equivalent formalisms provided by Analytical Mechanics. The use of these equations in engineering applications has begun to be reconsidered in recent years, offering advantages in terms of the number of calculations involved and reducing the cost of the modeling stage. Extension to systems with micro-structures and voids is a natural development of the method in the current context of the existing computational tools.

The use of robots has become a general phenomenon in all industries. It is a trend of the last few decades which requires an adaptation of the design of these systems to ensure adequate control. The latest developments have led to the design and manufacture of machines that work at high speeds and are subject to high forces. They need to be carefully designed, which is why many studies have begun to analyze various aspects of their operation. For such systems, the accelerations become important and can greatly influence operation. In this context, the use of the GA method becomes important, introducing the notion of acceleration energy. At this point, the method starts to become interesting for various engineering problems [62,63].

The method has proven to be interesting for a wide range of applications. An example of a flexible robot is presented in [64]. The theoretical results obtained by the GA method have been validated experimentally. Another application [65] concerns an N-flexible-link manipulator used in industrial applications. In [66], using the GA formalism, the evolution equations are established and, separately, an algebraic system provides the forces acting on the links [67,68].

An advantage of applying this set of equations is the reduced number of operations compared to other methods. Currently, the method is beginning to be reconsidered and several researchers have used it in their works [69–74]. The FEM has demonstrated its validity and utility in numerous problems in a very wide spectrum of domains. It is a powerful tool for studying the behavior of mechanical systems. For multibody systems, FEM has been used along with Lagrange's equations. FEM currently has computational procedures and models incorporated into available software that ensure a very wide range of applications are handled.

Many finite elements have been developed, along with powerful pre- and post-processing tools. The basic assumption for the application of this method remains the hypothesis of small deformations. In this paper, we address the problem of using the FEM together with an alternative Analytical Mechanics method to obtain the motion equations, namely, the GA method. For systems of such complexity, the use of micro-structured materials with voids requires the use of procedures in the analysis that require as few calculations as possible. We mention that, in the last twenty years, the classical methods of Analytical

Mechanics have begun to be reconsidered. This is because engineering applications have started to become more and more complex. In this context, in which the developed models are very sophisticated and involve a huge number of arithmetic calculations, some advantages offered by the particular form of some of the mechanical principles can have a major influence on the cost and the time required to achieve a high-performance design. The work is part of this trend of revaluing classical knowledge and reevaluating the advantages it can offer.

The accuracy issues of the obtained results are not presented in this paper. They are a field of study in themselves. In this research, we were mainly concerned with presenting an equivalent method for determining the set of equations. The justification for this is the opportunity to obtain some computational advantages, namely, a shorter modeling time and, consequently, lower costs for obtaining numerical results. The use of this method must also ensure relevant results in order to make sense from a technical point of view.

2. Energy of Accelerations and Basic Notions

The system is considered a mechanical system made up of N material points whose position is defined by n independent coordinates. These coordinates will be noted with q_i, where $i = \overline{1,n}$. If the studied system is a system with scleronoma links, the acceleration of one of the material particles, let us say i, of the system is expressed by the relation

$$\bar{a}_i = \sum_k \sum_j \frac{\partial^2 \bar{r}_i}{\partial q_k \partial q_j} \dot{q}_k \dot{q}_j + \sum_k \frac{\partial \bar{r}_i}{\partial q_k} \ddot{q}_k \ ; \ k,j = \overline{1,n} \ ; \ i = \overline{1,N}. \tag{1}$$

In this expression, $\bar{r}_i$ is the position vector of the point i. In the following, this will be denoted with a dot placed over a scalar, vector, or matrix size of the derivative of the considered size with respect to time. The energy of acceleration denoted by S is a basic notion used in the further considerations [72]:

$$S = \frac{1}{2} \sum_i m_i a_i^2 \ ; \ i = \overline{1,N}. \tag{2}$$

Formal Equation (2) is similar to the relation used to define the kinetic energy. However, the mechanical significance is obviously different. Considering a solid elastic body, Equation (2) for a system of material points can be extended for the solid under the for:

$$S = \frac{1}{2} \int_V a^2 dm. \tag{3}$$

If we consider the acceleration of a point arbitrary chosen, this has the expression

$$\bar{a} = \sum_k \sum_j \frac{\partial^2 \bar{r}}{\partial q_k \partial q_j} \dot{q}_k \dot{q}_j + \sum_k \frac{\partial \bar{r}}{\partial q_k} \ddot{q}_k \ ; \ k,j = \overline{1,n}. \tag{4}$$

Using Equations (3) and (4) we get

$$\begin{gathered} S = \frac{1}{2} \int\limits_V \rho a^2 dV = \frac{1}{2} \int\limits_V \rho \left(\sum_k \sum_j \frac{\partial^2 \bar{r}}{\partial q_k \partial q_j} \dot{q}_k \dot{q}_j + \sum_k \frac{\partial \bar{r}}{\partial q_k} \ddot{q}_k \right)^2 dV = \\ E_{ao}(\dot{q}) + E_{a1}(\dot{q}, \ddot{q}) + E_{a2}(\ddot{q}) \ , \ k,j = \overline{1,n}. \end{gathered} \tag{5}$$

where it is denoted by

$$E_{ao}(\dot{q}) = \frac{1}{2} \sum_k \sum_j \sum_l \sum_m \left(\int\limits_V \rho \frac{\partial^2 \bar{r}}{\partial q_k \partial q_j} \frac{\partial^2 \bar{r}}{\partial q_l \partial q_m} dV \right) \dot{q}_k \dot{q}_j \dot{q}_l \dot{q}_m \ ; \ j,k,l,m = \overline{1,n}, \tag{6}$$

which represents the part of the energy of accelerations that do not contains accelerations; by

$$E_{a1}(\dot{q},\ddot{q}) = \frac{1}{2}\sum_k\sum_j\sum_l\left(\int_V \rho\frac{\partial^2\overline{r}}{\partial q_k \partial q_j}\frac{\partial\overline{r}}{\partial q_l}dV\right)\dot{q}_k\dot{q}_j\ddot{q}_l \ ; \ k,j,l = \overline{1,n}. \tag{7}$$

which represents the part of the energy of accelerations that contains the linear terms in accelerations; and by

$$E_{a2}(\ddot{q}) = \frac{1}{2}\sum_k\sum_j\left(\int_V \rho\frac{\partial\overline{r}}{\partial q_k}\frac{\partial\overline{r}}{\partial q_j}dV\right)\ddot{q}_k\ddot{q}_j \ ; \ k,j = \overline{1,n}. \tag{8}$$

which represents the part that contains the quadratic terms in accelerations.

The classic forms of the GA equations are:

$$\frac{\partial S}{\partial \ddot{q}_i} = Q_i \ i = \overline{1,n}. \tag{9}$$

In Equation (9), Q_i represents the generalized force corresponding to the generalized coordinate q_i.

Now, we consider an elastic body that can present, in its volume, a series of voids. The density $\rho(x,y,z)$ of the body changes in every point, and can be expressed by the relation [34]

$$\rho(x,y,z) = v(x,y,z)\ \gamma(x,y,z). \tag{10}$$

Here, $\gamma(x,y,z)$ is the mass density of the solid if the voids do not exist, and $v(x,y,z)$ represents the volume fraction of the existing material, $(0 < \nu \leq 1)$. The volume fraction represents the fraction of the volume of voids over the total volume. We can consider the situation at an initial moment:

$$\rho_o(x,y,z) = \nu_o(x,y,z)\ \gamma_o(x,y,z). \tag{11}$$

Let us consider that the moving reference system, related to the studied finite element, has the angular velocity $\overline{\omega}$, the angular acceleration $\overline{\varepsilon}$, the velocity $\overline{v}_o$ of the origin $O(X_o, Y_o, Z_o)$, and $\overline{a}_o$ the acceleration of the point O. In the theory of the elastic body with voids, the position of an elementary element is described by the coordinate of the point around which is considered the elementary element and the third rotation of the element. The approximation made in FEM links the displacements of a certain point denoted M with the independent coordinates $\{\delta\}_L$, representing the displacement of the nodes of the finite elements, and $\{\phi\}_L$, representing the rotation of a reference frame situated in the point. The local kinematics of the finite element are therefore defined through the relation [34]

$$\{u\}_L = [N_\delta]\{\delta\}_L \ ; \ \{\phi\}_L = [N_\phi]\{\delta\}_L. \tag{12}$$

and the distribution of the percentage of voids can be written as

$$\nu_L = [N_\nu]\{\delta\}_L. \tag{13}$$

In these relations, $[N_\delta]$, $[N_\phi]$, and $[N_\nu]$ are shape function matrices. The quantity ν_L is scalar, and the shape matrix $[N_\nu]$ is a line matrix.

If $\{u\}_L$ represents the displacement of the point M that moves into M', it can be written

$$\{r_{M'}\}_G = \{r_O\}_G + [R](\{r\}_L + \{u\}_L)\,. \tag{14}$$

In Equation (14), $[R]$ represents the rotation matrix which realizes the transformation of a vector from the local coordinate system L to the global coordinate system G. Additionally,

$\{r_{M'}\}_G$ is the position vector of M' having the components expressed in a global reference frame. The velocity of M′ is

$$\{v_{M'}\}_G = \{\dot{r}_{M'}\}_G = \{\dot{r}_O\}_G + \left[\dot{R}\right](\{r\}_L + [N]\{\delta\}_L) + [R][N]\left\{\dot{\delta}\right\}_L. \tag{15}$$

Using Equations (12) and (13), we obtain

$$\left\{\dot{\phi}\right\}_L = [N_\phi]\left\{\dot{\delta}\right\}_L, \tag{16}$$

$$\dot{\nu}_L = [N_\nu]\left\{\dot{\delta}\right\}_L. \tag{17}$$

With Equations (15)–(17), the kinetic energy of a finite element, considered as a part of a micro-structured material with voids, is:

$$E_c = \frac{1}{2}\int_V \rho_0\{v_{M'}\}_G^T\{v_{M'}\}_G dV + \frac{1}{2}\int_V \rho_0\left\{\dot{\phi}_{M'}\right\}_G^T[Y]\left\{\dot{\phi}_{M'}\right\}_G dV + \frac{1}{2}\int_V \rho_0\kappa_\nu\dot{\nu}_{M'G}^2 dV. \tag{18}$$

It is denoted with κ_ν the so called "equilibrated inertia" [34], and with $[Y]$, the matrix of the coefficients of inertia [1–3,5,10,12].

The classical form of the elastic potential energy is [58]

$$E_p = \frac{1}{2}\int_V \{\sigma\}^T\{\varepsilon\}dV. \tag{19}$$

The classical Hooke's law is [54]

$$\{\sigma\} = [H]\{\varepsilon\}. \tag{20}$$

and it exists the following relations:

$$\{\varepsilon\} = [b_1]\{u\} + [b_2]\{\phi\} = ([b_1][N_\delta] + [b_2][N_\phi])\{\delta\}_L = [N_s]\{\delta\}_L, \tag{21}$$

where $[b_1]$ and $[b_2]$ are two differential operators, and

$$[N_s] = [b_1][N_\delta] + [b_2][N_\phi] \tag{22}$$

(see [54]).

So, the potential energy can be written

$$E_p = \frac{1}{2}\{\delta\}_L^T\left(\int_V [N_s]^T[H]^T[N_s]dV\right)\{\delta\}_L. \tag{23}$$

Equation (11) can be expressed as

$$E_p = \frac{1}{2}\{\delta\}_L^T[k]\{\delta\}_L. \tag{24}$$

In Equation (24), $[k]$ represents the stiffness matrix.

The term of energy due to the voids is

$$E_{pv} = \frac{1}{2}\{\delta\}_L^T[k_v]\{\delta\}_L. \tag{25}$$

In reference [53], E_{pv} is represented as

$$E_{pv} = \frac{1}{2}\begin{bmatrix} \frac{\partial v}{\partial x} & \frac{\partial v}{\partial y} & \frac{\partial v}{\partial z} \end{bmatrix} \begin{bmatrix} d_{11} & d_{12} & d_{13} \\ d_{21} & d_{22} & d_{23} \\ d_{31} & d_{32} & d_{33} \end{bmatrix} \begin{Bmatrix} \frac{\partial v}{\partial x} \\ \frac{\partial v}{\partial y} \\ \frac{\partial v}{\partial z} \end{Bmatrix}. \tag{26}$$

Using Equations (12) and (13), it gives

$$\begin{aligned} \frac{\partial v}{\partial x} &= \frac{\partial}{\partial x}([N_v]\{\delta\}_L) = [N_{v,x}]\{\delta\}_L, \\ \frac{\partial v}{\partial y} &= \frac{\partial}{\partial y}([N_v]\{\delta\}_L) = [N_{v,y}]\{\delta\}_L, \\ \frac{\partial v}{\partial z} &= \frac{\partial}{\partial z}([N_v]\{\delta\}_L) = [N_{v,z}]_L\{\delta\}_L, \end{aligned} \tag{27}$$

or

$$\begin{Bmatrix} \frac{\partial v}{\partial x} \\ \frac{\partial v}{\partial y} \\ \frac{\partial v}{\partial z} \end{Bmatrix} = \begin{bmatrix} [N_{v,x}] \\ [N_{v,y}] \\ [N_{v,z}] \end{bmatrix} \{\delta\}_L, \tag{28}$$

or:

$$\begin{bmatrix} \frac{\partial v}{\partial x} & \frac{\partial v}{\partial y} & \frac{\partial v}{\partial z} \end{bmatrix} = \{\delta\}_L^T \begin{bmatrix} [N_{v,x}]^T & [N_{v,y}]^T & [N_{v,z}]^T \end{bmatrix}. \tag{29}$$

and

$$E_{pv} = \frac{1}{2}\{\delta\}_L^T \begin{bmatrix} [N_{v,x}]^T & [N_{v,y}]^T & [N_{v,z}]^T \end{bmatrix} [d] \begin{bmatrix} [N_{v,x}] \\ [N_{v,y}] \\ [N_{v,z}] \end{bmatrix} \{\delta\}_L. \tag{30}$$

Considering a homogeneous and isotropic body, the coefficients d_{ij} are equal, and an estimate for them is presented in [34]. The matrix $[d]$ is the unit matrix premultiplied with a coefficient for the most practical cases [34].

The work produced by concentrated load $\{q_t\}_L$ and moments $\{q_r\}_L$ is

$$W^c = \{q\}_L^T\{\delta\}_L. \tag{31}$$

where it is denoted

$$\{q\}_L^T = \{q_t\}_L^T + \{q_r\}_L^T. \tag{32}$$

and that produced by the volume forces and moments is

$$W^d = \{q^*\}_L^T\{\delta\}_L. \tag{33}$$

It is noted as

$$\{q^*\}_L^T = \left[\int_V \{p\}_L^T[N_\delta]dV\right]\{\delta\}_L + \left[\int_V \{m\}_L^T[N_\phi]dV\right]\{\delta\}_L. \tag{34}$$

The potential energy due to the existence of voids is

$$E_{pv} = \frac{1}{2}\{\delta\}_L^T[k_v]\{\delta\}_L. \tag{35}$$

In what follows, the method of LE is presented to determine the evolution equations [75].

The Lagrangean [21] has the classical form

$$L = E_c - E_p + W^d + W^c + W^v. \quad (36)$$

In this formula, W^d is the work of distributed forces, W^c is the work of concentrated forces, and W^v is the work determined by the existence of voids.

We use the notations

$$[m] = \int_V [N_\delta]^T [N_\delta] \rho_o dV; \ [J] = \int_V [N_\phi]^T [Y][N_\phi] \rho_o dV; \ [m_v] = \int_V [N_v]^T [N_v] \kappa \, \rho_o dV; \quad (37)$$

$$[c] = 2\int_V [N_\delta]^T \left[\dot{R}\right]^T [R][N_\delta] \rho_o dV; \ \left[k(\varepsilon) + k(\omega^2)\right] = \int_V [N_\delta]^T \left(\left[\ddot{R}\right]^T [R]\right) [N_\delta] \rho_o dV. \quad (38)$$

$$\left[m_O^i\right] = \int_V [N_\delta]^T \rho_o dV; \ \left\{q^i(\varepsilon)\right\} + \left\{q^i(\omega^2)\right\} = \int_V [N_\delta]^T [R]^T \left[\ddot{R}\right] \{r\}_L \rho_o dV. \quad (39)$$

If we use the LE, it results in

$$\begin{aligned} &([m] + [J] + [m_v])\left\{\ddot{\delta}\right\}_L + [c]\left\{\dot{\delta}\right\}_L + ([k] + [k_v] + [k(\varepsilon)] + [k(\omega^2)])\{\delta\}_L \\ &= \{q\}_L^T + \{q^*\}_L^T + \{q_v\}^T - [m_O^i]\{\ddot{r}_O\}_L - \{q^i(\varepsilon)\} - \{q^i(\omega^2)\}. \end{aligned} \quad (40)$$

Considering the static case, it obtains

$$\left([k] + [k_v] + [k(\varepsilon)] + \left[k(\omega^2)\right]\right)\{\delta\}_L = \{q\}_L^T + \{q^*\}_L^T + \{q_v\}^T. \quad (41)$$

3. Results

In the following, the GA method is presented to obtain the evolution equations for a solid composed of such a material. Using the GA equations, it is necessary to write the energy of the accelerations. The acceleration of a point of the solid is

$$\{a_{M'}\}_G = \{\ddot{r}_O\}_G + \left[\ddot{R}\right]\{r\}_L + \left[\ddot{R}\right][N]\{\delta\}_L + 2\left[\dot{R}\right][N]\left\{\dot{\delta}\right\}_L + [R][N]\left\{\ddot{\delta}\right\}_L. \quad (42)$$

and the energy of the accelerations is given by the relation

$$E_c = \frac{1}{2}\int_V \rho_0 \{a_{M'}\}_G^T \{a_{M'}\}_G dV + \frac{1}{2}\int_V \rho_0 \left\{\ddot{\phi}_{M'}\right\}_G^T [Y] \left\{\ddot{\phi}_{M'}\right\}_G dV + \frac{1}{2}\int_V \rho_0 \kappa_v \ddot{v}_{M'G}^2 dV. \quad (43)$$

The second order derivative of Equation (12) are used in Equation (41):

$$\left\{\ddot{\phi}\right\}_L = [N_\phi]\left\{\ddot{\delta}\right\}_L. \quad (44)$$

Performing all the necessary calculations within the expression (43) using the notations (37)–(39) and applying Equation (9), we finally obtain Relations (40) and (41). The number of operations used to obtain them is less than in the case of using LE.

An example will illustrate our theoretical consideration. We consider a circular bar in which gaps of material will be inserted at percentages of 1, 2, 3, and 4% (Figure 1). The bar has 1 m length and a diameter equal to 1 cm. To achieve this, consider the discretized bar in three-dimensional finite elements. In a cross section of the bar, with a circular shape, 32 finite elements are considered (Figure 2). Statistically, one element is extracted from this structure to assure a percentage of 1, 2, 3, or 4%. The extraction of these elements to create the voids is done statistically. For example, if the structure is divided into 3200 elements,

32 elements will be extracted to achieve 1% voids. Thus, with this procedure, a bar with 1% voids is first made, then the number of voids is successively increased until the last variant containing 4% voids is obtained. For each of these variants, the strain and stress calculation is performed to obtain the maximum values. The studied material is considered to have the Young's modulus of 125 GPa, with $\nu = 0.3$. The force value F is 100 N. The bar is clamped at both ends.

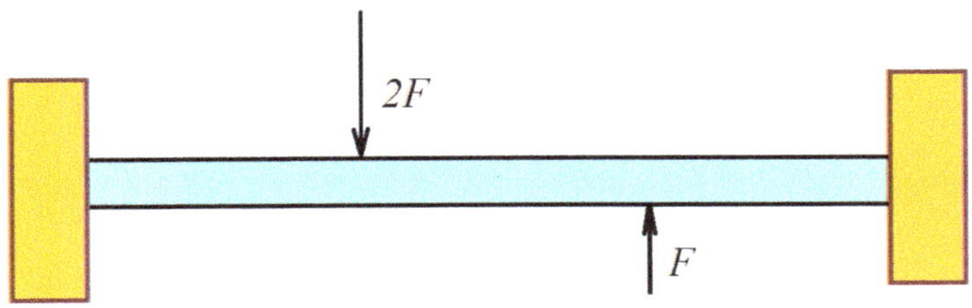

Figure 1. The studied truss loaded with two forces.

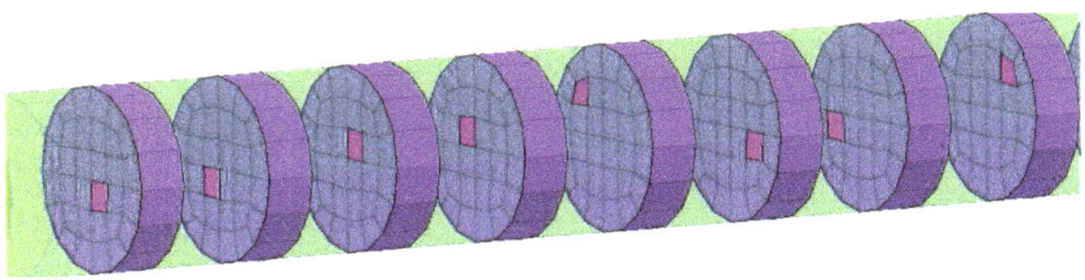

Figure 2. Voids inside the body of the bar.

Considering the distribution of voids in Figure 2, a calculation of stresses and deformations was performed in the four considered cases and the results were compared with the situation of a homogeneous bar without voids. Figure 3 contains the maximum displacements of the bar in the studied cases. Figure 4 contains the maximum von Mises stresses of the bar in the studied cases.

In Table 1, these results are synthetized for a global image of the displacements and stresses.

Table 1. The displacements and von Mises stresses.

	Homogeneous Bar	1% Voids	2% Voids	3% Voids	4% Voids
Displacements [mm]	0.5126	0.5322	0.5524	0.5586	0.5723
Variation of displacements [%]	----	3.82	7.76	8.97	11.64
von Mises stress [GPa]	22.995	23.541	24.213	24.805	25.323
Variation of von Mises stress [%]	----	2.37	5.39	7.86	10.12

A calculation of the eigenfrequencies of the system was made in two cases: for 0% voids and for 4% voids. The results are presented in Table 2. It can be concluded that the existence of a percentage of voids in the material will have an insignificant influence on the vibrations of the studied body.

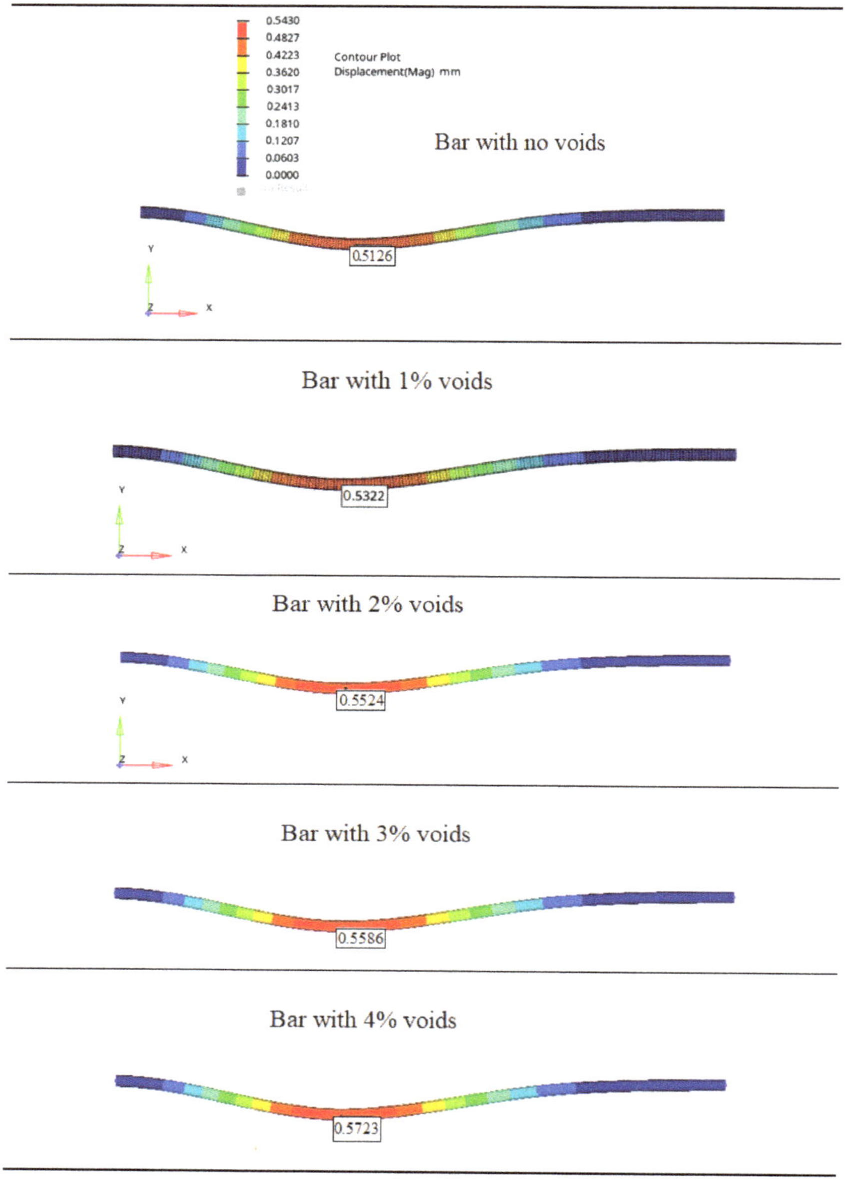

Figure 3. Maximum displacements of the bar, in mm.

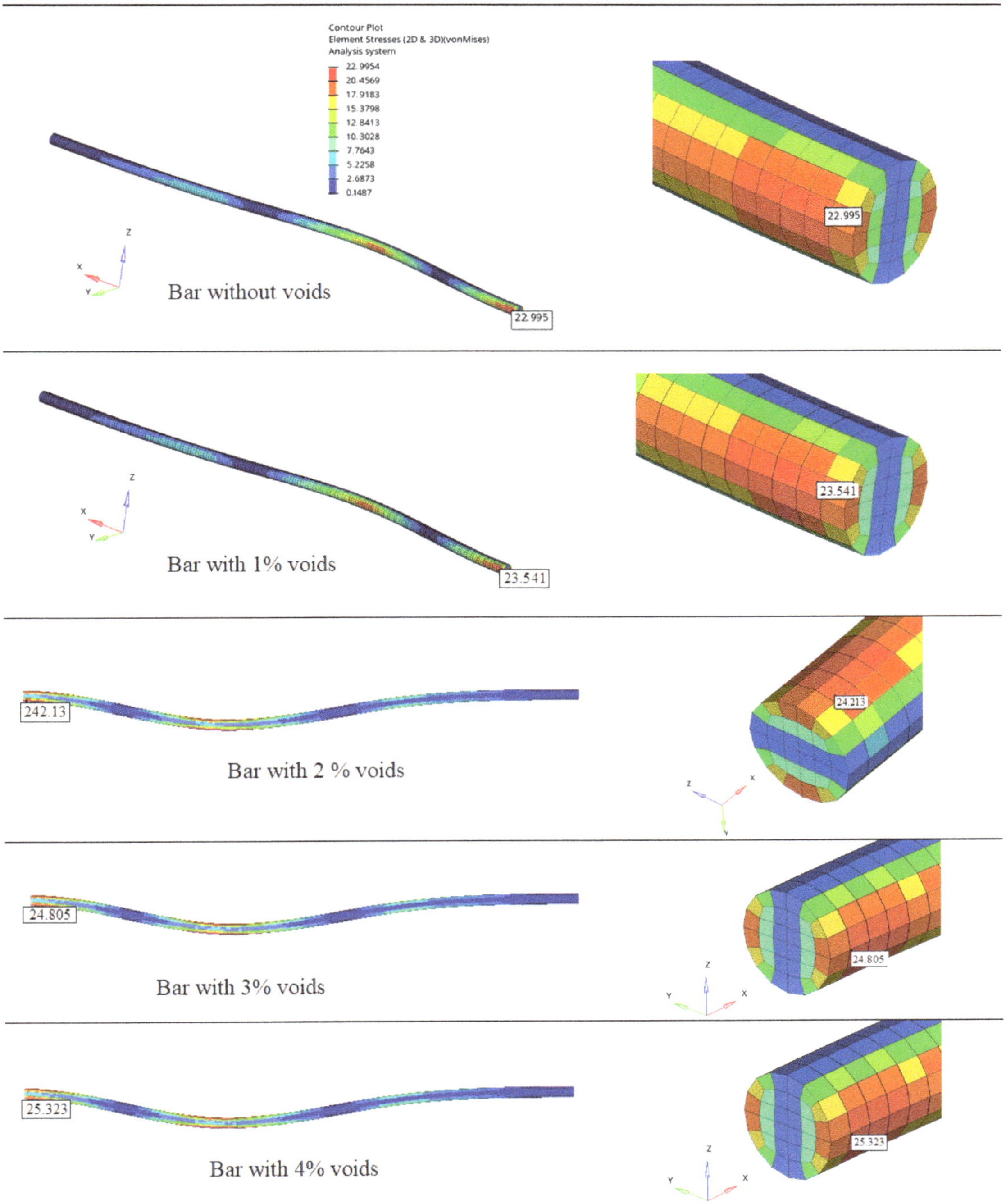

Figure 4. Maximum von Mises stress, in GPa.

Table 2. The eigenmodes of the bar with voids.

Mode	Representation	Frequency for 0% Voids [Hz]	Frequency for 4% Voids [Hz]
1		139.0319	139.9093
2		139.0319	139.9093
3		382.3166	382.3166
4	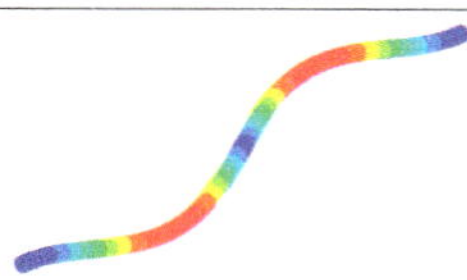	382.3166	382.3166
5		747.0574	747.0574
6		747.0574	747.0574
7		1229.853	1229.853
8		1229.853	1229.853
9		1828.136	1828.136

Table 2. *Cont.*

Mode	Representation	Frequency for 0% Voids [Hz]	Frequency for 4% Voids [Hz]
10		1828.136	1828.136

4. Discussion

If LE are applied to determine the set of the equations of motion, there will be fewer mathematical differentiation operations if the GA equations are applied. The use of these equations makes the calculations easier, which for large systems can be significant. It is difficult to estimate the number of operations, this depends on the size of the system and the type of finite elements that was chosen, which determines the number of degrees of freedom that will be taken into account.

The LE is

$$\frac{d}{dt}\left\{\frac{\partial L}{\partial \dot{\delta}_e}\right\} - \left\{\frac{\partial L}{\partial \delta_e}\right\} = 0 \tag{45}$$

From a qualitative point of view, it can be observed that it is necessary to perform four differentiation operations for the expressions $\left\{\partial L/\partial \dot{\delta}_e\right\}$, another four for the expressions $\{\partial L/\partial \delta_e\}$, and then the derivatives in relation to time of the terms $\left\{\partial L/\partial \dot{\delta}_e\right\}$.

However, if we use the Gibbs–Appell equations, it is necessary to differentiate the energy of the accelerations. In that case, it is necessary to make only five operations. These operations in both cases are related to the components of a vector; for this reason, they will also depend on the number of degrees of the system. In the case of the Gibbs–Appell formalism, only five differentiations will be made.

It can therefore be concluded that if the Gibbs–Appell equations and the acceleration energy are applied, the number of operations that must be performed is less than if the Lagrange equations and the kinetic energy are used. In most applications, Lagrange's method is used. This is due to the fact that most researchers are very familiar with the notion of kinetic energy and less so with the notion of acceleration energy. This method can therefore also be used when studying a mechanical system that has in its composition elements made of materials with micro-structure and voids. The use of the Gibbs-Appell formalism has the advantage of reducing the calculation time and, consequently, the cost of the analysis stage of such a mechanical system. In general, it can be considered that the number of operations can be halved. In the case of complex structures, of large dimensions and operating in difficult conditions, this reduction can be important.

Previous studies have shown that the existence of voids, even in small percentages, can cause a significant variation in the mechanical properties [75,76] (see Table 3).

The results obtained in our analysis are presented in Table 4.

From this table, it can be seen that voids can lead to a significant reduction in the mechanical properties. It follows that the study of their influence in different situations has become a very important thing. So, the study of these materials becomes important for practical applications.

Table 3. The mechanical effect of the existence of voids in structure.

Increase in Percentage of Voids	Reduction in Flexural Rigidity/[Reference]
1%	10%/[21]
0% to 5%	25%/[21]
2.5%	20%/[20]
1%	10%/[20]
3%	17%/[77]
1%	35%/[78]
6%	40%/[78]

Table 4. The results obtained for the studied model.

Increase in Percentage of Voids	Variation of Displacement [%]	Variation of Von Mises Stress [%]
0%	0	0
1%	3.82	2.37
2%	7.76	5.39
3%	8.97	7.86
4%	11.64	10.12

5. Conclusions

In this paper, the authors sought to extend the application of the Gibbs–Appell formalism to analyze systems consisting of materials with micro-s and voids. In a previous paper, the authors extended the area of FEM to apply it to MBS bodies with microstructure and voids. The method used to do this was the Lagrange Equations. As for other mechanical systems, usually made by rigid bodies, there are a lot of papers proving that using other methods such as the Lagrange formalism can be useful in some cases. We extended this observation to MBS with microstructure and voids. We found that this is possible with little effort. As a result, it is also possible for this type of material to apply the Gibbs–Appell equations and consequently benefit from the advantages of using these equations. The developed model takes into account both the microstructural properties of the material and the embedded voids.

Advantages of using the Gibbs–Appell method are mentioned in a series of papers [61,63,65,67]. The present work aims to expand this area of application of the method. If most of the works that approach this formalism refer to bodies with rigid elements, the authors tried to extend the method to elastic mechanical systems. The models used for these systems lead to a large number of operations and, as a result, any method to shorten the calculation time (and costs) is extremely beneficial. Obviously, at this stage, the work can form the basis of further developments for the study of mechanical engineering systems used in practice.

Author Contributions: Conceptualization, S.V., M.M. and C.I.; methodology, S.V., M.M. and C.I.; software, S.V., M.M. and C.I.; validation, S.V., M.M. and C.I.; formal analysis, S.V., M.M. and C.I.; investigation, S.V., M.M. and C.I.; resources, S.V., M.M. and C.I.; writing—original draft preparation S.V., M.M. and C.I.; writing—review and editing, S.V., M.M. and C.I.; visualization, S.V., M.M. and C.I.; supervision, S.V., M.M. and C.I.; project administration, S.V., M.M. and C.I.; funding acquisition S.V., M.M. and C.I.; All authors have read and agreed to the published version of the manuscript.

Funding: The APC was funded by Transilvania University of Brasov (cf. HBS 1543/2020).

Institutional Review Board Statement: Not applicable.

Informed Consent Statement: Not applicable.

Data Availability Statement: Data are contained within the article.

Conflicts of Interest: The authors declare no conflicts of interest.

References

1. Mehdikhani, M.; Gorbatikh, L.; Verpoest, I.; Lomov, S.V. Voids in fiber-reinforced polymer composites: A review on their formation, characteristics, and effects on mechanical performance. Judd NCW and Wright WW. Voids and their effects on mechanical-properties of composites—Appraisal. *J. Compos. Mater.* **2019**, *53*, 1579–1669. [CrossRef]
2. Rohatgi, V.; Patel, N.; Lee, L.J. Experimental investigation of flow-induced microvoids during impregnation of unidirectional stitched fiberglass mat. *Polym. Compos.* **1996**, *17*, 161–170. [CrossRef]
3. Teodorescu-Draghicescu, H.; Scutaru, M.L.; Rosu, D.; Calin, M.R.; Grigore, P. New Advanced Sandwich Composite with twill weave carbon and EPS. *J. Optoelectron. Adv. Mater.* **2013**, *15*, 199–203.
4. Marin, M.; Hobiny, A.; Abbas, I. The Effects of Fractional Time Derivatives in Porothermoelastic Materials Using Finite Element Method. *Mathematics* **2021**, *9*, 1606. [CrossRef]
5. Schell, J.S.U.; Deleglise, M.; Binetruy, C.; Krawczak, P.; Ermanni, P. Numerical prediction and experimental characterisation of mesoscale-voids in liquid composite moulding. *Compos. Part. A Appl. Sci. Manuf.* **2007**, *38*, 2460–2470. [CrossRef]
6. Helmus, R.; Kratz, J.; Potter, K.; Hubert, P.; Hinterhölzl, R. An experimental technique to characterize interply void formation in unidirectional prepregs. *J. Compos. Mater.* **2017**, *51*, 579–591. [CrossRef]
7. Hernandez, S.; Sket, F.; Gonzalez, C.; Llorca, J. Optimization of curing cycle in carbon fiber-reinforced laminates: Void distribution and mechanical properties. *Compos. Sci. Technol.* **2013**, *85*, 73–82. [CrossRef]
8. Campbell, F.C.; Mallow, A.R.; Browning, C.E. Porosity in carbon-fiber composites—An overview of causes. *J. Adv. Mater.* **1995**, *26*, 18–33.
9. Naganuma, T.; Naito, K.; Kyono, J.; Kagawa, Y. Influence of prepreg conditions on the void occurrence and tensile properties of woven glass fiber-reinforced polyimide composites. *Compos. Sci. Technol.* **2009**, *69*, 2428–2433. [CrossRef]
10. Gladysz, G.M.; Chawla, K.K. *Intrinsic Voids in Polymers. Voids in Materials: From Unavoidable Defects to Designed Cellular Materials*; Elsevier: Amsterdam, The Netherlands, 2015; pp. 37–48.
11. Sung, B.J.; Yethiraj, A. Structure of void space in polymer solutions. *Phys. Rev. E* **2010**, *81*, 237. [CrossRef]
12. Liang, J.; Chen, R.; Zhang, J.F. Geometry and statistics of voids in lattice polymers. *Biophys. J.* **2002**, *82*, 471A–477A.
13. Nie, L.; Lee, K.; Liao, G.L. Void control in adhesive bonding using thermosetting polymer. *Sens. Actuator A-Phys.* **2011**, *167*, 398–405. [CrossRef]
14. Lee, J.W.; Wang, C.S.; Price, G.E. Void Formation in Coagulated Rigid-Rod Polymer Thin-Films. *Polymer* **1995**, *36*, 955–958. [CrossRef]
15. Gerhard-Multhaupt, R. Voided polymer electrets—New materials, new challenges, new chances. In Proceedings of the 11th International Symposium on Electrets (ISE 11), Melbourne, VIC, Australia, 3 October 2002; pp. 36–45.
16. Murray, B.R.; Leen, S.B.; Bradaigh, C.M.O. Void distributions and permeability prediction for rotationally moulded polymers. *Proc. Inst. Mech. Engineers. Part L-J. Mater.-Des. Appl.* **2015**, *229*, 403–418. [CrossRef]
17. Shen, T.F. Void damage model and service life prediction for solid high polymer. *Chin. Sci. Bull.* **2001**, *46*, 1842–1845. [CrossRef]
18. Summerscales, J.; Fry, S.A. Poisson Ration in Fiber-Reinforced Polymer Composites with a High Void Content. *J. Mater. Sci. Lett.* **1994**, *13*, 912–914. [CrossRef]
19. Wu, Y.N.; Shivpuri, R.; Lee, L.J. Effect of macro and micro voids on elastic properties of polymer composites. *J. Reinf. Plast. Compos.* **1998**, *17*, 1391–1402. [CrossRef]
20. Hocine, N.A.; Hamdi, A.; Zairi, F. Experimental and finite element investigation of void nucleation in rubber-like materials. *Int. J. Solids Struct.* **2011**, *48*, 1248–1254. [CrossRef]
21. Tang, J.-M.; Lee, W.I.; Springer, G.S. Effects of cure pressure on resin flow, voids, and mechanical properties. *J. Compos. Mater.* **1987**, *21*, 421–440. [CrossRef]
22. Liu, L.; Zhang, B.-M.; Wang, D.-F.; Wu, Z.-J. Effects of cure cycles on void content and mechanical properties of composite laminates. *Compos. Struct.* **2006**, *73*, 303–309. [CrossRef]
23. Ghiorse, S. Effect of void content on the mechanical properties of carbon/epoxy laminates. *Sample Q.* **1993**, *24*, 54–59.
24. Cinquin, J.; Triquenaux, V.; Rousne, Y. Porosity influence on organic composite material mechanical properties. In Proceedings of the 16th International Conference on Composite Materials (ICCM16), Kyoto, Japan, 8–13 July 2007.
25. Hou, M.; Ye, L.; Mai, Y.-W. Effect of moulding temperature on flexure, impact strength and interlaminar fracture toughness of CF/PEI composite. *J. Reinf. Plast. Compos.* **1996**, *15*, 1117–1130. [CrossRef]
26. Flavin, J.N.; Knops, R.J. Some decay estimates in continuum dynamics. *J. Elast.* **1987**, *17*, 249–264. [CrossRef]
27. Goodman, M.A.; Cowin, S.C. A continuum theory for granular materials. *Arch. Ration. Mech. Anal.* **1972**, *44*, 249–266. [CrossRef]
28. Chirita, S.; Arusoaie, A. Thermoelastic waves in double porosity materials. *Eur. J. Mech. A Solids* **2021**, *86*, 104177. [CrossRef]
29. Abbas, I.; Hobiny, A.; Marin, M. Photo-thermal interactions in a semi-conductor material with cylindrical cavities and variable thermal conductivity. *J. Taibah Univ. Sci.* **2020**, *14*, 1369–1376. [CrossRef]
30. Marin, M. On the minimum principle for dipolar materials with stretch. *Nonlinear Anal. RWA* **2009**, *10*, 1572–1578. [CrossRef]

31. Modrea, A.; Vlase, S.; Calin, M.R.; Peterlicean, A. The influence of dimensional and structural shifts of the elastic constant values in cylinder fiber composites. *J. Optoelectron. Adv. Mater.* **2013**, *15*, 278–283.
32. Vlase, S.; Teodorescu-Draghicescu, H.; Calin, M.R.; Serbina, L. Simulation of the elastic properties of some fibre-reinforced composite laminates under off-axis loading system. *Optoelectron. Adv. Mater. Rapid Commun.* **2011**, *5*, 424–429.
33. Öchsner, A. *Computational Statics and Dynamics: An Introduction Based on the Finite Element Method*; Springer: Singapore, 2020.
34. Iesan, D. *Thermoelastic Models of Continua*; Kluwer Academic: Dordrecht, The Netherlands, 2004.
35. Nguyen, V.T.; Hwu, C. A Review on Modelling Polymer Composites via Anisotropic Viscoelasticity. *J. Aeronaut. Astronaut. Aviat.* **2021**, *53*, 387–402.
36. Raju, K.; Tay, T.E.; Tan, V.B.C. A review of the FEM method for composites. *Multiscale Multidiscip. Model. Exp. Des.* **2021**, *4*, 1–24. [CrossRef]
37. Sharma, A.; Bagha, A.K.; Shukla, D.K.; Bahl, S. Finite element model updating of metallic and composite structures-A state of the art review. *AIMS Mater. Sci.* **2021**, *8*, 390–415. [CrossRef]
38. Jagadeesh, G.V.; Setti, S.G. A review on micromechanical methods for evaluation of mechanical behavior of particulate reinforced metal matrix composites. *J. Mater. Sci.* **2020**, *55*, 9848–9882. [CrossRef]
39. Muzel, S.D.; Bonhin, E.; Guimaraes, N.M.; Guidi, E.S. Application of the Finite Element Method in the Analysis of Composite Materials: A Review. *Polymers* **2020**, *12*, 818. [CrossRef] [PubMed]
40. Teodorescu-Draghicescu, H.; Stanciu, A.; Vlase, S.; Scutaru, L.; Calin, M.R.; Serbina, L. Finite Element Method Analysis of Some Fibre-Reinforced Composite Laminates. *Optoelectron. Adv. Mater. Rapid Commun.* **2011**, *5*, 782–785.
41. Stanciu, A.; Teodorescu-Drăghicescu, H.; Vlase, S.; Scutaru, M.L.; Calin, M.R. Mechanical behavior of CSM450 and RT800 laminates subjected to four-point bend tests. *Optoelectron. Adv. Mater. Rapid Commun.* **2012**, *6*, 495–497.
42. Niculiţă, C.; Vlase, S.; Bencze, A.; Mihălcică, M.; Calin, M.R.; Serbina, L. Optimum stacking in a multi-ply laminate used for the skin of adaptive wings. *Optoelectron. Adv. Mater. Rapid Commun.* **2011**, *5*, 1233–1236.
43. Nunziato, J.W.; Cowin, S.C. Linear elastic materials with voids. *J. Elast.* **1983**, *13*, 125–147.
44. Othman, M.I.A.; Fekry, M.; Marin, M. Plane waves in generalized magneto-thermo-viscoelastic medium with voids under the effect of initial stress and laser pulse heating. *Struct. Eng. Mech.* **2020**, *73*, 621–629.
45. Chang, X.; Ren, M.F.; Li, T.; Guo, X. Evaluation of mechanical behaviour of unidirectional fibre-reinforced composites considering the void morphology. *J. Reinf. Platics Compos.* **2017**, *36*, 1817–1828. [CrossRef]
46. Dong, C.S. Effects of Process-Induced Voids on the Properties of Fibre Reinforced Composites. *J. Mater. Sci. Technol.* **2016**, *32*, 597–604. [CrossRef]
47. Erdman, A.G.; Sandor, G.N.; Oakberg, A. A General Method for Kineto-Elastodynamic Analysis and Synthesis of Mechanism. Journal of Engineering for Industry. *ASME Trans.* **1972**, *94*, 1193.
48. Bagci, C. Elastodynamic Response of Mechanical Systems using Matrix Exponential Mode Uncoupling and Incremental Forcing Techniques with Finite Element Method. In Proceedings of the Sixth Word Congress on Theory of Machines and Mechanisms, New Delhi, India, 15–20 December 1983; p. 472.
49. Bahgat, B.M.; Willmert, K.D. Finite Element Vibrational Analysis of Planar Mechanisms. *Mech. Mach. Theory* **1976**, *11*, 47. [CrossRef]
50. Cleghorn, W.L.; Fenton, E.G.; Tabarrok, K.B. Finite Element Analysis of High-Speed Flexible Mechanisms. *Mech. Mach. Theory* **1981**, *16*, 407. [CrossRef]
51. Christensen, E.R.; Lee, S.W. Nonlinear finite element modelling of the dynamics of unrestrained flexible structures. *Comput. Struct.* **1986**, *23*, 819–829. [CrossRef]
52. Midha, A.; Erdman, A.G.; Frohrib, D.A. Finite element approach to mathematical modeling of high-speed elastic linkages. *Mech. Mach. Theory* **1978**, *13*, 603–618. [CrossRef]
53. Nath, K.; Ghosh, A. Steady-state response of mechanism with elastic links by finite element methods. *Mech. Mach. Theory* **1980**, *15*, 199. [CrossRef]
54. Vlase, S.; Marin, M.; Öchsner, A.; Scutaru, M.L. Motion equation for a flexible one-dimensional element used in the dynamical analysis of a multibody system. *Continuum Mech. Thermodyn.* **2019**, *31*, 715–724. [CrossRef]
55. Vlase, S. Dynamical Response of a Multibody System with Flexible Elements with a General Three-Dimensional Motion. *Rom. J. Phys.* **2012**, *57*, 676–693.
56. Vlase, S.; Dănăşel, C.; Scutaru, M.L.; Mihălcică, M. Finite Element Analysis of a Two-Dimensional Linear Elastic Systems with a Plane "rigid Motion". *Rom. J. Phys.* **2014**, *59*, 476–487.
57. Deü, J.-F.; Galucio, A.C.; Ohayon, R. Dynamic responses of flexible-link mechanisms with passive/active damping treatment. *Comput. Struct.* **2008**, *86*, 258–265. [CrossRef]
58. Hou, W.; Zhang, X. Dynamic analysis of flexible linkage mechanisms under uniform temperature change. *J. Sound. Vib.* **2009**, *319*, 570–592. [CrossRef]
59. Neto, M.A.; Ambrósio, J.A.C.; Leal, R. Composite materials in flexible multibody systems. *Comput. Methods Appl. Mech. Eng.* **2006**, *195*, 6860–6873. [CrossRef]
60. Piras, G.; Cleghorn, W.L.; Mills, J.K. Dynamic finite-element analysis of a planar high-speed, high-precision parallel manipulator with flexible links. *Mech. Mach. Theory* **2005**, *40*, 849–862. [CrossRef]
61. Gibbs, J.W. On the fundamental formulae of dynamics. *Am. J. Math.* **1879**, *2*, 49–64. [CrossRef]

62. Appell, P. Sur une forme générale des equations de la dynamique. *C.R. Acad. Sci. Paris.* **1899**, *1900*, 129.
63. Mirtaheri, S.M.; Zohoor, H. The Explicit Gibbs-Appell Equations of Motion for Rigid-Body Constrained Mechanical System. In Proceedings of the 2018 6th RSI International Conference on Robotics and Mechatronics (IcRoM), Tehran, Iran, 23–25 October 2018; pp. 304–309.
64. Mehrjooee, O.; Dehkordi, S.F.; Korayem, M.H. Dynamic modeling and extended bifurcation analysis of flexible-link manipulator. *Mech. Based Des. Struct. Mach.* **2020**, *48*, 87–110. [CrossRef]
65. Korayem, M.H.; Dehkordi, S.F. Motion equations of cooperative multi flexible mobile manipulator via recursive Gibbs-Appell formulation. *Appl. Math. Model.* **2019**, *65*, 443–463. [CrossRef]
66. Shafei, A.M.; Shafei, H.R. A systematic method for the hybrid dynamic modeling of open kinematic chains confined in a closed environment. *Multibody Syst. Dyn.* **2017**, *38*, 21–42. [CrossRef]
67. Amini, S.; Dehkordi, S.F.; Fahraji, S.H. Motion equation derivation and tip-over evaluations for K mobile manipulators with the consideration of motors mass by the use of Gibbs-Appell formulation. In Proceedings of the 5th RSI International Conference on Robotics and Mechatronics (IcRoM), Tehran, Iran, 25–27 October 2017.
68. Korayem, M.H.; Dehkordi, S.F. Derivation of dynamic equation of viscoelastic manipulator with revolute-prismatic joint using recursive Gibbs-Appell formulation. *Nonlinear Dyn.* **2017**, *89*, 2041–2064. [CrossRef]
69. Shafei, A.M.; Korayem, M.H. Theoretical and experimental study of dynamic load-carrying capacity for flexible robotic arms in point-to-point motion. *Optim. Control. Appl. Methods* **2017**, *38*, 963–972. [CrossRef]
70. Marin, M.; Seadawy, A.; Vlase, S.; Chirila, A. On mixed problem in thermoelasticity of type III for Cosserat media. *J. Taibah Univ. Sci.* **2022**, *16*, 1264–1274. [CrossRef]
71. Vlase, S.; Negrean, I.; Marin, M.; Scutaru, M.L. Energy of Accelerations Used to Obtain the Motion Equations of a Three-Dimensional Finite Element. *Symmetry* **2020**, *12*, 321. [CrossRef]
72. Negrean, I.; Crișan, A.-D.; Vlase, S. A New Approach in Analytical Dynamics of Mechanical Systems. *Symmetry* **2020**, *12*, 95. [CrossRef]
73. Vlase, S. Elimination of Lagrangian Multipliers. *Mech. Res. Commun.* **1987**, *14*, 17. [CrossRef]
74. Scutaru, M.L.; Mitrica, B. Dynamical Analysis of the Mechanical System with Two Degrees of Freedom Applied to the Transmission of the Wind Turbine. *Math. Probl. Eng.* **2016**, *2016*, 3821083. [CrossRef]
75. Vlase, S.; Marin, M.; Öchsner, A.; Itu, C. Elastic response of a hollow cylinder with voids and micropolar structure. *Contin. Mech. Thermodyn.* **2022**, *34*, 855–866. [CrossRef]
76. Katouzian, M.; Vlase, S.; Scutaru, M.L. Finite Element Method-Based Simulation Creep Behavior of Viscoelastic Carbon-Fiber Composite. *Polymers* **2021**, *13*, 1017. [CrossRef]
77. Iesan, D. A theory of thermoelastic materials with voids. *Acta Mech.* **1986**, *60*, 67–89. [CrossRef]
78. Rusu, G. On existence and uniqueness in thermoelasticity of bodies with voids. *Bull. Acad. Polon Sci.* **1987**, *35*, 339–346.

mathematics

MDPI

Article

Investigating Behavior of Slider–Crank Mechanisms with Bearing Failures Using Vibration Analysis Techniques

Mofareh Hassan Ghazwani [1] and Van Vinh Pham [2,*]

[1] Department of Mechanical Engineering, Jazan University, P.O. Box 114, Jazan 45142, Saudi Arabia
[2] Institute of Energy & Mining Mechanical Engineering, Nha Trang 57100, Vietnam
* Correspondence: phamvv1978.iemm@gmail.com

Abstract: This study focuses on investigating the behavior of slider–crank mechanisms with different bearing failures using a vibration analysis technique. The reliability and lifespan of bearings are crucial for such mechanisms, which convert rotary motion to reciprocating motion. Previous research primarily addressed ball-bearing failures, neglecting needle bearings due to their specific applications. To bridge this gap, our experimental setup integrated both roller and ball bearings within a slider–crank mechanism. Vibration data were collected during normal operation, as well as under failure conditions of the ball and roller bearings. By analyzing the vibration signatures during simultaneous multiple failures, we gained insights into the nature of vibrations in the system. Furthermore, a mathematical model based on Hertzian contact was employed to calculate the theoretical frequency of ball bearings; however, due to the variable motion of the needle bearing, a novel mathematical model was proposed to estimate the defective impulse frequency, considering the inter-impact time between two impacts. The experimental results were compared with the healthy crank mechanism setup to draw meaningful conclusions. This research contributes to a comprehensive understanding of bearing failures in slider–crank mechanisms and provides valuable insights for designing reliable and long-lasting systems.

Keywords: vibrational analysis; ball bearing; needle bearing; slider–crank mechanism; frequency analysis

MSC: 35A24; 65D25; 65F18; 74H15

1. Introduction

The slider–crank mechanism is one of the most versatile and common assemblies in machines. It is a four-bar chain mechanism with one sliding joint and three revolute joints. Pumps, compressors, internal combustion engines, quick return mechanisms, punches, etc., are some inversions of slider–crank mechanisms. The slider–crank mechanism converts rotational motion into linear motion. The motion of the slider–crank mechanism is possible due to the free movement of the revolute joints held together by bearings. These components are designed to have a long life without any failures. This mechanism supports various loads and allows relative motions among the crank, connecting rod, and slider. Therefore, bearings used in the mechanism undergo cyclic loading; as a result, they have a high chance of failure. There are two types of failure with a high probability of occurrence: cracks in parts containing bearings like races or cages and surface failures like abrasive wear, corrosive wear, pitting, and scoring. For this reason, many studies have been conducted to analyze the failures in vibration signature analyses of bearings. A detailed literature survey on failures in bearings is summarized below.

Butler [1] used the shock pulse method to detect damage in ball bearings, for which a stethoscope or any listening stick was used to listen to the shock pulses of damaged bearings. Gupta [2,3] analyzed the dynamics of cylindrical rolling element bearing. An analytical formulation for the rolling element bearing and the interaction of the rolling element races with normal and moment vectors were proposed. The electro-hydrodynamic traction model was considered to calculate the roller race tractive forces during this analysis. Toersen [4] presented an experiment on damaged bearings and implemented an envelope technique to detect defects in ball bearings. The experimental results revealed that the defects depend upon the speed of the bearing corresponding to the frequency of the impact in the outer race, inner race, and ball uniquely. Mcfadden and Smith [5] developed a model to explain the vibrations caused by a single point defect in a bearing caused by a constant radial load. An impulse caused by a single point defect was considered an impulse function. The effect of the impulse function can be controlled by changing the magnitude of the impulse function. As the rolling elements roll over the defects, it causes an impulse with a fixed frequency in the bearing. The frequency depends on various parameters like bearing geometry, shaft speed, bearing load distribution, and location. When an impulse is generated in the bearing due to the defect, it creates a resonance between the bearing and the machine part to which it is fixed.

Patil et al. [6] presented research on localized bearing defects. The bearing was assumed to be a nonlinear spring, and the input force was considered a contact force whose calculations are carried out using Hertzian contact theory. The defect was assumed as a half-sine wave in which several readings are taken for different defect sizes and at various speeds. Vibration data were acquired in the time-domain signal and further converted into the frequency domain by fast Fourier transform analysis to find the exact resonance frequency. Tandon and Choudhury [7] proposed an analytical model for calculating the frequency and amplitudes of localized bearing under radial and axial bearing loads. For the inner race defect, sidebands were found around the peaks. The effect of load and pulse shape was also considered in the model and predicted that the magnitude of amplitude for the outer race is higher than that of the inner race. Liu et al. [8] developed a dynamic simulation model to study the effect of localized bearing defects, considering it as a two-degree-of-freedom system using piecewise functions and the Hertzian contact mechanism. The research found that it is essential to establish a relationship between impulse response and the defect's shape and size for its operation in a bearing. Choudhury and Tandon [9] have conducted several experiments using both good and defective bearings. An acoustic emission technique was applied to detect the roller bearing defect and compare the measured acoustic signals to find the flaws. Rubini and Meneghetti [10] presented a paper on applying envelope and wavelet transform analysis for fault diagnosis. The bearing defects can be analyzed by spectral analysis in classical vibrational analysis; however, this becomes very difficult if the forcing function is deficient.

Kiral and Karagulle [11] proposed a novel technique to use computer programming to perform the vibration response using a finite element analysis by applying a forcing function. The time and frequency domain analyses could be performed for healthy and damaged conditions followed by a comparison of the results to identify the exact cause of failures. Rai and Mohanty [12] applied the fast Fourier transform (FFT) of intrinsic mode functions in the Hilbert–Huang transform (HHT) technique to determine the failures in the bearing. Discrete Fourier transform and wavelet transform are beneficial for identifying the defect of bearings. Lu et al. [13] presented a paper on the fault diagnosis of motor bearings under variable speed using angular resampling of transient sound signals (TSA). A transient signal analysis tool was used to find the defect in the bearings; however, it is not a popular nor correct method for variable speed in a bearing analysis. Cui et al. [14] established a nonlinear vibration analysis technique to diagnose severe faults in bearings. The defect size is controlled in the outer race of the bearing; vibration signals are simulated and then analyzed for the defect impacts whose time interval gives the impact characteristics. Patel et al. [15] developed a dynamic model for vibration studies for deep-groove ball bearings with defects in multiple inner and outer races. In the analysis, the masses of the shaft, housing, races, and balls in their modelling are considered a parameter that influences the vibration characteristics. Salunkhe et al. [16] presented a study to analyze the vibration of deep-groove ball bearing using finite element analysis (FEA) and the dimension analysis technique (DAT). Experimental work was performed to investigate the vibration characteristics of ball bearings. The FEA, DAT, and experiment results show that vibration amplitude is a critical function of surface fault size. Their study was found to be effective in estimating vibration amplitude and defect frequency within reasonable error. Nan et al. [17] improved a new model to investigate the dynamic analysis of a rolling ball-bearing rotor. Hou et al. [18] presented a comparative study using an acoustic emission and vibration analysis for the bearing fault diagnosis of high-speed trains. Their research was the first to compare the effectiveness of applying acoustic emission (AE) and vibration methods to diagnose a naturally degraded high-speed train bearing. Abdulbary et al. [19] analyzed fault diagnosis in a rotating system based on vibration analysis. Their goal of was to assist researchers in implementing identification, diagnosis, and repair techniques of common fault types using vibration analysis. Several fundamental techniques were provided for the condition monitoring of rotating systems, including fast Fourier transform, the frequency domain decomposition method, wavelet transform, stochastic subspace identification, and deep learning. Xiao et al. [20] developed a computational framework to investigate the fault-clearing failure mechanism of a reciprocating compressor system, and ADAMS software (version 2013.3) is used to create a simulation model of the mechanism. Jangra [21] listed a summary of the many gearbox issues and the methods used to diagnose them using vibration. The equipment was subjected to various loads, and the environment might cause deterioration. Many failures were detected by the methods used.

The present research contributed to understanding the internal dynamic mechanism of the rolling ball bearing and needle ball bearing through simulations which are practically helpful for predicting the impeding faults in rolling ball and needle bearings. This paper highlighted the mathematical equation analyses of the ball and needle ball bearings, which were further solved using MATLAB programming. In order to verify the mathematical results, experimental investigations were conducted using a vibration monitoring technique on the crank–chain mechanism. Further, small cracks were induced, and variations in vibration parameters such as amplitude and frequencies were observed concluded.

2. Mathematical Model

2.1. System Modeling for the Ball Bearings

Each ball bearing was assumed to be a nonlinear spring-mass damper system during analysis. The inner race of the bearing was connected to the shaft, and the outer race was kept fixed. A constant radial load was applied to the bearings. It was also presumed that the forces were applied when there was contact between the rolling element and the races. The differential equations are formed, and computer programs are written to solve them.

The forces which arise due to the contact of rolling elements with the races can be given as

$$F = k\delta^n \tag{1}$$

where F is the contact force, k is the Hertzian load deflection factor, δ is the deflection, and n is the exponent whose value is $3/2$ for the ball bearing and $10/9$ for the roller bearing. The value of k, i.e., Hertzian load factor, is calculated to be $7.0701 \times 10^9 \mathrm{N/m^{3/2}}$. A cross-section of the bearing with different parameters is shown in Figure 1.

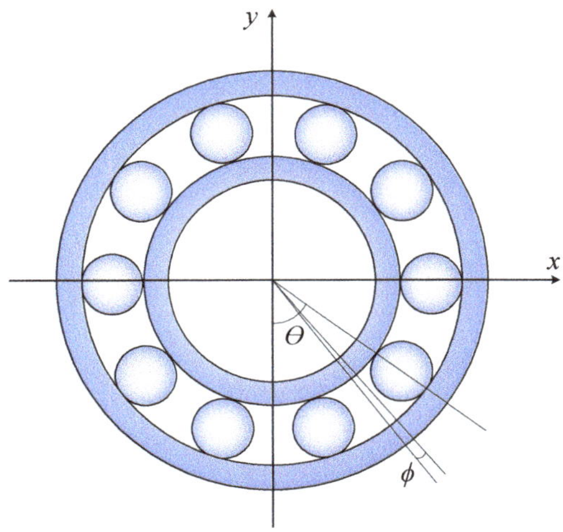

Figure 1. Cross-section of bearing showing different parameters.

2.2. Calculating the Forces

Using the Hertzian contact stress, we can calculate the forces applied by the individual ball on the races.

$$F = k[xcos(\theta_i) + ysin(\theta_i) - Cr]^{3/2} \tag{2}$$

where x is the displacement in the x direction, y is the displacement in the y direction, and θ_i is the angular position of the i-th bearing. This force can be resolved into x and y components for all the bearings as follows:

$$Fx = \sum_{i=1}^{z} k[xcos(\theta_i) + ysin(\theta_i) - Cr]^{3/2}\cos(\theta i) \tag{3}$$

$$Fy = \sum_{i=1}^{z} k[xcos(\theta_i) + ysin(\theta_i) - Cr]^{3/2}\sin(\theta i) \tag{4}$$

Now the defect for the inner and outer race is modeled as a sine function. The forces which arise in the defect region are as given as below

$$FFdx = \sum_{i=1}^{z} k\left[xcos(\theta_i) + ysin(\theta_i) - \left(Cr - Hd\sin\left(\frac{\pi}{\varphi}(\theta t - \theta i)\right)\right)\right]^{3/2}\cos(\theta i) \tag{5}$$

$$FFdy = \sum_{i=1}^{z} k\left[xcos(\theta_i) + ysin(\theta_i) - \left(Cr - Hd\sin\left(\frac{\pi}{\varphi}(\theta t - \theta i)\right)\right)\right]^{3/2}\sin(\theta i) \tag{6}$$

where

$$\varphi = \frac{Defect\ size}{Raceway\ size} \tag{7}$$

and for the inner race defect, φ yields

$$\theta t = \omega_c t + \frac{2\pi}{z(z-i)} \tag{8}$$

and for outer race defect

$$\theta t = (\omega_c - \omega)t + \frac{2\pi}{z(z-i)} \tag{9}$$

For the ball defect

$$\theta t = (\omega_b / z)t + \frac{2\pi}{z(z-i)} \tag{10}$$

where i depend on the number of defects. When the rolling elements are not in the defect region, the equations of motion are given as

$$m\ddot{x} + c\dot{x} + Fx = w \tag{11}$$

$$m\ddot{x} + c\dot{x} + Fy = 0 \tag{12}$$

When the rolling elements are in the defect region, the equations of motion are

$$m\ddot{x} + c\dot{x} + Fdx = w \tag{13}$$

$$m\ddot{x} + c\dot{x} + Fdy = 0 \tag{14}$$

where m is mass of the race based on which forces are to be calculated, c is the damping coefficient, and w is the load on the bearing.

2.3. MATLAB Program to Determine the State Variables for Roller Bearings

The MATLAB program (MATLAB R2018b) consists of two parts: one of them is the main program which calculates each time interval and stores the data, and the other is a function that solves the force equations. The differential equations are solved using the built-in function, ODE45, which uses a fourth-order Ranga–Kutta numerical differential approach. For the program, the following algorithm, as shown in Figure 2, was used. The parameters used in the program for all ball bearings are given Table 1.

Table 1. Specifications of the for ball bearing under investigation.

Quantities	Values
Hertzian contact load	7.0701×10^9 N/m^2
Radial clearance	20.5×10^{-6} m
Radial load	19.62 N
Damping coefficient	200 Ns/m
Mass of outer race	0.058 kg
For inner race	
Shaft speed	298 rpm = 31.2064 rad/s
Relative cage speed $(\omega_c - \omega_s)$	11.6292 rad/s
Length of defect	1 mm
Angular length of defect	71.942×10^{-3} rad
Height of defect	26.3890×10^{-3} mm
For outer race	
Shaft speed	304 rpm
Cage speed (ω_c)	11.8634 rad/s
Length of defect	2 mm
Angular length of defect	85.470×10^{-3} mm
Height of defect	106.456×10^{-3} mm
For rolling element	
Shaft speed	300 rpm
Cage speed (ω_b/z)	8.2391 rad/s
Length of defect	1 mm
Average angular length of defect	57.3387×10^{-3} rad
Height of defect	26.389×10^{-3} mm
Initial displacement in x	10^{-6} m
Initial velocity in x	0 m/s
Initial displacement in y	10^{-6} m
Initial velocity in y	0 m/s
Time for simulation	0–0.7 s
Time step	10^{-4} s

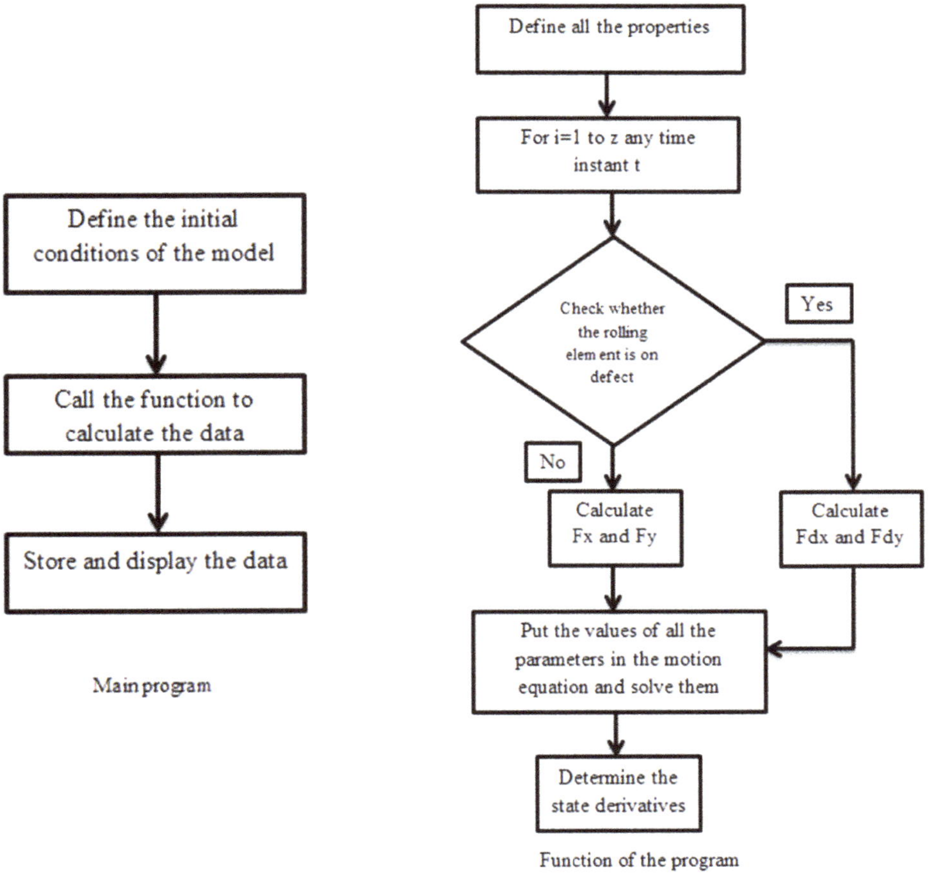

Figure 2. Algorithm to calculate state variables.

2.4. System Modeling for the Roller Bearings

The method described below is applied for the fault diagnosis of the needle roller bearing. It is located at the connection of the crank pin and connecting rod. The motion of the bearing is cyclic. A line defect has been induced in the pin and the connecting rod for the fault diagnosis. As the rolling elements roll over the defect, it generates an point of impact. The inter-impact time interval changes through a crank rotation, but the angle between the two defects remains constant. The inter-impact time is calculated for this analysis, and the frequency range is found. This range is relatively small for the crank pin defect compared to the defect on the connecting rod. Since the frequency range for the connecting rod defect is high, only the high- and low-frequency components are found.

2.5. The MATLAB Program to Determine the Frequency Range

Figure 3 shows how the MATLAB program (MATLAB 2018b) calculates the frequency, and the parameters used are given in Table 2.

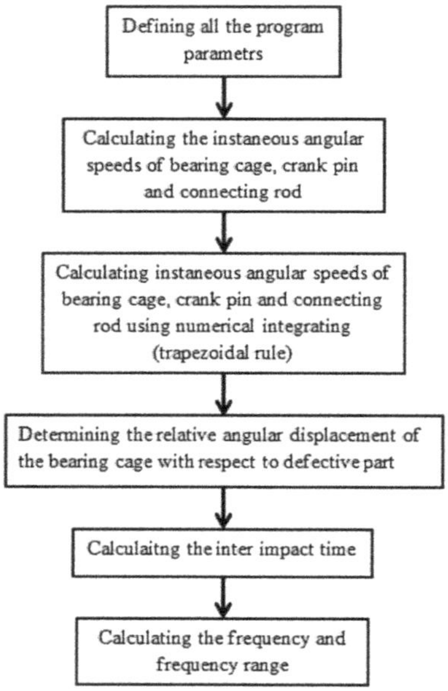

Figure 3. Algorithm to calculate frequency range.

Table 2. Parameters used to calculate the frequency range of bearing.

Quantity	Values
Crank radius	24.5 mm
Connection rod length	94 m
Rolling element diameter	2.5 mm
Pitch diameter	27.5 m
Number of rolling element	20
Inter-impact angular distance	0.314159265
Shaft speed for crack pin defect	314 rpm
Shaft speed for connecting rod defect	313 rpm

3. Experimental Setup

The experimental setup consists of a slider–crank mechanism obtained from a 100cc bike engine (Victor Enterprise, Kalamazoo, MI, USA). It contains two types of bearings, namely ball and needle bearings. Experimental work has been carried out on both of them. To support the deep crankshaft groove, ball bearings have been used to facilitate revolutions between the crank pin and connecting rod. Defects are induced at different locations of the bearings and evaluated for their diagnosis. The following are the parts that have been used to construct the setup.

3.1. Experiment Equipment

I. Engine block: Figure 4 shows the engine block used in this study. The piston slides on the cylinder of the engine block. The dimensions of the cylinder in the engine block are 5 cm in diameter and 9 cm in length.

Figure 4. Engine block.

II. Crank, connecting rod, and piston: The crank, the connecting rod, and the piston help to convert the reciprocating motion to rotational motion, as shown in Figure 5. One end of the connecting rod is connected at a length of 2.5 cm from the center of the crank, thus giving it a stroke length of 5 cm. With the connecting rod, the piston is attached with the help of a piston pin. The diameter of the piston is 4.9 cm, thus giving an actual swept volume of approximately 100 cm^3.

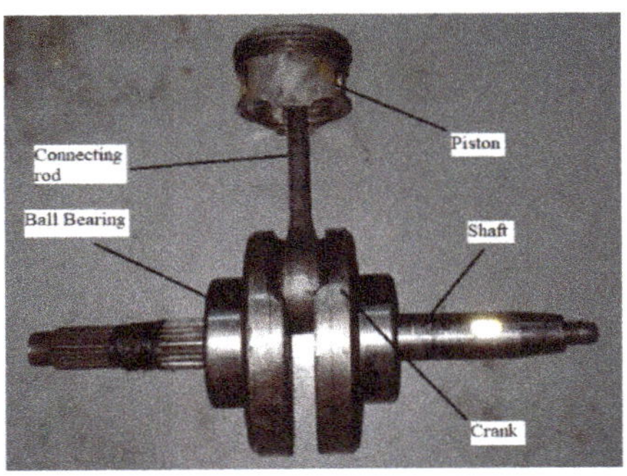

Figure 5. Crank, connecting rod, and piston.

III. Bearings: Each of the two ball bearings supports the two ends of the crankshaft. Bearings are used between the crank pin and the connecting rod to transfer the load torque from the piston to the crankshaft needle roller, as illustrated in Figure 6.

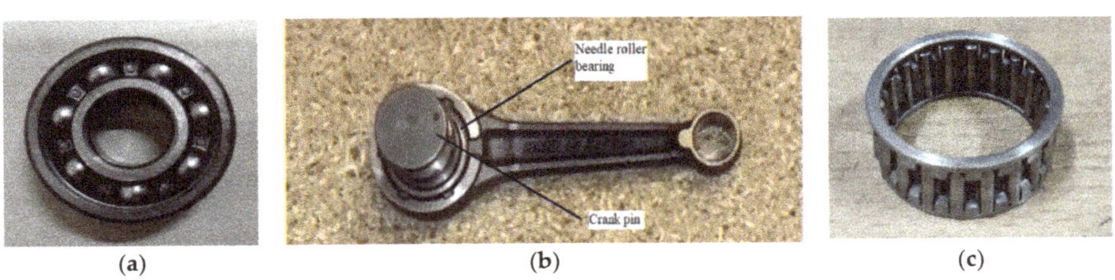

Figure 6. The construction of connecting rod: (a) ball bearing, (b) needle roller bearing between crank pin and connecting rod, and (c) ball bearing.

IV. Motor, gear, and pinion: An electric motor provides the motion in this setup. The whole setup is run with the help of a 220 volt, 3A ac motor (SMK0A-3A, Kalamazoo, USA).

The maximum rated rpm is 1400. A voltage regulator is attached to the motor to control the speed of the motor. For practical running purposes, the motor runs at 1200 rpm. A gear and pinion mechanism has been used to transmit the motion from the engine to the crank. The gear and pinion's pitch circle diameter are 64 mm and 16 mm, respectively, thus giving a gear ratio of 4. Though the rpm fluctuates from observation to observation, it stays around 300 rpm for most trials.

V. Stand and Frame: A frame and a stand are constructed to hold all the parts together.

3.2. Experimental Procedure

Five deep-groove ball bearings, SKF 6304, (VEXTA, Kalamazoo, USA) were used in this experiment. Among them, two are without any defects, and the rest have defects on the inner race, outer trace, and ball, respectively. Since the cage is permanently joined, there was no other way to access the inner race, balls, and outer race. So, the bearings had to be dismantled and then joined again. Similarly, to make observations on the defects in the needle roller bearing K 25 × 30 × 14, defects were induced in the pin and the connecting rod, and then observations are taken simultaneously.

3.3. Inducing Damage

Various methods were used to induce defects inside each part of the experiment. A hand-operated cutting tool was used to induce defects in the inner race. The width of the defect is about 2 mm. Figure 7 shows the defect in the inner race. Figure 8 shows the bearing with the outer race defect. The defect in the outer race was induced using a welding machine.

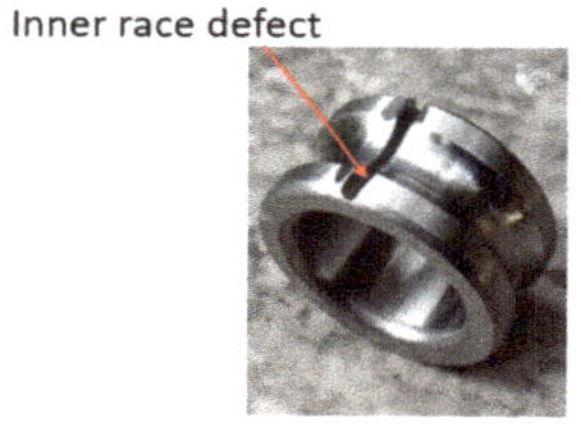

Figure 7. Inner race defect.

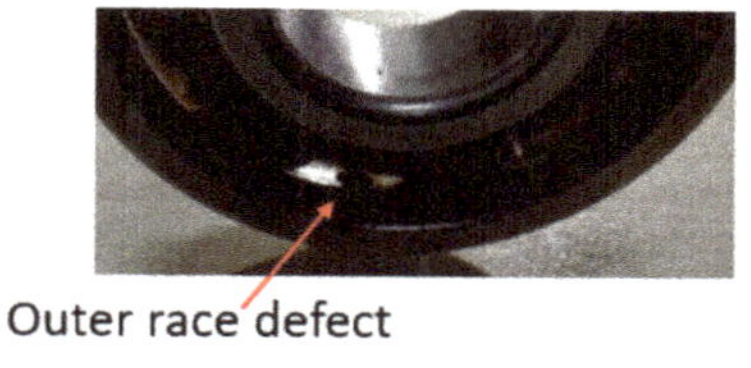

Figure 8. Outer race defect.

For the ball, the defect was induced with a hand tool, as illustrated in Figure 8. The defect's width is about 2 mm.

A wire EDM machine was used to induce a defect in the crank pin and connecting rod, as presented in Figure 9. The defect's width is 0.5 mm and is across the length of the crank pin and connecting rod.

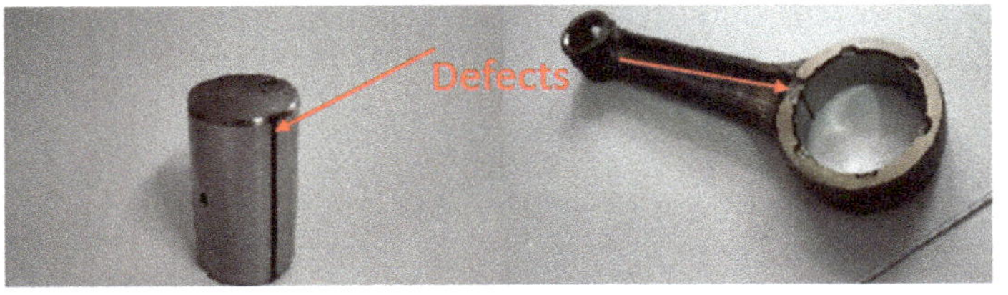

Figure 9. Crank pin and connecting rod defect.

3.4. Data Acquisition and Accelerometer

The vibrational data acquisition is performed using a PRUFTECHNIK VibXpert 2 (PRUFTECHNIK, Kalamazoo, USA) channel FFT analyzer and is recorded on Omnitrend software (OMNITREND2.5.0). Table 3 summarizes the vibration signal characteristics observed using the VibXpert analyzer (PRUFTECHNIK, Kalamazoo, USA) during test.

Table 3. Signal characteristics used in VibXpert analyzer during experiment.

Setup Class	Bearing Spectrum
Quantity	Acceleration
HP/LP Filter	1000/40,000
Frequency	400 Hz
Line No.	800
Window	Hanning
Envelope	On
Averages	3 (Linear)

A complete test setup with an VibXpert FFT analyzer, an accelerometer for acquiring the vibration data, and a laser tachometer used for measuring the rpm of the crankshaft, as shown in Figure 10.

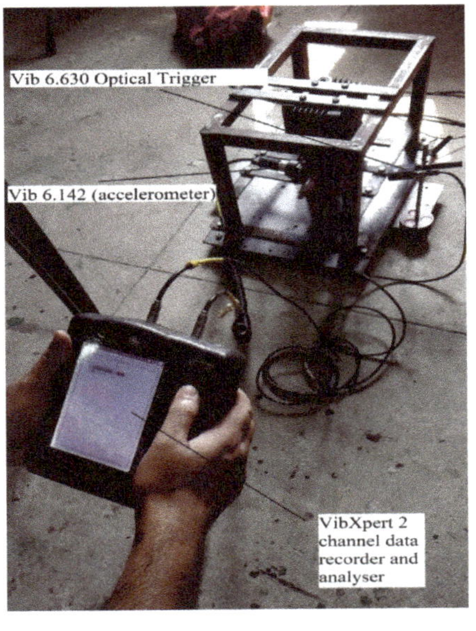

Figure 10. Experimental setup with accelerometer and laser stroboscope.

The acceleration transducer, VIB 6.142 DEX (FLUKE, Kalamazoo, USA), was mounted on bearing housings using a magnetic base. The specifications of the transducer (accelerometer), as given by OEM, are as follows: sensitivity, 1 mA/ms^{-2}; frequency range, from 1 Hz to 20,000 Hz; and resonance frequencies, about 360,000 Hz. The signals are collected using a VibXpert analyzer and analyzed using FFT. The corresponding signal peak is then calculated and matched with the experimental value.

4. Results and Discussions

4.1. Results for the Analysis of Defect in Ball Bearing

After solving the nonlinear differential equations, the radial displacement is obtained. The displacement vs. time plot obtained after running the simulation is given below. All the parameters are given in Table 1. The simulation was run for 0.7 s with a time step of 4–10 s, providing a good graph resolution.

The time between any two peaks was calculated to determine the defect frequency. Figure 11 represents the time for the second and third peaks, which was calculated to be 0.0474 s and 0.0932 s, respectively. The difference between the time intervals comes out to be 0.0458 s. The inverse of this time gives us the defect frequency, which is given as:

$$\frac{1}{T} = \frac{1}{0.0458\ \text{s}} = 21.83\ \text{Hz} \tag{15}$$

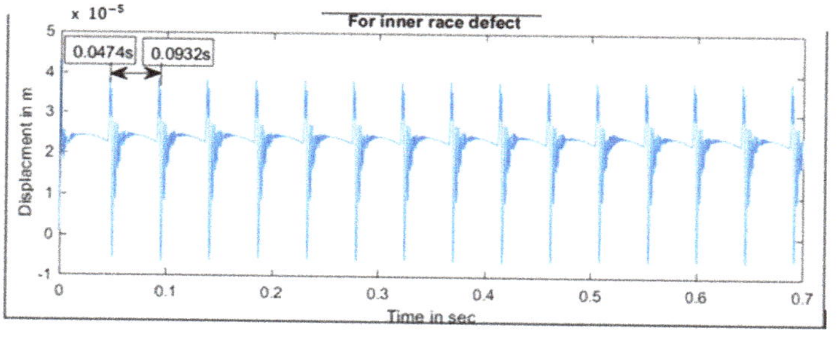

Figure 11. Displacement vs. time for inner race defect for ball bearing.

The experimental value for the defect as measured from the detector and the acceleration vs. frequency is plotted in Figure 12. As shown, the fundamental frequency for the inner race defects is 21.5 Hz. Additionally, the harmonics appear at 43 Hz. The balls enter and leave the defective region, causing deflections. In the load zone, the amplitudes of the impacts are the highest. They are reduced as the defect leaves the load zone.

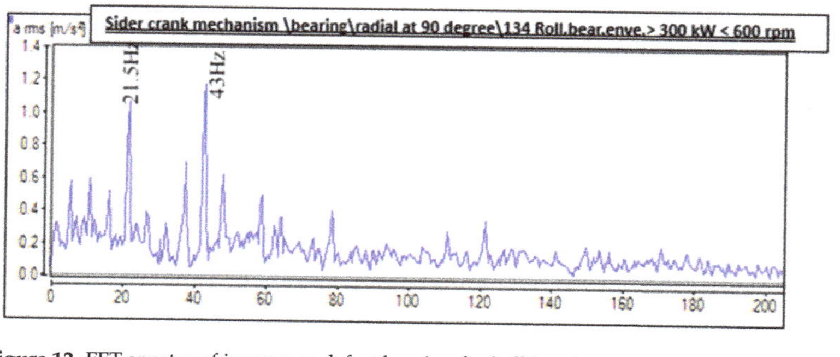

Figure 12. FFT spectra of inner race defect bearing for ball bearing.

Similarly, the displacement versus time data for the outer race defect of the ball bearing are plotted in Figure 13 using the nonlinear differential equations for the outer race. The time between any two peaks was again calculated to find out the defect frequency.

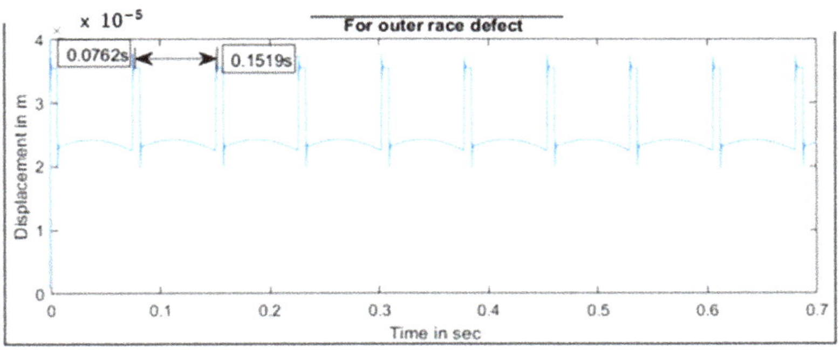

Figure 13. Displacement vs. time for outer race defect for ball bearing.

It can be seen that the time for the second and third peaks is 0.0762 s and 0.1519 s, respectively. The difference between the time intervals comes out to be 0.0757 s. The inverse of this time is the defect frequency, which is

$$\frac{1}{0.0757\text{ s}} = 13.21\text{ Hz} \tag{16}$$

The experimental value of the acceleration vs. frequency data of the outer race defect, as measured from the detector, is given in Figure 14. The fundamental frequency for the inner race defect is 13 Hz, and the harmonic appears at 26 Hz.

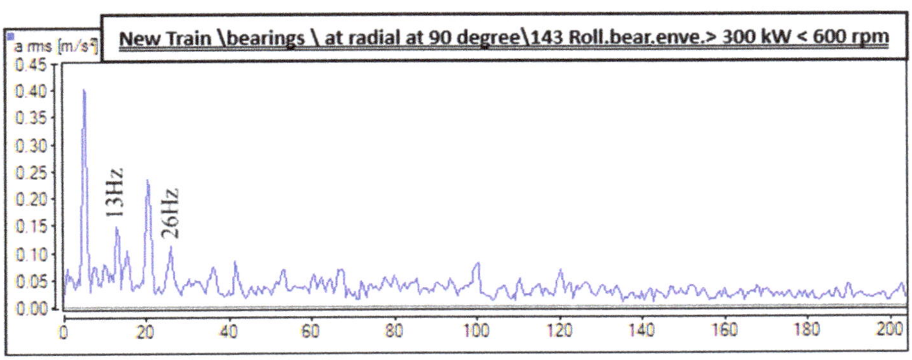

Figure 14. FFT spectrum of outer race defect bearing for ball bearing.

By solving the nonlinear differential equations for the ball bearing defect, the plotted in Figure 15 is obtained.

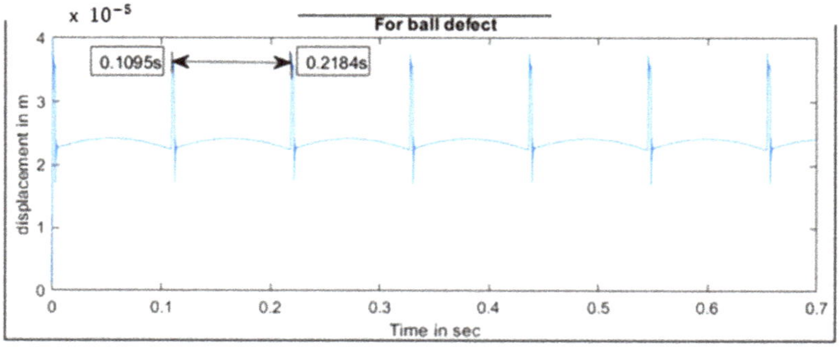

Figure 15. Displacement vs. time for ball race defect for ball bearing.

The time between any two peaks was again calculated to determine the defect frequency. Figure 15 shows that the time for the second and third peaks is 0.1095 s and 0.2184 s, respectively. The difference between the time intervals comes out to be 0.1089 s. The inverse of this time gives the defect frequency, which is

$$\frac{1}{0.1089\ \text{s}} = 9.18\ \text{Hz} \tag{17}$$

The experimental value of the acceleration versus frequency data of the outer race defect, as measured from the detector, is represented in Figure 16. The fundamental frequency for the inner race defect is 9.5 Hz, and the harmonics occur at 19 Hz.

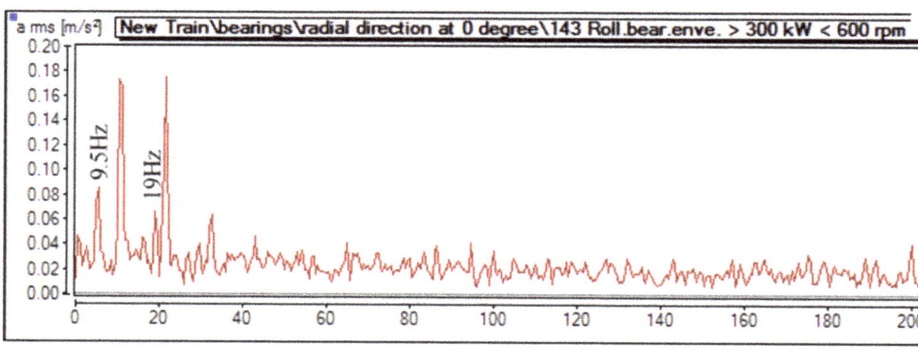

Figure 16. Spectrum of ball bearing.

4.2. Results for the Analysis of Defects of Needle Roller Bearing

After running the MATLAB code in Section 2.5, the frequency range is first calculated for the defect induced in the needle roller bearing. This is achieved by calculating the inter-impact time and then the frequency. Observations from the healthy bearing given in Figure 17 are also added for comparison.

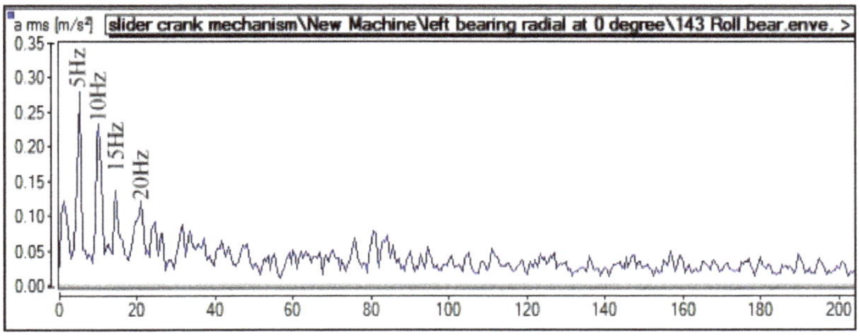

Figure 17. Spectrum of healthy ball bearing.

While the bearing runs at 5 Hz, the spectrum spike is seen at 5 Hz, and the harmonics of the fundamental vibrations are also visible at 10 Hz, 15 Hz, and 20 Hz. This may have arisen due to looseness in the bearing.

Figure 18 shows the FFT spectrum of the pin defect in the needle roller bearing. For the defect induced in the pin, the frequency range comes out to be between 137 and 167 Hz.

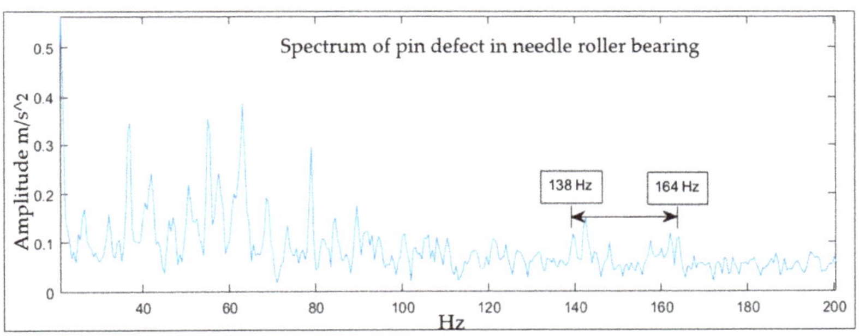

Figure 18. Spectrum of pin defect in needle roller bearing.

From the obtained data, relatively higher amplitudes are seen between 138 Hz and 164 Hz. The amplitudes appeared to be not very high because the accelerometer is attached to the ball bearing housing and not directly above the defective parts.

For the defect induced in the connecting rod, the frequency range comes out to be between 14 Hz and 82 Hz, as shown in Figure 19. Since the frequency range is high, it is complicated to predict the frequency components due to the defect in the connecting rod. Therefore, the extreme frequency components are only shown.

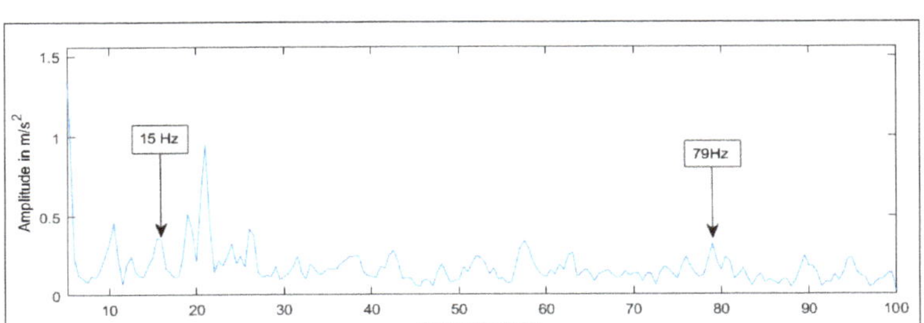

Figure 19. Spectrum of connecting defect in needle roller bearing.

From the result, the fault frequencies were calculated, which have been tabulated in Table 4. It can be noted that the calculated and the actual value of ball defect frequency was found to be varying because of the slippage of the rolling element within the races.

Table 4. Comparison of experimental and calculated data (Inner race defect Vs. Outer race defect Vs. Ball defect).

Defect Types	Calculated Defective Operating Frequency	Experimental Frequency
Inner race defect	21.83 Hz	21.5 Hz
Outer race defect	13.21 Hz	13 Hz
Ball defect	9.18 Hz	9.5 Hz

The motion of the bearing is cyclic, and a range of fault frequencies was computed instead of a single frequency. A straightforward approach to determine the fault frequency was proposed. This was based on inter-impact time when the rolling element rolls over the fault. To calculate the frequency range, a MATLAB program was written. The findings are summarized in Table 5.

Table 5. Comparison of experimental and calculated data (Pin defect Vs. Connecting rod defect).

Defect Types	Calculated Defective Frequency Range	Experimental Defective Frequency Range
Pin defect	137–167 Hz	138–164 Hz
Connecting rod defect	14–82 Hz	15–79 Hz

5. Conclusions

For the ball bearing, a mathematical model was developed. The bearing was modeled as a set of nonlinear spring-mass damper systems. The forces arising from the contact between the rolling element and the races were modeled using Hertzian contact theory.

The study was aimed to diagnose the impeding faults at the crank pin and the connecting rod in which the ball and needle roller bearings are used. The motion of the bearing is cyclic, and a range of fault frequencies was computed instead of a single frequency. A straight forward algorithm was proposed to determine the fault frequency. The experimental vibration data in terms of the spectra were used to identify the fault frequencies. Both theoretical and test results were compared with the healthy bearings. The average values of the vibration amplitude for the defective bearing was observed to be much higher than those of the healthy one for the same frequency range. Further, for the defect in the crank pin, the frequency range was small, and therefore, a range of fault frequencies was seen. The frequency range was high for the defect in the connecting rod; therefore, only the extreme frequencies were shown. The amplitude was minimal as the detector was not attached directly over the part containing the fault but to the ball bearing housing attached over the shaft.

Author Contributions: Conceptualization, methodology, software, validation, formal analysis, and investigation, M.H.G. and V.V.P.; resources, data curation, and writing—original draft preparation, M.H.G.; writing—review and editing, visualization, supervision, and project administration, M.H.G. and V.V.P.; funding acquisition, M.H.G. All authors have read and agreed to the published version of the manuscript.

Funding: The authors extend their appreciation to the Deputyship for Research & Innovation, Ministry of Education in Saudi Arabia, for funding this research work through project number ISP23-69.

Data Availability Statement: All data were included in this study. Data sharing is not applicable to this article.

Acknowledgments: The authors extend their appreciation to the Deputyship for Research & Innovation, Ministry of Education in Saudi Arabia, for funding this research work through project number ISP23-69.

Conflicts of Interest: The authors declare no conflicts of interest.

References

1. Butler, D.E. The Shock-pulse method for the detection of damaged rolling bearings. *Non-Destr. Test.* **1973**, *6*, 92–95. [CrossRef]
2. Gupta, P.K. Dynamics of rolling-element bearings part I: Cylindrical roller bearing analysis discussion. *J. Tribol.* **1979**, *101*, 293–302. [CrossRef]
3. Gupta, P.K. Dynamics of Rolling Element Bearings—2. Cylindrical Roller Bearing Results. *Am. Soc. Mech. Eng.* **1978**, *101*, 305–311. [CrossRef]
4. Toersen, H. Application of an envelope technique in the detection of ball bearing defects in a laboratory experiment. *TriboTest* **1998**, *4*, 297–308. [CrossRef]
5. McFadden, P.D.; Smith, J.D. Model for the vibration produced by a single point defect in a rolling element bearing. *J. Sound Vib.* **1984**, *96*, 69–82. [CrossRef]
6. Patil, M.S.; Mathew, J.; Rajendrakumar, P.K.; Desai, S. A theoretical model to predict the effect of localized defect on vibrations associated with ball bearing. *Int. J. Mech. Sci.* **2010**, *52*, 1193–1201. [CrossRef]
7. Tandon, N.; Choudhury, A. An analytical model for the prediction of the vibration response of rolling element bearings due to a localized defect. *J. Sound Vib.* **1997**, *205*, 275–292. [CrossRef]
8. Liu, J.; Shao, Y.; Lim, T.C. Vibration analysis of ball bearings with a localized defect applying piecewise response function. *Mech. Mach. Theory* **2012**, *56*, 156–169. [CrossRef]
9. Choudhury, A.; Tandon, N. Application of acoustic emission technique for the detection of defects in rolling element bearings. *Tribol. Int.* **2000**, *33*, 39–45. [CrossRef]
10. Rubini, R.; Meneghetti, U. Application of the envelope and wavelet transform analyses for the diagnosis of incipient faults in ball bearings. *Mech. Syst. Signal Process.* **2001**, *15*, 287–302. [CrossRef]
11. Kiral, Z.; Karagülle, H. Simulation and analysis of vibration signals generated by rolling element bearing with defects. *Tribol. Int.* **2003**, *36*, 667–678. [CrossRef]
12. Rai, V.K.; Mohanty, A.R. Bearing fault diagnosis using FFT of intrinsic mode functions in Hilbert-Huang transform. *Mech. Syst. Signal Process.* **2007**, *21*, 2607–2615. [CrossRef]
13. Lu, S.; Wang, X.; He, Q.; Liu, F.; Liu, Y. Fault diagnosis of motor bearing with speed fluctuation via angular resampling of transient sound signals. *J. Sound Vib.* **2016**, *385*, 16–32. [CrossRef]
14. Cui, L.; Zhang, Y.; Zhang, F.; Zhang, J.; Lee, S. Vibration response mechanism of faulty outer race rolling element bearings for quantitative analysis. *J. Sound Vib.* **2016**, *364*, 67–76. [CrossRef]
15. Patel, V.N.; Tandon, N.; Pandey, R.K. Dynamic model for vibration studies of deep groove ball bearings considering single and multiple defects in races. *J. Tribol.* **2010**, *132*, 041101. [CrossRef]
16. Salunkhe, V.G.; Desavale, R.G.; Kumbhar, S.G. Vibration Analysis of Deep Groove Ball Bearing Using Finite Element Analysis and Dimension Analysis. *J. Tribol.* **2022**, *144*, 081202. [CrossRef]
17. Nan, G.; Jiang, S.; Yu, D. Dynamic analysis of rolling ball bearing-rotor based on a new improved model. *SN Appl. Sci.* **2022**, *4*, 173. [CrossRef]
18. Hou, D.; Qi, H.; Luo, H.; Wang, C.; Yang, J. Comparative study on the use of acoustic emission and vibration analyses for the bearing fault diagnosis of high-speed trains. *Struct. Health Monit.* **2022**, *21*, 1518–1540. [CrossRef]
19. AbdulBary, M.; Embaby, A.; Gomaa, F. Fault Diagnosis in Rotating System Based on Vibration Analysis. *ERJ. Eng. Res. J.* **2021**, *44*, 285–294. [CrossRef]
20. Xiao, S.; Xiao, Q.; Song, M.; Zhang, Z. Dynamic analysis for a reciprocating compressor system with clearance fault. *Appl. Sci.* **2021**, *11*, 1295. [CrossRef]
21. Jangra, D. A Review on Different Faults in Gearbox and Vibration Based Diagnosis. *Int. J. Curr. Eng. Technol.* **2022**, *12*, 315–325. [CrossRef]

mathematics

Article

A Novel Method for Predicting the Behavior of a Sucker Rod Pumping Unit Based on the Polished Rod Velocity

Jiaojian Yin * and Hongzhang Ma

College of Science, China University of Petroleum (East China), Qingdao 266580, China; mahzh@upc.edu.cn
* Correspondence: yinjiaojian@upc.edu.cn

Abstract: Fault dynamometer cards are the basis of the diagnosis technique for sucker rod pumping systems. Predicting fault cards with a pumping condition model is an economical and effective method. The usual model is described by a mixed function of the pump displacement and pump load, and it is difficult to use in the prediction method based on the analytical solution of the sucker rod string wave equation. In this paper, a normal pumping condition model described by a function of polished rod velocity is proposed. For the analytical solution of the sucker rod wave equation, an iterative prediction algorithm with pumping condition models is proposed, its convergence is analyzed, and then it is validated by classical finite difference method simulated cards and measured surface dynamometer cards. The results show that the proposed algorithm is accurate. The algorithm has a maximum relative error of 0.10% for the classical method simulated card area and 1.45% for the measured card area. The research of this paper provides an effective scheme for the design, prediction, and fault diagnosis of a sucker rod pumping system with an analytical solution.

Keywords: surface dynamometer card; downhole card; pumping condition model; Rotaflex pumping unit; simulation

MSC: 35L05

1. Introduction

A sucker rod pumping system is an artificial lift instrument that is commonly installed worldwide [1]. It comprises a surface unit, a sucker rod string, and a subsurface pump [2,3]. The subsurface pump consists of a standing valve at the bottom of the well and a traveling valve attached to a rod [4]. A sucker rod pumping system is usually set up in an open-air environment and requires a long operation time, so monitoring its working conditions is very important for oil production [5]. However, its working condition is difficult to monitor directly because it operates in a small-diameter oil tube thousands of meters underground. In production practice, the pumping condition is usually identified by analyzing the surface dynamometer card [6], which is called the diagnosis technology. Many advanced analytical methods have been applied in diagnosis technology based on fault dynamometer cards [7–11]. It is impossible to have all kinds of fault dynamometer cards in a real oil well. One of the most economical and effective methods for obtaining the card is simulation based on the wave equation of the sucker rod string with the establishment of a pumping condition model, which is called prediction technology [12,13].

As early as 1963, a one-dimensional wave equation of a sucker rod string under normal and gas interference pumping conditions was built by Gibbs [14]. Then, for different pumping conditions, a two-dimensional wave equation [15,16], a three-dimensional wave equation [17,18] and other wave equations [19–23] were established. In 2020, Xiaoxiao et al. [24] simulated the working process of a sucker rod pumping system under fault conditions based on the three-dimensional wave equation of a sucker rod string by adopting operating characteristic models of the pump valves.

Usually, pumping condition models are described by the mix function of the pump displacement (or velocity) and pump load. Due to unknown pump positions at the beginning of pumping, the finite difference method is employed to solve the wave equation [14–20,24]. It should first be determined where the pump is in its stroke, and then the pump load should be determined within one time step [14,25]. However, the finite difference method should satisfy the stability conditions [26]. The analytical solution method based on the Fourier series for the one-dimensional wave equation of a sucker rod string can overcome this shortcoming, but it requires the pump load–time function within one pumping cycle as the boundary condition [26,27]. It is difficult to use traditional pumping condition models.

To overcome this shortcoming, a normal pumping condition model with the polished rod velocity as a function is established. An iterative prediction algorithm is proposed. The novelty of this work is that the algorithm can use the analytical solution of the wave equation to predict the behavior of pumping units and is based only on the polished rod velocity.

The remainder of the paper is organized as follows: Section 2 describes the mathematical problem of this work. Section 3 describes the approach to the problem solution. Section 4 presents the results and discussion. Section 5 presents the conclusions of the paper.

2. Mathematical Problem

2.1. One-Dimensional Sucker Rod String Wave Equation

In the actual production of oilfields, multi-tapered rod string is the majority used. The wave equation of the i-th stage rod string, along with its boundary and continuity conditions, is provided below [26]:

$$\begin{cases} \frac{\partial^2 u_i}{\partial t^2} - c_i^2 \frac{\partial^2 u_i}{\partial x^2} + v_i \frac{\partial u_i}{\partial t} = 0 \quad l - L_i < x < l \\ u(0,t) = -u_a(t) \\ E_{rK} A_{rK} \frac{\partial u(x,t)}{\partial x}\Big|_{x=L} = P_p(t) \\ u_i(l,t) = u_{i+1}(l,t) \\ E_{ri} A_{ri} \frac{\partial u_i(x,t)}{\partial x}\Big|_{x=l} = E_{ri+1} A_{ri+1} \frac{\partial u_{i+1}(x,t)}{\partial x}\Big|_{x=l} \end{cases} \tag{1}$$

where $c_i = \sqrt{E_{ri} g / \rho_i}$, $l = \sum_{k=1}^{i} L_k$, E_r represents Young's modulus of the rod, g represents the gravitational constant, ρ represents the density of the rod material, and L represents the length of the rod string.

When the weight of the sucker rod in the fluid is considered separately, the pump load is described as follows [21,23]:

$$P_p(t) = A_p[p_d - p(t)] - A_{re} p_d \tag{2}$$

where A_p is the plunger area, p_d is the pump discharge pressure, p is the pump pressure, and A_{re} is the cross area of the last section of the rod string.

2.2. Traditional Normal Pumping Conditions

Under normal pumping conditions with the tubing string anchored, only the sucker rod string undergoes elastic changes during the plunger movement caused by polished rod movement. Based on the assumption of the normal pumping condition and its movement rule [28], the relation between the pump displacement and load can be expressed as follows:

$$\begin{cases} u_p(t) = 0, P_p(t) < W_0, 0 \le t \le t_m \\ P_p(t) = W_0, P_p(t) \ge W_0, 0 \le t \le t_m \\ u_p(t) = u_m, P_p(t) > 0, t_m < t \le T \\ P_p(t) = 0, P_p(t) \le 0, t_m < t \le T \end{cases} \tag{3}$$

where $W_0 = A_p(p_d - p_s)$, t_m is the downstroke start time, u_m is the plunger position at the downstroke start time, and T is the pumping period. Equation (3) can be described as the famous Robin boundary condition [14,29]. Obviously, the time-varying mixed boundary of displacement and load is a complex, which switches automatically according to the pump load.

2.3. Analytical Solution of the One-Dimensional Sucker Rod String Wave Equation

After, the polished rod displacement and the pump load are approximated by the truncated Fourier series as follows [26]:

$$\begin{cases} u_a(t) = \frac{\nu_0}{2} + \sum\limits_{n=1}^{N} (\nu_n \cos n\omega t + \delta_n \sin n\omega t) \\ P_p(t) = \frac{\sigma_0}{2} + \sum\limits_{n=1}^{N} (\sigma_n \cos n\omega t + \tau_n \sin n\omega t) \end{cases} \tag{4}$$

where N is the number of Fourier series; ν_0, ν_n, δ_n, σ_0, σ_n, and τ_n are the Fourier coefficients; and $\omega = 2\pi n/T$, $n = 1, 2, 3, \ldots$

Equation (1) is solved by a matrix expression of analytical solutions in predictive analysis by our team. Further details are given in Reference [26]. The main results are as follows:

$$\begin{cases} u_i(x,t) = \xi_i + \eta_i x + \sum\limits_{n=1}^{N} [Q_{in}(x) \cos n\omega t + P_{in}(x) \sin n\omega t] \\ D_i(x,t) = E_{ri}A_{ri}\eta_i + E_{ri}A_{ri} \sum\limits_{n=1}^{N} [Q_{in}'(x) \cos n\omega t + P_{in}'(x) \sin n\omega t] \end{cases} \tag{5}$$

where

$$\begin{cases} \begin{bmatrix} Q_{in}(x) & P_{in}(x) & Q_{in}'(x) & P_{in}'(x) \end{bmatrix}^T = \left[MF_{inx}^{4\times4}\right]\left[C_{in}^{4\times1}\right] \\ \left[MF_{inx}^{4\times4}\right] = \begin{bmatrix} M_{1inx} & M_{2inx} \\ F_{1inx} & F_{2inx} \end{bmatrix} \\ \left[C_{in}^{4\times1}\right] = \begin{bmatrix} \varepsilon_{in} & \pi_{in} & \kappa_{in} & \mu_{in} \end{bmatrix}^T \end{cases} \tag{6}$$

$$\begin{cases} M_{1inx} = \begin{bmatrix} \cosh\beta_{in}x\cos\alpha_{in}x & \sinh\beta_{in}x\sin\alpha_{in}x \\ -\sinh\beta_{in}x\sin\alpha_{in}x & \cosh\beta_{in}x\cos\alpha_{in}x \end{bmatrix}_{in}^{x} \\ M_{2inx} = \begin{bmatrix} \cosh\beta_{in}x\sin\alpha_{in}x & \sinh\beta_{in}x\cos\alpha_{in}x \\ \sinh\beta_{in}x\cos\alpha_{in}x & -\cosh\beta_{in}x\sin\alpha_{in}x \end{bmatrix}_{in}^{x} \\ F_{1inx} = \frac{\partial M_{1inx}}{\partial x}, F_{2inx} = \frac{\partial M_{2inx}}{\partial x} \\ \beta_{in} = \frac{n\omega}{c_i\sqrt{2}}\sqrt{-1+\sqrt{1+\left(\frac{v_i}{n\omega}\right)^2}}, \alpha_{in} = \frac{n\omega}{c_i\sqrt{2}}\sqrt{1+\sqrt{1+\left(\frac{v_i}{n\omega}\right)^2}} \end{cases} \tag{7}$$

Considering the boundary conditions, the coefficients of $\left[C_n^{4K\times1}\right]$ can be obtained as follows:

$$\begin{cases} \left[C_n^{4K\times1}\right] = \left[TM_n^{4K\times4K}\right]^{-1}\left[UD_n^{4K\times1}\right] \\ \left[C_n^{4K\times1}\right] = \begin{bmatrix} C_{1n}^{4\times1} & \cdot & C_{in}^{4\times1} & \cdot & C_{Kn}^{4\times1} \end{bmatrix}^T \\ \left[UD_n^{4K\times1}\right] = \begin{bmatrix} U_n^{2\times1} & 0^{2\times1} & \cdot & 0^{4\times1} & \cdot & 0^{2\times1} & D_n^{2\times1} \end{bmatrix}^T \\ \left[U_n^{2\times1}\right] = -\begin{bmatrix} v_n & \delta_n \end{bmatrix}^T, \left[D_n^{2\times1}\right] = \begin{bmatrix} \sigma_n & \tau_n \end{bmatrix}^T / E_{rK}A_{rK} \end{cases} \tag{8}$$

Thus, the pump displacement and the polished rod load can be given as follows:

$$\begin{cases} u_p(t) = \frac{v_0}{2} - \frac{\sigma_0}{2} \sum\limits_{k=1}^{K} \frac{L_{rk}}{E_{rk} A_{rk}} - \sum\limits_{n=1}^{N} [Q_{Kn}(L) \cos n\omega t + P_{Kn}(L) \sin n\omega t] \\ PRL(t) = \frac{\sigma_0}{2} + E_{r1} A_{r1} \sum\limits_{n=1}^{N} [Q'_{1n}(0) \cos n\omega t + P'_{1n}(0) \sin n\omega t] \end{cases} \tag{9}$$

where

$$\begin{array}{l} \begin{bmatrix} Q_{Kn}(L) & P_{Kn}(L) \end{bmatrix}^T = \begin{bmatrix} M_{1KnL} & M_{2KnL} \end{bmatrix} \begin{bmatrix} C_{Kn}^{4\times1} \end{bmatrix} \\ \begin{bmatrix} Q_{1n}'(0) & P_{1n}'(0) \end{bmatrix}^T = \begin{bmatrix} F_{11n0} & F_{21n0} \end{bmatrix} \begin{bmatrix} C_{1n}^{4\times1} \end{bmatrix} \end{array} \tag{10}$$

The analytical solution is mainly based on the complex theory and separation of variables to solve the wave equation proposed by Gibbs in 1967 [30]. Obviously, this analytical solution is a frequency domain method that requires a periodic pump load-time function and cannot be used to solve the definite solution problem of Equations (1) and (3).

3. Approach to the Problem Solution

To solve the definite solution problem using the analytic method, an iterative algorithm, which ranges from static to dynamic, can be employed. In the algorithm, the sucker rod string is equivalent to a spring, and a periodic pump load-time function of polished rod velocity is obtained. Taking the polished rod displacement and pump load as the initial values, the pump displacement can be calculated according to the analytical solution. According to the calculated pump displacement, the new polished rod velocity can be obtained according to the modified method. Thus, the new periodic pump load-time function of polished rod velocity is obtained. After several iterations, the pump load will become a dynamic load to meet the requirements.

3.1. Model of Normal Pumping Conditions

There are four stages in a pumping cycle: the first stage is the loading portion of the upstroke, the second is the fully loaded portion of the upstroke, the third is the unloading portion of the downstroke, and the last is the unloaded portion of the downstroke [25].

The normal pumping condition model should consider the anchored state of the tubing string. With the tubing string anchored, only the sucker rod string undergoes elastic changes during the plunger movement; meanwhile, in the anchored state, the sucker rod string and the tubing string also exhibit elastic changes caused by polished rod movement [28]. Considering the elastic movement, the sucker rod string and the tubing string can be equivalent to springs. A schematic diagram during the loading portion of the upstroke is shown in Figure 1.

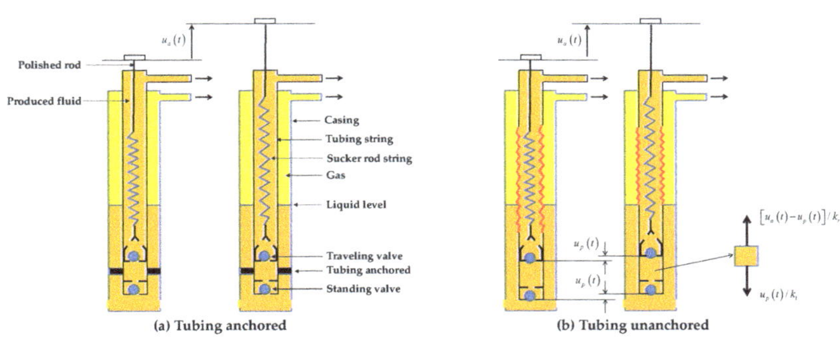

Figure 1. Schematic diagram of the normal pumping condition model.

As shown in Figure 1a, when the pumping speed is low enough, it has a pump load (i.e., pump plunger load) as follows:

$$P_p(t) = u_a(t)/k_r \tag{11}$$

where $u_a(t)$ is the polished rod displacement, k_r is the flexibility of the equivalent spring of the sucker rod string (i.e., the derivative of stiffness), and $k_r = L_r/(E_rA_r)$. The pump load in the unloading portion of the downstroke differs only by a constant from Equation (11).

According to Figure 1b, when the pump displacement (i.e., the position of the pump plunger) derived from the elastic movement of the tubing string is $u_p(t)$,

$$P_p(t) = u_a(t)/k_e \tag{12}$$

$$u_a(t) = u_p(t)k_e/k_t \tag{13}$$

where $k_e = \delta_t k_t + k_r$, k_t is the flexibility of the tubing string, $k_t = L_t/(E_tA_t)$, and L_t, E_t, and A_t are the length, Young's modulus, and cross area of the tubing string, respectively. The $\delta_t = 0$ represents the state of tubing anchored while $\delta_t = 0$ represents the state of tubing unanchored. Obviously, the equivalent springs of the sucker rod string and the tubing string are in series. It is a static model of the sucker rod string system. When considering the dynamic characteristics, the spring-mass-damper system [22] can be considered as an alternative, which is under study.

Considering Equation (12) and differentiating Equation (2) yields

$$v_a(t) = -A_pk_e\frac{dp(t)}{dt} \tag{14}$$

where $v_a(t)$ is the velocity of the polished rod. Equation (14) is suitable for both the loading portion and the unloading portion.

When the pump pressure is less than the intake pressure, which is p_s, the standing valve will open. When the pump pressure is greater than the discharge pressure, the traveling valve will open. Considering these valve opening conditions and Equation (14), the pump pressure can be given by the recurrent equation as follows:

$$\begin{cases} p_{fd}(t_i) = p(t_{i-1}) - \frac{\Delta t}{A_pk_e}v_a(t_{i-1}) \\ p(t_i) = \begin{cases} p_{fd}(t_i) & , p_{fd}(t_i) > p_s, 0 \le t_i < t_m \\ p_s & , p_{fd}(t_i) \le p_s, 0 \le t_i < t_m \\ p_{fd}(t_i) & , p_{fd}(t_i) < p_d, t_m \le t_i \le T \\ p_d & , p_{fd}(t_i) \ge p_d, t_m \le t_i \le T \end{cases} \end{cases} \tag{15}$$

where $\triangle t$ is the time increment.

$$u_p(t_i) = u_a(t_i) - k_rA_p[p_d - p(t_i)] \tag{16}$$

The initial value is

$$\begin{cases} p(t_0) = p_d \\ v_p(t_0) = 0 \end{cases} \tag{17}$$

The advantage of the recurrent Equation (15) is that it does not consider the constant u_m in the downstroke of Equation (3), and it is easy to include other fault conditions. For example, considering the leakage state of the pump valve, Equation (15) can be modified as follows:

$$p_{fd}(t_i) = p(t_{i-1}) - \frac{\Delta t}{A_pk_e}\left[v_a(t_{i-1}) - v_{pl}(t_{i-1})\right] \tag{18}$$

where v_{pl} is the plunger velocity due to leakage of the pump valve. For the standing valve and traveling valve, the plunger velocity is given as follows [24]:

$$\begin{cases} v_{pls} = \frac{\zeta_s \zeta_p}{A_p}[p(t_{i-1}) - p_s]^{e_s} \\ v_{plt} = \frac{\zeta_t \zeta_p}{A_p}[p_d - p(t_{i-1})]^{e_t} \\ \zeta_p = \frac{\pi D_p \delta^3}{12\mu l_p} \end{cases} \tag{19}$$

where D_p represents the diameter of the plunger, l_p represents the length of the plunger, δ represents the clearance between the plunger and pump barrel, ζ_s and ζ_t are the leakage coefficients of the standing valve and traveling valve, respectively, and e_s and e_t are the leakage exponents of the standing valve and traveling valve, respectively.

3.2. Iterative Algorithm

The pumping condition model proposed in the paper is a static model. If it is used in the pump displacement and the polished rod load resolution of Equation (9), an error will be introduced. The higher the pumping speed is, the greater the error.

To solve the definite solution problem by the analytic method, the iterative algorithm should consist of the following steps:

Step 1: Calculate the pump pressure and pump load according to the pumping model based on the polished rod velocity.

$$\begin{cases} p^0(t) = f[v_p(t)] \\ P_p^0(t) = A_p[p_d - p^0(t)] - A_{re}p_d \end{cases}$$

Step 2: Approximate the polished rod displacement and the pump load by the truncated Fourier series according to Equation (4).

Step 3: Calculate the pump displacement $u_p{}^0(t)$ and the polished rod load according to Equation (9).

Step 4: Modify the polished rod displacement as follows:

$$u_a^0(t) = u_p^0(t) + k_r A_p\left[p_d - p^0(t)\right]$$

Step 5: Calculate the tolerance error as follows:

$$\Delta u_a = \max\left|u_a(t) - u_a^0(t)\right|$$

Step 6: Evaluate the tolerance error.

If $\triangle u_a > \varepsilon$, update the polished rod displacement as follows, and return to step 1.

$$u_a(t) = \frac{u_a(t) + u_a^0(t)}{2}$$

Otherwise, if $\triangle u_a \leq \varepsilon$, stop the program, and obtain the results of the surface dynamometer card, i.e., $[u_a{}^0(t), PRL(t)]$, and the downhole card, i.e., $[u_p{}^0(t), P_p{}^0(t)]$.

The flowchart of the algorithm is shown in Figure 2.

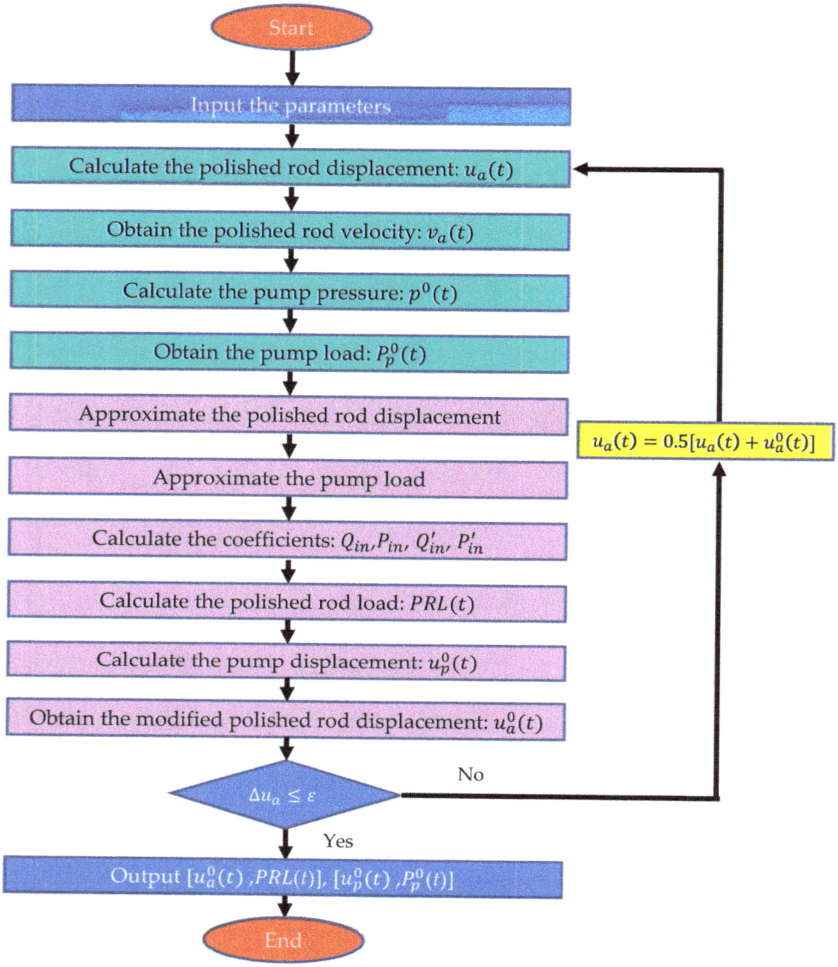

Figure 2. Flowchart of the prediction algorithm.

The computer program used in this paper is MATLAB R2021a, and the pseudocode of the algorithm is shown in Algorithm 1.

Algorithm 1: Prediction algorithm with iteration

Input: n_p, K, and a series system parameter
Calculate: c_i, p_d, p_s, W_0, k_s, k_t, T (i.e., $60/n_p$), ω, and v_i
Set: $J = 400$, t = linspace(0, T, $J + 1$), $N = J/2$
Calculate: $u_a(t)$ according to kinematic equation of pumping unit's movement
Approximated by Fourier series with trpaz function: $u_a(t) \rightarrow \nu_0$, ν_n, and δ_n refer to Equation (4)

Set: $\varepsilon = 0.1\%$, $u_a{}^0(t) = u_a(t)$
For j **= 1:300**
  Set: $u_a(t) = 0.5[u_a(t) + u_a{}^0(t)] \rightarrow v_a(t)$
  Calculate: p^0 refer to Equation (15) $\rightarrow P_p{}^0(t) = A_p(p_d - p) - A_r(\text{end})p_d \rightarrow q_t = P_p{}^0(t)./(E_r(\text{end})^*A_r(\text{end}))$
  Approximated: $q_t(t) \rightarrow \sigma_0$, σ_n and τ_n refer to Equation (4)
  for n **= 1:**N
    $i = 1{:}K \rightarrow \beta_{in}, \alpha_{in} \rightarrow M_{1inx}, M_{2inx}, F_{1inx}, F_{2inx} \rightarrow TM_n{}^{4K\times 4K}$ refer to Equation (7)
    UD_n = zeros(4K,1); $U_n = [\nu_n\ \delta_n]'$; $D_n(4K\text{-}1{:}4K) = [\sigma_n\ \tau_n]'$; $UD_n(1{:}2) = U_n \rightarrow UD_n(4^*K\text{-}1{:}4^*K) = D_n$
    $C_n{}^{4K\times 1} = TM_n{}^{4K\times 4K} \backslash UD_n$ refer to Equation (8)
    $[Q_{Kn}(L)\ P_{Kn}(L)]' = [M_{1KnL}, M_{2KnL}] \times C_{Kn}{}^{4K\times 1}$; $[Q_{1n}(0)\ P_{1n}(0)]' = [F_{11n0}, F_{21n0}] \times C_{1n}{}^{4K\times 1}$ refer to Equation (10)
  end
  Calculate: $PRL(t)$, $u_p{}^0(t)$ refer to Equation (9)
  Modify: $u_a{}^0(t) = u_p{}^0(t) + k_r P_p{}^0(t) \rightarrow \triangle u_a = \max(\text{abs}(u_a(t) - u_a{}^0(t)))$
  If $\triangle u_a <= \varepsilon$
    break
  end
end

Output: $u_a{}^0(t)$, $PRL(t)$, $u_p{}^0(t)$, $P_p{}^0(t)$

Note: The equation for v_i is given in Reference [26].

3.3. Theoretical Analysis of the Prediction Algorithm

To prove the algorithm, the normal pumping condition with the tubing anchored and a single rod is considered as an example. During the loading portion, the pump is stationary [14], that is, $u_p(t) = 0$. Next, it needs be proven that the pump displacement approaches 0 during the loading portion after iteration.

3.3.1. Theoretical Basis

There is another analytical solution of the single rod wave equation, which is based on separating variables without using the complex method and has a clearer physical significance [27]. It is used to illustrate the mechanism of iteration. The pump displacement based on the single rod wave equation can be given as follows:

$$\begin{cases} u_{pr}(t) = u_a(t) + \Delta_1 u_a(t) - k_r P_p(t) - k_r \Delta_2 P_p(t) \\ \Delta_1 u_a(t) = \sum\limits_{m=0}^{\infty} u_{am}(t) \sin \omega_m l \\ \Delta_2 P_p(t) = k_r \sum\limits_{m=0}^{\infty} P_{pm}(t) \sin \omega_m l \end{cases} \tag{20}$$

where

$$\begin{cases} u_{am}(t) = \sum\limits_{n=1}^{\infty} P_{smn} \cos \eta_n t + Q_{smn} \sin \eta_n t \\ P_{pm}(t) = \sum\limits_{n=1}^{\infty} P_{pmn} \cos \eta_n t + Q_{pmn} \sin \eta_n t \end{cases} \tag{21}$$

$$\begin{cases} \begin{bmatrix} A_{smn} \\ B_{smn} \end{bmatrix} = \frac{2}{l\omega_m} \begin{bmatrix} \eta_n^2 & -\nu\eta_n \\ \nu\eta_n & \eta_n^2 \end{bmatrix} \begin{bmatrix} \nu_n \\ \delta_n \end{bmatrix} \\ \begin{bmatrix} P_{smn} \\ Q_{smn} \end{bmatrix} = \begin{bmatrix} (\omega_m c)^2 - \eta_n^2 & \upsilon\eta_n \\ -\upsilon\eta_n & (\omega_m c)^2 - \eta_n^2 \end{bmatrix}^{-1} \begin{bmatrix} A_{smn} \\ B_{smn} \end{bmatrix} \end{cases} \tag{22}$$

$$\begin{cases} \begin{bmatrix} A_{pmn} \\ B_{pmn} \end{bmatrix} = \frac{2(-1)^m}{l\omega_m{}^2} \begin{bmatrix} \eta_n^2 & -\nu\eta_n \\ \nu\eta_n & \eta_n^2 \end{bmatrix} \begin{bmatrix} \sigma_n \\ \tau_n \end{bmatrix} \\ \begin{bmatrix} (\omega_m c)^2 - \eta_n^2 & \upsilon\eta_n \\ -\upsilon\eta_n & (\omega_m c)^2 - \eta_n^2] \end{bmatrix} \begin{bmatrix} P_{pmn} \\ Q_{pmn} \end{bmatrix} = \begin{bmatrix} A_{pmn} \\ B_{pmn} \end{bmatrix} \end{cases} \tag{23}$$

where l is the length of the rod string; ω_m is the eigenfrequency; and $\omega_m = (2m + 1)\pi/(2l)$, m = 0, 1, 2, ...

Obviously, in the static state, $\triangle_1 u_a(t) = \triangle_2 P_p(t) = 0$, and Equation (20) is reduced to Equation (16).

3.3.2. Results of the Iterative Process

In step 1 of the iterative process,

$$P_p^0(t) = \frac{u_a(t)}{k_r}$$

Thus, the pump displacement can be calculated according to step 3, i.e., Equation (20), as follows:

$$u_p^0(t) = \Delta_1 u_a(t) - \Delta_2 u_a(t)$$

The pump displacement is not zero when it is not in the static state. The aim of the iteration is to ensure that the pump displacement is 0 during the loading portion, i.e., $u_p(t) = 0$.

According to step 4, the modified polished rod displacement is as follows:

$$u_a^0(t) = u_a(t) + \Delta_1 u_a(t) - \Delta_2 u_a(t)$$

Then, the new pump load according to step 1 is as follows:

$$P_p^1(t) = \frac{u_a^0(t)}{k_r}$$

The new pump displacement is calculated according to step 3, i.e., Equation (20), as follows:

$$u_p^1(t) = -\Delta_2 u_p^0(t)$$

According to step 4, the modified polished rod displacement is as follows:

$$u_a^1(t) = u_a(t) + \Delta_1 u_a(t) - \Delta_2 u_p^0(t) - \Delta_2 u_a(t)$$

Then, the new pump load is obtained according to step 1.

$$P_p^2(t) = \frac{u_a^1(t)}{k_r}$$

It has the new calculated pump displacement according to step 3, i.e., Equation (20), as follows:

$$u_p^2(t) = \Delta_2^2 u_p^0(t)$$

where $\triangle_2$ is an operator. The $\triangle_2{}^2 = \triangle_2\triangle_2$, i.e., $\triangle_2{}^2 u_p{}^0(t) = \triangle_2[\triangle_2 u_p{}^0(t)]$.

Therefore, by generalizing this derivation, the following expression can be obtained after the i-th iteration.

$$u_p^i(t) = (-1)^i \Delta_2^i u_p^0(t) \tag{24}$$

If the operator $\triangle_2$ can reduce the value of $u_p{}^0(t)$, the value of $u_p{}^i(t)$ will approach zero after the i-th iteration, i.e., the iteration is convergence. Next, is the discussion of the convergence of iterations.

3.3.3. Convergence of Iterations

Considering the tubing anchored state, i.e., Equations (12) and (16), and according to Equations (21)–(23), the iterative matrix of the operator $\triangle_2$ can be written as the following expression:

$$[M_n] = \frac{k_r}{k_e}\frac{\sigma_0}{2E_{rK}A_{rK}}\sum_{m=0}^{\infty}\frac{2(-1)^m}{l\omega_m{}^2}\sin\omega_m l\begin{bmatrix} A_{mn} & -B_{mn} \\ B_{mn} & A_{mn}\end{bmatrix} \tag{25}$$

where

$$\begin{cases} A_{mn} = \dfrac{\left[(\omega_m c)^2-\eta_n^2\right]\eta_n^2-(v\eta_n)^2}{\left[(\omega_m c)^2-\eta_n^2\right]^2+(v\eta_n)^2} \\ B_{mn} = \dfrac{\left[(\omega_m c)^2-\eta_n^2\right]v\eta_n+v\eta_n\eta_n^2}{\left[(\omega_m c)^2-\eta_n^2\right]^2+(v\eta_n)^2} \end{cases} \tag{26}$$

The role of $\sigma_0/(2E_{rK}A_{rK})$ is to adjust the order of magnitude.

Obviously, when the maximum value of M_n is less than 1, the iteration converges. When only m = 0, the value of $\omega_m{}^{-2}$ is the largest. Equations (25) and (26) show the convergence mechanism, which is that the maximum value of M_n occurs when m = 0 and $\eta_n = \sqrt{(\omega_0 c)^2 - \frac{v^2}{2}}$, i.e., harmonic resonance. The disadvantage is that Equations (25) and (26) are only applicable to the case of a single rod. Further study of the case of multi-tapered rods is ongoing.

To visualize the relation between the iterative matrix elements M_n and the Fourier series number n, especially for multi-tapered rods, the iterative matrix in the matrix expression of the analytical solution [26] is given as follows:

$$[M_n] = \frac{k_r}{k_e}\frac{\sigma_0}{2E_{rK}A_{rK}}\left[M_{nL}^{2\times 4}\right]\begin{bmatrix} M_{n0}^{2\times 4} \\ F_{nL}^{2\times 4}\end{bmatrix}^{-1} \text{ for single rod;} \tag{27}$$

$$[M_n] = \frac{k_r}{k_e}\frac{\sigma_0}{2E_{rK}A_{rK}}\left[M_{nL}^{2\times 4}\right]\left[TM_{inv1}^{4\times 4}\right] \text{ for multi-tapered rod} \tag{28}$$

where $\left[TM_{inv1}^{4\times 4}\right] = [TM_{inv}(4K-3:4K, 4K-3:4K)]$, $[TM_{inv}] = \left[TM_n^{4K\times 4K}\right]^{-1}$.

Thus, the convergence curve between the iterative matrix elements M_n and Fourier series number n can be drawn when solving the wave equation with Equations (4)–(10).

4. Results and Discussion

4.1. Validation Study

Two methods are used to validate the prediction algorithm. One is to validate the prediction algorithm by comparison with the simulated results of the classical finite differential solution [14,25,26], and the other is based on the measured surface dynamometer card. The reason for the comparison with the finite difference method is that it is a well-known and proven solution for the predictive analysis of sucker rod pumping systems. The further details of the finite differential solution are given in reference [26] and are not repeated here.

The measured data are from two different kinds of wells belonging to an oilfield of the Sinopec Oilfield Company of China. The basic parameters of the wells are listed in Table 1.

In the analytical solution, the time increment is $T/400$, the Fourier series number is 200, and the tolerance error is 0.1%. In the finite differential solution, the time increment is $0.95L_{min}/c$, which can satisfy the stability conditions, and the tolerance error is 0.1%.

Table 1. Basic parameters of oil well.

Items	Values	Values
Pumping unit	Long-stroke pumping unit (Rotaflex)	Beam pumping unit (CYJ14-4.8-73HB)
Pump stroke, m	6.0	4.2
Pumping speed, min^{-1}	1.4	4.1
Sucker rod string, mm×m	25 × 372.5 + 22 × 518.2	22 × 986.2
Tubing string, mm×m	76 × 856.7, unanchored	62 × 980.6, unanchored
Pump diameter, mm	63	57
Pump depth, m	900.6	997.3
Fluid density, kg/m^3	998.46	990.30
Dynamic liquid level, m	629	579
Oil pressure, MPa	0.9	0.1
Casing pressure, MPa	0	0
Fluid viscosity, mPa.s	800	747.5
Gas/oil ratio, m^3/m^3	0	0
Rod and tube's density, kg/m^3	7850 (Steel)	7850 (Steel)
Rod and tube's Young's modulus, GPa	210 (Steel)	210 (Steel)

4.1.1. Comparison with the Finite Differential Solution

Well 1 is used here as an example for comparative study. After two iterations, the finite difference solution satisfies the accuracy requirement, and the simulation results are shown in Figure 3. After the first iteration, the results simulated by the analytical solution are also shown in Figure 3. The first iteration of the analytical solution means that the pumping condition model is a static model. Figure 3 shows that the surface dynamometer cards and downhole cards simulated by both solutions are consistent. The relative area error of the surface card and downhole card is 0.02%. This demonstrates the feasibility of the proposed prediction algorithm using only the static pumping condition model at a speed of 1.4 min^{-1}. In this paper, the relative area error is defined as $(A_f - A_a)/A_f \times 100\%$, where A_f is the card area of the finite difference solution, and A_a is that of the analytical solution.

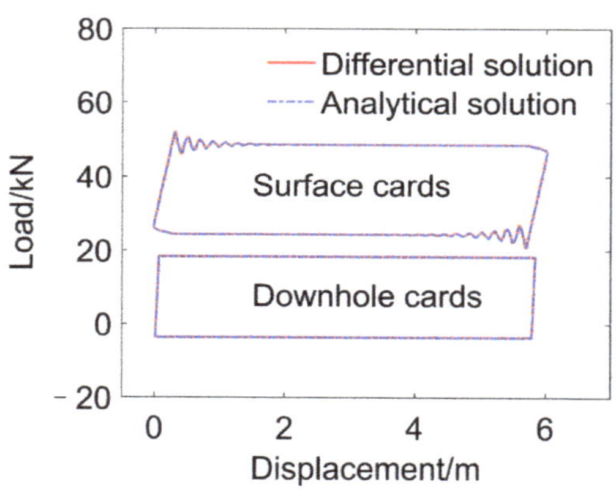

Figure 3. Simulated cards with a pumping speed of 1.4 min^{-1}.

To further demonstrate the applicability of the algorithm proposed in this paper, the cards at a pumping speed of 5.0 min^{-1} are simulated by both solutions. The simulation results of the analytical solution after the first iteration are shown in Figure 4. As illustrated in Figure 4, for the downhole cards, the loading and unloading portions of the analytical solution are significantly smaller than those of the finite difference solution. In the surface dynamometer card, the amplitude of the fluctuation in the upper stroke and downstroke of the analytical solution is slightly smaller than that of the finite difference solution.

Hence, the use of the static pump simulation model at this pumping speed will result in a larger error.

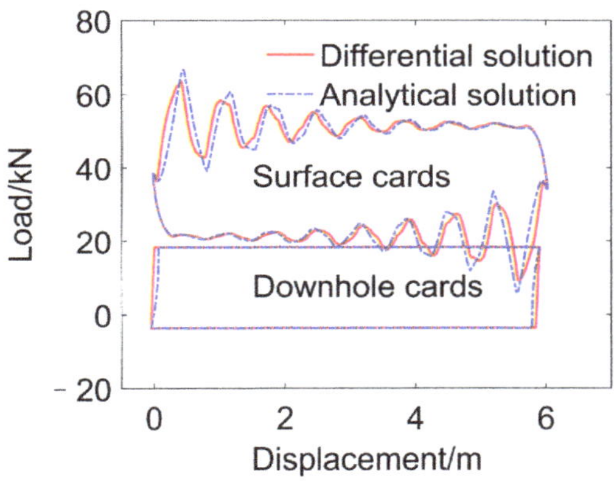

Figure 4. Simulated cards with a pumping speed of 5.0 min^{-1} and the first iteration of the analytic solution.

After eight iterations, the accuracy requirement of the analytical solution is met, and the results are shown in Figure 5. As shown in Figure 5, the surface dynamometer cards and downhole cards simulated by both solutions are consistent, and the area relative errors of the surface card and downhole card are −0.10% and 0.01%, respectively, which demonstrates that the iterative algorithm proposed in this paper can eliminate the error of the static model and achieve the same accuracy as the finite difference solution.

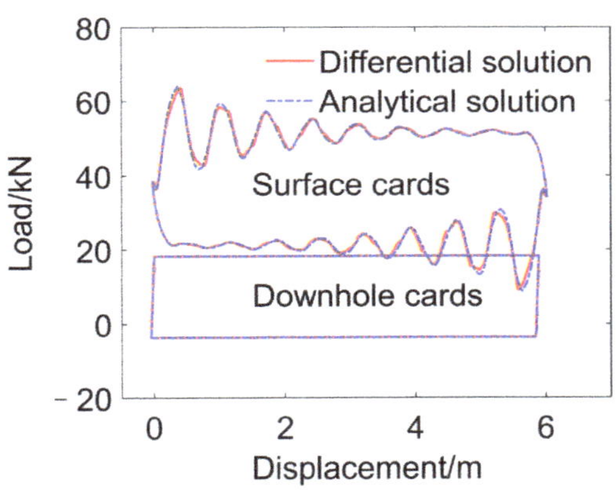

Figure 5. Simulated cards with the pumping speed of 5.0 min^{-1}.

4.1.2. Comparison with the Measured Card

The surfaces and downhole cards simulated by the analytical solution and the measured surface dynamometer cards of well 1 and well 2 are shown in Figures 6 and 7, respectively. Table 2 compares the data taken from the simulated surface dynamometer card and the measured data, which are recorded by the dynamometer.

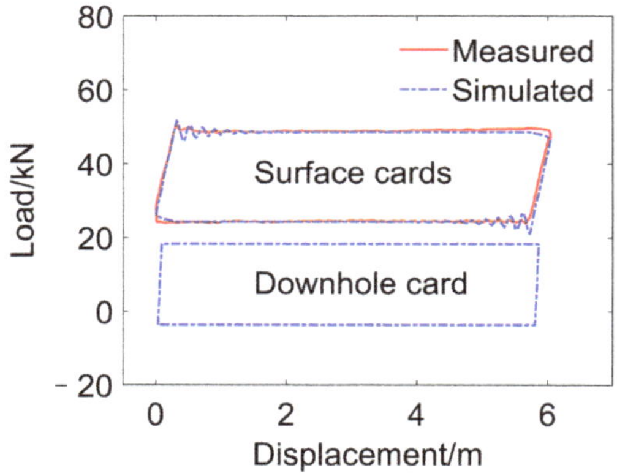

Figure 6. Measured surface dynamometer card and simulated cards of well 1.

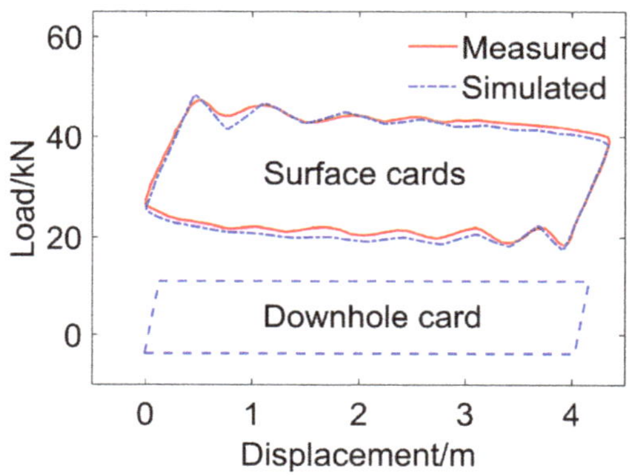

Figure 7. Measured surface dynamometer card and simulated cards of well 2.

Table 2. Comparison of the data predicted from the algorithm with the dynamometer recorded data.

Well Number		Min Load (kN)	Max Load (kN)	Area (kNm)
Well 1	simulated	20.90	51.90	140.35
	measured	23.77	50.81	142.19
Well 2	simulated	17.46	48.28	92.11
	measured	18.38	47.25	90.80

As illustrated in Figure 6, the simulated surface dynamometer card has good consistency with the measured card. As shown in Table 2, the loads and area predicted by the analytical solution closely matched the actual loads, especially for the card area, and the relative area error to the measured card area is 1.30%. The difference may come from errors due to dynamometer resolution.

According to the simulated surface dynamometer card by the analytical solution of well 2, the buoyant rod weight was adjusted by −0.91 kN. This error may be due to calculation method of the rod buoyancy weight different from the actual. As illustrated in Figure 7, there is little difference between the two surface dynamometer cards. Table 2 shows that the loads and area predicted by the analytical solution also closely match the actual loads, and the relative area error to the measured card area is 1.45%. These results indicate that the prediction algorithm is feasible. These differences may be due to dynamometer resolution or the neglect of hydrodynamic effects. Further research is ongoing.

4.2. Convergence Study

The convergence characteristics of the algorithm are studied for wells 1 and 2 at different pumping speeds. For well 1 at pumping speeds of 1.4 min^{-1} and 5.0 min^{-1}, iterative matrix elements M_n with the increasing Fourier series are calculated according to Equation (28) and are shown in Figures 8 and 9. The relative characteristic data are given in Table 3. The resonant frequency is calculated according to $2n\pi/T$.

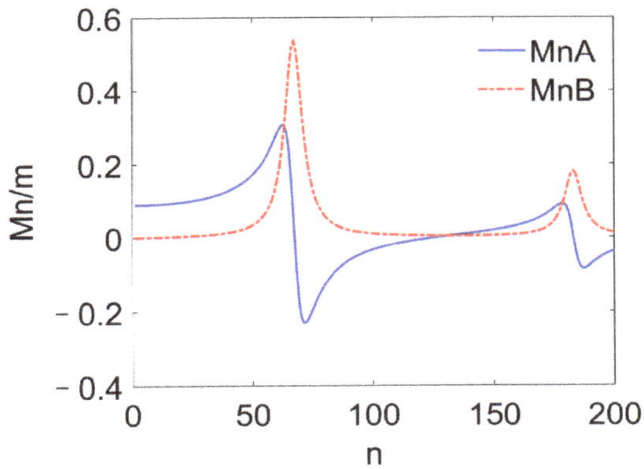

Figure 8. Convergence curve of well 1 at a pumping speed of 1.4 min^{-1}.

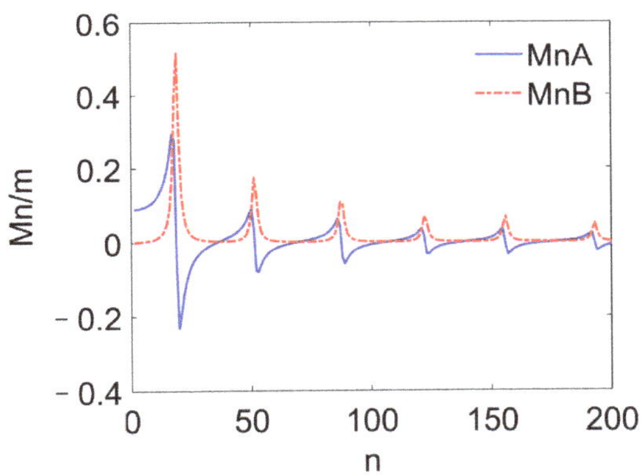

Figure 9. Convergence curve of well 1 at a pumping speed of 5.0 min^{-1}.

Table 3. Comparison of the data convergence results.

Well Number	Pumping Speed (min^{-1})	Iteration Number	Resonance Position	Resonance Frequency (Hz)	Max $\lvert MnA \rvert$ (m)	Max $\lvert MnB \rvert$ (m)
Well 1	1.4	3	67	9.8227	0.3064	0.5386
	5.0	8	19	9.9484	0.2933	0.5159
Well 2	4.1	3	19	8.1577	0.1228	0.2009
	6.0	3	13	8.1681	0.1174	0.2010

Figures 8 and 9 show that the values of the iterative matrix elements are less than one; so, the iterations converge. A comparison of Figures 8 and 9 also shows that the number of harmonics increases, and the resonance position decreases, as the pumping speed increases. Table 3 shows that despite the different pumping speeds, the frequency of the resonance and the maximum value of the iterative matrix element are almost constant. The mechanism is shown in Equations (25) and (26), i.e., the convergence of the algorithm depends on the material of the rod, its length, the fluid viscosity, and the tube anchoring state. Table 3 also shows that the number of iterations at a pumping speed of 5.0 min^{-1} is greater than that at a pumping speed of 1.4 min^{-1}. The number of iterations of the algorithm depends on the initial value and the structure of the algorithm. A comparison of Figures 4 and 5 shows that the initial value at a pumping speed of 5.0 min^{-1} is far from the true solution. This may be the reason for the greater number of iterations at a speed of 5.0 min^{-1}.

Figures 10 and 11 show the convergence curves of well 2 at pumping speeds of 4.1 min^{-1} and 6.0 min^{-1}, which are calculated according to Equation (27). The relative characteristic data are also shown in Table 3. The results show that there is the same convergence law between well 1 and well 2. The difference is that the algorithm of well 2 is more likely to converge because the maximum value of the iterative matrix elements is smaller. The resonance frequency calculated from η_n is 8.1267, which is very close to the resonance frequency in Table 3. The error is due to too few Fourier series.

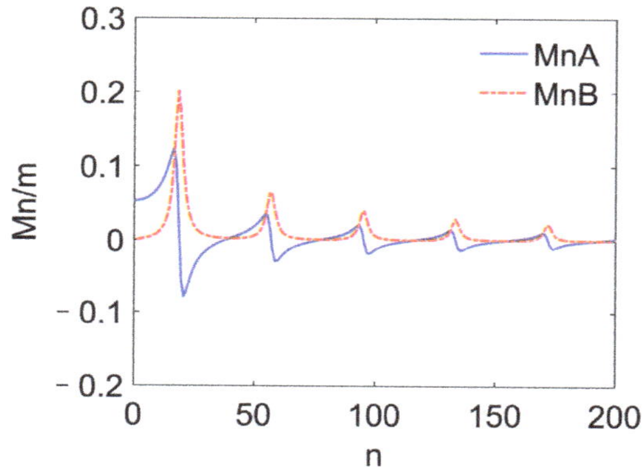

Figure 10. Convergence curve of well 2 at pumping speed of 4.1 min^{-1}.

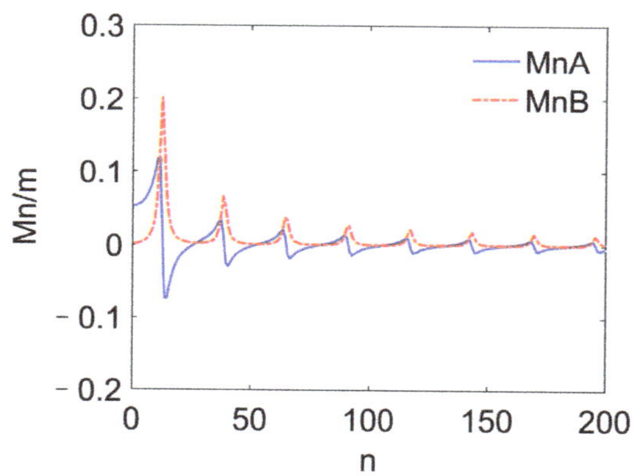

Figure 11. Convergence curve of well 2 at pumping speed of 6.0 min^{-1}.

5. Conclusions

This paper establishes a normal pump condition model based on the polished rod velocity. The iterative prediction algorithm proposed in this paper predicts the behavior of a sucker rod pumping unit based on an analytical solution. The algorithm is validated by classical finite difference method simulated cards and measured surface dynamometer cards. The convergence of the algorithm is analyzed theoretically and numerically. The following conclusions can be drawn:

(1) In the normal pump condition model, the recursive equation for pump pressure is based on the polished rod velocity, which can easily provide the pump load–time function within one pumping cycle, naturally consider the anchoring state of the tubing, and include other fault conditions.
(2) The algorithm can use the analytical solution of the wave equation to predict the behavior of the pumping unit only based on the polished rod velocity. Comparison with the simulated cards of the classical finite difference method shows that the maximum area relative error is 0.10%, and the proposed algorithm can achieve the same level of accuracy as the classical finite difference method. When compared with the measured surface cards, the area relative error is 1.45%, indicating that the algorithm is feasible.
(3) The convergence of the algorithm is analyzed theoretically. An expression for the iteration matrix is given, which can be applied to both single rod and multi-tapered rods. The expression shows that the convergence of the algorithm depends on the material of the rod, its length, the fluid viscosity, and the tube anchoring state. Numerical results show that the algorithm converges in the two wells given in this paper. The smaller the maximum value of the iterative matrix elements, the easier it is for the algorithm to converge. The convergence analysis provides assurance of the accuracy and reliability of the algorithm.

Based on the limitations of this study, the authors would like to propose the following directions for future research: (a) a more widely applicable iterative algorithm; (b) a theoretical study of the convergence of multi-tapered sucker rod pumping systems; and (c) an iterative algorithm study of multi-fault pumping conditions.

Author Contributions: Conceptualization, J.Y.; methodology, J.Y.; software, J.Y.; validation, J.Y.; formal analysis, J.Y.; investigation, J.Y.; resources, J.Y.; data curation, J.Y.; writing—original draft preparation, J.Y.; writing—review and editing, J.Y.; visualization, J.Y.; supervision, J.Y.; project administration, H.M.; funding acquisition, H.M. All authors have read and agreed to the published version of the manuscript.

Funding: This research was supported by the Shandong province Natural Science Foundation of China (Grant No. ZR2021MD067), the Fundamental Research Funds for the Central Universities (Grant No. 22CX03011A).

Data Availability Statement: The data presented in this study are available on request.

Acknowledgments: Comments and suggestions from the editor and reviewers are very much appreciated.

Conflicts of Interest: The authors declare no conflicts of interest.

References

1. Takacs, G. A critical analysis of power conditions in sucker-rod pumping systems. *J. Petrol. Sci. Eng.* **2022**, *210*, 110061. [CrossRef]
2. Ramos, A.J.A.; Almeida Júnior, D.S.; Santos, A.R.; Araújo, E.A.; Aum, P.T. Energy dissipation analysis of oil wells sucker rod string. *J. Braz. Soc. Mech. Sci. Eng.* **2020**, *42*, 108. [CrossRef]
3. Langbauer, C.; Langbauer, T.; Fruhwirth, R.; Mastobaev, B. Sucker rod pump frequency-elastic drive mode development–from the numerical model to the field test. *Liq. Gas. Energy Resour.* **2021**, *1*, 64–85. [CrossRef]
4. Bangert, P. Diagnosing and Predicting Problems with Rod Pumps using Machine Learning. In Proceedings of the SPE Middle East Oil and Gas Show and Conference, Manama, Bahrain, 18–21 March 2019. [CrossRef]
5. Wang, X.; He, Y.; Li, F.; Dou, X.; Wang, Z.; Xu, H.; Fu, L. A Working Condition Diagnosis Model of Sucker Rod Pumping Wells Based on Big Data Deep Learning. In Proceedings of the International Petroleum Technology Conference, Beijing, China, 26–28 March 2019. [CrossRef]
6. Xu, J. A Method for Diagnosing the Performance of Sucker Rod String in Straight Inclined Wells. In Proceedings of the SPE Latin America/Caribbean Petroleum Engineering Conference, Buenos Aires, Argentina, 27–29 April 1994. [CrossRef]
7. Zheng, B.; Gao, X. Sucker rod pumping diagnosis using valve working displacement and parameter optimal continuous hidden Markov model. *J. Process Cont.* **2017**, *59*, 1–12. [CrossRef]

8. Zheng, B.; Guo, X.; Ki, X. Diagnosis of Sucker Rod Pump based on generating dynamometer cards. *J. Process Cont.* **2019**, *77*, 76–88. [CrossRef]
9. Zhang, A.; Gao, X. Supervised dictionary-based transfer subspace learning and applications for fault diagnosis of sucker rod pumping systems. *Neurocomputing* **2019**, *338*, 293–306. [CrossRef]
10. He, Y.; Zang, C.; Zeng, P.; Wang, M.; Wan, G.; Dong, Q. Automatic Recognition of Sucker-Rod Pumping System Working Conditions Using Few-Shot Indicator Diagram Based on Meta-learning. In Proceedings of the International Conference on Intelligent Automation and Soft Computing, Chicago, IL, USA, 26–28 May 2021. [CrossRef]
11. Han, Y.; Li, K.; Ge, F.; Xu, W. Online fault diagnosis for sucker rod pumping well by optimized density peak clustering. *ISA Trans.* **2022**, *120*, 222–234. [CrossRef] [PubMed]
12. Takacs, G. Calculation of Operational Parameters. In *Sucker-Rod Pumping Handbook: Production Engineering Fundamentals and Long-Stroke Rod Pumping*; Gulf Professional Publishing: Houston, TX, USA, 2015; Chapter 4; pp. 247–376. [CrossRef]
13. Moreno, G.A.; Garriz, A.E. Sucker rod string dynamics in deviated wells. *J. Petrol. Sci. Eng.* **2019**, *184*, 106534. [CrossRef]
14. Gibbs, S.G. Predicting the behavior of sucker-rod pumping systems. *SPE J.* **1963**, *15*, 769–778. [CrossRef]
15. Doty, D.R.; Schmidt, Z. An Improved Model for Sucker Rod Pumping. *SPE J.* **1983**, *23*, 1. [CrossRef]
16. Lekia, S.D.L.; Evans, R.D. A Coupled Rod and Fluid Dynamic Model for Predicting the Behavior of Sucker-Rod Pumping Systems. *SPE Prod. Fac.* **1995**, *10*, 26–33. [CrossRef]
17. Yu, G.A.; Wu, Y.J.; Wang, G.Y. Three dimensional vibration in a sucker rod beam pumping system. *Acta Petrolei Sin.* **1989**, *10*, 76–83. (In Chinese) [CrossRef]
18. Lollback, P.A.; Wang, G.Y.; Rahman, S.S. An alternative approach to the analysis of sucker-rod dynamics in vertical and deviated wells. *J. Pet. Sci. Eng.* **1997**, *17*, 313–320. [CrossRef]
19. Khodabandeh, A.; Miska, S. A Simple Method for Predicting the Performance of a Sucker-Rod Pumping System. In Proceedings of the SPE Eastern Regional Meeting, Lexington, KY, USA, 22–25 October 1991. [CrossRef]
20. Khodabandeh, A.; Miska, S. A New Approach for Modeling Fluid Inertia Effects on Sucker-Rod Pump Performance and Design. In Proceedings of the SPE Rocky Mountain Regional Meeting, Casper, WY, USA, 18–21 May 1992. [CrossRef]
21. Xing, M.; Dong, S. An improved longitudinal vibration model and dynamic characteristic of sucker rod string. *J. Vibroeng.* **2014**, *16*, 3432–3448.
22. Xing, M. Response analysis of longitudinal vibration of sucker rod string considering rod buckling. *Adv. Eng. Softw.* **2016**, *99*, 49–58. [CrossRef]
23. Li, W.; Dong, S.; Sun, X. An Improved Sucker Rod Pumping System Model and Swabbing Parameters Optimized Design. *Math. Probl. Eng.* **2018**, *2018*, 4746210. [CrossRef]
24. Lv, X.; Wang, H.; Liu, Y.; Chen, S.; Lan, W.; Sun, B. A novel method of output metering with dynamometer card for SRPS under fault condition. *J. Pet. Sci. Eng.* **2020**, *192*, 107098. [CrossRef]
25. Schafer, D.J.; Jennings, J.W. An investigation of analytical and numerical sucker rod pumping mathematical models. In Proceedings of the SPE Annual Technical Conference and Exhibition, Dallas, TX, USA, 24 September 1987. [CrossRef]
26. Yin, J.; Sun, D.; Yang, Y. Predicting multi-tapered sucker-rod pumping systems with the analytical solution. *J. Pet. Sci. Eng.* **2021**, *197*, 108115. [CrossRef]
27. Yin, J.; Sun, D.; Yang, Y. A Novel Method for Diagnosis of Sucker-Rod Pumping Systems Based on the Polished-Rod Load Vibration in Vertical Wells. *SPE J.* **2020**, *25*, 2470–2481. [CrossRef]
28. Takacs, G. The Analysis of Sucker-Rod Pumping Installations. In *Sucker-Rod Pumping Handbook: Production Engineering Fundamentals and Long-Stroke Rod Pumping*; Gulf Professional Publishing: Houston, TX, USA, 2015; Chapter 6; pp. 423–503. [CrossRef]
29. DaCunha, J.J.; Gibbs, S.G. Modeling a Finite-Length Sucker Rod Using the Semi-Infinite-Wave Equation and a Proof to Gibbs' Conjecture. *Soc. Petrol. Eng.* **2009**, *14*, 112–119. [CrossRef]
30. Gibb, S.G. Method of Determining Sucker Rod Pump Performance. U.S. Patent 3343409, 26 September 1967.

mathematics

MDPI

Article

Improving the Reliability of Current Collectors in Electric Vehicles

Boris V. Malozyomov [1], Nikita V. Martyushev [2,*], Anton Y. Demin [2], Alexander V. Pogrebnoy [2], Egor A. Efremenkov [3], Denis V. Valuev [4] and Aleksandr E. Boltrushevich [2]

1 Department of Electrotechnical Complexes, Novosibirsk State Technical University, 630073 Novosibirsk, Russia; borisnovel@mail.ru
2 Department of Information Technology, Tomsk Polytechnic University, 634050 Tomsk, Russia; ad@tpu.ru (A.Y.D.); pogrebnoy@tpu.ru (A.V.P.); aeb20@tpu.ru (A.E.B.)
3 Department of Mechanical Engineering, Tomsk Polytechnic University, 634050 Tomsk, Russia; egorefr@tpu.ru
4 Yurga Technological Institute (Branch), Tomsk Polytechnic University, 652055 Yurga, Russia; valuev@tpu.ru
* Correspondence: martjushev@tpu.ru

Abstract: This article presents a mathematically grounded approach to increasing the operational reliability of current collectors in electric transport systems by ensuring a constant contact force between the collector shoe and the power rail. The core objective is achieved through the development and analysis of a mechanical system incorporating spring and cam elements, which is specifically designed to provide a nearly invariant contact pressure under varying operating conditions. A set of equilibrium equations was derived to determine the stiffness ratios of the springs and the geometric conditions under which the contact force remains constant despite wear or displacement. Additionally, the paper introduces a method for synthesizing the cam profile that compensates for nonlinear spring deformation, ensuring force constancy over a wide range of movement. The analytical results were validated through parametric simulations, which assessed the influence of wear depth, rail inclination, and external vibrations on the system's force output. These simulations, executed within a numerical framework using scientific computing tools, demonstrated that the deviation of the contact force does not exceed a few percent under typical disturbances. Experimental verification further confirmed the theoretical predictions. The study exemplifies the effective use of mathematical modeling, nonlinear mechanics, and numerical methods in the design of energy transmission components for transport applications, contributing to the development of robust and maintainable systems.

Keywords: modeling; electric transport; reliability; pantograph; contact pressure; constant contact force; subway; reduction of wear

MSC: 74K10; 70Q05; 74C10

1. Introduction

One of the key problems facing electric vehicles (EVs) is ensuring the stable and reliable operation of current collectors [1,2]. Satisfactory current collector quality, characterized by minimal sparking and stable electrical contact, directly affects the efficiency, safety, and durability of the ETS [3]. To achieve optimal current collection, it is necessary to maintain a stable contact pressure, which, on the one hand, must be sufficient to ensure continuous electrical contact and, on the other hand, must not be too large so as not to cause intensive mechanical wear of the contact elements of the pantograph (shoe in the subway or insert in the trolleybus) and the contact wire or contact rail [4,5].

The problem of maintaining optimal contact pressure is especially relevant for the current collectors of the lower type of current collectors, which are widely used in the metro. For example, the design of the current collector type 81-720/81-721 "Yauza", used in subway cars, uses springs to create contact pressure between the shoe and the contact rail [6]. However, the disadvantage of this design is the dependence of contact pressure on the force of the springs and the position of the shoe on the holder, which leads to its instability during the movement of the car. Insufficient pressure is fraught with contact disruption, the formation of an electric arc, overheating, melting, and, as a result, the destruction of contact parts [7]. Excessive pressure, on the contrary, causes accelerated wear of the shoe and contact rail and can also lead to the breakdown of pantograph parts, which ultimately reduces service life and increases operating costs [8].

The search for solutions to ensure stable contact pressure has led to the development of alternative pantograph designs. In particular, in [9], a current collector of the lower current collector type is proposed, in which a pneumatic rubber cord element is used instead of pressure springs. Although this solution allows one to adjust the contact pressure, it adds complexity to the design, requiring the implementation of an additional automatic pressure control system.

Modern research is aimed at developing more intelligent and adaptive current collection systems. For example, ref. [10] presents a pantograph that uses an active contact pressure control system based on data received from position, acceleration, and vibration sensors. Such a system, using optimal control algorithms, is able to compensate in real time for fluctuations in contact pressure caused by the unevenness of the contact rail, changes in travel speed, and other factors.

The problems of improving current collection systems are closely related to the development of methods for diagnosing and monitoring the condition of the contact network and packaging devices. In ref. [11], the use of machine learning methods to analyze data on current, voltage, and vibration in the current collector system is proposed in order to detect defects early and prevent accidents. The development and implementation of such predictive analytics systems will significantly improve the reliability and safety of ETS operation.

In addition, the use of new materials and technologies for the manufacture of contact elements is a promising direction. For example, ref. [12] discusses the use of composite materials with high wear resistance and electrical conductivity for the manufacture of pantograph shoes. This will reduce the wear of the contact rail and increase the service life of the pantograph while ensuring stable electrical contact.

In the context of the development of high-speed transport, the problem of current collection reliability is of particular relevance. In ref. [13], the authors propose the use of contactless methods of power transmission, such as inductive transmission, to provide power supply to high-speed trains, which will completely eliminate the problem of wear and damage to the contact network.

Thus, in order to ensure a reliable and efficient power supply to ETS, it is necessary to develop and implement innovative solutions in the field of current collection, combining advanced methods of control, diagnostics, and materials science. Improving current collection systems is an important step towards creating more environmentally friendly, safer, and more cost-effective transport systems [14,15].

To ensure a reliable, non-sparking current collector, the contact pressure must be within certain limits and, if possible, be constant regardless of the speed of the car. The purpose of the work is to increase the reliability of the pantograph for subway cars by providing a constant contact force.

2. Materials and Methods

In this study, a comprehensive method was developed and implemented to improve the reliability of current collectors of electric vehicles by providing a constant contact force between the pantograph shoe and the contact rail. As a basis, two design schemes of the pantograph are proposed: one based on a spring-lever mechanism, the other using cam-spring compensation. For both schemes, mathematical models were built, making it possible to determine the necessary ratios of spring stiffness and geometric parameters at which the contact force remains constant when the shoe wears out or changes its position. In particular, the cam profile compensating for the nonlinearity of elastic deformations was analytically derived. Next, parametric numerical simulations were carried out, which makes it possible to assess the stability of the contact force under characteristic operational deviations, such as wear, rail inclination, and vibrations. Modeling was implemented in the Python v3.9 environment using scientific libraries. To confirm the theoretical results, a laboratory experimental setup was assembled, which made it possible to record the behavior of the contact force in various modes. Next, a comparison of the calculated and experimental data was carried out. This comparison made it possible to evaluate the accuracy of the model and the stability of the clamp.

The authors propose developed versions of a current collector with a constant contact force. The proposed device (Figure 1) comprises a slipper shoe (1) that is in constant contact (from below) with the contact rail (2); a shoe holder (3) rigidly and perpendicularly fixed to the shoe, sliding inside a sleeve mounted on the beam; the guide rods (4) of the shoe for movements rigidly connected to the shoe, sliding inside the bushings mounted on the beam; two sliders (5) with the ability to slide along the horizontal guides, and two horizontal springs (6) connected to the sliders and the bar; two rods (7) connecting the sliders to the shoe holder; and a vertical spring (8) connecting the shoe holder to the bar. The proposed device (Figure 1) is based on our own conceptual design developed in this study. The structural principles partially refer to prior concepts discussed in [16], which served as an initial reference for mechanical arrangement but do not implement the constant-force functionality analyzed here.

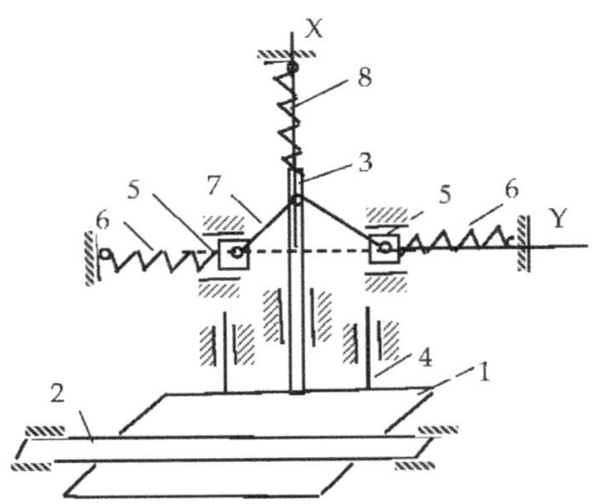

Figure 1. Constant contact force for pantograph option.

The device works as follows. In the initial position (the shoe is brought under the rail), the rods (7) occupy a horizontal position (dotted line). In this position, the spring (8) is stretched, and its tension force is equal to F_{8t}. With this force, the shoe acts on the rail. The springs (6) are compressed, and the tension forces are equal to F_{6t}.

When the thickness of the shoe or rail decreases, the spring (8) is compressed, the springs (6) begin to stretch, and the bars (7) take the position shown in Figure 1.

Let us determine at what ratio of spring stiffness the pressure force on the rail will remain constant and equal to F_{8t}. Let us make an equilibrium condition for the slider (5) (Figure 2a) with an explanation of all the forces:

$$S \cdot cos\alpha = F_{6t} - c_6 \cdot (l - l \cdot sin\alpha)$$

where the following applies: S—rod reaction (7); α—rod inclination angle; F_{6t}—initial spring tension (6), c_6—spring stiffness (6); l—rod length (7).

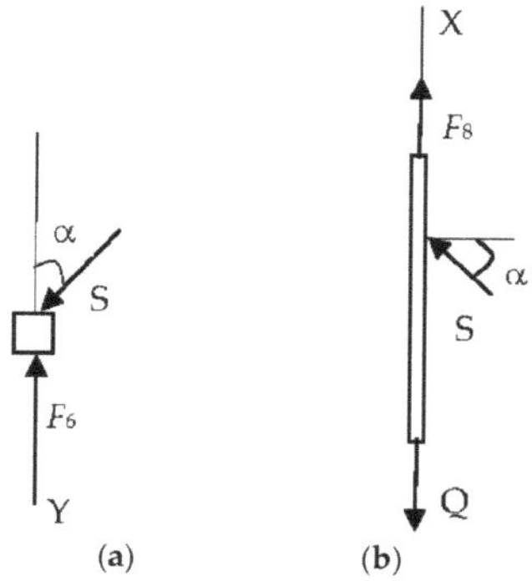

Figure 2. The ratio of spring stiffness and pressure forces: (**a**)—slide; (**b**)—shoe.

Let us take a look at the slider (5) separately (Figure 2a) and write down the equilibrium condition for it in the projection on the OY axis:

$$S \cos \alpha - F_6 = 0, \tag{1}$$

where

$$F_6 = F_{6t} - c_6 l(1 - \cos \alpha),$$

c_6—spring rate (6); l—rod length (7); S—rod reaction (7); α is the angle of inclination of the rod (7) to the OY axis.

To determine the force projections on the OY axis in the analysis of the slide (5) in Figure 2, a trigonometric relationship between the position of the pull rod length l and the horizontal displacement x from the vertical position was used. At small deflection angles, we see that

$$\sin \alpha = \frac{x}{l}, \ \cos \alpha = \frac{\sqrt{l^2 - x^2}}{l}$$

Here, α is the angle of inclination of the thrust to the vertical, and x is the horizontal displacement. These expressions follow from the geometric relations of a right-angled triangle and allow us to express the forces in projections on the coordinate axes. The simplification of the thrust reaction force and the subsequent substitution in (2) make it possible to arrive at Equation (3), from which it can be seen that when the conditions $F_{6t} - c_6 l = 0$ and $c_8 = 2c_6$, the contact force Q does not depend on the change in the coordinate x and remains constant.

Let us write down the equilibrium condition [17] of the holder (3) with the shoe (1) (Figure 2b) in the projection on the axis OX:

$$F_8 - Q + 2S \sin \alpha = 0, \tag{2}$$

where

$$F_8 = F_{8t} - c_8 x,$$

Q is the force with which the rail presses on the shoe, and c_8 is the spring stiffness (8).

The following is supplemented by an explanation of the balance of forces for the contact shoe holder 3 (Figure 2b):

$$Q = F_{8t} \ - c_8 \cdot \Delta h + 2S \cdot sin\alpha,$$

where Q is the force of contact with the rail, F_{8t} is the initial tension of the spring (8), $c_8 \cdot$ is the stiffness of the spring (8), and Δh is the displacement of the shoe due to wear.

The transition from (1) and (2) to the final constancy condition is as follows:

$$Q = F_{8t} \text{ at } F_{6t} - c_6 l = 0 \text{ and } c_8 = 2c_6$$

These conditions compensate for the change in spring force (8) due to the geometry of the lever and the spring rate (6), which guarantees a constant contact force Q during shoe wear.

From Equation (1), by expressing the reaction of the rod S, taking into account the fact that $\sin\alpha = x/l$, $\cos\alpha = \sqrt{l^2 - x^2}/l$ and substituting this into Equation (2), we get

$$F_{8t} - c_8 x - Q + 2\frac{x}{\sqrt{l^2 - x^2}}(F_{6t} - c_6 l) + 2xc_6 = 0. \quad (3)$$

From Equation (3), it can be seen that at $F_{6t} - c_6 l = 0$ and $c_8 = 2c_6$, the force of the pressure of the rail on the shoe will be constant for the entire time of the decrease in the thickness of the shoe, and this is equal to $Q = F_{8t}$.

Thus, in order for the pressure of the shoe on the rail to be constant and equal to $Q = F_{8t}$ during the reduction in shoe thickness, two conditions, $F_{6t} - c_6 l = 0$ and $c_8 = 2c_6$, must be met.

For the slide (5) (Figure 2a), the projection of forces on the OY axis gives Equation (1), where it is taken into account that at small angles α, the length of the spring (6) changes to $l \cdot sin\alpha$. The substitution S from (1) to (2) allows us to exclude the unknown reaction of the rod and obtain the final condition (3) for the constancy of the force Q.

3. Modeling of a Current Collector of Increased Reliability

Providing a constant force between the shoe and the contact rail, or constant contact, will prevent the formation of an electric arc, unacceptable heating, melting, and the destruction of the contact parts [18]. This will increase the service life of the shoe and, therefore, the entire pantograph [19].

The parameters of the elastic elements were selected on the basis of a combination of empirical data and recommendations from manufacturers of standard springs (ST SEV 5616-86—"Helical cylindrical compression and tension springs of class 1, category 3 made of round steel. The main parameters of the turns". At the same time, the permissible pressure force of 100–140 N was taken into account; a spring stiffness of c = 14,000 N/m provides a given force with preliminary deformation within 10 mm. A cam radius of R_0 = 0.01 m corresponds to the limitation on the dimensions of the structure and allows rotation within 2.3 rads. Choosing a variable radius cam is a trade-off between ease of manufacture and the need for constant force. Alternative shapes, such as linear-eccentric profiles, have been rejected due to increased force fluctuations with uneven wear.

To create a constant contact force in the second version of the current collector, a cam-spring device is used. The required force between the shoe of the current collector of the car and the contact rail, according to the requirements, is about 200 N [20]. The design diagram of such current collectors of the lower current collector type is shown in Figure 3.

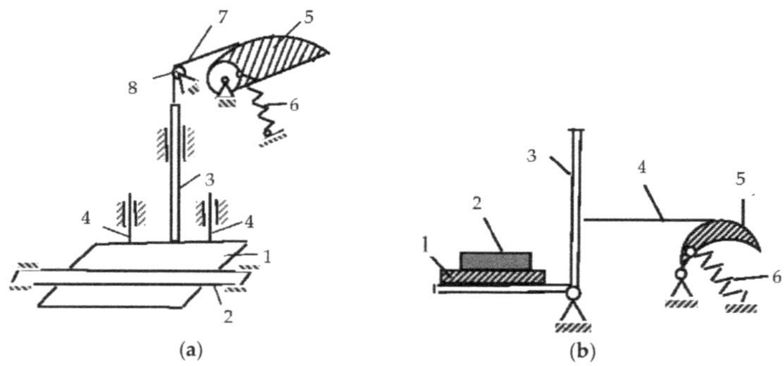

Figure 3. Structural diagram of the current collectors of the lower current collector type: (**a**)—with the forward movement of the bracket with a shoe; (**b**)—with the rotational movement of the bracket with the shoe.

As practice has shown, the first option is preferable in terms of durability (Figure 3a). The pantograph of the lower current collector type contains a slip shoe (1), which is in constant contact (from below) with the contact rail (2), and a shoe holder (3), rigidly and perpendicularly fixed to the shoe and sliding inside a sleeve mounted on a beam. Rods (4) are the guides for the movement of the shoe (3). One end of the spring (6) is attached to the cam drum, and the other to the beam. The cable (7), coming off the cam, is thrown over the fixed block (8) and connected to the shoe holder.

The initial position of the cam (5) corresponds to the rotation angle of ψ 1. In this position, the spring (6) is stretched to the specified value λ, and the pressure of the shoe (*1*) on the rail is equal to the specified Q_0. If the thickness of the shoe or rail decreases, the spring will be compressed, and the cam will rotate clockwise by an angle ψ, but the specified value of the shoe pressing Q_0 on the rail will remain constant. The constancy of the tension force of the cable (7) when turning the cam is ensured by the fact that the cam profile (5) is made with a variable radius of curvature [21].

Let us find the cam profile that provides a constant force Q for this case. The calculation scheme in this case is shown in Figure 4.

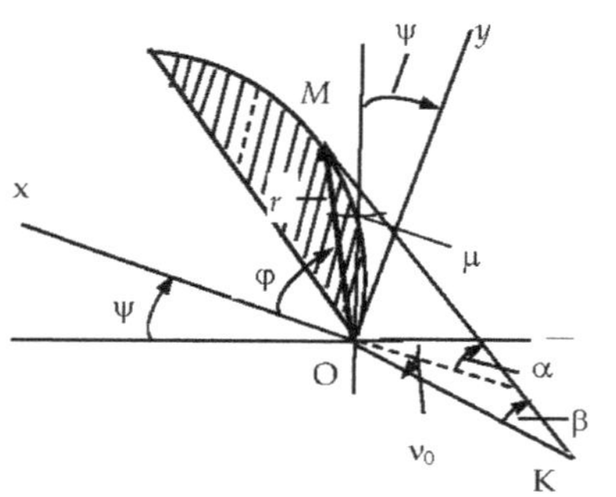

Figure 4. Cam profile design diagram.

As can be seen from the geometry of Figure 4, the relationship between the angles α, ν_0, β, and ψ is as follows:

$$\alpha = \nu_0 - \psi + \beta.$$

In addition,

$$d = r \cdot \sin(\varphi - \alpha) = L \cdot \sin\beta, \quad (4)$$

where L is the distance between the axes of the drum and the block.

For the constancy of the effort $Q = Q_0$, the equality of moments is necessary:

$$Qd = c(\lambda + R_0\psi)R_0 = c\lambda R_0(1 + R_0\psi/\lambda). \quad (5)$$

Here, c is the spring stiffness; R_0 is the radius of the drum; and λ is the initial deformation of the spring at $Q = Q_0$.

Since at $\psi = 0$, $Q_0 d_0 = c\lambda R_0$, from (4) and (5), we obtain that the length of the perpendicular lowered from the origin to the line of the filament (in order for the force Q to be constant) must vary according to the law

$$d = d_0\left(1 + R_0\frac{\psi}{\lambda}\right) = L\sin\beta. \quad (6)$$

From (4), and taking into account (6), we find

$$\varphi = \nu_0 + \beta - \left(\frac{\lambda}{R_0}\right)\left[\left(\frac{L}{d_0}\right)\sin\beta - 1\right] + \arcsin\left(\frac{L}{r}\sin\beta\right). \quad (7)$$

Take the differential from (7):

$$d\varphi = d\beta - \frac{\lambda}{R_0}\frac{L}{d_0}\cos\beta \cdot d\beta + \frac{r}{\sqrt{r^2 - L^2\sin^2\beta}}\left(\frac{L}{r}\cos\beta \cdot d\beta - \frac{L\sin\beta}{r^2}dr\right).$$

Hence, taking into account the fact that

$$\frac{dr}{d\varphi} = \frac{r}{\mathrm{tg}(\alpha - \varphi)},$$

We get

$$r = L\sqrt{\sin^2\beta + \frac{\cos^2\beta}{\left(\frac{\lambda}{R_0}\frac{L}{d_0}\cos\beta - 1\right)^2}}. \quad (8)$$

Then, the coordinates of the point M of the thread coming off the cam are

$$x = r\cos\varphi, \quad y = r\sin\varphi.$$

Using the x and y coordinates, we determine the cam profile (Figure 5).

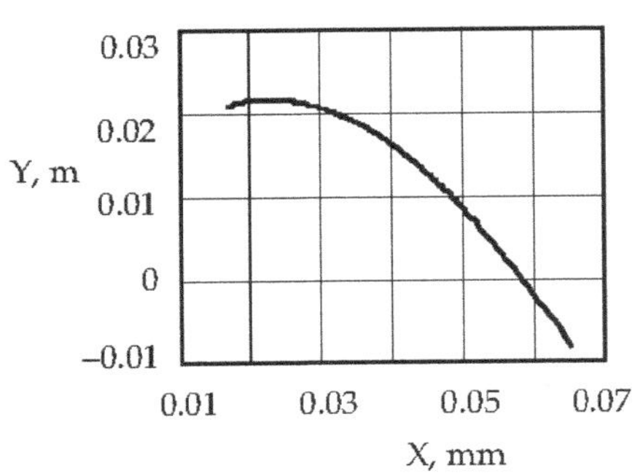

Figure 5. Cam profile with a linear spring.

To design a cam for a given force $Q = Q_0$, Equations (6) and (8) are conveniently written in a dimensionless form:

$$\tilde{r} = \sqrt{\sin^2\beta + \frac{\cos^2\beta}{(W_1\cos\beta - 1)^2}}, \quad \tilde{d} = \sin\beta = \frac{1}{W_1}\left(\frac{\lambda}{R_0} + \psi\right). \tag{9}$$

Here, $\tilde{r} = \frac{r}{L}$, $\tilde{d} = \frac{d}{L}$, $W_1 = \frac{LQ_0}{cR_0^2}$.

From here, one can obtain the limit value of the cam rotation angle

$$\psi_{\mathrm{rt}} = W_1 - \frac{\lambda}{R_0}.$$

When the shoe is moved, the cam (5) will begin to rotate clockwise (the spring (6), in this case, is stretched). However, the force in the cable (7) coming down from the cam (5) and attached to the shoe holder will be unchanged and equal to Q.

It is planned to use two parallel cam–spring mechanisms in one pantograph. Each such device shall provide a continuous force of 100 N.

When performing a numerical simulation of the cam, we set the following parameters. Let the stiffness of the linear spring be c = 14,000 N/m, the initial deformation of the spring at the force Q = 100 N be equal to $\lambda = 1 \times 10^{-2}$ m, $R_0 = 1 \times 10^{-2}$ m, and $L = 5 \times 10^{-2}$ m. Let us determine Equations (11)–(13) for the shape of the cam that produces a constant force Q = 100 N when the cam rotates within the range of $\psi = 0$ to the limit $\psi_{\mathrm{rt}} = \frac{\lambda}{R_0}\left(\frac{L}{d_0} - 1\right)$. In this case, $\psi\rho\tau$ = 2.3 rads (133°).

Based on the fact that the maximum displacement of the shoe is equal to S_m = 0.02 m, from the formula expressing the equality of the works of the elastic force and the force Q, we see

$$S_m = \frac{c}{2Q}[(\lambda + R_0\psi_1)^2 - \lambda^2],$$

Let us determine the required maximum angle of rotation of the cam [22]. In this case, it turns out to be equal to ψ_1 = 0.92, i.e., ψ_1 = 52.7°. It can be seen that the maximum required cam angle $\psi_1\ \iota\sigma$ is much smaller than the maximum realized angle $\psi\rho\tau$.

Let us dwell on the issues of spring and cable strength. Let us make the spring index c_1 equal to the ratio of the average diameter of the spring coil to the diameter of the wire bar from which the spring is wound $c_1 = \frac{D_0}{d} = 4.6$. The number of required spring coils will be determined by the formula

$$n = \frac{Gd^4}{8D_0^3 c} \approx 18 \text{ coils.}$$

Here, $G = 8 \times 10^{10}$ MPa is the shear modulus [23]. With a spring index of $c_1 \geq 4$, the correction factor k, which takes into account the influence of the curvature of the turns and the shear force, is calculated using the formula

$$k = \frac{4c_1 - 1}{4c_1 - 4} + \frac{0.65}{c_1} = 1.35.$$

We check the fulfillment of the condition for the strength of a spring made of round wire under the action of static or slowly changing variable loads:

$$\tau_{\max} = k8F\frac{c_1}{\pi d^2} = 709{\cdot}10^6 \text{ N/m}^2.$$

That is, for the value $\tau_{\max} < [\tau]$, for springs made of steel 60C2, 60C2A, and 50HFA, the value is taken to be equal to $[\tau] = 750{\cdot}10^6 \text{ N/m}^2$, which means that the condition of the spring strength is met [24]. Here, τ denotes the allowable value of the shear stress for calculating the shear strength of the spring. The value of 750×10^6 N/m^2 corresponds to the shear strength for spring steels of the 60C2, 60C2A, and 50HFA types, which are widely used in mechanical engineering. Steel 60S2 and 50HFA are alloy structural spring steels according to ISO 8458-3-92 [25]—which are rolled from spring-loaded carbon alloy steel, providing high fatigue strength.

It is necessary to check the condition of the strength of the cable with a diameter of $d = 1 \times 10^{-3}$ m at a load of $Q = 100$ N. Let us calculate the stress in the cable for $\sigma = \frac{Q}{S} = 127.4{\cdot}10^6$ N/m^2. Since $\sigma < \sigma_m = 160{\cdot}10^6$ N/m^2, the condition of the strength of the cable is met.

Thus, the possibility of using cam–spring devices in current collectors in order to create a constant contact force within certain limits is shown [26].

Let us investigate the effect of dry friction on the dynamic properties of the considered systems with zero stiffness. Let us consider the motion of the mass m on such a suspension, taking into account the dry friction N with the harmonic perturbation a_0 sinωt (Figure 6a).

$$m\ddot{y} + N\text{sign}\dot{y} = ma_0\omega^2 \sin \omega t. \tag{10}$$

Here, y is a deviation from the position of static equilibrium.

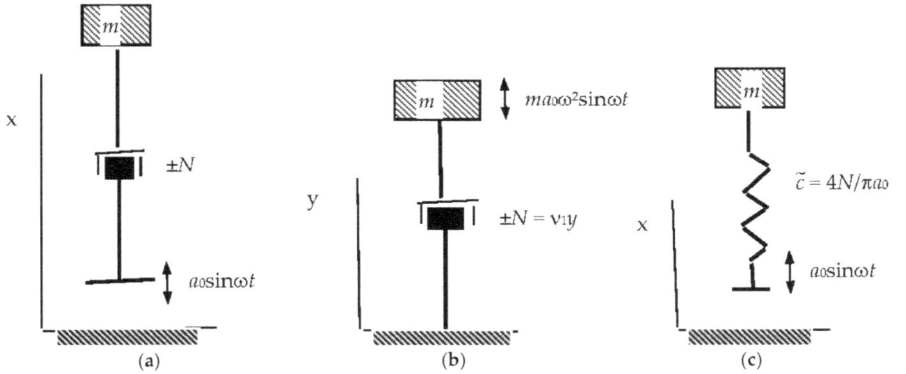

Figure 6. Kinematic scheme of the influence of dry friction on the dynamic properties of the considered systems with zero rigidity: (**a**)—Mechanical model of a mass on a zero-stiffness suspension subject to dry friction and harmonic excitation; (**b**)—Equivalent damping model showing the force–displacement diagram accounting for energy dissipation due to dry friction; (**c**)—Reduced system with equivalent stiffness and damping used for comparative dynamic analysis.

Let us replace the second term on the left side of the equation with an equivalent term $\nu_1\dot{y}$, where the coefficient ν_1 is determined from the condition of equality of work for one period of the actual drag force and the equivalent force [27]:

$$4Ny = \nu_1 \int_0^{\frac{2\pi}{\omega}} \dot{y}^2 dt = \nu_1 \omega y_0^2 \int_0^{\frac{2\pi}{\omega}} \cos^2 \omega t d(\omega t) = \nu_1 \omega y_0^2 \pi,$$

From here, we find

$$\nu_1 = \frac{4N}{\pi \omega y_0}, \tag{11}$$

where y_0 is the amplitude of relative displacement.

As a result, we get (Figure 6b)

$$m\ddot{y} + \nu_1 \dot{y} = m a_0 \omega^2 \sin \omega t. \quad (12)$$

From this equation and correlation, we find

$$y_0 = a_0 \sqrt{1 - N_c^2}, \quad (13)$$

where

$$N_c = \frac{4N}{\pi n a_0 \omega^2}. \quad (14)$$

Using the relation $y = x - a_0 \sin \omega t$, convert Equation (12) to the form

$$\ddot{x} + \nu \dot{x} = a_0 \omega \nu \cos \omega t, \quad (15)$$

where

$$\nu = \frac{\nu_1}{m} = \frac{4N}{\pi m \omega y_0}. \quad (16)$$

Taking $x = x_0 \cos(\omega t + \varphi)$, into account for (16) and (13), we find the value of the vibration damping coefficient:

$$\delta = \frac{a_0}{x_0} = \frac{\pi m a_0 \omega^2}{4N} = \frac{1}{N_c}. \quad (17)$$

According to the value of the dimensionless parameter N_c, it is possible to estimate the effect of dry friction on a current collector with zero rigidity.

Let us write Equation (17) in the following form:

$$\delta = \frac{\omega^2}{\frac{\widetilde{c}}{m}}, \quad (18)$$

where

$$\widetilde{c} = \frac{4N}{\pi a_0}. \quad (19)$$

Let us call the value $\widetilde{c}$ the reduced rigidity of the system under consideration.

Let us replace the original system (Figure 6a) with the reduced system (Figure 6c).

In this case, the equation of motion of the object has the form

$$m\ddot{x} + \widetilde{c}x = \widetilde{c}a_0 \sin \omega t \text{ and } \delta = \frac{\omega^2}{\frac{\widetilde{c}}{m}} - 1. \quad (20)$$

A comparison of Equations (20) and (18) allows us to conclude that the value of the damping coefficient of an elastic system of low rigidity [28,29], in the first approximation, is one more than the corresponding reduced elastic system (Figure 6c), the stiffness of which $\widetilde{c}$ is determined by the ratio (19).

To evaluate the performance of the proposed pantograph mechanism, with constant force, in real operating conditions, numerical simulations were carried out. The simulation evaluated the stability of the contact force under three key scenarios: contact shoe wear, the inclination of the contact rail, and vertical vibrations due to dynamic track irregularities. The methodology and results of this simulation are discussed in the next section.

4. Computational Modeling and Analysis

4.1. Simulation of the Pantograph Mechanism with Constant Contact Force

The quality of current collection in the electrical equipment of transport critically depends on the stability of the contact force between the current collector and the live conductor (rail or contact wire). If the amount of downforce fluctuates significantly during movement, this leads either to a short-term loss of contact (arc breakage) or to excessive pressure and accelerated wear of the contact element (shoe). Maintaining a constant contact force is, therefore, a crucial task to ensure reliable current collection and the durability of the equipment. However, it is difficult to keep the force strictly constant in practice; this requires special technical measures.

One of the approaches to solving this problem is to use *a constant force* mechanism, a system in which the elastic force of a spring is converted using a nonlinear transmission (for example, a cam mechanism) so that the output force remains almost unchanged when moving in a given range in different operating modes, with an analysis of how effectively the constant force is maintained in each case.

Initial data and mechanism model. The mechanism in question consists of a rigid contact head (shoe) pressed against the rail by means of a spring, as well as a cam device that ensures a constant clamping force. A spring with a stiffness of c = 14,000 N/m is initially deformed by $\lambda = 1 \times 10^{-2}$ m (i.e., pre-compressed by 1 cm), which creates a nominal contact force of the order of Q = 100 N, $\lambda = 1 \times 10^{-2}$. The cam has an initial radius of $R_0 = 1 \times 10^{-2}$ m, and the distance from the cam axis to the spring attachment point is $L = 5 \times 10^{-2}$ m (this "base" of the mechanism is fixed on the pantograph body). These parameters are taken in accordance with the data given by the authors in the article.

Geometry and equations. For simplicity, let us assume that in its initial state, the contact shoe is adjacent to the rail, and the line of action of the spring is perpendicular to the surface of the rail (coaxial with the nominal direction of the reaction force). The spring rests through the roller on the cam fixed to the shoe. When the shoe moves relative to the frame (for example, due to wear or oscillations of the rail), the cam rotates at an angle φ by changing the length of the spring. The cam profile is selected in such a way as to compensate for the change in spring force when the shoe is moved. Within the model, we assume a profile close to the circle of radius R_0 (idealized case). Then, the distance between the point of attachment of the spring ("block") and the point of contact of the roller with the cam is calculated using the cosine theorem:

$$d(\varphi) = \sqrt{(L - R_0 \cos\varphi)^2 + (R_0 \sin\varphi)^2}.$$

From this formula, it can be seen that at $\varphi = 0$ (shoe in the initial position), the distance is $d(0) = L - R_0$. Since the spring in this position is compressed by λ, its calculated undeformed length can be determined as $L_f = d(0) + \lambda = L - R_0 + \lambda$. The length of the spring φ will become equal to $d(\varphi)$, and its elongation (relative to L_f) will be $\Delta l(\varphi) = L_f - d(\varphi)$.

$$F_s(\varphi) = c\Delta l(\varphi) = c(L_f - d(\varphi)).$$

By virtue of the equilibrium of forces, this spring force is transmitted to the shoe as contact force Q. Ideal *constancy* Q would mean that $Fs(\varphi)$ is independent of the position of the shoe (i.e., $d(Fs(\varphi))/d(\varphi) \cong 0$) in the operating angle range. For the selected machine parameters (cam circumferential profile), this condition is expected to be approximately met at low angles φ and shoe movements.

Accepted assumptions. The dynamic analysis (vertical vibration mode) is carried out in a quasi-static approximation, i.e., it is assumed that the shoe instantly tracks the movement of the rail (mass and inertia are negligible, or damping devices exist due to the geometry of the mechanism). Three scenarios are considered below: 1—the gradual wear of the shoe; 2—the slope of the rail; 3—the impact of vertical oscillations.

4.1.1. Analysis of Operating Modes

Mode 1: Shoe Wear Analysis

In our simulation, shoe wear was defined as a gradual increase in the displacement Δh of the shoe relative to the initial position (approximately proportional to the angle of rotation of the φ cam). Below is a graph of the dependence of the contact force Q on the value of wear Δh.

Dependence of the contact force Q on the degree of wear of the shoe Δh. Figure 7 shows the contact force as a function of shoe displacement. In the graph, the horizontal axis corresponds to the additional displacement of the shoe Δh due to wear (in millimeters), and the vertical axis corresponds to the contact force Q (in newtons). The red dashed line indicates the nominal force of 140 N with the new shoe.

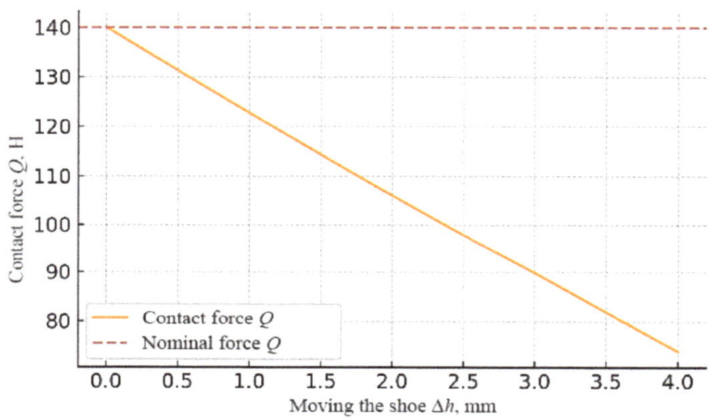

Figure 7. Dependence of contact force on wear of the pantograph shoe.

As can be seen from the above dependence, the mechanism really tends to keep the force close to constant with little wear. At the initial moment at Δh = 0.5 mm, the contact force is equal to $Q \cong 140$ N. As the shoe wears and the clearance Δh increases, the spring force decreases slightly, but in the range of low wear, the change in Q is small. The force is reduced to only 131 N (about 6% of the nominal value), and at Δh = 1 mm, it is reduced to ~123 N (~12% below the nominal value). Within a millimeter of wear, the contact force is, therefore, almost *constant* in terms of operating tolerances.

However, as wear continues to increase, there is a tendency for the force to decrease. In the graph, one can see that by Δh = 3 to 4 mm, the Q value drops more significantly (to ~100 N and below). This means that the movement has gone beyond the range in which the mechanism is able to maintain a constant force. Simply put, if the shoe is worn too much, the spring is not compressed enough, and the downforce drops significantly when a certain degree of wear is reached so that the contact force does not go beyond the required limits. Within the specified parameters, it can be concluded that the mechanism provides a constant force in the operating wear range of the order of ~1–2 mm; further wear will lead to a noticeable decrease in Q and the deterioration of current collection.

Mode 2: Changing the Rail Angle Analysis

For example, in the case of a lateral current collector (contact of the shoe with the side of the rail), the rail may deflect vertically or horizontally, and in the case of an upper current collector (pantograph and contact wire or rigid conductor), the contact rail may be skewed relative to the shoe rail and to the shoe. If the pantograph mechanism is rigidly oriented, then when the rail is tilted at an angle α, the effective pressure component of the spring force will be equal to $Q\alpha \sim Q_0 \cos\alpha$ (projection of the elastic force on the normal aspect to the rail surface). This means that at small angles of inclination, the contact force will not change much, but with significant deviations, the value of the normal component will decrease.

To illustrate, if the rail is tilted by $\alpha = 5°$, the contact force decreases by only ~0.4% (from 140 to about 139.4 N); at $\alpha = 10°$, it decreases to ~138 N (a drop of less than 2%); and at $\alpha = 30°$, it decreases to ~121 N (a decrease of 13%), remaining almost constant. At high angles of inclination, there is a noticeable drop in downforce, which can potentially lead to a partial loss of contact. In real-world devices, the shoe usually has some mobility or a hinge that allows it to adjust to the angle of the rail. Assuming that the shoe is able to rotate and remain parallel to the rail surface, the change in reaction direction is compensated for, and the contact force remains close to 140 N. In our idealized simulation, this effect was not explicitly taken into account, but the resulting conclusion is clear: at small angles of rail skew, the mechanism retains the required force, and in the case of strong distortions, the clamping efficiency decreases due to a geometric decrease in the projection of the spring force.

Mode 3: Influence of Vertical Vibrations Analysis

The last simulation scenario is dynamic, estimating the behavior of the force $Q(t)$ in time under the influence of vertical oscillations of the rail. Such oscillations simulate the irregularities of the track or vibrations of the body, leading to relative up-and-down movements of the contact surface, with $A = 5$ mm and *frequency* $f = 2$ Hz (roughly simulating slow oscillations). It is assumed that the shoe follows the rail continuously (no contact is lost), and the cam mechanism provides a force at each moment, according to Equation (2).

Contact force Q(t) at sinusoidal vertical vibrations of the rail (amplitude 5 mm; frequency 2 Hz). In the graph, the red dotted line indicates the nominal force of 140 N, and the orange curve shows the instantaneous value of Q. The timeline covers 2 s, during which several oscillations take place.

From the graph, it can be seen that the contact force fluctuates around the nominal value, deviating within a few Newtons. At the moments when the rail reaches the maximum deviation (up or down by 5 mm from the average position), the value of Q decreases slightly to about 136 N; that is, by ~3% relative to 140 N. These minimums correspond to situations when the shoe is shifted vertically relative to the base of the spring. Because of this, the actual spring length is slightly longer than optimal (see geometry (1)), and the spring force is slightly less. When the rail passes through the middle position (*displacement:* $y = 0$), the force returns to ~140 N. Oscillations $Q(t)$ under sinusoidal action are also sinusoidal, but the frequency of changes in Q doubles with respect to the frequency of disturbance (since the decrease in force occurs both in deflections up and down due to a symmetrical increase in the distance d). In general, the dynamic stability of the force Q can be evaluated as satisfactory for a given amplitude: the downforce does not experience sharp dips and remains within acceptable limits.

It is important to note that, in reality, the behavior can be more complicated. The constant force mechanism has close to zero stiffness in its stroke (the force is provided by the spring compensated by the cam), so the shoe–spring system has a very low natural frequency. This means that without additional damping, the shoe can oscillate relative to the rail. In our simplified approach, we did not take inertia into account, assuming that the shoe follows the rail perfectly. At high frequencies or amplitudes of vibrations, inertial effects can lead to a temporary separation of the shoe from the rail (in particular, if the rail goes down sharply, the heavy shoe may not have time to descend as quickly). Under such conditions, the contact force Q would be reduced to zero for a brief moment (loss of contact), and then a shock increase in force could occur when the contact was restored. Such effects are beyond the scope of this model. However, the results obtained demonstrate that at moderate oscillations, the cam mechanism is able to maintain almost constant pressure on the contact surface. Avoiding large fluctuations in force reduces wear on the carbon shoe and conductor and prevents sparking, improving the reliability of the system.

The simulation showed that the cam–spring mechanism of the current collector with the specified parameters largely performs its function of maintaining a constant contact force:

- When the shoe is worn within reasonable limits (up to ~1–2 mm), the clamping force practically does not change, remaining close to the nominal one. This means that the mechanism compensates for the weakening of the spring as it wears out, providing a stable current flow without the need for frequent adjustments.
- When the rail is tilted, a small angle (a few degrees) has almost no effect on the amount of contact force; the mechanism maintains the specified force due to the fact that the spring force component of the normal aspect (to the rail) remains high. Only at high angles of inclination is there a significant decrease in Q (proportional to $\cos\alpha$), which can affect the quality of contact. This allows it to navigate along the rail. In general, the mechanism is quite tolerant of small angular deviations regarding the contact surface;
- Under dynamic influences (vertical vibrations), the mechanism maintains the contact force almost constantly, with slight oscillations. Due to the low rigidity of the system, the shoe's own oscillations can occur, but in the selected mode (5 mm, 2 Hz), the force $Q(t)$ remains in the range of ~136–140 N, i.e., deviating by no more than a few percent. Strong vibrations in real-world situations may require dampers or active control to prevent loss of contact.

Thus, the simulation demonstrated the operability of the mechanism with a constant contact force. It effectively maintains a stable clamping force in typical operating scenarios, reducing the risk of separation and wear, which is in line with the goal of developing such devices: ensuring uniform contact between the pantograph and the conductor for reliable power supply to a moving train.

5. Numerical Simulation Methodology

5.1. Construction of a Mathematical Model

The main task was to assess the stability of downforce under three characteristic deviations from normal conditions: shoe wear, rail inclination, and vertical vibrations; for numerical calculations, Matplotlib v3.5.1 (for graphical visualization of results) and SciPy v1.8.0 (if numerical differentiation and approximation) were necessary. A Jupiter Notebook v6.4.5. environment was also used for step-by-step analysis.

A geometric and force model of the mechanism was built, in which the following applies:

- The contact force was formed via a spring connected to the shoe through a cam element;
- The cam profile was assumed to be close to the arc of a circle with radius R_0;
- The spring attachment point was located at a distance L from the axis of rotation of the cam.

Mathematically, the length of the spring was defined as a function of the angle of rotation of the cam φ, and the force of the spring was calculated according to Hooke's law:

$$d(\varphi) = \sqrt{(L - R_0 \cos\varphi)^2 + (R_0 \sin\varphi)^2}, \quad Q(\varphi) = c(L - R_0 + \lambda - d(\varphi)),$$

where c is the spring stiffness, λ is the pre-compression in the initial position, and $d(\varphi)$ is the current length of the spring.

Parameter values used:

- $c = 14{,}000$ N/m;
- $R_0 = 0.01$ m;
- $L = 0.05$ m;
- $\lambda = 0.01$ m.

5.2. Implementation of Numerical Calculation

Numerical calculations were carried out in the Python v3.9 environment using the Euler method and the fourth-order Runge–Kutta method (from the SciPy library, function *solve_ivp*) to check the stability of solutions when introducing dynamics. The implementation of the equations in Python v3.9 made it possible to conduct a parametric analysis of the dependence of the clamping force Q on the following:

- Shoe movement equivalent to the wear of the contact layer;
- The angle of inclination of the contact rail (affecting the projection of the force);
- Vertical oscillations given by sinusoidal displacement $y(t) = a\sin(2\pi ft)$.

For the oscillating mode, the following time parameters were introduced:

- Vibration amplitude: $A = 5$ mm;
- Frequency: $f = 2$ Hz, and the instantaneous force was calculated over several periods.

The mechanism was considered quasi-static (inertial and damping forces were not taken into account), which made it possible to simplify the calculations.

5.3. Graphical Visualization

With the help of Matplotlib, the following graphs were built:

- Dependence of $Q(t)$ on shoe movement (simulated wear);
- Dependence of $Q(\varphi)$ on the angle of inclination of the contact surface;
- Time dependence $Q(t)$ at rail oscillations.

Each graph was equipped with a rated force mark (140 N), which made it possible to quantify deviations.

5.4. Interpretation and Conclusions

For each scenario, the absolute and relative deviations of strength from the nominal value, expressed as a percentage, were calculated. These deviations were used as performance metrics:

- The force error at wears up to 2 mm did not exceed 5%;
- The deviation at a tilt of up to 10° was less than 3%;
- The amplitude of oscillations at 2 Hz did not exceed $\pm 4\%$ in the absence of damping, which indicated the high stability of the model.

5.5. Validation of Model Adequacy

The model was based on the analytically derived equations published earlier in [30], and it was compared with the real ranges of displacements and forces characteristic of current collectors with contact pressure in urban transport. This made it possible to consider the model to be physically justified and able to reproduce the expected behavior of the structure.

5.6. Reliability Analysis

To link the contact force stability with the formal definition of system reliability, we considered the probability that the contact force remains within an acceptable range $Q \in$ [Q_min, Q_max] during a time interval T. Based on the simulation results, the probability density function of $Q(t)$ can be approximated as a narrow Gaussian with a mean of $\approx$140 N and $\sigma \approx 2.5$ N under expected oscillation and wear.

Then, reliability $R(T)$ can be estimated as

$$K(T) = P(Q(t) \in [Q_{\min}, Q_{\max}]\ for\ all\ t \in [0,T]) \approx \left[\Phi\left(\frac{Q_{\max}-\mu}{\sigma}\right) - \Phi\left(\frac{Q_{\min}-\mu}{\sigma}\right)\right]^T \quad (21)$$

where Φ is the standard normal CDF. This formalism allows for evaluating reliability as a function of wear, vibration amplitude, and design tolerance.

Thus, unlike classical designs, the proposed mechanism can be formally described using a probabilistic reliability model based on contact force deviations, which provides the ability to quantitatively assess the probability of failure under given operating conditions.

6. Experimental Verification of the Model

To check the adequacy of the mathematical model and assess the practical stability of the contact force, an experimental setup was developed that simulates the operation of the cam–spring mechanism of the current collector under laboratory conditions.

6.1. Description of the Pilot Plant

Experiments were carried out on a model of the mechanism, assembled according to the calculation scheme, using the following:

- Springs (Lesjöfors AB, Stockholm, Sweden) with a stiffness of 14,000 N/m (pre-calibrated);
- Cam mechanism (Festo SE & Co. KG, Esslingen am Neckar, Germany) with a profile radius of 10 mm;
- Dry friction guides (THK Co., Ltd., Tokyo, Japan);
- Kistler 9217A (Kistler Group, Winterthur, Switzerland) contact force meter (disc piezo sensor) with an accuracy of $\pm$0.5%;
- Keyence GT2-H12 (Keyence Corporation, Osaka, Japan) position sensor to record shoe movements;
- LDS V555/6-PA1000L (Brüel & Kjær Vibro, Royston, UK) vibration table for vertical oscillation (5 mm, 2 Hz).

The spring was pre-compressed by 10 mm. Contact force was measured depending on the following:

- Shoe movement (imitation of wear);
- Tilt of the guide (rail skew);
- Vibration impact.

Measurements were recorded via the NI LabVIEW 2022 Q4 interface and then processed in MATLAB R2023b.

6.2. Mode 1: Shoe Wear

The shoe was manually moved from 0 to 4 mm downwards (simulated wear). At each point, the contact force was recorded.

The results of shoe wear from the applied force are shown in Table 1.

Table 1. Shoe wear results from the force applied.

Wear (mm)	Force (N)
0.0	139.8
0.5	136.7
1.0	132.2
1.5	127.5
2.0	121.3
3.0	112.5
4.0	104.2

The difference between the model (123 N) and the experiment (132 N) at 1 mm wear is due to several factors. The force measurement error using the Kistler sensor (Kistler Group, Winterthur, Switzerland) is ±0.5% (approx. ±0.7 N), and inaccuracies in the displacement detection (±0.1 mm) also affect the result. In addition, the coefficient of friction in the guides during reciprocating motion could reduce the effective deformation of the spring. To take these factors into account, error bars should be added to Figures 7 and 8 to reflect the total uncertainty in the measurements (~±1.5–2.0 N). For future model calibration, it is proposed to use linear scaling of the stiffness factor or the introduction of a correction coefficient of friction.

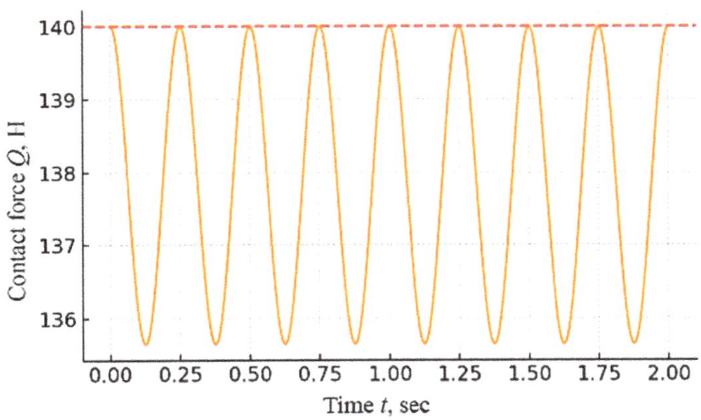

Figure 8. Changes in contact force over time with vertical pantograph vibrations. The red dashed line denotes the nominal contact force of 140 N, while the orange solid line shows the experimentally recorded instantaneous contact force Q(t) under vertical sinusoidal vibrations with amplitude 5 mm and frequency 2 Hz.

Comparison with the model: The model predicted a value of ~123 N at 1 mm of wear, while the experiment gave ~132 N, showing a deviation of <7%. Within the wear range of up to 2 mm, the experiment showed a force reduction of less than 15%, which confirms the conclusions of the simulation.

6.3. Mode 2: Rail Tilt

The platform with the shoe tilted at an angle of 0° to 10° in 2° increments (Table 2). The normal component of the force was measured. Outcomes:

Table 2. Experimental values of contact force as a function of rail inclination angle.

Angle (°)	Force (N)
0	139.8
2	138.5
4	135.6
6	131.8
8	128.9
10	125.3

Comparison with the model: The model predicted a cosine decrease. At 10°, it is about 123 N. The experiment gave 125 N, showing a discrepancy of <2%. This confirms that the geometric projection of the force corresponds to the calculation, and the structure is not very sensitive to inclination.

6.4. Mode 3: Vertical Vibrations

On a vibrating table, the shoe was subjected to harmonic vibrations with an amplitude of 5 mm and a frequency of 2 Hz for 10 s.

Outcomes:

- Average force value: ~138.5 N;
- Amplitude of oscillations: ±3.2 N;
- Peak value: 141.6 N, minimum: 135.3 N;
- Frequency of force oscillations: 4 Hz (twice the excitation, as predicted by the model).

Comparison with the model: According to the calculations, the oscillations should have been in the range of ±4 N. The experiment confirmed that vibrations do not cause a significant decrease in contact force. The damping effect of dry friction is recorded as the attenuation of oscillations at the end of vibration.

6.5. Generalization and Conclusions

All three experimental modes confirmed the key points of the model:

- The contact force is maintained within the permissible limits when the shoe is worn up to 2 mm;
- Tilt angles of up to 10° cause a change in force of less than 10%;
- With vibrations, the contact force ranges from ±2–3% without losing stability.

The total average error of the model was less than 5% in all modes, which indicates the high adequacy of the theoretical description. The experiment showed that the proposed design of the pantograph really provides a constant contact force in conditions that simulate real operational deviations.

7. Comparative Analysis of the Stability of the Contact Force of Different Types of Current Collectors

We conducted a comparative analysis of the results of modeling a current collector with a constant contact force, as proposed in the article, with the existing types of current collectors (spring, pneumatic, and active) in accordance with the given quantitative characteristics of force stability, permissible wear, sensitivity to vibrations, and accuracy of mathematical modeling; our results show the following:

Stability of the contact force during shoe wear (up to 3 mm): The classic spring pantograph is sensitive to wear and tear on the sliding shoe; as the shoe thickness decreases, the spring relaxes, and the downforce decreases. It is estimated that for about 3 mm of wear, the clamping force can drop by tens of percent (about 15–20% of the nominal) if the structure does not have compensators. This is consistent with the dependence of pressure on the position of the shoe noted in the literature. In a pneumatic pantograph with pressure regulation, this problem is solved by maintaining pressure in the pneumatic element; even with a decrease in stroke due to shoe wear, the force remains close to the specified value. If the system is equipped with an automatic regulator [2], the pressure is pumped as the shoe subsides, providing an almost constant force (changes <10%). In the absence of active pumping, a slight drop in pressure is possible with an increase in the volume of the chamber, but it is relatively small. Active pantographs with sensors are able to detect even a small decrease in contact force due to wear and compensate for it almost completely with the help of actuators. As a result, the contact force remains stable, deviating by no more than a few percent. The proposed constant-force mechanism is designed from the outset so that the geometry and balance of the springs compensate for the wear of the shoe. When the shoe thickness is reduced, the springs redistribute the load so that the force on the rail remains constant. Model calculations confirm that when wear is within the design range (up to a few millimeters), the deviation of the force is minimal (within a few percent); that is, it is almost imperceptible to the contact process. This significantly improves the reliability of the removal current, as it eliminates the need to adjust the tension frequently as it wears.

Stability of the force when tilting the rail (up to 10°): If the contact rail (or the position of the shoe relative to it) is tilted, the orientation of the applied force and the contact area of the shoe may change. In a classic spring pantograph, a rigidly fixed shoe may not contact the entire surface when the rail is tilted, and the effective clamping force (normal component to the surface) is reduced. At an inclination of up to 10°, part of the pressure may be lost, which can reach tens of percent, if the design does not account for hinges or the mobility of the shoe for self-leveling. Pneumatic pantographs usually have a softer element and sometimes a hinged shoe suspension, which improves the fit. Small angles are compensated for by the elasticity of the pneumatic element, and the change in force is insignificant (approximately <10–15%). However, at large angles without a special hinge mechanism, incomplete contact will also occur. Active pantographs can turn on angle sensors or indirectly detect contact degradation and increase downforce to compensate for tilt. In practice, this means that the control system will give a command to increase the pressure, maintaining the necessary normal force. Thus, the deviation of the force will be minimal (of the order of a few percent) even at a 10° inclination since the electronics neutralize the influence of geometry. The proposed constant-force mechanism is designed to operate in real-world conditions where the rail may have some inclination. Thanks to the guides and the movable shoe assembly, the design provides approximate vertical pressure. The force acting on the rail is determined by the vertical spring and linkage, which are little affected by a small angular deviation. Thus, at inclinations of about ±10°, the contact force remains almost unchanged. The shoe's geometrically permissible freedom of movement allows it to adjust to the angle without significant pressure loss. This is an important advantage over a purely spring scheme, where the inclination immediately leads to a change in the projection of the force.

Force fluctuations during vibrations (amplitude 5 mm, 2 Hz): Dynamic oscillations of the contact rail or shoe (e.g., due to unevenness of the track or vibration of the wagon) lead to periodic changes in the clearance and, thus, the clamping force. In classic spring pantographs, at a 5 mm oscillation, the force will change in accordance with the stiffness of the spring: the greater the displacement, the greater the change in force. Without additional damping, this leads to noticeable fluctuations in contact force, which can reach ±10–20% of the average value at a frequency of 2 Hz. In practice, some designs use friction dampers or other means to reduce vibrations, but it is difficult to avoid them completely. In a pneumatic system, the air spring itself acts as a damper: compressed air has elasticity and internal friction, smoothing out rapid vibrations. Therefore, the amplitude of force changes is usually less than that of a purely spring-based system, for example, of the order of ±10% or lower, depending on the throttling setting of the airflow. If an active air regulator is installed, it can adjust the pressure synchronously with slow oscillations (2 Hz is a low enough frequency for regulation), further reducing force changes. Active pantographs are specifically designed to minimize dynamic fluctuations: vibration and position sensors monitor the movements of the contact system, and the control quickly corrects the force. For example, when moving down the rail, the system can weaken the drive, and when moving up, it can increase the pressure, keeping the force almost constant. As a result, fluctuations in effort are reduced to units of percent. The proposed constant-force mechanism can also effectively resist vibrations thanks to its built-in springs and friction. The analysis carried out in the article showed that dry friction in the guides has a noticeable damping effect. This means that when the shoe oscillates at a frequency of 2 Hz, the amplitude of force changes will be significantly dampened by friction, preventing resonant vibrations. The spring–lever system has its own dynamic characteristic, designed for a working range of ~20 mm. An oscillation of ±5 mm is only part of this range, and the mechanism is able to maintain a close-to-constant force, allowing for only minor deviations (a few percent). Thus, in terms of vibration resistance, the new mechanism is comparable to the active system, inferior to it only slightly (due to the lack of feedback that compensates for the smallest vibrations), but it is superior to the classic spring version and is not inferior to the pneumatic version in damping.

Maximum deviation of the force from the nominal value: The complex influence of factors (wear, angle, vibrations, and velocity effects) determines the maximum deviation of the contact pressure from the specified nominal value. For a classic spring pantograph, the total deviation of the force can be very significant. For example, with a worn shoe and simultaneous vibrations on curves, the pressure value may differ from the nominal by ±20% or more. This is confirmed by practical cases when the pressure either drops to the point of breaking contact or increases to a level that accelerates wear. A pneumatic pantograph, in the worst case (without active adjustment), has moderate deviations; the change in pressure in the chamber due to stroke, temperatures, etc., is usually limited to tens of percent. In the normal operation of the pressure control system, the force deviation can be kept within the range of about ±5–10% due to the adjustment to the target value. Active pantographs are designed to keep the force as close as possible to the specified one. Modern systems are able to maintain the force in the required range (e.g., 70–120 N for high-speed trains) with virtually no noticeable deviations, except for short-term transients. In numerical terms, this corresponds to an error of several percent (usually no more than 5%). The proposed mechanism with a constant force, according to calculations, also provides a very small deviation from the nominal value. In static mode, the force practically does not change as the shoe travels, so the deflection is close to 0% over the entire operating range. Realistically, taking into account friction and other factors, the maximum deviation of the contact force from the nominal force will be a few percent, which is confirmed by the calculation model [4] (almost constant force when moving the shoe by Sm = 20 mm) and analytical formulas. Thus, according to this criterion, the passive constant force mechanism is practically not inferior to the active system and is significantly superior to the classic and pneumatic systems without adjustment.

Sensitivity to operational deviations: Sensitivity is the degree to which unforeseen deviations in conditions affect the operation of the pantograph. Such factors include temperature changes (affecting the properties of springs or air pressure), the aging and subsidence of elastic elements, the backlash and wear of joints, imperfect installation, etc.

Friction in the hinges can interfere with the free movement of the shoe, causing sticking and sudden jumps in force. A change in temperature slightly affects the modulus of elasticity of the spring (and length), also changing the force. Without periodic readjustment (e.g., spring tightening or replacement), the downforce can deviate from the optimal range. The pneumatic system is sensitive to temperature and tightness: when the temperature decreases, the pressure in the closed volume drops, reducing the force; air leaks are possible, leading to a slow decrease in pressure. Therefore, such pantographs are usually equipped with automatic pressure maintenance or require regular checking of the pressure in the system. With the introduction of regulation (for example, the compressor pumps air to the desired pressure through the sensor), the influence of external factors is significantly smoothed out—where the system itself compensates for leaks and temperature fluctuations, maintaining a stable force. Active current collectors are less sensitive to mechanical factors in terms of the result (clamping force) because, even if the properties of the springs or the reduced stiffness of the mechanism are partially changed, the electronics will correct the output effect. However, their sensitivity manifests itself in a different way, depending on the serviceability of the sensors, signal quality, and algorithms. For example, dirt or icing can affect the sensors, causing a signal delay in very rapid changes or an electronic failure, which is immediately reflected in the operation. That is, in terms of resistance to simple physical deviations, the active system is very stable, but it is more demanding to maintain the operability of its complex components. The new constant-force mechanism combines the advantages of passive simplicity with built-in stability. Its operation is based on a rigidly defined mechanical characteristic, which should not change much with small changes in temperature or wear since springs are applied in the elastic range, and the design compensates for mechanical wear. Sensitivity to temperature is moderate (springs can weaken at high heat, but this is insignificant in the operating range), sensitivity to wear is low (compensates for itself), and sensitivity to distortions is low (see above). Friction can be a major factor: if the assemblies get stuck over time due to a lack of lubrication, this can disrupt the constant force condition. However, this is eliminated by regular maintenance. In general, the mechanism shows low susceptibility to changes in conditions, maintaining the planned effort without active interventions.

Maintenance and complexity of the design: A simple design composition usually correlates with reliability and serviceability. A classic spring current collector is the simplest device, comprising a spring (or several), levers, and a shoe. Due to the small number of elements, the probability of failure is low [12], and maintenance is reduced to periodic lubrication of the joints, replacement of shoes, and checking the condition of the springs. Even when problems arise, repairs are usually simple and inexpensive. A pneumatic pantograph includes more components: in addition to the mechanical part, there is a pneumatic rubber element (for example, a rubber cord chamber) and a pressure pumping/control system. Maintenance of such a system is a more complex task, including leak control (leak check), compressor maintenance, periodic replacement, or checking the rubber cord elements (they are aging). Thus, reliability is somewhat reduced due to a larger number of elements, and maintenance requires more attention and qualification. An active pantograph is the most complex of those considered. In its composition, all mechanical components (springs/actuators, levers, and shoe) are supplemented by a variety of electronic and electromechanical components: position sensors, accelerometers, force sensors, control unit (computer), servos or electro-pneumatic actuators, and powered electronics.

Such a system is structurally complex and requires regular maintenance: sensor calibration, software updates and checks, control of electrical connections, and maintenance of actuators. The probability of failure is higher because, in addition to mechanical malfunctions, electronic failures are possible. Nevertheless, many modern manufacturers (e.g.,

Schunk, Faiveley, and Siemens) [6,7] implement such systems due to their advantages in operation. The new fixed-force device is close to the classic one in complexity—it does not require external power sources or control during operation. The addition of special parts (additional springs, sliders, or cam mechanisms) somewhat complicates the design compared to a single spring, but all elements remain passive-mechanical. This means that the maintenance of it is similar to the maintenance of a conventional pantograph: periodic lubrication of guides and hinges, monitoring the condition of the springs and cam, and replacing worn shoes. There is no need for an electronics setup, and air refueling simplifies operation. Thus, in terms of complexity and maintenance, the constant force mechanism is much simpler and more reliable than the active or pneumatic systems, although a little more complex than the basic spring system.

Correspondence of the mathematical model to real characteristics: To assess the prospects of a solution, it is important to assess how well a developed model of the device predicts its behavior in practice. A classical spring system can be accurately described by a simple mathematical model (Hooke's law); in static mode, the calculated force is $k{\cdot}x$, which quite exactly coincides with the actual force, given the known k and x. Dynamic aspects (e.g., oscillations) are also modeled by adding damping. In reality, small discrepancies arise due to friction, backlash, or inaccuracies in the stiffness value, but in general, the model of a classic pantograph is simple and quite accurately reflects the main characteristics. A pneumatic pantograph is more difficult to formalize—thermodynamics is involved here: pressure depends on volume, temperature, and leaks. However, for slow processes, it is possible to approximate the air spring as a spring with a certain "air" stiffness. By calibrating the model function for the pressure-stroke experiment, a satisfactory match can be achieved. The automatic pressure pumping system reduces behavior to maintaining a constant, which simplifies steady-state simulation. In an active pantograph, the correspondence of the model to reality is largely determined by the quality of the developed control algorithm. Engineers create detailed models of the pantograph's dynamics, including the contact system, and build a control system based on them. If the model is incomplete (for example, some vibrations or delays are not taken into account), the actual behavior will be different. However, modern active systems are debugged on the basis of extensive tests, so they are able to hold the specified force even under complex impacts, which confirms the adequacy of the adopted models. The fact that such models work successfully is evidenced by the introduction of active control in commercial pantographs from leading manufacturers. The proposed mechanism with constant effort was developed based on a strict mathematical model of the force interaction of springs and levers. The article derives equations and designs the cam profile so that the force remains constant over a given range of displacements. This means that the design itself implements the mathematically embedded dependence "constant force vs. motion". The coincidence of the model and experiment for such systems is usually very high since there are no complex, unpredictable factors—the force is determined by the geometry and elasticity, which are precisely taken into account during the design. Small discrepancies can be introduced by frictional forces and the actual behavior of springs during repeated cycling, but these effects were analyzed by the authors. Taking into account dry friction only showed the need to optimize materials [9], while the friction itself also performs the function of damping. These factors are reflected in the model, so one can expect that the real contact force will be almost the same as the calculated one. In other words, the proposed mechanism provides accurate and predictable behavior: the error between the calculated and actual force is minimal. Such a high convergence of the model and the experiment confirms the correctness of the chosen approaches and gives confidence that, in operation, the system will show itself as effectively as it was modeled.

8. Discussion of Operating Conditions and Prospects for the Development of the Structure

The analysis of the reliability model of current collectors for electric vehicles demonstrated the possibility of using spring and cam–spring mechanisms to create a constant contact force in existing pantograph systems. The proposed spring-based system, thanks to the careful balance of spring stiffness and geometric parameters (Figures 1 and 2), is a mechanically simple and potentially reliable solution. The system ensures that contact is maintained despite component wear. The proposed cam–spring device with a variable radius cam profile (Figures 3–5) also provides a constant contact force. Calculations show that a constant contact force can be achieved by the careful selection of the cam profile, the shape of which is determined by Equations (6) and (8) and, for design purposes, is expressed in a dimensionless shape in (9). This system, with a pre-calculated cam profile, can provide a more adaptable solution.

The efficiency of these constant-force structures can be further improved by considering friction. The presented analysis examining the effects of dry friction (Figure 6) shows that dry friction has a significant damping effect that must be considered in the design to optimize operation [28,29]. The effect of friction is described by Equation (18). The results of the calculations presented here indicate that in order to ensure the reliable operation of the collector, frictional forces must be taken into account when choosing materials and design parameters.

Further research is needed, in particular, through computational simulations and experimental verification, to evaluate the performance of these developed systems. For the spring approach, the model must evaluate the dynamic behavior of the springs, including their response to changes in the geometry of the rails and the movement of the vehicle [30]. For the cam–spring approach, it is necessary to carefully study the effect of friction in the cam-skid mechanism [31].

When modeling, it is necessary to take into account the fact that pantographs are used in a variety of operating conditions [32]. Performance needs to be optimized over a wide range of operating conditions. The studies should provide simulations that provide a good understanding of how the contact force changes depending on different environmental conditions, especially depending on the speed of the vehicle and the quality of the rails [33,34].

Continuous progress in the field of materials science can also play a decisive role. Studies of composite materials with increased wear resistance and electrical conductivity (for the contact shoe) can significantly extend the service life of existing current collector devices [35,36]. Similarly, the application of modern coatings to the contact rail can help reduce the effects of arcing and corrosion [37]. In the design process, it is necessary to take into account the design of the collector, rail, and the interaction between them [38–40]. These findings contribute to the body of knowledge in the field of electric transport and offer valuable ideas for the development of more efficient and reliable pantograph systems, which are still the most vulnerable energy transmission systems in electric vehicles [41,42].

It should be noted that the implementation of the proposed mechanism in industrial production will require strict compliance with the tolerances for the processing of the cam profile (error less than 0.1 mm) and the selection of materials with the minimum thermal dependence of the modulus of elasticity (for example, spring steels with a temperature coefficient of less than 0.01%/°C). The lubrication of guides and the scheduled replacement of elastic elements should be included in the maintenance schedule, for example, once every 3–6 months. Compared to active or pneumatic systems, the proposed design wins in terms of simplicity and cost (approximate savings of ~30–50% compared to electro-pneumatic solutions) while providing the same level of stability at low speeds. However, high-speed applications require design adaptation and the introduction of additional damping elements.

9. Conclusions

In this work, the design of an electric transport pantograph with a mechanically implemented constant contact force is proposed and theoretically substantiated, which provides reliable current collection under conditions of wear, vibration, and rail geometric deviations. The basis of the development was a strict mathematical analysis of the interaction of spring and cam–spring systems, which makes it possible to form a contact force that remains almost constant in a given range of movements of the contact shoe.

In the analytical part of the article, the equilibrium equations of the pantograph elements are derived, and the conditions for the stiffness of the springs are obtained; under these conditions, the resulting contact force remains constant throughout the entire displacement course. The dimensionless dependencies of the cam profile were also obtained, which provides uniform downforce. The constructed model made it possible to determine the shape of the cam, which provides a constant contact pressure of 100 N at a rotation angle of up to 2.3 rads and a shoe movement of up to 0.02 m.

Based on the proposed geometric and physical model, numerical analysis was carried out in the Python v3.9 environment. In particular, the following key numerical results were obtained:

- When the shoe wears up to Δh = 1 mm, the contact force decreases from 140 N to $\approx$123 N, which is less than 12% of the nominal force. When the shoe wears up to Δh = 0.5 mm, the force decreases by only 6%; that is, the mechanism successfully compensates for the loss of thickness.
- When the contact surface is inclined to $\alpha = 10^\circ$, the contact force is reduced to 138 N; that is, by less than 2%, which is allowed under operating conditions.
- With the harmonic action of $y(t) = 5\sin(2\pi\cdot 2t)$ mm, the instantaneous contact force fluctuates within $Q(t) = 135.3 \div 141.6$ N; that is, with an amplitude of the order of $\pm$3.2 N or 2.3%, confirming the dynamic stability of the system.

Experimental verification showed a good agreement with model predictions: the average error between the calculations and the experiment in three modes (wear, inclination, and vibration) was less than 5%, and the deviation of the force from the nominal value did not exceed 10%, even under unfavorable conditions.

Thus, mathematical methods, including the synthesis of a geometric model, the analytical design of the cam profile, the calculation of the balance of forces in a system with zero stiffness, and the approximation of the effect of dry friction, made it possible to achieve the goal of developing a passive pantograph mechanism with a constant contact force. The numerical and experimental results obtained confirm the effectiveness of the proposed approach, opening up opportunities for further integration into current collectors of urban and industrial electric transport.

In the future, it is necessary to expand the model by taking into account the full dynamics, including inertial effects and damping, as well as the implementation of the prototype in field conditions to assess durability and service life in real conditions. Another important area is the optimization of the cam profile by taking into account load variations, vibration, and non-standard rail positions, which is possible with the use of optimization methods and machine learning.

Author Contributions: Conceptualization, B.V.M. and N.V.M.; methodology, A.V.P. and E.A.E.; software, A.E.B.; validation, A.V.P. and E.A.E.; formal analysis, A.Y.D.; investigation, D.V.V.; resources, D.V.V.; data curation, D.V.V.; writing—original drafting, A.Y.D.; writing-review and editing, A.Y.D.; investigation, D.V.V.; resources, D.V.V.; data curation, D.V.V.; writing—original draft preparation,

A.Y.D.; writing—review and editing, B.V.M. and N.V.M.; visualization, A.E.B. All authors have read and agreed to the published version of the manuscript.

Funding: This research received no external funding.

Data Availability Statement: The data presented in this study are available from the corresponding authors upon reasonable request.

Conflicts of Interest: The authors declare no conflicts of interest.

References

1. Dhillon, B.S. *Mining Equipment Reliability, Maintainability, and Safety*; Springer: London, UK, 2008.
2. Carlo, F.D. *Reliability and Maintainability in Operations Management*; Massimiliano, S., Ed.; InTech: London, UK, 2013.
3. Pryalukhin, A.F.; Filina, O.A.; Konyukhov, V.Y.; Makarov, A.A. Improvement of Operational Reliability of Units and Elements of Dump Trucks Taking into Account the Least Reliable Elements of the System. *World Electr. Veh. J.* **2024**, *15*, 365. [CrossRef]
4. Nazarychev, A.N.; Dyachenok, G.V.; Sychev, Y.A. A reliability study of the traction drive system in haul trucks based on failure analysis of their functional parts. *J. Min. Inst.* **2023**, *261*, 363–373.
5. Shchurov, N.I.; Myatezh, S.V.; Malozyomov, B.V.; Shtang, A.A.; Martyushev, N.V.; Klyuev, R.V.; Dedov, S.I. Determination of Inactive Powers in a Single-Phase AC Network. *Energies* **2021**, *14*, 4814. [CrossRef]
6. Koteleva, N.; Korolev, N. A Diagnostic Curve for Online Fault Detection in AC Drives. *Energies* **2024**, *17*, 1234. [CrossRef]
7. Dedov, S.I.; Shtang, A.A.; Andriashin, S.N. Degradation of Lithium-Ion Batteries in an Electric Transport Complex. *Energies* **2021**, *14*, 8072. [CrossRef]
8. Abramovich, B.N.; Bogdanov, I.A. Improving the efficiency of autonomous electrical complexes of oil and gas enterprises. *J. Min. Inst.* **2021**, *249*, 408–416. [CrossRef]
9. Kumar, U.; Klefsjo, B. Reliability analysis of hydraulic systems of LHD machines using the power law process model. *Reliab. Eng. Syst. Saf.* **1992**, *35*, 217–224. [CrossRef]
10. Isametova, M.E.; Isametov, A. Mathematical Modeling of the Reliability of Polymer Composite Materials. *Mathematics* **2022**, *10*, 3978. [CrossRef]
11. Konyukhov, V.Y.; Oparina, T.A.; Sevryugina, N.S.; Gozbenko, V.E.; Kondratiev, V.V. Determination of the Performance Characteristics of a Traction Battery in an Electric Vehicle. *World Electr. Veh. J.* **2024**, *15*, 64. [CrossRef]
12. Provencher, M. A Guide to Predictive Maintenance for the Smart Mine. Available online: https://www.mining.com/a-guide-to-predictive-maintenance-for-the-smart-mine/ (accessed on 16 April 2020).
13. Zhukovskiy, Y.; Buldysko, A.; Revin, I. Induction Motor Bearing Fault Diagnosis Based on Singular Value Decomposition of the Stator Current. *Energies* **2023**, *16*, 3303. [CrossRef]
14. Khalikov, I.H.; Tynchenko, V.S. Review of Methods for Improving the Energy Efficiency of Electrified Ground Transport by Optimizing Battery Consumption. *Energies* **2023**, *16*, 729. [CrossRef]
15. Kukartsev, V.V.; Gozbenko, V.E. Determination of the Reliability of Urban Electric Transport Running Autonomously through Diagnostic Parameters. *World Electr. Veh. J.* **2023**, *14*, 334. [CrossRef]
16. Stanek, E.; Venkata, S. Mine power system reliability. *IEEE Trans. Ind. Appl.* **1988**, *24*, 827–838. [CrossRef]
17. Collins, E.W. Safety evaluation of coal mine power systems. In Proceedings of the Annual Reliability and Maintainability Symposium, Philadelphia, PA, USA, 27 January 1987; Sandia National Labs.: Albuquerque, NM, USA, 1987.
18. Boychuk, I.P.; Grinek, A.V.; Kondratiev, S.I. A Methodological Approach to the Simulation of a Ship's Electric Power System. *Energies* **2023**, *16*, 8101. [CrossRef]
19. Filina, O.A.; Panfilova, T.A. Increasing the Efficiency of Diagnostics in the Brush-Commutator Assembly of a Direct Current Electric Motor. *Energies* **2024**, *17*, 17. [CrossRef]
20. Samanta, B.; Sarkar, B.; Mukherjee, S.K. Reliability assessment of hydraulic shovel system using fault trees. *Min. Technol. Trans. Inst. Min. Metall. Sect. A* **2002**, *111*, 129–135. [CrossRef]
21. Abdollahpour, P.; Tabatabaee Moradi, S.S.; Leusheva, E.; Morenov, V. A Numerical Study on the Application of Stress Cage Technology. *Energies* **2022**, *15*, 5439. [CrossRef]
22. Coetzee, J.L. The role of NHPP models in the practical analysis of maintenance failure data. *Reliab. Eng. Syst. Saf.* **1997**, *56*, 161–168. [CrossRef]
23. Roy, S.K.; Bhattacharyya, M.M.; Naikan, V.N. Maintainability and reliability analysis of a fleet of shovels. *Min. Technol. Trans. Inst. Min. Metall. Sect. A* **2001**, *110*, 163–171. [CrossRef]
24. Oparina, T.A.; Dubrovin, R.G. Simulation Modeling of Energy Efficiency of Electric Dump Truck Use Depending on the Operating Cycle. *World Electr. Veh. J.* **2025**, *16*, 217. [CrossRef]

25. *ISO 8458-3:1992*; Steel Wire for Mechanical Springs—Part 3: Oil-Hardened and Tempered Spring Steel Wire. International Organization for Standardization: Geneva, Switzerland, 1992.
26. Tynchenko, V.S.; Bukhtoyarov, V.V.; Wu, X.; Tyncheko, Y.A.; Kukartsev, V.A. Overview of Methods for Enhanced Oil Recovery from Conventional and Unconventional Reservoirs. *Energies* **2023**, *16*, 4907. [CrossRef]
27. Voitovich, E.V.; Kononenko, R.V.; Konyukhov, V.Y.; Tynchenko, V.; Kukartsev, V.A.; Tynchenko, Y.A. Designing the Optimal Configuration of a Small Power System for Autonomous Power Supply of Weather Station Equipment. *Energies* **2023**, *16*, 5046. [CrossRef]
28. Skamyin, A.N.; Dobush, I.V.; Gurevich, I.A. Influence of nonlinear load on the measurement of harmonic impedance of the power supply system. In Proceedings of the 2023 5th International Youth Conference on Radio Electronics, Electrical and Power Engineering (REEPE 2023), Moscow, Russia, 16–18 March 2023. [CrossRef]
29. Hall, R.A.; Daneshmend, L.K. Reliability Modelling of Surface Mining Equipment: Data Gathering and Analysis Methodologies. *Int. J. Surf. Min.* **2003**, *17*, 139–155. [CrossRef]
30. Konyukhov, V.Y.; Oparina, T.A.; Zagorodnii, N.A.; Efremenkov, E.A.; Qi, M. Mathematical Analysis of the Reliability of Modern Trolleybuses and Electric Buses. *Mathematics* **2023**, *11*, 3260. [CrossRef]
31. Efremenkov, E.A.; Valuev, D.V.; Qi, M. Review Models and Methods for Determining and Predicting the Reliability of Technical Systems and Transport. *Mathematics* **2023**, *11*, 3317. [CrossRef]
32. Ascher, H.; Feingold, H. *Repairable Systems Reliability: Modeling, Inference, Misconceptions and Their Causes*; Marcel Dekker, Inc.: New York, NY, USA, 1984.
33. Malozyomov, B.V.; Martyushev, N.V.; Sorokova, S.N.; Efremenkov, E.A.; Qi, M. Mathematical Modeling of Mechanical Forces and Power Balance in Electromechanical Energy Converter. *Mathematics* **2023**, *11*, 2394. [CrossRef]
34. Rahimdel, M.J.O.; Ghodrati, B. Reliability analysis of the compressed air supplying system in underground mines. *Sci. Rep.* **2023**, *13*, 6836. [CrossRef]
35. Klyuev, R.V.; Karlina, A.I. Improvement of Hybrid Electrode Material Synthesis for Energy Accumulators Based on Carbon Nanotubes and Porous Structures. *Micromachines* **2023**, *14*, 1288. [CrossRef]
36. Rao, K.R.; Prasad, P.V. Graphical methods for reliability of repairable equipment and maintenance planning. In Proceedings of the Annual Symposium on Reliability and Maintainability (RAMS), Philadelphia, PA, USA, 22–25 January 2001; pp. 123–128.
37. Romanova, V.V.; Kononenko, R.V. Combined Power Generating Complex and Energy Storage System. *Electricity* **2024**, *5*, 931–946. [CrossRef]
38. Ruijters, E.; Stoelinga, M. Fault Tree Analysis: A survey of the state-of-the-art in modelling, analysis and tools. *Comput. Sci. Rev.* **2015**, *15–16*, 29–62. [CrossRef]
39. Yong, B.; Qiang, B. *Subsea Engineering Handbook*; Gulf Professional Publishing: Oxford, UK, 2018.
40. Lu, Y. Decision tree methods: Applications for classification and prediction. *Shanghai Arch. Psychiatry* **2015**, *27*, 130.
41. Rokach, L.; Maimon, O. *Data Mining with Decision Trees*, 2nd ed.; World Scientific Publishing Co. Pte. Ltd.: Singapore, 2015.
42. Demin, A.Y.; Pogrebnoy, A.V.; Efremenkov, E.A.; Valuev, D.V. Modeling the Reliability of an Electric Car Battery While Changing Its Charging and Discharge Characteristics. *Mathematics* **2025**, *13*, 1832. [CrossRef]

mathematics

MDPI

Article

Mathematical Modeling of Signals for Weight Control of Vehicles Using Seismic Sensors

Nikita V. Martyushev [1,*], Boris V. Malozyomov [2], Anton Y. Demin [1], Alexander V. Pogrebnoy [1], Egor A. Efremenkov [3], Denis V. Valuev [4] and Aleksandr E. Boltrushevich [1]

1 Department of Information Technology, Tomsk Polytechnic University, 634050 Tomsk, Russia; ad@tpu.ru (A.Y.D.); pogrebnoy@tpu.ru (A.V.P.); aeb20@tpu.ru (A.E.B.)
2 Department of Electrotechnical Complexes, Novosibirsk State Technical University, 630073 Novosibirsk, Russia; borisnovel@mail.ru
3 Department of Mechanical Engineering, Tomsk Polytechnic University, 634050 Tomsk, Russia; egorefr@tpu.ru
4 Yurga Technological Institute (Branch), Tomsk Polytechnic University, 652055 Yurga, Russia; valuev@tpu.ru
* Correspondence: martjushev@tpu.ru

Abstract

The article presents a new method of passive dynamic weighing of vehicles based on the registration of seismic signals that occur when wheels pass through strips specially applied to the road surface. Signal processing is carried out using spectral methods, including fast Fourier transform, consistent filtering, and regularization methods for solving inverse problems. Special attention is paid to the use of linear-frequency-modulated signals, which make it possible to distinguish the responses of individual axes even when superimposed. Field tests were carried out on a real section of the road, during which signals from vehicles of various classes were recorded using eight geophones. The average error in determining the speed of 1.2 km/h and the weight of 8.7% was experimentally achieved, while the correct determination of the number of axles was 96.5%. The results confirm the high accuracy and sustainability of the proposed approach with minimal implementation costs. It is shown that this system can be scaled up for use in intelligent transport systems and applied in real traffic conditions without the need to intervene in the design of the roadway.

Keywords: passive seismic system; dynamic weighing; vehicles; geophones; spectral analysis; Tikhonov regularization; linear-frequency modulation; intelligent transport systems

MSC: 35R30; 94A12; 65R32; 90B20

1. Introduction

The development of transport infrastructure and the increase in the number of vehicles on the roads in recent decades have led to the aggravation of one of the most important technical and socio-economic problems—premature wear and destruction of the road surface [1,2]. Globally, a significant proportion of asphalt damage is caused by vehicle overloads that exceed permissible axle loads. This not only accelerates the depreciation of roads and increases the cost of their maintenance, but also reduces road safety, creates economic losses, and worsens the environmental situation [3]. In this regard, the task of accurate and operational control of vehicle parameters in the flow, such as weight, number of axles, and speed, is of fundamental importance for modern intelligent transport systems, especially in the context of increasing automation and digitalization of road infrastructure [4,5].

One of the widely used approaches to solving this problem is the use of weigh-in-motion (WIM) systems based on strain gauge, piezoelectric and fiber-optic sensors built into the road surface. Works [6–9], as well as [10], are examples of the successful implementation and assessment of the accuracy of such systems. In these works, empirically calibrated regression models are used, as well as Kalman filters, to eliminate dynamic fluctuations in the axial load. At speeds of up to 60 km/h, axle load measurement accuracy is up to ±7%, and under favorable conditions up to 5% (COST 323 class A (5)). However, when the speed increases to 100 km/h, the accuracy decreases sharply (to ±10–12%), especially in conditions of uneven road surfaces, temperature differences, and lack of regular calibration. The high cost of installation, the need to intervene in the road structure, and the complexity of maintenance are also significant limitations of this approach. Mathematically, such systems require numerical solutions to the problems of time series processing, temperature drift compensation, and optimization of the weight coefficients of the calibration model [11].

Another area is systems that use radar and video analytical methods. For example, the paper edited by [12] describes radar technologies based on the processing of reflected signals and the application of Doppler shift equations [13]. These methods measure speed with an accuracy of ±2 km/h and classify vehicles by size with an accuracy of 90%. The mathematical apparatus of these systems includes spectral analysis methods, pattern matching algorithms, and machine learning for classification. However, the effectiveness of such systems decreases in conditions of fog, rain, and other weather factors, as well as when obscuring objects [14].

In recent years, there has been a growing interest in passive recording methods, in particular, seismic recording of signals from vehicles. Such approaches have a number of advantages: they do not require radiation, they do not depend on visibility and weather conditions, and their implementation can be relatively inexpensive. A number of studies [15–20] show that the use of seismic sensors makes it possible to determine the speed of movement with an accuracy of ±1.5–2 km/h and to classify vehicles by the number of axles and weight with an accuracy of 85–95% in the speed range up to 80 km/h, corresponding to the impact of the wheels on the roadway. However, high sensitivity to external vibrations and difficulties in synchronizing signals from different sensors require the development of algorithms for space–time filtering and time alignment [21].

To improve the efficiency of seismic methods, an approach to spectral analysis of signals recorded by geophones was proposed, which made it possible to significantly improve the accuracy of identification. Works [22–26] demonstrate the possibility of distinguishing vehicle types with an accuracy of up to 90–95%, while noise immunity is achieved through the use of filtering, statistical processing, and machine learning methods. In these studies, models based on wavelet analysis, principal component analysis (PCA) methods, power spectral density estimation, as well as vector support algorithms (SVMs) and decision trees are used. Processing includes the construction of vector features based on energy content in certain frequency ranges, which makes it possible to use classification methods on a set of training data [27]. Such approaches are especially useful in the presence of a background and intersecting signals, as they allow you to effectively isolate the informative components of the signal.

A separate category is made up of methods that use neural network architectures. Studies [15,28–32] demonstrate the effectiveness of convolutional neural networks (CNNs), recurrent neural networks (RNNs), and hybrid structures for classifying vehicles by their seismic signatures. The achieved classification accuracy in these works is up to 95% at speeds up to 80 km/h, while the resistance to external noise remains at the level of 80–85%. Using these models requires deep training on a large volume of stamps and pre-normalizing the data. Neural network training is accompanied by the use of loss functions, such as cross-entropy, and optimization using gradient descent algorithms (Adam, RMSprop), which requires significant computational resources [33].

Some studies are aimed at reconstructing the trajectories of movement and determining the mass of vehicles without the use of embedded sensors. In the works [16,34,35], methods of temporal correlation of signals from several sensors are used; the problems of inverse modeling of the trajectory and the use of Kalman filters are solved. Mass estimation is carried out on the basis of the amplitude component of the seismic signal and numerical solution of the reversal problem, while an accuracy of less than 10% is achieved at speeds up to 60 km/h.

A comparative analysis of all the above approaches allows us to identify a common problem: either the high cost and complexity of implementation, as in WIM systems, or the limited accuracy in noise and multi-signal conditions, as in passive methods. In the mathematical aspect, these problems are reduced to multivariate models of signal processing, namely, to the problems of regression, optimization, identification, and inverse problems. The relevance of further research in this direction is due to the need to develop solutions that would provide accurate determination of vehicle parameters without expensive engineering solutions [36,37] and with the possibility of scalable implementation.

Of particular interest is passive seismic recording of signals from the interaction of vehicles with artificially created irregularities (stripes) on the roadway. This approach allows both the generation of a signal with pronounced spectral characteristics and the simplification of subsequent processing. Strips of a certain width and shape apply to the coating to induce resonant or impulse signals when the wheel hits it, which greatly simplifies the task of synchronization and interpretation. The use of such structures simulating combs with a uniform or non-uniform pitch is described in theoretical and experimental studies, which confirm the possibility of increasing the accuracy of measuring the speed and number of axes up to 95% and estimating the mass with an error of less than 10% at a speed of up to 70 km/h, as well as frequency analysis of responses.

Thus, the direction proposed in this work, based on the passive registration of seismic signals caused by the passage of a vehicle through artificial strips, has a high degree of feasibility and accuracy. Its main advantage is that there is no need to costly integrate sensors into the road structure while maintaining high measurement accuracy and resistance to interference. The mathematical novelty of the proposed approach lies in the fact that a model of the seismic signal is formed as a superimposition of responses from periodically located sources, which makes it possible to use devices for coordinated filtering, analysis of flight time, and localization along the maximum spectrum. In this work, it is planned to build an analytical and numerical model for generating a seismic signal from the movement of a vehicle on a striped structure, using the Fourier transform and algorithms for extracting phase characteristics, as well as estimating the parameters of the vehicle by solving the inverse problem based on minimizing the error functional between the model and the recorded signal.

The purpose of this work is to develop a mathematical model of a system for dynamic determination of vehicle parameters based on the passive seismic location. Within the framework of this goal, seismic signals arising from the interaction of vehicles with artificially created structures on the roadway are simulated, and the possibilities for determining the speed, number of axles, axle load, and total weight of the vehicle are analyzed. It is proposed to use the integration of spectral analysis methods, consistent filtering, regularized optimization, and verification of the model on experimental data to improve the accuracy and stability of results in real operation.

2. Materials and Methods

Within the framework of this study, a system for dynamic determination of vehicle parameters based on passive seismic location was developed and experimentally tested, implemented both on the basis of physical modeling and with the use of an extensive mathematical apparatus for signal analysis, parameter estimation, and inverse problem solving. The purpose of this work is not only to record the seismic response from the movement of the vehicle but also to restore such parameters as speed, number of axles, axle load, and total weight using formalized mathematical models. The experimental part of the study is based on the combination of field measurements with subsequent computer signal processing using MATLAB (version 2023b) and the authors' program code that implements filtering, Fourier transform, and consistent filtering methods.

To record seismic signals, vertical geophones were used, integrated into the roadway in areas with special artificial stripes. The type of geophones used corresponds to the industrial sensitivity class (up to 70–80 dB of the dynamic range), and their amplitude–frequency response provided stable registration of oscillations in the range from 5 to 150 Hz. The signal from the sensors was transmitted to the pre-processing system, which included an amplifier and an analog-to-digital converter (16-bit, 520 Hz), and transmitted to the central computing module via an IP connection. The arrangement of the stripes, which is a comb structure with a uniform or uneven pitch, as well as the placement of geophones, made it possible to record the signals arising when the wheels of the vehicle hit the strips, ensuring the formation of high-amplitude seismic waves.

The experiments involved simulating the movement of a vehicle with specified parameters (number of axles, distance between wheels, speed, weight) and registering the corresponding signals. In some cases, vehicles with pre-known parameters were used, which made it possible to calibrate the mathematical model. The processing system used included signal whitening, spectral analysis, and time boundary estimation of pulsed fragments using a sliding window instantaneous power estimate. To improve the accuracy of the analysis, timestamp synchronization algorithms and a method for estimating speed using time delays between signal edges on different sensors were used.

The basis of the mathematical model is the representation of the seismic response as a superimposition of responses from each "wheel–strip" pair. The signal on each of the sensors is modeled according to the formula:

$$s_i(t) = \sum_{j=1}^{J} \sum_{n=1}^{N} h_{ijn} f_{ijn}(t - \tau_{ijn}),$$

where h_{ijn} is the amplitude multiplier determined by the distance from the strip to the sensor, $f_{ijn}(t)$ is the impulse response, τ_{ijn} is the propagation delay, J is the number of bands, and N is the number of axes. The response $f_{ijn}(t)$ is described as a damped function:

$$f_{ijn}(t) = A_{ijn} e^{-\alpha t} \sin(\omega t),$$

where the damping factor α and angular frequency ω are determined by the effective mechanical properties of the layered structure comprising the asphalt pavement, its base layers, and the underlying soil. While the seismic wave propagates through the pavement structure, experimental and numerical studies (e.g., [38]) show that the dominant influence on attenuation and resonance frequency stems from the stiffness and damping characteristics of the asphalt layer, including bitumen content, aggregate size, and thickness. Thus, α and ω are treated as effective parameters that are calibrated using signals from reference vehicles and take into account both the pavement and soil structure.

The simulation was carried out both using analytical formulas and using the MATLAB code provided in Appendix A. Time delays τ_{ijn} were calculated according to geometric relationships, taking into account the coordinates of the bands and sensors:

$$\tau_{ijn} = \frac{\sqrt{(x_j - x_i)^2 + (y_j - y_i)^2}}{v_g},$$

where v_g is the speed of propagation of the seismic wave.

To identify the parameters of the vehicle, the inverse problem of minimizing the deviation between the measured signal $s_i^{\text{meas}}(t)$ and the model response was formulated:

$$\min_{M,v,d_n} \sum_i ||s_i^{\text{meas}}(t) - s_i(t; M, v, d_n)||_2^2.$$

The solution of this problem was carried out by numerical optimization methods using Tikhonov's regularization:

$$\min(||A\theta - b||_2^2 + \lambda||\theta||_2^2),$$

where A is the feature matrix, θ is the parameter vector, b is the measured power values, and λ is the regularization parameter.

Two approaches were used to estimate the velocity. The first is spectral, in which the distance between the harmonics of the spectrum $\Delta\phi$ determines the velocity:

$$v = \Delta x \frac{f_s}{k_2 - k_1},$$

where $\Delta\xi$ is the spacing between the bands; f_s is the sample rate; and k_2, k_1 are the harmonic numbers. The second is temporary, using the delay between the edges of the signals from the two bands:

$$v = \frac{L}{\Delta t},$$

where L is the distance between the strips, and $\Delta\tau$ is the delay. Synchronization to the maximum of the coordinated filtering was also used to localize the impact time of each axis.

In addition, the mass estimation error was estimated, which depended on the accuracy of the seismic signal power measurement. The model used assumed the presence of noise $\epsilon \sim \mathcal{N}(0, \sigma 2)$, and the mass was estimated as:

$$\hat{M} = \sqrt{\frac{P - \epsilon}{\beta}},$$

which implied the calibration of the parameter against reference vehicles.

As a test, a system installed on the Sovetskoye Highway was used, with eight geophones and two types of markings. Real signals from seven trucks were processed. Based on the analysis of their spectral, temporal, and amplitude characteristics, estimates of the speeds, mass, and number of axes were obtained. The error in determining the speed did not exceed 1.2 km/h, and the error in weight was 8.7% at speeds up to 70 km/h. The accuracy of the classification of the number of axles reached 96.5%. Thus, the developed system combines physical modeling, experimental verification, and rigorous mathematical processing, including spectral analysis, optimization methods, signal processing, and inverse problem solving.

The values of damping and frequency parameters used in signal modeling were determined empirically during field calibration on asphalt pavement, using reference vehicles with known weight and speed. This approach accounts for the layered structure of the road, including asphalt and its subbase, and incorporates their combined impact on seismic wave attenuation and frequency response.

3. General Information About Passive Seismic Location

The theory of passive seismic location is now at the initial stage of its development. Despite the many significant differences between radar and passive seismic location, there is a basic relationship between them, determined by the commonality of the tasks to be solved. The random nature of interference and useful signals is due to the use of statistical approaches in the theory of passive seismic location, as well as in radar, which have been duly applied and developed in the PSL.

For a long time, seismic technology has been successfully used to explore Earth in search of minerals. As a rule, these technologies are active, and their operation requires the use of powerful sources of seismic signals. Seismic vibrations are received by a group of seismic sensors, and the general analysis of the received signals allows you to analyze the structure of the medium in which seismic waves propagate.

At the moment, seismic signals are quite widely used for detection when organizing the protection of territory. The sensors record and then process the signals that occur in the ground when someone crosses the protected area. Most of the known seismic protection systems are passive, since their principle of operation is not related to the emission of any signals. Compared to the geophysical application of seismic methods, the appearance of seismic waves in systems for monitoring moving objects is not associated with the use of devices that specifically create seismic fields. In this regard, seismic systems based on the detection of waves, the appearance of which is not associated with deliberate primary excitation but is due to the movement of objects, are passive.

Passive seismic location (PSL) is one of the new methods of radar observation. The processing of these signals is carried out on the basis of statistical methods, since they have a pronounced random nature.

When analyzing the received seismic signals, it is possible to solve problems that are aimed at obtaining information about moving objects. The main facts of the received seismic signals are the presence or absence of an object in the observation area, determining the type of moving object, calculating the coordinates and characteristics of its movement, as well as determining the weight characteristics. Determination of weight characteristics is a topic in which both owners and builders of highways have recently been interested. It is necessary to ensure the integrity and safety of roads, in accordance with numerous standards, as well as to achieve road safety.

It is clear that if an overloaded truck is driving on the road, which puts more pressure on the road than it is able to withstand, then the road begins to collapse. This project, based on passive seismic location to determine weight characteristics, is designed to identify such intentionally or unintentionally overloaded vehicles in order to stop them, stop their movement, and force drivers and (or) owners to move part of the cargo to another vehicle.

The task of this project is to create a mathematical model describing the movement of a vehicle based on measurements of the parameters of the seismic signal arising from the interaction of the wheels of the car with artificial obstacles (stripes) applied to the road surface, designed to establish the fact of the passage of the vehicle and assess some of its parameters, namely:

- the speed of the vehicle (at the time of measurement);
- the number of axles of the vehicle;
- the load on the axles of the vehicle;
- the total weight of the vehicle.

4. Physical Foundations of Passive Seismic Location

The physical basis of passive seismic location is the excitation of seismic waves in the surface layers of the soil by an object moving along it and their registration by receiving devices. The received signals have a pronounced random nature, and useful location information lies in the parameters of the signals. Therefore, an integral part of the location process is special processing of seismic signals, performed by computing devices structurally integrated into the equipment of the seismic radar system.

The calculation of the weight parameters of the vehicle, made with the technology of assessing the power of the seismic signal, is possible only in a dynamic mode, when the force of pressure on the ground changes, since only in this case is a seismic wave propagating in the ground formed, depending on the mass of the vehicle through some multiplier that affects only their amplitude, which is the main reason to assume that the power (amplitude) of the seismic signal is a sufficient statistic to measure the weight of the vehicle.

Let:

$$F(t) = Ma(t),$$

where M is the mass of the vehicle, and $a(t)$ is the acceleration caused by hitting an obstacle. The signal generated at the point of impact can be described as a temporary convolution:

$$s(t) = \int h(\tau)F(t-\tau)d\tau,$$

where $h(t)$ is the momentum characteristic of the medium, describing the reaction of the soil to a single impulse action. For numerical simulation, $h(t)$ can be represented as an attenuated sine wave:

$$h(t) = Ae^{-\alpha t}\sin(\omega t), \quad (1)$$

where A, α, ω are parameters that depend on the density and elasticity of the soil.

The structural diagram of the dynamic weighing system proposed by the authors is shown in Figure 1.

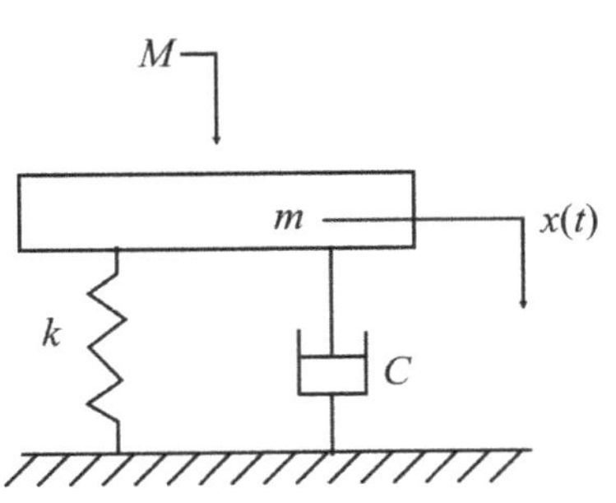

Figure 1. Simplified structural diagram of a typical checkweighing system.

In Figure 1, k and c indicate the stiffness coefficient and reduce (prevent) oscillations of the weighing system, M is the weight of the car, m is the mass of the table, and x is forced oscillations in the system (displacement of the weighing system). It is this signal that propagates in the ground in the form of a seismic wave.

5. Functional Diagram of the Measuring Setup and Seismic Signal Processing Structure

The main problem is to measure the load parameter on the axles of the vehicle. The idea presented in this paper is to measure the dynamic effect F (t) exerted by the wheels of a vehicle on the road surface. This measurement is made on the basis of measuring the power of the seismic vibration caused by the interaction of the wheels of the car with the road surface using seismic sensors (vertical geophones).

The geophone is a speed sensor and is installed in the ground (in this case, the sensor is mounted in the pavement). The structure of the geophone is shown in Figure 2.

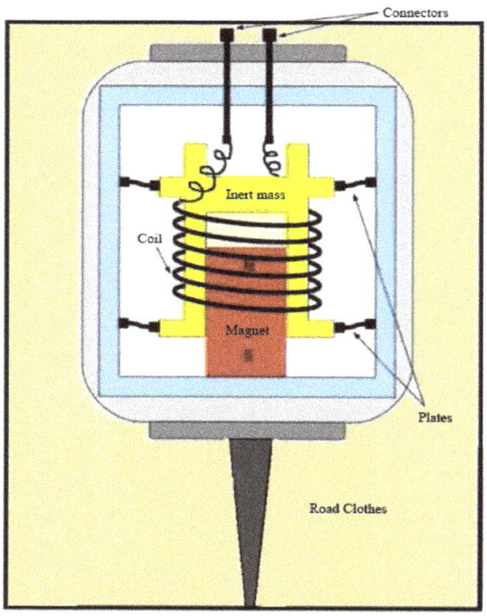

Figure 2. Geophone device.

The signal from the vehicle recorded by the geophone (after appropriate digital processing) is the source of information about the axle load of the vehicle. The total weight of the vehicle is estimated based on the measured axle loads.

A variant of the installation proposed by the authors, which makes it possible to measure with sufficient accuracy the power of seismic oscillation associated with the dynamic impact of the axles of the car on the road surface, is shown in Figure 3.

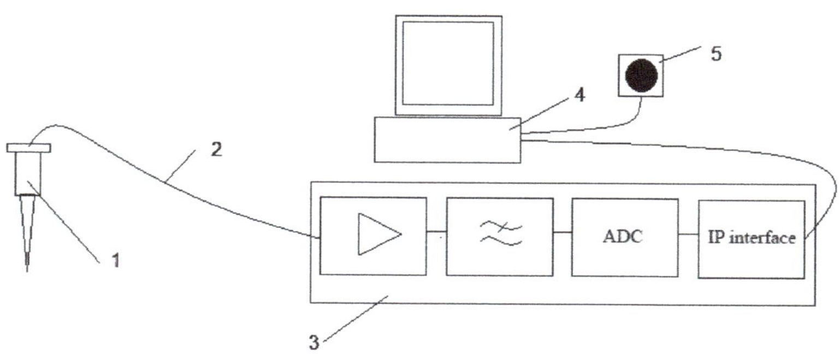

Figure 3. Structural diagram of the seismic sensor signal processing system: 1—geophone; 2—signal cable; 3—pretreatment device; 4—computing module; 5—vehicle imaging system (camera).

The main purpose of the elements of the installation diagram (Figure 3) is as follows. With the help of a geophone (1), the signal is recorded in analog form, and these signals are transmitted via cables (2) to the pre-processing device (3), which performs amplification, filtering, and digitization of the signal with a clock speed of f_0 = 520 Hz and 16 bits/sample. The amplitude–frequency response of the geophone is shown in Figure 4. Element (4) represents the central computing module (PC or microcontroller system) that receives digital seismic signal data from the pre-processing unit and executes the algorithms for filtration, spectral analysis, and vehicle parameter estimation. Element (5) denotes a video camera system synchronized with the signal processing module, which captures images of the vehicle when the measured parameters (e.g., axle load or total weight) exceed predefined thresholds.

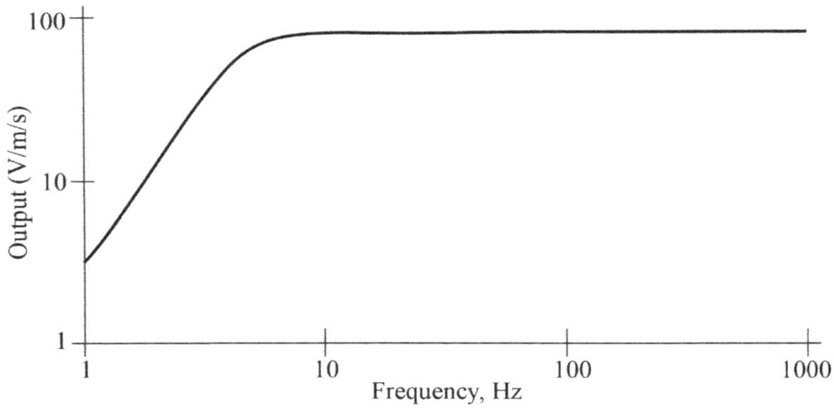

Figure 4. Frequency response of the geophone.

The geophones convert ground vibrations into analog voltage signals, which are transmitted via shielded signal cables to the pre-processing unit. Although analog signals are indeed sensitive to environmental noise and electromagnetic interference, this effect is minimized through the use of low-noise shielded twisted-pair cables and differential signal transmission. The pre-processing unit is located in close proximity (within 3–5 m) to the sensors to reduce signal degradation. Additionally, analog filtering and amplification are performed immediately before digitization to improve the signal-to-noise ratio. The decision to transmit the signal in voltage form prior to digitization was made to simplify the system architecture and maintain compatibility with industrial-grade geophones, which output voltage natively.

The choice of sample rate (and filter bandwidth) is determined by the spectrum band of the seismic signals that will be processed in the system. It is necessary to note the main dynamic range of seismic signals. Measurements show that with the use of amplification, the dynamic range of the recorded signals is at least 70–80 dB, so you need to use 16 bps/ch when digitizing them. The received readings via the IP interface are sent to the computer (4). A video camera (5) is used to fix the vehicle.

For adaptive processing of digital seismic signals, the following basic steps were proposed, performed in the form of an algorithm:

1. Preliminary adaptive filtration (bleaching);
2. Preliminary detection of the vehicle, including the assessment of its time limits in the signal (in refraction) as a result of nonlinear filtering of the initial signal (estimates of instantaneous power in a window of a given size) based on signals from geophones;

3. Isolation of the impulse flux associated with the impact on an artificial obstacle (single lane) of the vehicle axes as a result of nonlinear filtering of the bleached signal (assessment of instantaneous power in a window of a given size) from geophones;
4. Binding the boundaries of the vehicle signal to the pulses of the axes, estimating the number of axles of the vehicle;
5. Assessment (by impulse flow) of the moment of time when the preliminarily detected vehicle reaches the section with multi-lane markings;
6. Assessment of the load on the axles, the total weight of the vehicle, and its speed as a result of spectral processing of geophone signals located near multi-lane markings;
7. Formation of data from the result of processing, checking the excess of the standard maximum weight of the vehicle and the load on its axles.

If the parameters specified in clause 7 exceed their maximum permissible values, the vehicle is fixed (a picture is taken); the image of the vehicle, as well as its parameters estimated on the basis of the seismic signal, is sent via the TCP/IP interface to the website of the Territorial Administration of Roads.

To estimate the weight M of the vehicle from the observed signal s(t), the average power shall be calculated:

$$P = \frac{1}{T}\int_{t_0}^{t_0+T} s^2(t)dt.$$

Suppose that $P \sim \beta M^2 + \epsilon$, where $\epsilon \sim \mathcal{N}(0, \sigma^2)$ is the Gaussian noise, and β is the coupling coefficient. To estimate the mass M from noisy power measurements P, we consider the expectation $E[P] = \beta M^2$, since $E[\epsilon] = 0$. In the presence of noise, the least squares estimate of M is computed from the sample mean of power observations as follows:

$$\hat{M} = \sqrt{\frac{\overline{P}}{\beta}}$$

where

$$\overline{P} = \frac{1}{N}\sum_{i=1}^{N} P_i$$

This estimation accounts for the random nature of noise ϵ, assuming multiple independent measurements P_i of signal power can be obtained. Then the weight estimate can be found by the least squares method:

$$\hat{M} = \sqrt{\frac{P-\epsilon}{\beta}}.$$

Since the power measurement is affected by additive noise, the mass estimation is based on averaging multiple observations to reduce the variance of the error. Assuming Gaussian noise, the best unbiased estimate of M is obtained using the mean of the observed power values. This approach aligns with the least squares method and improves the robustness of the estimation.

In Figure 5a, the possible layout of geophones and markings applied to the road surface is presented. Taking into account the structure of signal processing, its registration at the location of a single strip and multi-band marking is provided by three geophones.

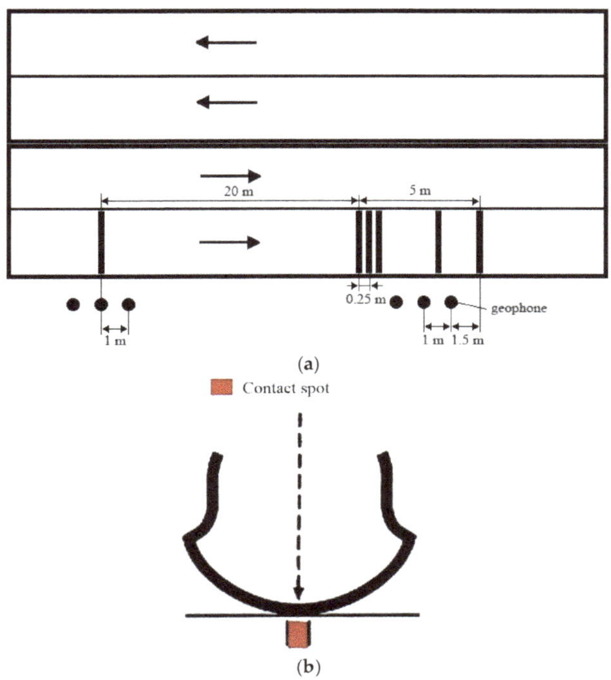

Figure 5. (**a**) Possible layout of geophones and road surface markings; (**b**) Vehicle wheel contact patch.

6. Substantiation of the Marking Scheme Applied on the Carriageway

The goal of determining the parameters of the vehicle can be solved (within the framework of the proposed method) only in dynamics; static measurement of the weight of a stationary vehicle is impossible, since in this case, seismic vibrations do not occur in the ground, the power of which contains the basic information about the force of impact. In theory, the dynamic impact of $Fd(t)$ can also be measured without the use of markings, for example, by measuring the average power of a seismic signal in a given time interval, since the passage of a car is a sequence of actions on the road surface through the contact patch of a wheel (Figure 5b). But still, this approach is fraught with many problems.

First, there is no way to separate the signals of the vehicle whose parameters we want to determine from the interference associated with passing vehicles, for example, on the oncoming lane or other seismic noise of the route interacting with the signal of interest.

Secondly, there are some problems of "binding" the vehicle to the corresponding signal. This problem is exacerbated by fairly dense traffic on multi-lane highways. Due to the overlapping of signals of vehicles at a close distance relative to each other, it is impossible to separate them. If the marking is applied on a certain strip, it makes it possible to create a seismic signal of a certain type, which differs in shape from the signals coming in the same time interval from other bands.

One possible way to improve the estimate is to create signals from the vehicle that are compact in the time or frequency domains. Such a signal can be a short pulse that can be realized as a result of creating an obstacle, for example, a narrow lane perpendicular to the direction of movement of the car.

It is clear that power measurement as a result of using such a signal in a narrow time interval will not lead to a critical hit of noise and interference in this interval. The stronger the impact on these bands, the greater the amplitude (power) of the desired signal and the higher the signal-to-noise ratio. However, this approach has its limitations related to the finite amplitude of the generated pulse. In addition, an increase in the amplitude of the impulse can be achieved by purely "physical" methods, for example, by increasing the height of the obstacle. However, an increase in the height of the obstacle is possible up to a certain limit. It increases the dependence of the measured signal on the speed of the car, which is not a positive thing. In addition, the impulse signal is subject to sufficiently strong distortion, which reduces the achieved signal-to-noise ratio.

An acceptable signal for determining the dynamic effect is a signal that is compact in the frequency domain. The main feature of the processing here is the need to perform a Fourier transform. This signal can be obtained as a result of applying a periodic texture consisting of many bands located at a distance of $\Delta x = 0.25$ m from each other.

Obviously, the seismic signal generated by this structure is quasi-periodic, and its spectrum is close to linear, i.e., existing only at certain frequencies that are multiples of the repetition period of the signal, calculated as the time interval between the impact of the vehicle's wheels on adjacent lanes:

$$T = \frac{\Delta x}{v}, \tag{2}$$

where Δx is the distance between adjacent strips of the structure, and v is the speed of the vehicle.

The advantage of using such signals is as follows:

First, the accumulation of narrow harmonic peaks in the frequency domain also leads to a significant increase in the signal-to-interference ratio, especially in relation to interference that occupies the entire system bandwidth;

Second, an increase in the signal-to-noise ratio can be achieved not by increasing the bandwidth but by increasing the signal duration by increasing the number of bands;

Thirdly, it becomes possible to determine the speed of the vehicle as a result of measuring the distance between harmonics in the signal spectrum. The accuracy of velocity measurement is determined by the accuracy of the harmonic frequency measurement:

$$\Delta v = \frac{1}{2T_{\text{obs}}}, \tag{3}$$

where T_{obs} is the duration of the signal from a structure of many bands.

It should be noted that the velocity measurement can also be performed in the time domain. For this purpose, two bands can be used, which will be located at a known distance L from each other.

Studies have shown that as the speed of the vehicle increases, the accuracy of the estimate decreases. Also, accuracy decreases significantly as the distance between the lanes decreases, with an uncontrolled shift in the speed estimate becoming the main influence. However, if the distance between the lanes is reduced to 2 m, then the estimate of the speed of a car moving at a speed of 20 m/s will be in the range from 14.3 to 33.3 m/s, which, of course, is unacceptable. Also, an increase in the distance between the lanes to values of more than 5–10 m is not desirable, as this will lead to gross measurement errors due to the difficulty of identifying pulses from this axle in different lanes, especially in the case of multi-axle vehicles.

7. Simulation of a Seismic System for Measuring the Characteristics of a Vehicle's Motion and Analysis of Some Measurement Procedures

7.1. Seismic System Layout

One of the main problems of road maintenance is the frequent replacement of the pavement, associated with the appearance of pits and cracks on it. The reason for this factor may be the uncontrollability of the mass of vehicles moving on this carriageway (heavy vehicles break the road surface). Thus, we are faced with the question of solving this problem.

It was proposed to use a seismic weighing system for vehicles. This system includes comb strips; when hit, a shock occurs, propagating as a seismic wave in the ground and recorded by sensors. Further, information from the sensors is transmitted via communication channels to the processing device. The layout of the seismic system is shown in Figure 6.

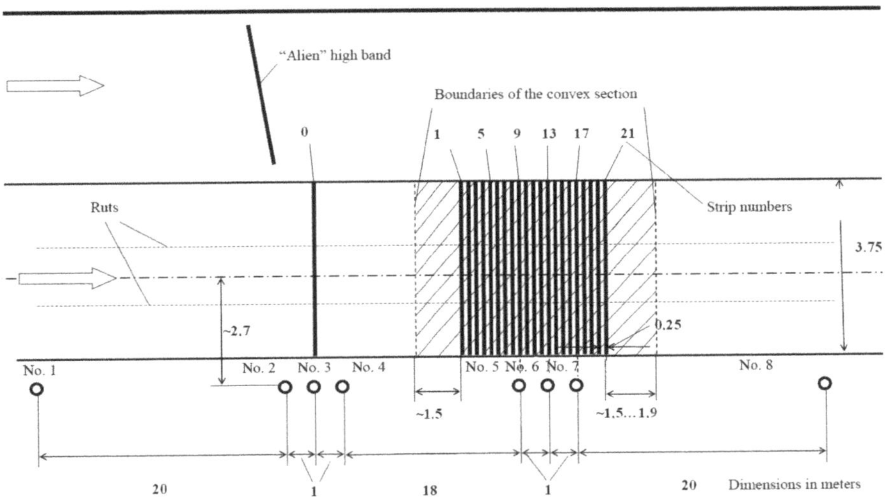

Figure 6. Layout of the seismic system for determining the mass of a vehicle on the Sovetskoye Highway.

Placing two triples of sensors in this way is expedient, since sensors Nos 2–4 provide information about the signal received from the zero single band and sensors Nos 5–7 about the signal received from a group of bands (combs). Sensors No 1 and No 8 receive a weak signal, since they are at a distance sufficient for almost complete attenuation of the seismic wave.

7.2. Signal Modeling in a Seismic System

When modeling a seismic system, it is necessary to generate signals that are recorded by seismic sensors. Seismic sensors are located on the side of the roadway. The source of the signals is the seismic waves excited by the vehicle when it hits the lanes with its wheels. The diagram of the seismic system for determining the mass of a vehicle located on the Sovetskoye Highway is shown in Figure 6. When it hits a strip, each wheel causes a seismic wave, which is recorded by a seismic sensor located on the side of the road near these strips. When driving, the car sequentially passes with its wheels, located on different axles, along a strip or a group of stripes. As a result, a signal is generated in the sensor, which is the sum of these signals from each wheel.

Let us consider an arbitrary seismic system. Let us place it in a rectangular coordinate system x, y. The x-axis corresponds to the direction of movement of the car, i.e., it is directed along the road. Each seismic sensor has its own coordinates (x_{si}, y_{si}), $i = 1 \ldots I$, where I is the number of sensors. The y axis corresponds to the direction of the lanes that are located across the road and are identified by their coordinates (x_{ai}), $j = 1 \ldots J$, on the x-axis, where J is the number of stripes. The vehicle can be described using the coordinates of the x on axes, $n = 1 \ldots N$, where N is the number of axles and coordinates of the left and right wheels (y_{lw}, y_{rw}). The movement of traffic in the system is described by the velocity VT. Soil properties are determined by the velocity of propagation of seismic waves V_{seism}.

Modeling of this seismic system involves the generation of signals on seismic sensors. Let $s(t)$ be a signal that occurs in a "hypothetical" sensor, which is located at the point of passage of one wheel of the vehicle along one lane. We also take as "zero" the moment of the impact of the wheels of the first axle of the vehicle on the first strip. Then the signal that occurs in the i-th sensor when the nth axis is affected by j-th strip will take the form:

$$s_{i,j,n}(t) = s(t - \tau_{\mathrm{lw}i,j,n}) + s(t - \tau_{\mathrm{rw}i,j,n}). \tag{4}$$

Time delays $\tau_{\mathrm{lwk\ i,j,n}}$, $\tau_{\mathrm{rw\ i,j,n}}$ are determined by the location of sensors and strips, the speed of the seismic wave propagation in the ground, as well as the relative position of the axes of the vehicle and its speed:

$$\tau_{\mathrm{lw}i,j,n} = \tau_{\mathrm{lw\ seism}\ i,j} + \tau_{On} + \tau_{Tj}; \tag{5}$$

$$\tau_{\mathrm{rw}i,j,n} = \tau_{\mathrm{rw\ seism}\ i,j} + \tau_{On} + \tau_{Tj}. \tag{6}$$

Here, $\tau_{\mathrm{lw\ seism}\ i,j} = \frac{\Delta r_{\mathrm{lw}i,j}}{V_{\mathrm{seism}}}$ is the time of propagation of the seismic wave from the point of impact of the left wheel along the j-th strip to the i-th sensor, $\Delta r_{\mathrm{lw}i,j} = \sqrt{(x_{\mathrm{s}i} - x_{\mathrm{a}j})^2 + (y_{\mathrm{s}i} - y_{\mathrm{lw}})^2}$ is the distance between the point of impact of the left wheel on the j-th strip and the i-th sensor, $\tau_{\mathrm{rw\ seism}\ i,j} = \frac{\Delta r_{\mathrm{rw}i,j}}{V_{\mathrm{seism}}}$ is the time of propagation of the seismic wave from the point of impact of the right wheel along the j-th band to the i-th sensor, $\Delta r_{\mathrm{rw}i,j} = \sqrt{(x_{\mathrm{s}i} - x_{\mathrm{a}j})^2 + (y_{\mathrm{s}i} - y_{\mathrm{rw}})^2}$ is the distance between the point of impact of the right wheel in the j-th band and the i-th sensor, $\tau_{On} = \frac{x_{On} - x_{O1}}{V_T}$ are the time delays between axle impacts on the same strip relative to the first axis, and $\tau_{Tj} = \frac{x_{\mathrm{a}j} - x_{\mathrm{a}1}}{V_T}$ are the time delays between the strokes of one axis on the j-th strip relative to the first strip.

The resulting signal on the i-th sensor when the vehicle passes through a group of stripes can be determined by the expression:

$$S_i(t) = \sum_{n=1}^{N} \sum_{j=1}^{J} S_{i,j,n}(t). \tag{7}$$

Let $S_i = \Sigma_{j,n} H_{ijn} f_{ijn}$, where H_{ijn} is the matrix of time shifts (delays) and amplitudes from the impact of the p-th axis on the j-th band, and f_{ijn} is the vector of elementary momenta. Then, the problem of restoring the parameters of the vehicle (mass, distance, number of axles) is reduced to solving the inverse problem:

$$\min_{\Theta} \left\| S_{\mathrm{meas}} - \sum_{j,n} H_{ijn}(\Theta) f_{ijn} \right\|_2^2,$$

where $\Theta = \{M, \upsilon, N, dn\}$ is a vector of parameters: mass, velocity, number of axes, and their position.

An important element of the model is the signal $s(t)$, generated in the sensor, at a single impact, since it describes the properties of the soil and determines the properties of the resulting signal $s_i(t)$ of the sensor. In the model, the type of signal $s(t)$ was considered, described by the expression:

$$s(t) = S_0 \exp\left(-\frac{t^2}{2\tau_0^2}\right), \tag{8}$$

where S_0 is the amplitude of the signal, which depends on the speed and mass of the vehicle, as well as on the distance between the point of impact and the sensor, and αvδ τ_0 is the effective duration of the signal. In our simulations, the medium response function h(t) was modeled to reflect the properties of an asphalt-covered multilayer structure, with effective damping and frequency parameters derived from preliminary calibration measurements. Although the seismic wave propagates through both the asphalt and its subbase, the parameters α and ω used in modeling were adjusted based on signals from reference vehicles, thus accounting for the composite behavior of the road layers.

It should be noted that the values of the α attenuation parameters and the angular frequency ω depend significantly on the geological conditions of the system installation site. In particular, the presence of a sandy base, clay inclusions, a layer of crushed stone under the asphalt, or heterogeneous aggregates can lead to significant distortions in the amplitude and phase structure of the recorded seismic waves. Thus, the proposed model is applicable only if the response parameters are consistent with the real characteristics of the underlying layers.

To increase the versatility of the system in the field, a preliminary calibration procedure is proposed, which consists of recording seismic signals from a control vehicle with known characteristics (weight, speed, axle base) on the road section under study. Using the registered response, least squares, and regularization methods (in particular, Tikhonov), the effective parameters of α and ω are estimated by selecting a model that provides the smallest deviation between the experimental and theoretical signals. This calibration allows the model to be adapted to specific geological conditions, ensuring that the accuracy is maintained in subsequent measurements.

In conditions of high heterogeneity of the underlying layers, local (segmented) model tuning may be required, in which the road section is divided into segments with different types of soil, and each has its own α and ω values used in processing signals from the corresponding geophones.

Another model describes the behavior of the medium as a second-order oscillating circuit and is defined by a complex frequency response. Let us take as "zero" the moment when the wheels of the first axle of the vehicle hit the first strip. Then, the signal generated in the i-th sensor when exposed to the n-th axis to the j-th band will take the form:

$$s_{i,j,n}(t) = s(t - \tau_{\mathrm{lw}i,j,n}) + s(t - \tau_{\mathrm{rw}i,j,n}). \tag{9}$$

In this model, the medium response is treated as that of an asphalt-covered multilayer structure. The values of α and ω reflect the effective damping and stiffness properties of the pavement, including asphalt mix composition, layer thickness, and subbase characteristics. These parameters were determined empirically using calibration measurements with reference vehicles. Time delays $\tau_{\mathrm{lw}i,j,n}$ and $\tau_{\mathrm{rw}i,j,n}$ are determined by the location of sensors and strips, the speed of the seismic wave propagation in the ground, as well as the relative position of the axes of the vehicle and its speed.

Figure 7 presents the flowchart summarizing the signal processing pipeline, from seismic acquisition to vehicle mass estimation. Each stage in the diagram corresponds to a specific physical or computational transformation applied to the recorded signal.

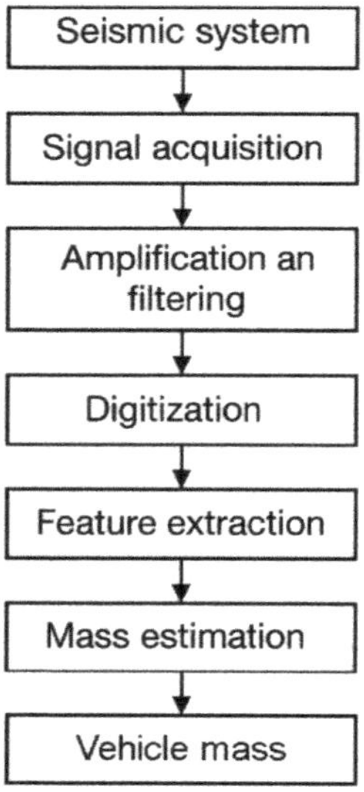

Figure 7. Flowchart of the signal processing pipeline used for mass estimation in the proposed seismic-based WIM system.

The signal generated in the 3rd sensor when one wheel hits a single strip is shown in Figure 8. Figure 8 shows the signal described by this expression (number 7). The signals generated in the 3rd sensor when two wheels, i.e., one axle of the vehicle, are exposed to a single lane are shown in Figure 9. As can be seen in Figure 8, the signals of the individual wheels are separated, and the time shift is determined by the V_{seism} seismic wave propagation velocity and the wheel spacing Δd:

$$\Delta\tau = \frac{\Delta d}{V_{\text{seism}}}. \tag{10}$$

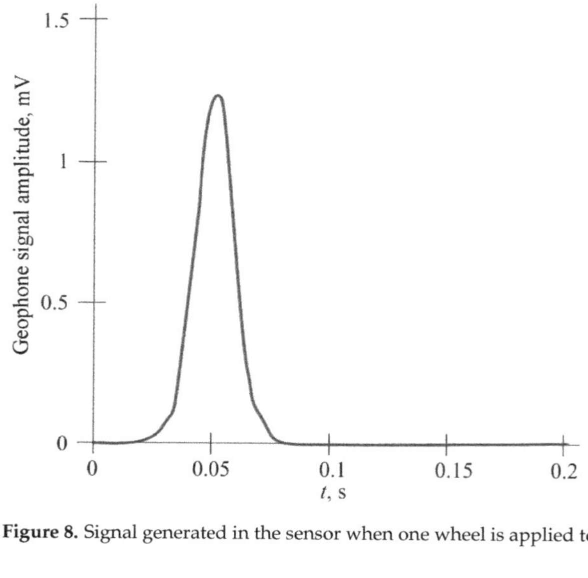

Figure 8. Signal generated in the sensor when one wheel is applied to a single strip.

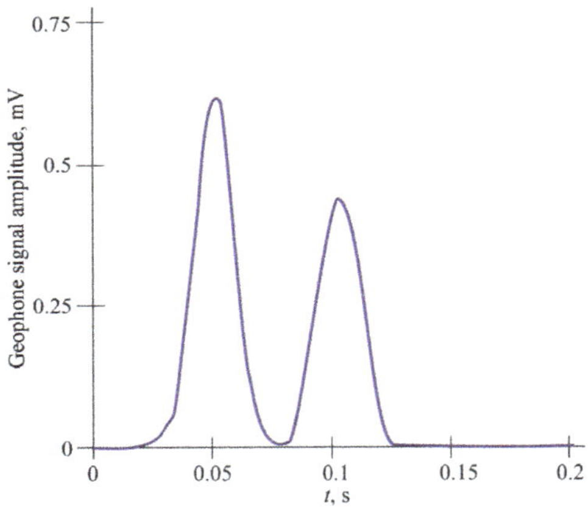

Figure 9. Signals generated in the 3rd sensor when one axis affects a single lane.

In this experiment, the distance between the wheels Δd = 2.5 m, and the velocity of the V_{seism} wave = 125 m/s.

$$\Delta\tau = 0.021\text{s}.$$

It is also seen that the amplitude of the second pulse is smaller, because it occurs when the strip of the far wheel is impacted, i.e., the wave travels a greater distance and, therefore, attenuates more.

Figure 10 shows the signal on the 6th sensor when moving along a group of stripes of the same axis. Figure 10 shows that when a vehicle affects a group of lanes, a periodic signal is generated in the sensor. The fundamental frequency of the signal depends on the distance between the strips $\Delta\lambda$ and the transport speed V_T.

$$f_0 = \frac{V_T}{\Delta l}. \tag{11}$$

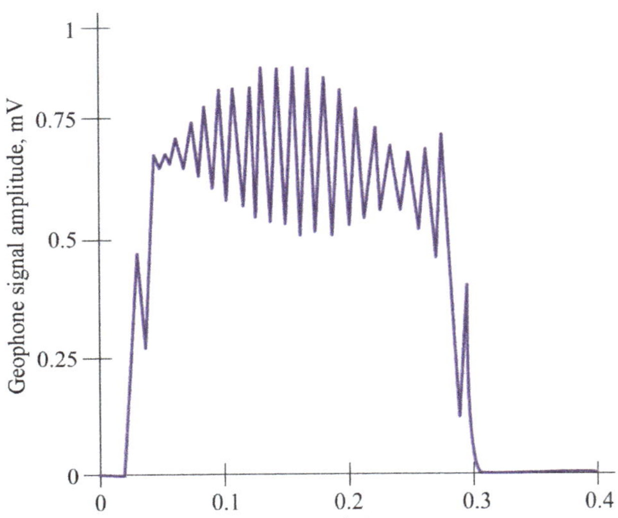

Figure 10. Signal on the 6th sensor when moving along a group of stripes of one axis.

Next, waveforms were constructed for the diagram in Figure 6. For the third (Figure 11) and sixth (Figure 12) sensors. The signals described the movement of a two-axle vehicle with two wheels on each axle.

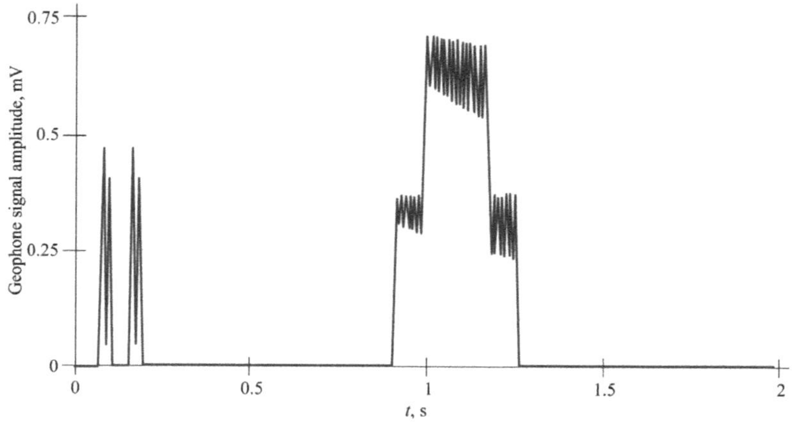

Figure 11. Waveform for the third sensor.

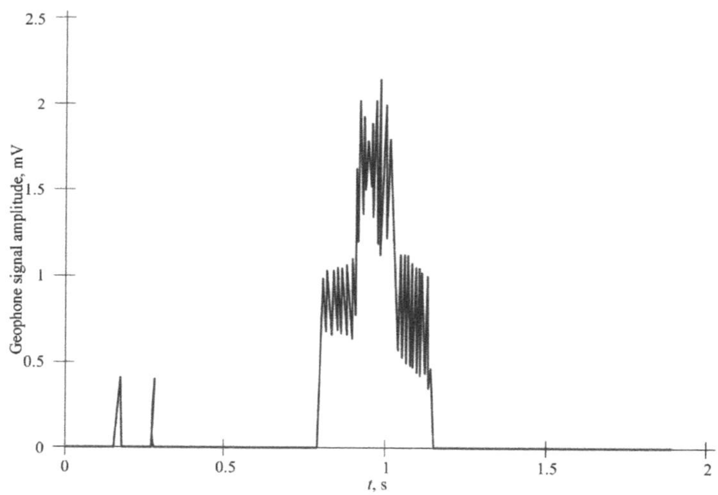

Figure 12. Signal waveform for the sixth sensor.

Since the third sensor is in the top three (Figure 12), the signal from the zero band reaches it with a greater amplitude than the sixth sensor in the second three. Two short-term jumps are observed on the waveforms. At the same time, as we can see from the graph shown in Figure 11, each of them contains two maximums, which characterizes the movement on the zero lane by two wheels; in the waveform illustrated in Figure 13, these pulses do not have two maxima due to the low strength of the signals coming from the zero band. That is, the signals from the two wheels are summed up and go to the sixth sensor in the form of a single pulse.

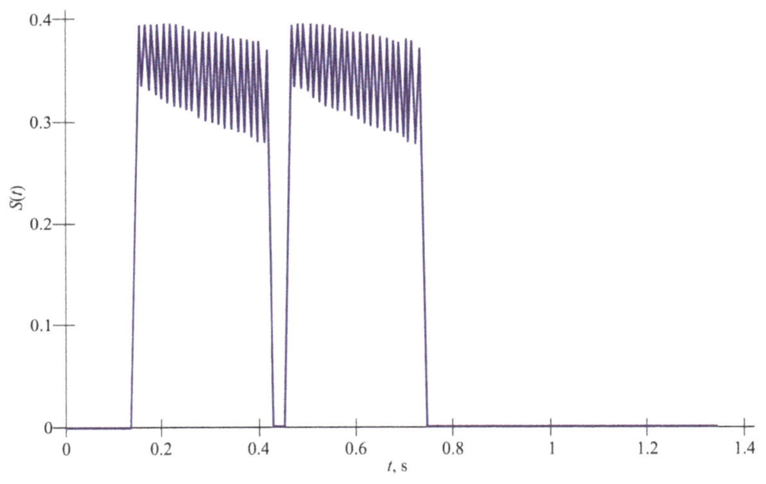

Figure 13. Simulated signal for a car with two axles spaced 7 m apart.

Further, the movement of the vehicle along the comb is traced. On the sensors, the movement of the vehicle is observed first by the first axle; then by both; then, after the departure of the first axle, by the second axle. The amplitude of the signal received from the sixth sensor is greater than the amplitude of the signal received from the third sensor. This is due to the fact that the sixth sensor is located in the second three; therefore, it is closer to the band group. The variable increase and decrease in the amplitude of the comb signal on the sixth sensor is due to delays between the wheels and axles, which were not taken into account in the third sensor due to the distance of its location relative to the group of lanes.

7.3. Signal Compression During Processing Due to the Use of "Combs" with Special Characteristics

When using a uniform comb with a band spacing of 0.25 m and a total comb length of about 5 m, we encounter the problem of signal interference. When a car with several axles passes along a uniform comb (5 m long), and the distance between the axles is less than the size of this comb, then signals from the first and second axles are superimposed.

Appendix A contains the MATLAB function, which implements a mathematical model of seismic signal generation when a vehicle crosses specially applied convex stripes on the roadway for various configurations of combs formed by strips. Figure 12 shows a simulated signal for a car with two axles located at a distance of 7 m. Since the distance between the axles is greater than the length of the comb, we clearly see the signal from each axle separately.

Figure 14 shows a simulated signal for a car with two axles located at a distance of 3 m. Since the distance between the axles is less than the length of the comb, there is an overlap of signals from the first and second axles.

As a result, we see one very long signal, from the moment when the front axle drove to the moment when the rear axle moves. Due to the fact that we receive this signal continuously, we have no way of distinguishing between the signal from the first axis and the second. To solve this problem, it was proposed to use a non-uniform arrangement of bands in order to achieve a linear increase in the frequency of the signal.

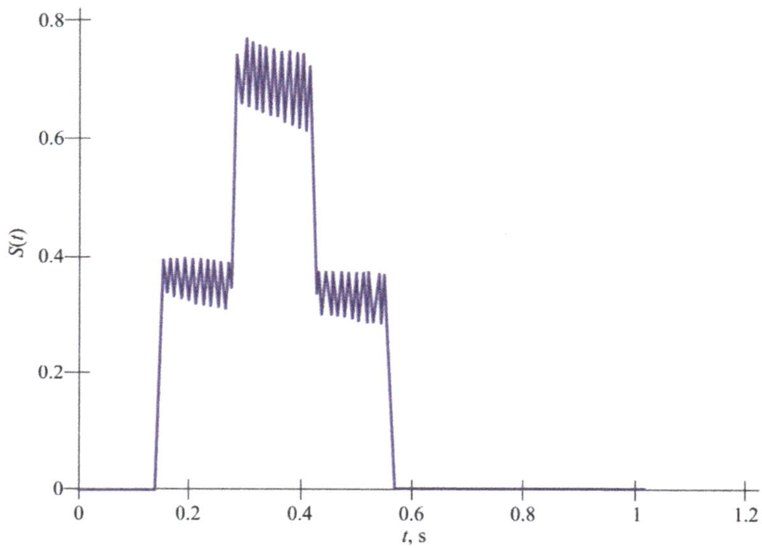

Figure 14. Simulated signal for a car with two axles located at a distance of 3 m.

The signal from an irregular comb can be described as a chirp signal:

$$s(t) = A\exp\left(2\pi i\left(f_0 i + \frac{Kt^2}{2}\right)\right),$$

where f_0 is the initial frequency, and K is the frequency modulation coefficient. Applying matched filtering:

$$h(t) = s^*(T + t)$$

provides an output response in the form of a narrow autocorrelation function, with the signal-to-noise ratio (SNR) amplified in proportion to the signal length. This idea originated from radar, since radar uses broadband signals of various types, including one of the most famous, which is a pulse with linear-frequency modulation (LFM). This idea allowed us to understand and distinguish between the front axle and the rear axle. Table 1 shows the coordinates according to which the comb with an uneven arrangement of stripes was made. The total length is 4.326 m.

Table 1. Coordinates of bands for an uneven comb.

0.5	**0.476**	**0.444**	**0.408**	**0.370**	**0.333**	**0.298**	**0.266**	**0.212**	**0.190**	**0.172**
0.154	0.139	0.126								

A series of tests was carried out on a sample of N = 60 vehicles to assess the stability of the speed and axle number algorithm. The mean error in determining the speed was $\sigma_\upsilon = 0.78$ km/h, with a standard deviation of $\Delta^{-}\upsilon$ of 1.14 km/h. The distribution of the error is close to normal (tested using the Shapiro–Wilk test, $p > 0.15$), which makes it possible to use the standard norm when constructing confidence intervals. Thus, with a confidence probability of 95%, the error in determining the speed does not exceed:

$$\Delta^{-}\upsilon + 1.96\frac{\sigma_\upsilon}{\sqrt{N}} \approx 0.78 + 0.29 = 1.07\text{km/h}.$$

A similar analysis was performed to determine the number of axes: the accuracy was 96.5%, with most of the errors occurring in cases of overlapping pulses from adjacent axes, which can be compensated for by the use of an improved detector based on phase coherence.

Figure 15 shows a simulated signal for a car that is driving along an irregular ridge. The car has two axles and two wheels on each of them. The axles are located at a distance of 5 m. In this graph, you can clearly see the signals from each wheel, as well as from each axle. Since the distance between the axes is greater than the length of the comb, these signals are not superimposed.

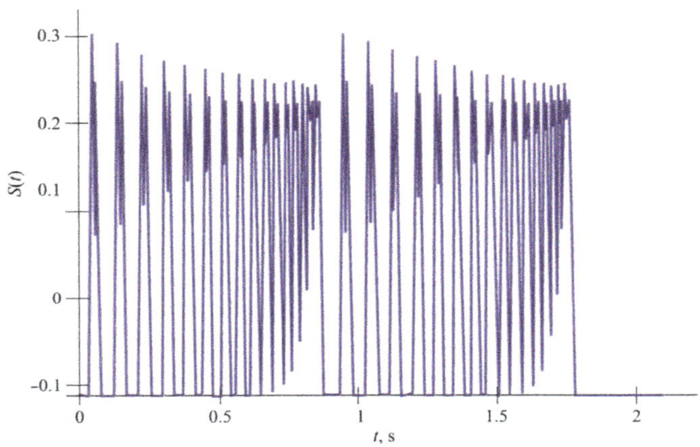

Figure 15. A simulated signal for a car that has two axles and two wheels on each. The axles are spaced at a distance of 5 m.

Figure 16 shows a simulated signal for a car that is driving on an irregular ridge. The car has two axles and two wheels on each of them. The axes are located at a distance of 3 m. Since the distance between the axes is less than the length of the comb, these signals are superimposed.

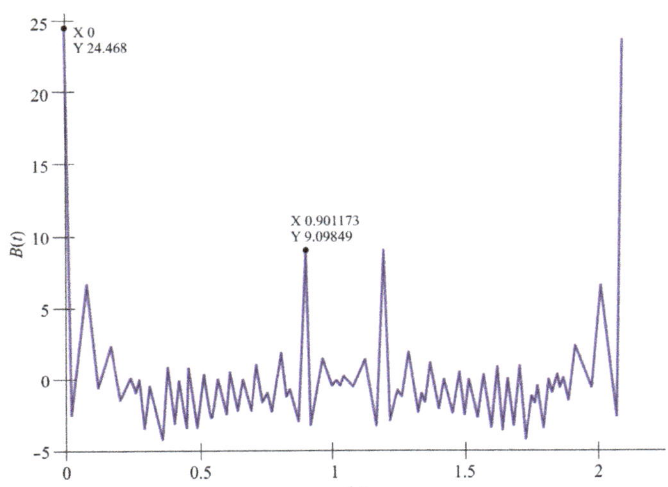

Figure 16. A simulated signal for a car that is driving on an irregular ridge.

We see the sum of the two signals from the front and rear axles, but since there is a linear increase in the frequency of the signal, we can distinguish these signals from each other. For example, in Figure 17, the first point equal to X = 0.58 indicates the beginning of the second signal from the rear axle, and the point X = 0.86 indicates the end of the first signal from the front axle.

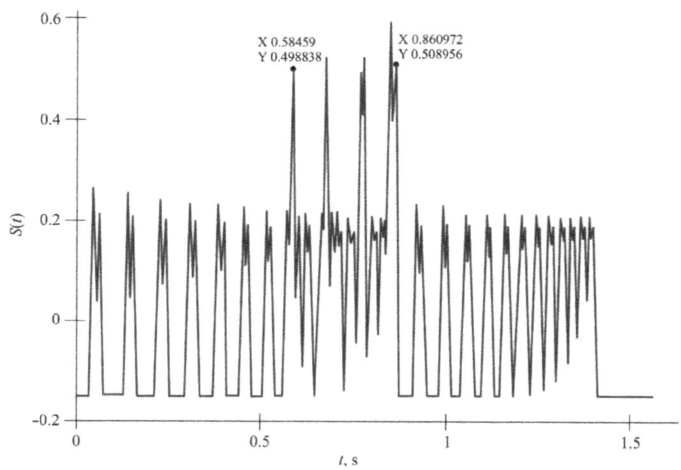

Figure 17. A simulated signal for a car that has two axles and two wheels on each. The axles are spaced 3 m apart.

The signal from each axis has its own feature (linear-frequency increase) and in order to implement it, we used a matched filter on the receiving side. It provides a response in the form of a correlation function. And the correlation function of a linear-frequency modulated pulse is a compressed signal (Figure 18).

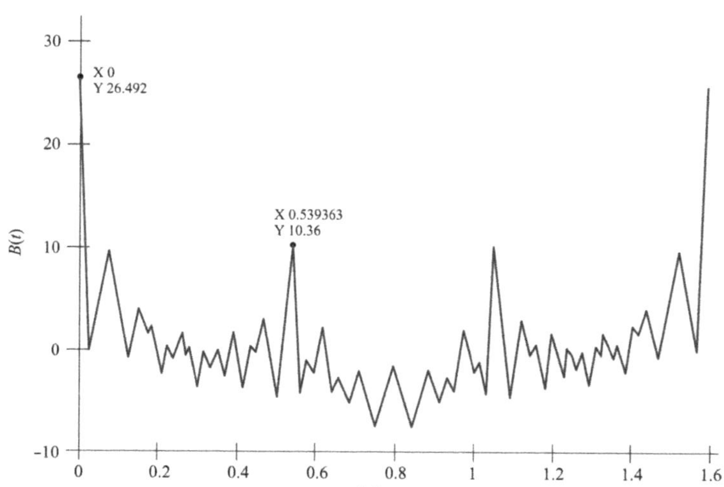

Figure 18. The result of coordinated filtering of the signal from two axes of the vehicle.

This method allows us to determine at what point in time the first and second axles hit the comb. This, in turn, will help us determine the speed of the car.

8. Working with Real Signals

To adjust the mathematical model, it was necessary to conduct a number of experiments to evaluate the operation of the current system. In this regard, further work was carried out based on real signals and existing databases. The databases include vehicle parameters: dimensions, class, approximate speed, axle load.

8.1. Measurement of Vehicle Speed

The power of the signal recorded by seismic sensors, which occurs when vehicles pass along the strips, depends on the weight and speed of the vehicle. Therefore, to determine the weight of a vehicle, it is necessary to know its speed. This section provides three methods for measuring the speed of transport from seismic signals. The speed was calculated in three ways:

(1) Spectral analysis;
(2) Measurement by timestamps;
(3) Measurement by the zero band.

In order to accumulate statistics, the vehicle speed measurement was carried out for seven known trucks, the parameters of which are taken from the database. The velocity values for them, measured in three ways, are stated in Table 2.

Table 2. Speed measurement results of known vehicles.

Vehicle Number	Spectral Method (km/h)	Time Method (km/h)	Axle Method (km/h)
A 449 XN 122	82.368 76.95 77.48	66.03	77.84
K 763 UA 154	68.72 66.75 62.67	54.6	64.49
E 611 OM 154	77.68 70.82 70.06	59.12	68.36
IN 268 TA 154	59.91 57.7 56.4 56.84	47.66	56.9
K 919 KO 22	79.2 76.84 76.74	64.02	81.86
E 012 UT 154	78.62 88.83 77.63	71.48	84.53
T 522 OM 154	62.45 61.37 60.8 60.47	51.59	65.48

8.1.1. Speed Measurement Using Spectral Analysis

One of the methods for measuring the speed of the vehicle is the spectral analysis of signals in the areas describing the movement along the ridge (readings of the sixth sensor). A program was developed that allows you to calculate the necessary parameters automatically.

Automatic measurement of harmonic parameters is effective only when the harmonics are located at frequencies that differ from each other by two times ±2 references. In other cases, in order to determine the reference (frequency) of the harmonic, it was necessary to carry out measurements according to graphs. Having received data on the parameters of the spectrum, they began to calculate the velocity. The following formula was derived:

$$v = \frac{f_f}{N}\frac{n_{\text{ave}}}{k}3.6l, \tag{12}$$

where f is the sample rate, N is the number of all counts, k is the harmonic number, l is the distance between the stripes, and N_{ave} is the average reading of the K-th harmonic:

$$n_{\text{ave}} = \frac{\frac{n_2}{2} + n_1}{2}. \tag{13}$$

The formula was determined on the basis that the frequency of collisions of the vehicle with each of the comb lanes determines its speed. As an example, let us consider the movement of a known vehicle, the parameters of which are known from the database, and denote it TC1. The TC1 has five axles with two wheels on each of them. Figure 19 shows a graph of the signal describing the movement of TC1 along the ridge. Figures 20–22 show graphs of the spectra for different portions of this signal with an indication of harmonics.

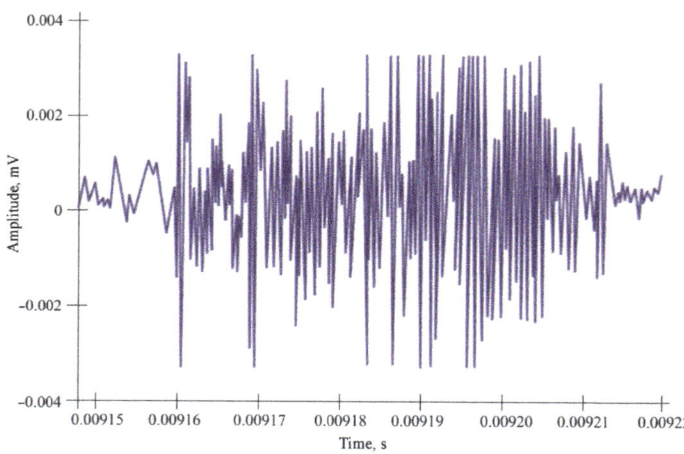

Figure 19. Signal TC1.

The velocity for the following sections was found (Formula (11)):

$$v_1 = \tfrac{528}{108}\frac{\frac{\frac{37}{2}+19}{2}}{1}3.6 \cdot 0.25 = 82.37\ \text{km/h};$$
$$v_2 = \tfrac{528}{176}\frac{\frac{\frac{56}{2}+29}{2}}{1}3.6 \cdot 0.25 = 76.95\ \text{km/h};$$
$$v_1 = \tfrac{528}{108}\frac{\frac{\frac{110}{2}+56}{2}}{1}3.6 \cdot 0.25 = 77.48\ \text{km/h}.$$

In order to avoid measurement errors when using this method, it is necessary to observe at least two harmonics. Since the second harmonic sample also increases with an increase in the speed of the vehicle, there is a possibility that this sample will exceed the central reference of the section when a certain speed is exceeded. Let us calculate the speed threshold:

$$v_{\text{threshold}} = \frac{f_d}{N}\frac{\frac{N}{2}}{2}3.6l = \frac{f_d}{4}3.6l = \frac{528}{4}3.6 \cdot 0.25 = 118.8\,\text{km/h}.$$

Thus, when exceeding the speed of 118.8 km/h, one harmonic will be observed. The disadvantage of this method is the ambiguous determination of the harmonics of the spectrum.

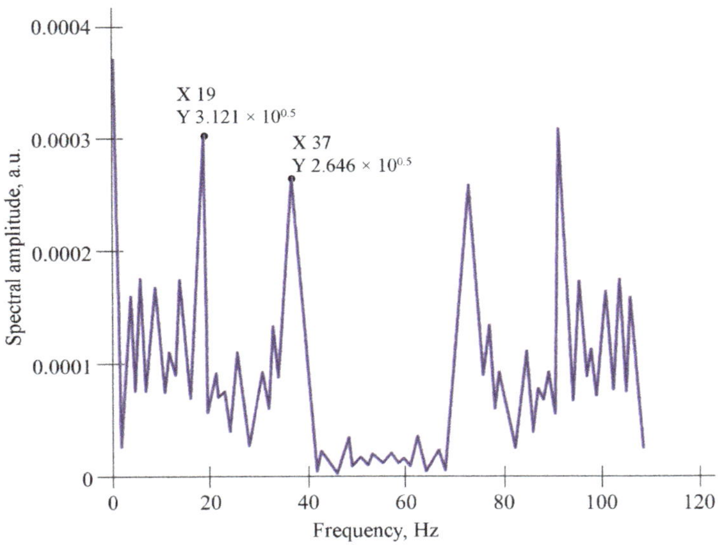

Figure 20. Spectrum of the first segment of the TS1 signal.

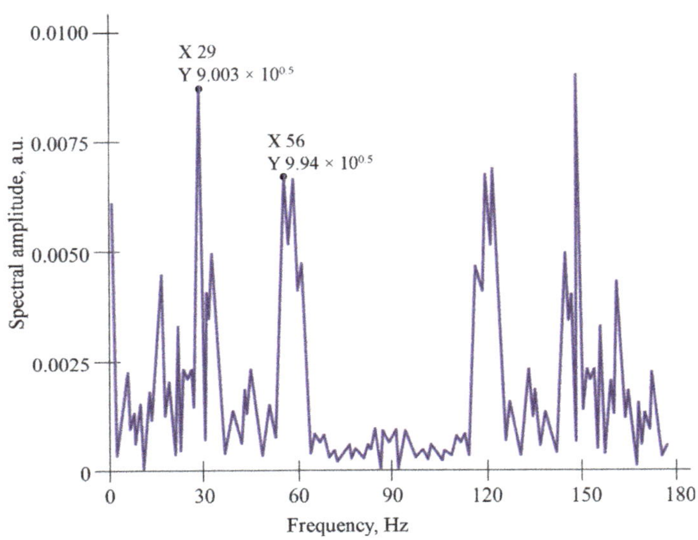

Figure 21. Spectrum of the second segment of the TS1 signal.

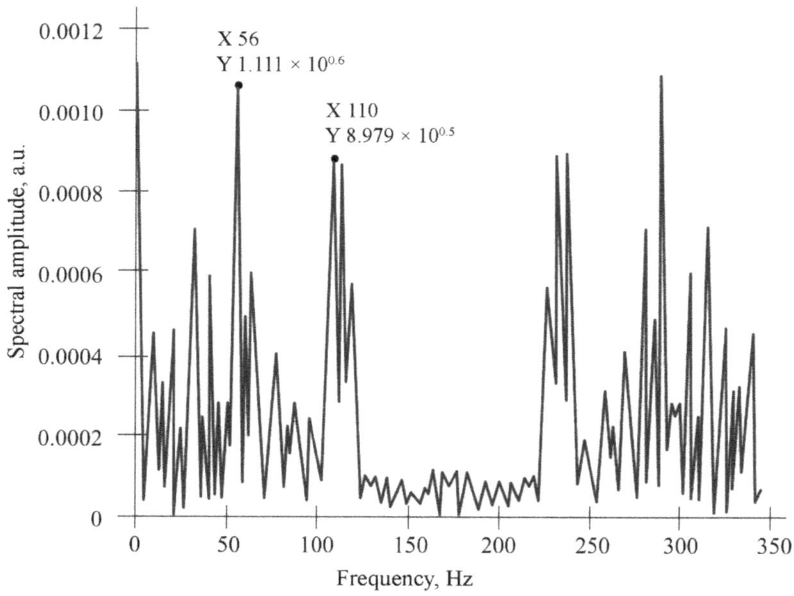

Figure 22. Spectrum of the third segment of the TS1 signal.

8.1.2. Timestamp Measurement of Vehicle Speed

To measure the speed of the vehicle in time, marks of the same pulse were taken on different sensors: the third and the sixth. The formula for determining the time delays of signals as a function of distances between the near wheel and the sensors is as follows:

$$t_{di} = \frac{\Delta r_{si}}{v_{pr}}, \tag{14}$$

where *TDI* is the delay time of signals, depending on the distances between the near wheel and the sensor; Δrsi is the distance between the *i*-th sensor and the near wheel; and upr = 120 m/s is the speed of wave propagation in the ground. The distance from the track obtained by the passage of the near wheel to the sensor line is 2.5 m. Then,

$$t_{d3} = \frac{2.5}{120} = 0.02083 \text{ s}; \; t_{d6} = \frac{\sqrt{2.5^2 + 4.5^2}}{120} = 0.0429 \text{ s}.$$

Let us consider the determination of the speed of the vehicle in this way using the example of the movement of TC1. Signals with timestamps are shown in Figure 23. The moments of collisions of the near wheel TC1 on the zero lane (Figure 23a) and on the convexity (Figure 23b) were established: 91,143 and 91,597 counts c, respectively. Let us find the time corresponding to these counts:

$$t_{h1} = \frac{91143}{528} = 172.619318 \, \text{s}; \; t_{h2} = \frac{91547}{528} = 173.47916 \, \text{s}.$$

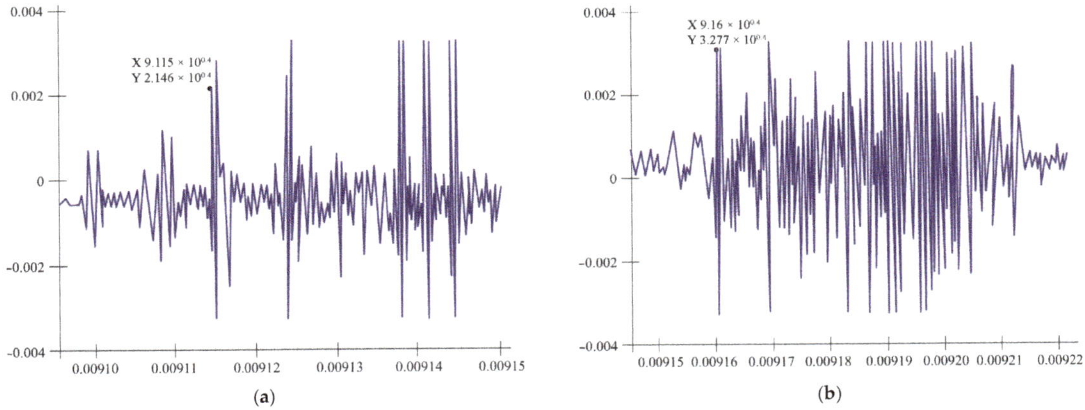

Figure 23. Signal TC1 on different sensors with indication of timestamps: (**a**) readings of the third sensor; (**b**) readings of the sixth sensor.

Then, let us determine the value of the moment of impact of the near wheel TC1 along the lanes (without taking into account delays):

Time difference between strikes:

$$t_1 = t_{\text{h}1} - t_{\text{d}3} = 172.619318 - 0.02083 = 172.598488\,\text{s};$$
$$t_2 = t_{\text{h}2} - t_{\text{d}6} = 173.47916 - 0.0429 = 173.43626\text{ s};$$
$$\Delta t = t_2 - t_1 = 173.43626 - 172.598488 = 0.837772\text{ s}.$$

This means that TC1 drove the section from the zero lane to the bulge in a time equal to 0.837772 s. Knowing the distance r between the zero lane and the convexity, it is possible to calculate the speed of the vehicle:

$$v = \frac{r}{\Delta t} \cdot 3.6. \tag{15}$$

For TC1:

$$v = \frac{15.5}{0.837772} \cdot 3.6 = 66.6\,\text{km/h}.$$

8.1.3. Measurement of Vehicle Zero Lane Speed

The determination of the speed of a vehicle on the zero lane is not the main one due to the use of known parameters (taken from the database) and is provided for the evaluation of speed measurement by the previous methods.

As an example, let us examine the movement of TC1 again. A graph of the signal is taken from the third sensor, labeled in Figure 24. The marks indicate the moment of impact of the near wheel of each axle on the zero stripe:

- First axis t1 impact: 17,263 s;
- Second axis impact *t2*: 17,280,871 s;
- Third axis t3 impact: 173,073,863 s;
- Fourth axis t4 strike: 17,313,447 s;
- Fifth Axis strike *T5*: 17,319,508 s.

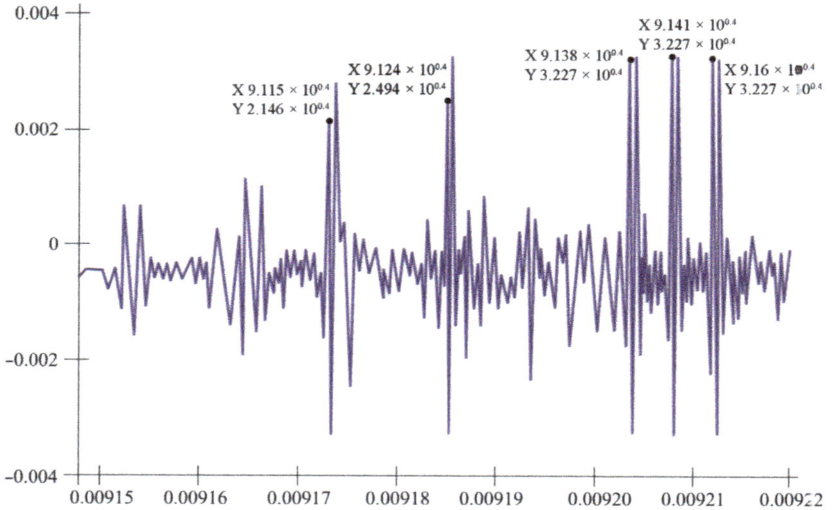

Figure 24. TC1 signal from the third sensor with tags.

Let us determine the time differences between the moments of impacts by adjacent axes:

$$\Delta t_{21} = t_2 - t_1 = 172.80871 - 172.63 = 0.17871 \text{ s};$$
$$\Delta t_{32} = t_3 - t_2 = 173.073863 - 172.80871 = 0.265153 \text{ s};$$
$$\Delta t_{43} = t_4 - t_3 = 173.13447 - 173.073863 = 0.060607 \text{ s};$$
$$\Delta t_{54} = t_5 - t_4 = 173.19508 - 173.13447 = 0.06061 \text{ s}.$$

Distances between adjacent axes taken from the database:

- Between the first and second axles $\Delta\rho 21$: 3.73 m;
- Between the second and third axes $\Delta\rho 32$: 5.67 m;
- Between the first and second axles $\Delta\rho 43$: 1.33 m;
- Between the first and second axles $\Delta\rho 54$: 1.34 m.

Let us take the time difference and the distance between the first and last axes.

In this case, the speed of the vehicle in the zero lane is determined by the formula:

$$v = \frac{\Delta r_{ji}}{\Delta t_{ji}} \cdot 3.6, \tag{15}$$

where j, i = 1 are the numbers of the last and first axes, respectively.

The speed of TC1 will be as follows:

$$v = \frac{\Delta r_{51}}{\Delta t_{51}} = \frac{1.34 + 1.33 + 5.67 + 3.73}{0.06061 + 0.060607 + 0.265153 + 0.17871} \cdot 3.6 = 76.9 \text{ km/h}.$$

8.2. Results of Vehicle Speed Measurements

To analyze the accuracy of each of the methods, let us enter the standard deviation metric:

$$\text{RMSE} = \sqrt{\frac{1}{N}\sum_{i=1}^{N} (\hat{v}_i - v_i)^2},$$

where $\hat{\upsilon}_i$ is the measured value of the speed, and $\upsilon\iota$ is the reference value. It is also possible to construct a confidence interval of the estimate:

$$\hat{\upsilon} \pm z_{\alpha/2}\frac{\sigma}{\sqrt{N}},$$

where σ is the standard deviation from the experiments, and $z_{\alpha/2}$ is the quantile of the normal distribution.

A comparison of the uniform and non-uniform comb showed that in the case of a uniform structure, the main signal energy is concentrated in a narrow frequency range of $f_0 \pm 15$ Hz, which contributes to a higher amplitude of the correlation response but reduces resolution at high speed. The non-uniform structure, on the contrary, creates a signal distributed over frequencies with maximum compression in the time domain—the width of the main lobe of the autocorrelation function is reduced from 0.45 to 0.22 s while increasing resistance to noise due to a more uniform spectrum. Based on the analysis of the RMS (root mean square error value), it can be concluded that the non-uniform comb is advantageous at speeds above 50 km/h and the number of axles from three and above.

It can be seen that the closest velocity values correspond to the spectral analysis and zero band measurements. The method of determining the speed of a vehicle by timestamps is inaccurate (it has a difference of about 10–15 km/h compared to other values of the speed of the same vehicle), since there is a possibility of incorrect determination of the numbering of sensors, as well as inaccurate measurement of the distance between the convexity and the zero stripe.

Measurement of the TC velocity by spectral analysis also has a disadvantage associated with the variable behavior of harmonics, as a result of which it is not always possible to determine the frequency at which they are located. There is also difficulty in choosing a "window" to automatically provide a solution to the problem of finding harmonic parameters. Another disadvantage of this method is the existence of a threshold value of velocity, above which the determination of velocity by spectral analysis is not relevant.

8.3. Comparative Analysis of Speed Measurement Methods

Within the framework of the study, three different methods for determining the speed of a vehicle based on recorded seismic signals were implemented and tested: the spectral, time, and zero band methods. Each of them is based on its own physical and mathematical model of data processing and is implemented at various stages of signal analysis (Table 3).

Table 3. Comparison of speed measurement methods.

Speed Measurement Method	Average Error (km/h)	Standard Deviation (km/h)	Advantages	Restrictions
Spectral method	1.2	0.78	High accuracy, noise resistance	Loss of stability at a speed of >118 km/h
Timestamp Method	3.8	2.1	Easy to implement	Highly dependent on the accuracy of dating and placement
Zero Stripe Method	1.3	0.9	Good consistency with the base	Requires database data and accurate labeling

The spectral method is based on the application of a fast Fourier transform to a signal received from a geophone located near the ridge with a uniform spacing of the bands. The periodic structure of the comb causes the formation of a quasi-harmonic signal, the spectrum of which contains pronounced harmonics. The distance between these harmonics is proportional to the speed of the vehicle. To calculate the velocity, a specially developed formula was used to link the frequency of harmonics, the spacing between bands, and the velocity, as well as a software module for automatic determination of spectral parameters. The spectral method has shown high accuracy at speeds up to 80 km/h and provides good immunity to background noise due to its narrow bandwidth, but its application is difficult at high vehicle speeds, when spectral harmonics begin to overlap.

The timestamping method is implemented by measuring the time delay between responses on different sensors when the same vehicle element (usually the near wheel) passes. In the course of the experiments, the moments of appearance of characteristic peaks in the signal from the third and sixth geophones, between which the exact spatial distance is known, were tracked. By determining the time interval between the peaks and knowing the distance between the sensors, the speed of movement was calculated. This method is simple and clear, but it turned out to be sensitive to the accuracy of time synchronization and to possible errors in determining the identity of signals from the same machine element, especially in a complex multi-signal structure.

The zero lane method involves the use of information about successive impacts of the vehicle axles on the initial (zero) ridge lane. By knowing the impact timestamps of each axle and the distances between them (taken from a database of known cars), it is possible to calculate the average speed between the axles. This approach was used in the work mainly to verify the results obtained by other methods, and it showed good agreement with the spectral method. Its main limitation is the need to have a priori data on the geometry of the vehicle, without which the calculation is impossible.

Thus, each of the presented methods has its own application features, advantages, and limitations, which are reflected in the table. Their combined use in the study made it possible to increase the reliability of speed estimates and cross-verify the results.

8.4. Noise Sensitivity Assessment and Threshold Level Determination

To analyze the stability of the proposed system to external disturbances, a series of numerical experiments were carried out with the superimposition of additive Gaussian noise of varied dispersion on real and synthetic seismic signals. The initial model of the $s(t)$ signal, obtained from the system with known vehicle parameters, was supplemented with the noise component $n(t) \sim \mathcal{N}(0, \sigma 2)$, after which the speed, mass, and number of axles were re-evaluated at different noise intensities.

The simulation looked at the range of signal-to-noise levels (SNRs) from +30 dB (low noise) to 0 dB (signal and noise are commensurate). In each case, the mean error in determining mass and velocity was evaluated, as well as the standard deviation of the results over 100 repetitions.

The results showed that at SNR > 15 dB, the system demonstrates stability: the error in estimating the mass does not exceed 10%, and the speed does not exceed 1.5 km/h (Table 4). When the SNR drops to 10 dB, the mass error reaches 14%, and when the SNR is < 5 dB, there is a sharp decrease in accuracy—the mass error exceeds 20%, and the detection of the number of axes becomes unstable (less than 80% of correct determinations).

The threshold noise level for the system is set at an SNR level of ≈ 8 dB. Below this limit, the accuracy of the mass estimate exceeds the permissible threshold of 15%, which makes it necessary to apply additional filtration measures.

Table 4. Dependence of accuracy on noise level.

SNR (dB)	Average Mass Error (%)	Art. Weight Deviation (%)	Speed Error (km/h)	Correctness of Determining the Number of Axes (%)
30	7.8	2.1	1.1	96.5
20	9.1	3.4	1.3	95.1
15	10.2	4.0	1.5	93.8
10	13.8	5.6	2.2	89.4
8	15.4	6.3	2.7	85.0
5	20.7	8.9	3.5	77.2
0	>30	—	>5.0	<60

8.5. Extended Validation of the Method on a Sample from Real Road Conditions

To improve the reliability of the results obtained, additional validation of the developed system was carried out on an extended sample of 180 vehicles of various categories. The sample included both light commercial vehicles (LCVs) and passenger vehicles (cars, minivans), as well as heavy trucks, trailers, and buses. The tests were carried out on two sections of the road with different types of pavement: asphalt concrete and cement concrete, as well as under variable weather conditions—dry and wet surfaces, air temperature from −1 to +28 °C. Additionally, the flow density was recorded: low (less than 500 tf/h), medium (500–1200 tf/h), and high (more than 1500 tf/h).

For each class of vehicles, the values of errors in determining the speed, mass, and number of axles were obtained, and standard deviations were calculated. The results of the analysis showed that the proposed method is resistant to changes in the road surface—the differences in the error in determining the weight did not exceed 1.5% between sections with asphalt and concrete. The influence of weather conditions was expressed in a slight increase in error (up to 9.3%) on a wet surface, which is explained by a change in the coefficient of adhesion and distortion of signal amplitudes. However, even under these conditions, the system retained the stability of peak response detection and acceptable recognition accuracy. At high traffic density (~1800 tf/h), signal overlap was observed, especially in passenger cars with a short baseline, but the use of filtering with phase coherence and response synchronization made it possible to minimize errors in the classification and isolation of individual events.

Thus, the extended validation showed high reproducibility of the results in various road and operational conditions. The average error in speed was 1.4 km/h and in weight 9.2%, and the correctness of the recognition of the number of axles remained at the level of 94.8%. These values confirm the applicability of the proposed approach in real operating conditions, including multi-axis machines and mixed flow.

9. Discussion

9.1. Accuracy of Determining the Parameters of Vehicles

In field tests, the system with eight geophones and artificial markings (stripes) was able to estimate the speed, weight, and number of axles of trucks with an error of no more than ~1.2 km/h in speed and ~8.7% in weight at speeds up to 70 km/h; the correctness of determining the number of axles reached 96.5%. In the authors' studies on passive vibration recording, it is reported that seismic sensors make it possible to measure the speed of movement with an error of about ±1.5–2 km/h and to classify vehicles by axle load/weight with an accuracy of ~85–95% (in the speed range up to ~80 km/h) [15,17]. In particular, methods based on two seismic sensors installed at the curb are able to determine speed and center distances, although the accuracy of such estimates is inferior—about 20% error in field tests [19]. Traditional WIM (weigh-in-motion) systems with sensors embedded in the coating provide a typical error in measuring the total weight of about 7–12% [6,8]. Although the best WIM systems approach the requirements of direct weight control (some studies aim for <5% error), in practice, even modern WIM systems are often used only for the pre-selection of overloaded vehicles. Thus, the accuracy achieved in our work (~8–9% by weight) is comparable to the level of the best dynamic weighing systems. Moreover, the high quality of recognition of the number of axes (≈96%) indicates the effectiveness of using artificial irregularities to generate distinct seismic signals from each axis. Doppler sensors are able to classify transport by size with an accuracy of about 90% [7], and inductive loops or magnetometers with a sufficient network of sensors achieve ~95–99% classification accuracy [38], but these methods do not directly measure mass. Thus, the proposed approach combines a high accuracy of mass and velocity estimation, comparable to WIM, and a classification accuracy close to the best non-contact sensors.

Table 5 summarizes the comparative characteristics of the approaches used in the work to determine the key parameters of the vehicle—speed, weight, and number of axles. The presented data demonstrate that the spectral method of velocity estimation turned out to be the most accurate and resistant to noise, while the mass estimation based on the measured power of the seismic signal provided an acceptable error under the condition of preliminary calibration. The number of axles is most effectively determined through impulse response analysis using structured roadway markings. This approach allows for accuracy comparable to industrial WIM systems at minimal infrastructure costs.

Table 5. Comparison of approaches to determining the parameters of the vehicle.

Parameter	Method/Approach	Average Error	Advantages	Restrictions
Speed	Spectral analysis	1.2 km/h	High accuracy with a stable spectrum	Speed limits (>118 km/h)
Speed	By timestamps	3.8 km/h	Simplicity	Synchronization errors
Mass	Through average signal strength	8.7%	Real-world applicability	Dependence on calibration and road performance
Number of axles	Highlighting signal peaks	96.5% correctness	High precision with separate axis response	Errors when applying signals from closely spaced axes

Model Applicability Limitations and Soil Type Calibratio

Despite the high accuracy achieved in the field tests, the proposed model has limitations related to sensitivity to the geological characteristics of the site. The attenuation and resonance frequency parameters that describe the response of the medium to a wheel impact vary depending on the density, humidity, and type of soil, as well as the construction of the pavement. Models calibrated on a rigid substrate (cement concrete, dense crushed stone) may lose accuracy when transferred to areas with a loose or water-saturated substrate (sand, clay).

To ensure the correct operation of the system in various geological conditions, a preliminary calibration procedure is required. It involves the recording of the seismic response from the reference vehicle, after which the parameters of the response model of the medium (attenuation and frequency) are numerically identified by minimizing the residual between the model and the measured signal. This procedure allows you to take into account the specific features of wave propagation in a particular layer and increase the accuracy of the mass and velocity estimates.

It should also be noted that in the event of a sudden change in geological conditions along the monitored section of the road, it is recommended to calibrate in segments, using separate values of model parameters for different zones. This allows you to maintain the stability of the algorithm under conditions of variable stiffness and base structure.

9.2. Resistance to External Noise and Weather Conditions

One of the important advantages of a passive seismic system is its independence from visibility and weather conditions [16]. Unlike video cameras or lidars, whose accuracy deteriorates when there is a lack of light, fog, rain, or obstruction of view by large vehicles, seismic sensors detect ground vibrations that are independent of illumination or atmospheric transparency. In addition, radar systems, although they can operate in any weather conditions, are also subject to interference (precipitation, third-party objects) and require signal emission [7]. Passive geophones are devoid of these disadvantages, which is confirmed by the growing interest in seismic methods in recent years [17]. At the same time, the high sensitivity of geophones means that they pick up not only signals from cars but also extraneous ground vibrations. It is noted in the literature that external vibrations (e.g., from the operation of machinery, other traffic flows, or natural sources) can reduce the accuracy of parameter determination [23]. In our system, this problem is partially solved by using artificial bumps (stripes): when the wheels run over them, they generate high-amplitude seismic pulses that stand out significantly against the background of noise. In addition, filtering and spectral analysis methods are used to increase the signal-to-noise ratio. It is known that the use of time–frequency processing (FFT, wavelet conversion) and statistical methods makes it possible to isolate the dominant components associated with wheel impacts and thereby improve the noise immunity of the classification [22,39,40]. Studies that used such approaches (e.g., [22,24–26]) reported achieving ~90–95% accuracy in recognizing vehicle types while rejecting interference using filtering, statistical signal processing techniques, and machine learning algorithms. Moreover, modern neural network algorithms (CNN, RNN, etc.) demonstrate high accuracy (up to ~95%) even at a significant noise level, maintaining classification correctness at the level of ~80–85% in difficult conditions [41–43]. Thus, thanks to the combination of engineering solutions (artificial roadway marking) and computational processing methods (filtration, spectral analysis, ML), the proposed system is highly resistant to external noise. It is important to emphasize that the operation of geophones is practically not affected by temperature and weather factors—unlike, for example, piezoelectric WIM sensors, the characteristics of which significantly depend on the temperature of the road surface and require corrections [8]. This indicates the potential reliability of our approach in a variety of climatic and operating conditions.

9.3. Cost and Complexity of Infrastructure Implementation

Classic WIM systems provide automatic weighing on the move at high speed and acceptable accuracy but at the cost of their implementation being complex and expensive [6]. It is necessary to mount strain gauges, quartz piezo strips, or fiber-optic sensors directly into the roadway, which implies the construction of a measuring section of the road, its regular maintenance, and calibration. The installation of such sensors is associated with blocking traffic during installation and violates the integrity of the road structure. In addition, over time, due to traffic and climatic factors, the coverage at the sensor installation site can degrade, deteriorating accuracy and requiring repairs. Alternative systems, such as bridge WIM (installation of deformation and vibration sensors on existing bridge structures), facilitate integration but are not applicable on all road sections and also require fine-tuning for each site [44]. Finally, over-road sensors (video cameras, radars, laser scanners) require the installation of poles, power supply, and network infrastructure, which is associated with significant costs on the scale of a long route [12]. Against this background, the proposed passive seismic system is favorably distinguished by its relative simplicity and low cost of deployment [1]. Geophones are compact and inexpensive, and their installation involves small recesses in the roadside or pavement, which minimizes interference with the road structure. In the paper [15], it is explicitly noted that seismic sensors for traffic monitoring are cost-effective and easy to install compared to most traditional sensors [1]. Our system, in addition to the geophones themselves, uses only small artificial bumps (stripes) on the pavement, the implementation of which is technically simple and financially incomparably cheaper than, for example, the embedding of load sensors over the entire width of the lane. Thus, the total cost of equipment and installation of a seismic system on a road section can be orders of magnitude lower compared to camera complexes or built-in WIM sensors. This is confirmed by the estimates of various authors: for example, Ahmad et al. note that seismic traffic monitoring provides higher efficiency at lower costs compared to existing methods [45]. Add to this the absence of radiating device costs (like radars) and minimal maintenance requirements (geophones have a simple design without moving parts, designed for long-term operation), we can expect a low total life cycle cost of the proposed system [46].

9.4. Technical Feasibility and Scalability

The results of the experiments confirm the practical feasibility of the proposed approach. The system successfully operated on a real road section, registering and correctly processing seismic signals from several trucks at speeds up to 70 km/h. A significant factor that ensured the efficiency of the method was the combination of several geophones into a local network (in this case, eight sensors). The use of an array of sensors and special marks on the road made it possible to solve the problem of synchronizing signals from the wheels and increase the reliability of parameter estimation. The difficulties of passive systems noted in the literature, for example, a decrease in accuracy when superimposing signals from several machines or when driving speed increases, can be overcome by increasing the density of sensors and improving the algorithms for extracting the signal [19,47] of each object. For example, ref. [18] proposed a method for correlation processing of signals from several geophones using a Kalman filter, which made it possible to reconstruct the trajectory of movement and estimate the weight of the car with an error of less than 10% at speeds up to 60 km/h [18]. This result is comparable to ours and confirms that with the correct installation of the sensor network and calibration of the model, it is possible to achieve high accuracy without direct measurement of the weight force. The scalability of the proposed solution is another significant advantage. Due to their low cost and ease of installation, such seismic monitoring nodes can be deployed at a large number of points in the road network. Unlike stationary weighing stations, which are installed at only a few control locations, geophones can be distributed over extended areas for continuous flow monitoring. In experimental projects abroad, it has already been demonstrated that a dense network of seismic sensors is capable of covering large areas: for example, an array of ~5200 geophones over an area of 7×10 km has been successfully used to record the movement of vehicles in urban conditions [34,48]. Of course, the practical deployment of such a system will require solutions for the collection and transmission of large amounts of data, but modern wireless technologies and distributed computing methods make this approach feasible. A general analysis of existing approaches shows that our system seeks to eliminate the key shortcomings of analogues: it avoids expensive engineering structures typical of WIM and, at the same time, minimizes the problematic aspects of passive methods (interference, multi-signaling) due to hardware and software. Thus, the possibility of creating a scalable network of passive control of vehicles is demonstrated, providing high-precision determination of their parameters in a wide range of conditions without significant infrastructure costs.

9.5. Comparative Analysis with Existing WIM Systems

To fully assess the effectiveness of the proposed method, it is important to compare it with recognized WIM technologies. Traditional "in-road" systems based on the installation of piezo and strain gauges in the road surface are characterized by an accuracy of about ±6–15%, in accordance with the requirements of ASTM E1318-09, while the most common piezo quartz and strain gauge elements provide an error of about ±10% [49]. Bridge-WIM systems (installed on bridges) demonstrate comparable accuracy ±5–10% and are used in areas with increased requirements for data reliability [49].

On-board systems that use accelerometers inside vehicles achieve significantly higher accuracy ±1–3% but require equipment in each vehicle and are economically and organizationally complex. For example, such solutions often use airborne telemetry data and are part of integrated transportation monitoring systems [50].

The method proposed in the article, based on seismic measurements using geophones, makes it possible to estimate the weight of the vehicle with an error of about 8–12% during the first field tests. This accuracy is already comparable to low-cost versions of WIM systems in the ASTM Type II class, where errors of ±10–15% are allowed [49,51]. These results are consistent with the limitations of ASTM E1318 for motion mass control systems [51,52].

The key advantage of our method is its non-invasiveness: geophones are installed on the surface of the road surface, which eliminates the need to cut asphalt, pour concrete, or install cable channels. Instead, compact shielded cables are used, and signal amplification and digitization are carried out in a central unit located in close proximity to the sensors. This makes the system particularly attractive for installation in the field, on temporary sites, or in areas with limited access to road infrastructure.

From a practical point of view, the proposed approach combines ease of installation and maintenance, low installation costs, and compliance with standard accuracy requirements. Pre-calibration with control vehicles is sufficient to provide results suitable for monitoring and pre-weighing, without expensive equipment and capital work.

Of course, the accuracy of the proposed method is inferior to top solutions, such as On-Board WIM, where the error is only ±1–3%. However, the advantages of rapid deployment, mobility, and cost-effectiveness make it suitable for everyday use by road services, especially with limited budgets and temporary installations.

In the future, field comparative tests are planned at locations with industrial WIM systems installed. These tests will allow for a direct comparison of results, refine calibration factors, and confirm that the proposed method complies with ASTM E1318-09 [52] and GOST 32348-2013 [53], paving the way for large-scale application.

10. Conclusions

In this study, a mathematical model of a passive seismic system for dynamic determination of the weight characteristics of vehicles in motion was developed and experimentally confirmed. The basis of the proposed approach is the registration of seismic signals arising from the collision of vehicle wheels with strips specially applied to the road surface, as well as their subsequent processing using a complex mathematical apparatus, including the Fourier transform, coordinated filtration, regularized methods for solving inverse problems, and parameter optimization models.

Thanks to the developed system, it was possible to achieve high accuracy indicators: the average error in determining the speed was 1.2 km/h, with a maximum recorded error of less than 2 km/h. The accuracy of determining the mass of vehicles based on the recorded seismic signals reached the level of 8.7% at a speed of up to 70 km/h. The correctness of determining the number of axles was 96.5%, while most of the errors occurred under the conditions of overlapping signals from several axes and were successfully eliminated using non-uniform combs and phase-coherent filtering methods. In addition, for a sample of 60 vehicles, the speed measurement error had a standard deviation of 0.78 km/h, which confirms the stability of the system.

Two independent approaches were used to determine the velocity: the frequency method, based on the analysis of the distance between the harmonics of the signal spectrum, and the time method, based on measuring the delay between the edges of signals recorded at different points. The estimates obtained were consistent, as evidenced by the standard deviation of less than 1.5 km/h between the results of both methods.

Particular attention was paid to the use of linear-frequency modulation signals generated when the wheels pass through specially formed combs with an uneven pitch. This made it possible to use consistent filtering, resulting in a narrow autocorrelation function of the signal. Due to this, it was possible to significantly improve the resolution of the system and increase the resistance to overlapping signals from different axes of vehicles.

Numerical experiments and full-scale tests have shown that the proposed model can be successfully applied in real traffic conditions. Testing on vehicles with different parameters has demonstrated the applicability of the method in the speed range from 30 to 80 km/h, with the number of axles from two to five, and a weight of up to 40 tons. Real signals obtained when driving along the measuring section on the Sovetskoye Highway were analyzed, and highly reliable results were obtained, coinciding with the database of reference data.

Thus, the use of spectral analysis methods, in combination with consistent filtering models, as well as the solution of regularized inverse problems, made it possible not only to restore the parameters of vehicles but also to ensure the stability of estimates against external interference, noise, and signal superimposition. The approach is highly feasible, low cost to implement, and can be scaled up for use in the road network, including integration with intelligent transport systems and digital twins of road infrastructure.

Author Contributions: Conceptualization, B.V.M. and N.V.M.; methodology, A.V.P. and E.A.E.; software, A.E.B.; validation, A.V.P. and E.A.E.; formal analysis, A.Y.D.; investigation, D.V.V.; resources, D.V.V.; data curation, D.V.V.; writing—original draft preparation, A.Y.D.; writing—review and editing, B.V.M. and N.V.M.; visualization, A.E.B. All authors have read and agreed to the published version of the manuscript.

Funding: This research received no external funding.

Data Availability Statement: The data presented in this study are available from the corresponding authors upon reasonable request.

Conflicts of Interest: The authors declare no conflicts of interest.

Appendix A

MATLAB program, which implements a mathematical model of seismic signals generation from vehicles.

```
close all
clc clear
K=[5; 7];%wheel coordinate matrix
G=[0; 3];%axis matrix
P=[38,38.5,38.976,39.42,39.828,40.198,40.531,40.829,41.095,41.333,41.545,41.735,41.907,42.061,42.2,42.326];%unev
                    en comb band matrix
```

```
N=1; %number of sensors
D=[35; 0];% sensors for uneven comb
Vm=20/3.6;%vehicle speed in m/s Vras=125;%wave propagation velocity tau=0.0042;%pulse duration fd=597;
                    %Sample Rate
T=(P-P(1))/Vm;%Lane Travel Time
M=950;%number of implementations t=(0:1/fd:(M-1)/fd);%time
S=zeros(N,M);
Am=1; %signal amplitude tzo=G/Vm; %Axis Delay Time

P2=[38:0.25:43];%uniform comb band matrix
N=1; %number of sensors
D2=[42.544; 0];% sensors for uniform comb
T2=(P2-P2(1))/Vm;%Lane Travel Time
S2=zeros(N,M);

for x=1:N
   for y=1:max(size(P))

      R1(x,y)=sqrt((P(y)-D(1,x))^2+(K(1)-D(2,x))^2);%distance from the first wheel to the sensor
      R2(x,y)=sqrt((P(y)-D(1,x))^2+(K(2)-D(2,x))^2);%distance from the second wheel to the sensor
      Z1=1/sqrt(R1(x,y)); %Signal attenuation in the ground
      Z2=1/sqrt(R2(x,y));%signal attenuation in the ground
      Tz1(x,y)=R1(x,y)/Vras; %Sensor Delay Time
      Tz2(x,y)=R2(x,y)/Vras;%sensor delay time
(top wheel) for i=1:max(size(G))
            %Latency
            Ti1 = Tz1(x,y)+T(y)+tzo(i);
            Ti2                    =                    Tz2(x,y)+T(y)+tzo(i);
                  S=(Z1*Am*exp(-(t-Ti1).^2/(2*tau^2)))+(Z2*Am*exp((t-Ti2).^2/(2*tau^2)))+S(1,:);%Envelop
                  e for two wheels and two axles
            B=abs(fft(S));%Fourier transform of the signal.
            % Filter Selected
            f1=fd*(0:(M-1))/M;%Set the frequency domain f
(For S2)
            H=conj(B);
            Sf=H.*B;
            B2=ifft(Sf);
                  end      end end    figure
plot(t,B2),title('Consistent filtering for non-uniform comb') xlabel('t(c)'), ylabel('B(t)');
  figure
plot(t,S), grid, title('Modulated signal from an uneven comb') xlabel('t(c)'), ylabel('S(t)');

for x=1:N
   for y=1:max(size(P2))

      R12(x,y)=sqrt((P2(y)-D2(1,x))^2+(K(1)-
D2(2,x))^2);%distance from the first wheel to the sensor R22(x,y)=sqrt((P2(y)-D2(1,x))^2+(K(2)-
D2(2,x))^2);%distance from the second wheel to the sensor
      Z12=1/sqrt(R12(x,y)); %Signal attenuation in the ground
      Z22=1/sqrt(R22(x,y));%signal attenuation in the ground
      Tz12(x,y)=R12(x,y)/Vras; %Sensor Delay Time
```

```
    Tz22(x,y)=R22(x,y)/Vras;%sensor delay time
(top wheel)
            for i=1:max(size(G))
            %Latency
            Ti12 = Tz12(x,y)+T2(y)+tzo(i);
            Ti22 = Tz22(x,y)+T2(y)+tzo(i);
            S2=(Z12*Am*exp(-(t-
Ti12).^2/(2*tau^2)))+S2(1,:);%Right Wheel Envelope
            %Aplut Spectrum
            B22=abs(fft(S2));%Fourier transform.
f1=fd*(0:(M-1))/M;%Set the frequency domain f
(For S2) end
    end end    figure
plot(f1,B22),title('Aplite spectrum from a uniform comb') xlabel('f(Hz)'), ylabel('B(t)');
  figure plot(t,S2), grid, title('Modulated signal from a uniform comb') xlabel('t(c)'), ylabel('S(t)');
  figure subplot(2,2,1); plot(t,S), grid, title('Modulated signal from an uneven comb') xlabel('t(c)'), ylabel('S(t)');
                subplot(2,2,3); plot(t,B2),title('Consistent filtering for non-uniform comb') xlabel('t(c)'),
                ylabel('B(t)');
subplot(2,2,2); plot(t,S2), grid, title('Modulated signal from a uniform comb') xlabel('t(c)'), ylabel('S(t)');
subplot(2,2,4); plot(t,B22),title('Apliteal spectrum from a uniform comb')
xlabel('f(Hz)'), ylabel('B(f)');
```

References

1. Martyushev, N.V.; Malozyomov, B.V.; Kukartsev, V.V.; Gozbenko, V.E.; Konyukhov, V.Y.; Mikhalev, A.S.; Kukartsev, V.A.; Tynchenko, Y.A. Determination of the Reliability of Urban Electric Transport Running Autonomously through Diagnostic Parameters. *World Electr. Veh. J.* **2023**, *14*, 334. [CrossRef]
2. Zhang, H.; Feng, J.; Shi, Q. Fatigue Damage in Asphalt Pavement Based on Axle Load Spectra and Temperature Variation. *Coatings* **2023**, *14*, 882. [CrossRef]
3. Kumar, A.; Suman, S.K. Effects of overloaded commercial traffic on pavement surface layer. *Intell. Transp. Infrastruct.* **2023**, *1*, 55–68. [CrossRef]
4. Filina, O.A.; Martyushev, N.V.; Malozyomov, B.V.; Tynchenko, V.S.; Kukartsev, V.A.; Bashmur, K.A.; Pavlov, P.P.; Panfilova, T.A. Increasing the Efficiency of Diagnostics in the Brush-Commutator Assembly of a Direct Current Electric Motor. *Energies* **2024**, *17*, 17. [CrossRef]
5. Malozyomov, B.V.; Martyushev, N.V.; Kukartsev, V.V.; Konyukhov, V.Y.; Oparina, T.A.; Sevryugina, N.S.; Gozbenko, V.E.; Kondratiev, V.V. Determination of the Performance Characteristics of a Traction Battery in an Electric Vehicle. *World Electr. Veh. J.* **2024**, *15*, 64. [CrossRef]
6. Gajda, J.; Burnos, P.; Sroka, R. Accuracy Assessment of Weigh-in-Motion Systems for Vehicle's Direct Enforcement. *IEEE Intell. Transp. Syst. Mag.* **2018**, *10*, 88–94. [CrossRef]
7. Jacob, B.; Cottineau, L.-M. Weigh-in-Motion for Direct Enforcement of Overloaded Commercial Vehicles. *Transp. Res. Procedia* **2016**, *14*, 1423–1432. [CrossRef]
8. Burnos, P.; Gajda, J. Thermal Property Analysis of Axle Load Sensors for Weighing Vehicles in Weigh-in-Motion System. *Sensors* **2016**, *16*, 2143. [CrossRef]
9. Meli, E.; Pugi, L. Preliminary development, simulation and validation of a weigh in motion system for railway vehicles. *Meccanica* **2024**, *48*, 2541–2565. [CrossRef]
10. Masud, M.M.; Haider, S.W.; Selezneva, O.; Wolf, D.J. Representative Weigh-In-Motion (WIM) System Accuracy and Guidelines for Equipment Selection Based on Sensor, Site, and Calibration-Related Factors. *Int. J. Pavement Res. Technol.* **2024**, *17*, 732–749. [CrossRef]
11. Malozyomov, B.V.; Martyushev, N.V.; Sorokova, S.N.; Efremenkov, E.A.; Valuev, D.V.; Qi, M. Mathematical Modelling of Traction Equipment Parameters of Electric Cargo Trucks. *Mathematics* **2024**, *12*, 577. [CrossRef]
12. Sil, S. CDMA Technology for Intelligent Transportation Systems. *arXiv* **2007**, arXiv:0705.2084. [CrossRef]
13. Hyun, E.; Jin, Y. Doppler-Spectrum Feature-Based Human–Vehicle Classification Scheme Using Machine Learning for an FMCW Radar Sensor. *Sensors* **2020**, *20*, 2001. [CrossRef]

14. Kim, J.; Park, B.-j.; Kim, J. Empirical Analysis of Autonomous Vehicle's LiDAR Detection Performance Degradation for Actual Road Driving in Rain and Fog. *Sensors* **2023**, *23*, 2972. [CrossRef]
15. Wang, H.; Quan, W.; Wang, Y.; Miller, G.R. Dual Roadside Seismic Sensor for Moving Road Vehicle Detection and Characterization. *Sensors* **2014**, *14*, 2892–2910. [CrossRef]
16. Tian, Y. Target Detection and Classification Using Seismic Signal Processing in Unattended Ground Sensor Systems. Ph.D. Thesis, University of Tennessee, Knoxville, TN, USA, 2001.
17. Jin, G. Vehicle Classification Based on Seismic Signatures with Weighted Intrinsic Mode Functions. *arXiv* **2019**, arXiv:1902.09981. [CrossRef]
18. Morozov, Y.V.; Raifel'd, M.A.; Spektor, A.A. Seismic Signal Processing for Estimating the Path of a Moving Vehicle. *Optoelectron. Instrum. Data Process.* **2018**, *54*, 237–242. [CrossRef]
19. Draayer, E.; Stracuzzi, D.; Ulmer, C.; McMahon, N. Pattern-of-Life Activity Recognition in Seismic Data. *Appl. Artif. Intell.* **2022**, *36*, 2057400. [CrossRef]
20. Wang, H.; Quan, W.; Liu, X.; Zhang, S. A Two Seismic Sensor Based Approach for Moving Vehicle Detection. *Procedia Soc. Behav. Sci.* **2013**, *96*, 2647–2653. [CrossRef]
21. Christensen, M.G.; Jensen, J.R.; Benesty, J.; Jakobsson, A. Spatio-Temporal Filtering Methods for Enhancement and Separation of Speech Signals. In Proceedings of the 2013 IEEE China Summit and International Conference on Signal and Information Processing (ChinaSIP), Beijing, China, 6–10 July 2013; pp. 303–307. [CrossRef]
22. Zhang, H.; Pan, Z.; Zhang, W. Acoustic–Seismic Mixed Feature Extraction Based on Wavelet Transform for Vehicle Classification in Wireless Sensor Networks. *Sensors* **2018**, *18*, 1862. [CrossRef]
23. Jin, G.; Ye, B.; Wu, Y.; Qu, F. Vehicle Classification Based on Seismic Signatures Using Convolutional Neural Network. *IEEE Geosci. Remote Sens. Lett.* **2018**, *99*, 1–5. [CrossRef]
24. Sun, Y.; Qian, D.; Zheng, J.; Liu, Y.; Liu, C. Seismic Signal Analysis Based on Variational Mode Decomposition and Hilbert Transform for Ground Intrusion Activity Classification. *Sensors* **2023**, *23*, 3674. [CrossRef] [PubMed]
25. Huang, J.; Zhou, Q.; Zhang, X.; Song, E.; Li, B.; Yuan, X. Seismic Target Classification Using a Wavelet Packet Manifold in Unattended Ground Sensors Systems. *Sensors* **2013**, *13*, 8534–8550. [CrossRef]
26. Sunu, J.; Percus, A.G. Dimensionality Reduction for Acoustic Vehicle Classification with Spectral Embedding. *arXiv* **2017**, arXiv:1705.09869.
27. Zhang, S.-Y.; Xue, X.; Zhang, X. Feature Extraction and Classification with Wavelet Transform and Support Vector Machines. In Proceedings of the 2005 IEEE International Geoscience and Remote Sensing Symposium (IGARSS), Seoul, Republic of Korea, 25–29 July 2005; pp. 3795–3798. [CrossRef]
28. Ahmad, A.B.; Tsuji, T. Traffic Monitoring System Based on Deep Learning and Seismometer Data. *Appl. Sci.* **2021**, *11*, 4590. [CrossRef]
29. Ertuncay, D.; de Lorenzo, A.; Costa, G. Deep Learning Based Earthquake and Vehicle Detection Algorithm. *J. Seismol.* **2025**, *29*, 269–281. [CrossRef]
30. Birnie, C.; Hansteen, F. Bidirectional Recurrent Neural Networks for Seismic Event Detection. *arXiv* **2020**, arXiv:2012.03009. [CrossRef]
31. Xing, K.; Wang, N.; Wang, W. A Ground Moving Target Detection Method for Seismic and Sound Sensor Based on Evolutionary Neural Networks. *Appl. Sci.* **2022**, *12*, 9343. [CrossRef]
32. Liu, G.; Kong, X.; Liu, H. Research on Vehicle Detection and Classification Algorithm Based on Wireless Sensor Networks. *J. China Precis. Instrum.* **2010**, *29*, 9–12. [CrossRef]
33. Ruder, S. An overview of gradient descent optimization algorithms. *arXiv* **2016**. [CrossRef]
34. Chen, X.; Yin, J.; Tang, K.; Tian, Y.; Sun, J. Vehicle Trajectory Reconstruction at Signalized Intersections Under Connected and Automated Vehicle Environment. *IEEE Trans. Intell. Transp. Syst.* **2022**, *23*, 17986–18000. [CrossRef]
35. Hostettler, R.; Birk, W.; Nordenvaad, M.L. Extended Kalman Filter for Vehicle Tracking Using Road Surface Vibration Measurements. In Proceedings of the 2012 IEEE 51st Conference on Decision and Control (CDC), Maui, HI, USA, 10–13 December 2012; pp. 5643–5648. [CrossRef]
36. Wong, J.N.; Yoon, D.J.; Schoellig, A.P.; Barfoot, T.D. Variational Inference with Parameter Learning Applied to Vehicle Trajectory Estimation. *IEEE Robot. Autom. Lett.* **2020**, *5*, 5291–5298. [CrossRef]
37. Koysuren, K.; Keles, A.F.; Cakmakci, M. Online Parameter Estimation Using Physics-Informed Deep Learning for Vehicle Stability Algorithms. In Proceedings of the 2023 American Control Conference (ACC), San Diego, CA, USA, 31 May–2 June 2023; pp. 466–471. [CrossRef]
38. Balid, W.; Refai, H.H. Real-Time Magnetic Length-Based Vehicle Classification: Case Study for Inductive Loops and Wireless Magnetometer Sensors in Oklahoma State. *Transp. Res. Rec.* **2018**, *2672*, 102–111. [CrossRef]
39. Evans, J.; Waterson, B.; Hamilton, A. Evolution and Future of Urban Road Incident Detection Algorithms. *J. Transp. Eng. Part A Syst.* **2020**, *146*, 04020036. [CrossRef]

40. Martyushev, N.V.; Malozyomov, B.V.; Demin, A.Y.; Pogrebnoy, A.V.; Efremenkov, E.A.; Valuev, D.V.; Boltrushevich, A.E. Modeling the Reliability of an Electric Car Battery While Changing Its Charging and Discharge Characteristics. *Mathematics* **2025**, *13*, 1832. [CrossRef]
41. Corera, I.; Piñeiro, E.; Navallas, J.; Sagues, M.; Loayssa, A. Long-Range Traffic Monitoring Based on Pulse-Compression Distributed Acoustic Sensing and Advanced Vehicle Tracking and Classification Algorithm. *Sensors* **2023**, *23*, 3127. [CrossRef]
42. Malozyomov, B.V.; Martyushev, N.V.; Demin, A.Y.; Pogrebnoy, A.V.; Efremenkov, E.A.; Valuev, D.V.; Boltrushevich, A.E. Improving the Reliability of Current Collectors in Electric Vehicles. *Mathematics* **2025**, *13*, 2022. [CrossRef]
43. Ahmad, A.B.; Saibi, H.; Belkacem, A.N.; Tsuji, T. Vehicle Auto-Classification Using Machine Learning Algorithms Based on Seismic Fingerprinting. *Computers* **2022**, *11*, 148. [CrossRef]
44. Taheri, A.; O'Brien, E.J.; Collop, A.C. Pavement Damage Model Incorporating Vehicle Dynamics and a 3D Pavement Surface. *Int. J. Pavement Eng.* **2012**, *13*, 374–383. [CrossRef]
45. Ma, R.; Zhang, Z.; Dong, Y.; Pan, Y. Deep Learning Based Vehicle Detection and Classification Methodology Using Strain Sensors under Bridge Deck. *Sensors* **2020**, *20*, 5051. [CrossRef]
46. Iqbal, N.; Masood, M.; Nasir, A.A.; Qureshi, K.K. Review of Contemporary Energy Harvesting Techniques and Their Feasibility in Wireless Geophones. *Int. J. Energy Res.* **2022**, *46*, 5703–5730. [CrossRef]
47. Sharma, N.; Kumar, A.; Singh, B.; Gupta, A. Detection of Various Vehicles Using Wireless Seismic Sensor Network. In Proceedings of the International Conference on Advances in Mobile Network, Communication and Its Applications (MNCAPPS), Bangalore, India, 1–2 August 2012; pp. 37–41. [CrossRef]
48. Wang, X.; Shen, S.; Huang, H.; Zhang, Z. Quantitative Assessment of the Pavement Modulus and Surface Crack using the Rayleigh Wave Dispersion Curve. *Transp. Res. Rec.* **2020**, *2674*, 259–269. [CrossRef]
49. Birgin, H.B.; Laflamme, S.; D'Alessandro, A.; Garcia-Macias, E.; Ubertini, F. A Weigh-In-Motion Characterization Algorithm for Smart Pavements Based on Conductive Cementitious Materials. *Sensors* **2020**, *20*, 659. [CrossRef] [PubMed]
50. O'Brien, E.; Žnidarič, A.; Ojio, T. Bridge Weigh-In-Motion—Latest Developments and Applications Worldwide. In Proceedings of the International Conference on Heavy Vehicles, Paris, France, 19–22 May 2008.
51. Rys, D. Investigation of Weigh-In-Motion Measurement Accuracy on the Basis of Steering Axle Load Spectra. *Sensors* **2019**, *19*, 3272. [CrossRef]
52. *ASTM E1318-09*; Standard Specification for Highway Weigh-In-Motion (WIM) Systems with User Requirements and Test Methods. ASTM International: West Conshohocken, PA, USA, 2009.
53. *GOST 32348-2013*; Automobile Roads. Weigh-In-Motion of Vehicles. General Technical Requirements. Standartinform: Moscow, Russia, 2013.

mathematics

MDPI

Article

The Effects of Shear Stress Memory and Variable Viscosity on Viscous Fluids Flowing Between Two Horizontal Parallel Plates

Dumitru Vieru [1,2,*], Constantin Fetecau [3] and Zulkhibri Ismail [4]

1 Department of Mathematics, Saveetha School of Engineering, Saveetha Institute of Medical and Technical Sciences, Saveetha University, Chennai 602105, Tamil Nadu, India
2 Department of Theoretical Mechanics, Technical University of Iasi, 700050 Iasi, Romania
3 Academy of Romanian Scientists, 3 Ilfov, 050044 Bucharest, Romania; fetecau@math.tuiasi.ro
4 Centre for Mathematical Sciences, College of Computing and Applied Sciences, Universiti Malaysia Pahang Al-Sultan Abdullah, Lebuh Persiaran Tun Khalil Yaacob, Kuantan 26300, Pahang, Malaysia; zulkhibri@umpsa.edu.my
* Correspondence: dumitru.vieru@academic.tuiasi.ro or dumitru_vieru@yahoo.com

Abstract

This article investigates a mathematical model with the Caputo derivative for the transient unidirectional flow of an incompressible viscous fluid with pressure-dependent viscosity. The fluid flows in the spatial domain bounded by two parallel plates extended to infinity. The plates translate in their planes with time-dependent velocities, and the fluid adheres to the solid boundaries. The generalization of the model consists of formulating a fractional constitutive equation to introduce the memory effect into the mathematical model. In addition, the fluid's viscosity is assumed to be pressure-dependent. More precisely, in this article, the viscosity is considered a power function of the vertical coordinate of the channel. Analytic solutions of the dimensionless initial and boundary value problems have been determined using the Laplace transform and Bessel equations. The inversion of Laplace transforms is conducted using both the methods of complex analysis and the Stehfest numerical algorithm. In addition, we discuss the explicit solution in some meaningful particular cases. Using numerical simulations and graphical representations, the results of the ordinary model ($\alpha = 1$) are compared with those of the fractional model ($0 < \alpha < 1$), highlighting the influence of the memory parameter on fluid behavior.

Keywords: pressure-dependent viscosity; Caputo fractional derivative; analytical solution; Laplace transform

MSC: 76A02; 26A33

1. Introduction

In many fluid flow problems, the influence of gravity must be taken into account. One such example is the Benard convection problem, which exists in important flow problems in geophysics and astrophysics. It is also known that in elastodynamics or in geological fluid flows, the material moduli that characterize the fluid vary significantly with pressure. In such situations, the effects of gravity cannot be ignored a priori. In situations where the pressure range is significant, gravity effects can become pronounced; the pressure will vary along the direction in which gravity acts, and, consequently, the fluid's viscosity will also vary significantly [1]. Since the properties of polymers depend on pressure, problems of processing polymeric materials have been intensively studied [2]. The flow of fluids with pressure-dependent viscosity between two parallel plane plates rotating about axes perpendicular to the plates, taking into account the effect of gravitational acceleration, was studied by Kannan and Rajagopal [3].

Alharbi et al. [4] investigated two-dimensional flows of a fluid with pressure-dependent viscosity through a porous structure with variable permeability. Exact solutions were obtained for a Riabouchinsky-type flow.

Vasudevaiah and Rajagopal [5] analytically studied flows of fluids with pressure-dependent viscosity in a pipe under sufficiently high pressures. The authors showed that the pressure depends logarithmically on the radial coordinate and exponentially on the axial coordinate. Bulicek et al. [6] investigated three-dimensional flows of a class of fluids with pressure- and shear-rate-dependent viscosity. The authors established the existence of a weak solution for the Cauchy problem for flows in unbounded domains. By using the perturbation method, Chen et al. [7] studied the electrokinetic flow of fluids with pressure-dependent viscosity in a nanotube. They found that pressure-dependent viscosity can enhance the magnitude of the streaming potential.

The Hele-Shaw flow of fluids whose viscosity depends on pressure, known as piezo-viscous fluids, near the tip of a sharp edge was investigated by Calusi and Palade [8] by considering both symmetric and antisymmetric two-dimensional flows. Using a procedure based on the method of separation of variables, the authors provided a general procedure to determine the pressure field of piezo-viscous fluids in Hele-Shaw flows.

Housiadas [9] studied the isothermal steady-state and pressure-driven flows of a Maxwell fluid in a straight channel and a circular tube under the assumption that the shear viscosity and the relaxation time of the fluid vary exponentially with pressure. Analytical solutions for the pressure and velocity fields were obtained by using a regular perturbation scheme with the non-dimensional pressure-viscosity coefficient as a small parameter. The author demonstrated that the pressure-dependent viscosity and relaxation time enhance the pressure gradient along the main flow direction, generate another along the wall-normal direction, and cause vertical motion of the fluid.

The mathematical modeling of physical phenomena using fractional calculus is a recent concern of researchers and has interesting applications in the description of viscoelasticity and diffusion problems [10–12]. By generalizing the rheological constitutive equations by replacing the integer derivative with respect to time with the fractional Caputo derivative, the memory formalism is introduced into the studied problem.

Garra and Polito [13] investigated a fractional model for the unidirectional unsteady flow of an incompressible viscous fluid with time-dependent viscosity described by the Riemann–Liouville fractional integral. The authors determined the analytical solution for the fluid velocity and investigated the influence of the memory kernel's fractional order on the fluid motion. The transient flows of incompressible generalized upper-convected Maxwell fluids with pressure-dependent viscosity of exponential form within a rectangular channel were studied by Shah et al. [14]. The authors of this work considered memory effects by generalizing constitutive equations of Maxwell fluids in the form of fractional differential equations with the time-fractional Caputo–Fabrizio derivative. Numerical solutions for the fluid velocity and shear stress are determined using the Stehfest algorithm for the Laplace transform inversion coupled with an appropriate numerical algorithm for the Caputo–Fabrizio time-fractional derivative.

An interesting review of viscoelastic models based on fractional calculus is presented by Mainardi and Spada [15]. They analyzed fractional models in relation to relaxation and creep properties, as well as the variation in fluid viscosity. The authors of reference [15] generalized some classical mechanical models, namely the Kelvin–Voigt model, Maxwell, Zener, anti-Zener, and Burgerssi, and investigated the role of the fractional derivative order in modifying the properties of classical models related to viscosity, creep, and relaxation.

Liu and Jiang [16] developed a time-fractional coupled model to characterize the heat transfer and magneto-hydrodynamic flow of Maxwell fluids with a modified dynamic viscosity and formulated an efficient numerical algorithm suitable for the studied model.

In this paper, we analyze an uncertain unidirectional flow model of an incompressible fluid with pressure-dependent viscosity and examine the influence of stress memory. We primarily consider a generalized constitutive equation of viscous Newtonian fluids by introducing an integro-differential term that characterizes memory effects.

The proposed mathematical model introduces a rheology based on a generalized stress–strain relationship by means of integro-differential Riemann–Liouville and Caputo operators.

The flow domain is a spatial domain bounded by two horizontal, parallel flat plates extended to infinity. Both plates translate in their planes with time-dependent velocities, and the fluid does not slip on the solid boundaries.

The viscosity of the fluid is assumed to be pressure-dependent. More precisely, in this article, we consider the viscosity to be a power function of the channels' vertical coordinate. Analytic solutions of the dimensionless initial and boundary value problems have been determined using the Laplace transform and Bessel equations. The inversion of Laplace transforms is conducted using both the methods of complex analysis and the Stehfest numerical algorithm. In addition, we discuss the explicit solution in some meaningful particular cases.

Using numerical simulations and graphical representations, the results of the ordinary model ($\alpha = 1$) are compared with those of the fractional model ($0 < \alpha < 1$), highlighting the influence of the memory parameter on fluid behavior.

2. Statement of the Problem

An incompressible viscous fluid fills the rectangular domain between two infinitely extended parallel horizontal plates located at distance d from each other. Let $OX_1X_2X_3$ be a Cartesian coordinate system with fundamental unit vectors $\vec{E}_1, \vec{E}_2, \vec{E}_3$. The unit vectors $\vec{E}_1$ and $\vec{E}_2$ are situated in the lower plate located in the plane $X_3 = 0$. The unit vector $\vec{E}_3$ is perpendicular to the two plates. The gravitational acceleration vector is $\vec{g} = -g\vec{E}_3$, and the flow domain is $D = \{(X_1, X_2, X_3), (X_1, X_2) \in R^2, X_3 \in [0, d]\}$.

The Cauchy stress tensor of the viscous fluid studied in this paper is given by [1]

$$\boldsymbol{T} = -\widetilde{p}\boldsymbol{I} + \boldsymbol{\Sigma} = -\widetilde{p}\boldsymbol{I} + \widetilde{\mu}(\widetilde{p})\boldsymbol{A}, \tag{1}$$

where $\widetilde{p}$ is hydrostatic pressure, $\boldsymbol{I}$ is the unit tensor, $\boldsymbol{A} = \nabla\vec{V} + \left(\nabla\vec{V}\right)^T$ is the first Rivlin–Ericksen tensor, and $\vec{V} = V_i(X_1, X_2, X_3, \widetilde{t})\vec{E}_i$, $i = 1, 2, 3$ is the velocity vector field (the summation convention is accepted in our notations).

The function $\widetilde{\mu}(\widetilde{p})$ in Equation (1) is the fluid viscosity, which is dependent on pressure according to the law [1,2]

$$\widetilde{\mu}(\widetilde{p}) = \mu_0[1 + \lambda(\widetilde{p} - p_0)]^n, \ \lambda > 0, \ n \geq 0, \tag{2}$$

where μ_0 is the fluid viscosity at the reference pressure p_0.

The continuity equation and the linear momentum balance are written as [1,6]

$$\frac{\partial V_i}{\partial X_i} = 0,\ i = 1,2,3, \tag{3}$$

$$\rho\left(\frac{\partial V_j}{\partial \tilde{t}} + V_i\frac{\partial V_j}{\partial X_i}\right) = -\frac{\partial \tilde{p}}{\partial X_j} + \frac{\partial \Sigma_{ji}}{\partial X_i} + f_j,\ i,j = 1,2,3, \tag{4}$$

where ρ is the density of the fluid, and $f_1 = 0,\ f_2 = 0,\ f_3 = -\rho g,$ are the body force components.

We search for solutions of (3) and (4) of the form $\vec{V} = \vec{V}(X_3,\ \tilde{t})$, along with the initial and boundary conditions

$$\begin{aligned}&\vec{V}(X_3,0) = 0,\\ &\vec{V}(0,\tilde{t}) = \tilde{f}_0(\tilde{t})\vec{E}_1, \vec{V}(d,\tilde{t}) = \tilde{f}_d(\tilde{t})\vec{E}_1,\ \tilde{t} > 0,\\ &\tilde{p}|_{X_3=d} = p_0,\ \tilde{t} > 0,\end{aligned} \tag{5}$$

where $\tilde{f}_0(\tilde{t})$ and $\tilde{f}_d(\tilde{t})$ are differentiable functions and $\tilde{f}_0(0) = 0, \tilde{f}_1(0) = 0$.

From the above assumptions, it is easy to show that

$$\begin{aligned}&V_1 = V_1(X_3,\tilde{t}),\ V_2 = V_3 = 0,\\ &\tilde{p} = \rho g(d - X_3) + p_0.\end{aligned} \tag{6}$$

Now, the initial-boundary value problem (3)–(5) reduces to

$$\begin{aligned}&\rho\tfrac{\partial V_1(X_3,\tilde{t})}{\partial \tilde{t}} = \tfrac{\partial \Sigma_{13}(X_3,\tilde{t})}{\partial X_3},\\ &\Sigma_{13}(X_3,\tilde{t}) = \tilde{\mu}(\tilde{p})\tfrac{\partial V_1(X_3,\tilde{t})}{\partial X_3},\end{aligned} \tag{7}$$

$$\begin{aligned}&V_1(X_3,0) = 0,\ 0 \le X_3 \le d,\\ &V_1(0,\tilde{t}) = \tilde{f}_0(\tilde{t}),\ V_1(d,\tilde{t}) = \tilde{f}_d(\tilde{t}),\ \tilde{t} > 0.\end{aligned} \tag{8}$$

By introducing the dimensionless quantities

$$\begin{aligned}&z = \tfrac{X_3}{d}, u = \tfrac{V_1}{V_0}, t = \tfrac{V_0\tilde{t}}{d}, p = \tfrac{\tilde{p}-p_0}{\rho d g} = 1 - z, \tau = \tfrac{d\Sigma_{13}}{\mu_0 V_0},\\ &Re = \tfrac{\rho d V_0}{\mu_0}, f_0(t) = \tilde{f}_0(dt/V_0), f_1(t) = \tilde{f}_d(dt/V_0),\end{aligned} \tag{9}$$

into Equations (7) and (8), we obtain the following dimensionless equations for the problem:

$$\begin{aligned}&Re\tfrac{\partial u(z,t)}{\partial t} = \tfrac{\partial \tau(z,t)}{\partial z},\ \tau(z,t) = \mu(z)\tfrac{\partial u(z,t)}{\partial z},\\ &u(z,0) = 0,\ 0 \le z \le 1,\\ &u(0,t) = f_0(t),\ u(1,t) = f_1(t),\\ &\mu(z) = [\beta(1-z) + 1]^n.\end{aligned} \tag{10}$$

In the above relations, V_0 is the characteristic velocity, and Re is the Reynolds number and $\beta = \lambda\rho g d$.

Generalized Fractional Mathematical Model

Let us consider the mathematical model with the dimensional constitutive equation given by the following fractional differential equation:

$$\Sigma_{13}(X_3,\tilde{t}) = \tilde{\mu}(\tilde{p})\sigma_0^{1-\alpha}\,{}^{C}\mathcal{D}_{\tilde{t}}^{1-\alpha}\frac{\partial V_1(X_3,\tilde{t})}{\partial X_3},\ 0 < \alpha \le 1, \tag{11}$$

where σ_0 is a material coefficient with the dimension of time and the differential operator ${}^{C}\mathcal{D}_{\tilde{t}}^{\alpha}\varphi(X_3,\tilde{t})$ means the time-fractional Caputo derivative operator defined by [17,18]

$$ {}^{C}\mathcal{D}_{\tilde{t}}^{\alpha}\varphi(X_3,\tilde{t}) = \begin{cases} \frac{\tilde{t}^{-\alpha}}{\Gamma(1-\alpha)} * \frac{\partial\varphi(X_3,\tilde{t})}{\partial\tilde{t}},\ 0 \leq \alpha < 1,\ \tilde{t} > 0, \\ \frac{\partial\varphi(X_3,\tilde{t})}{\partial\tilde{t}},\ \alpha = 1,\ \tilde{t} > 0. \end{cases} \tag{12} $$

The symbol "$*$" signifies the convolution product.

The scaling coefficient σ_0 was introduced to ensure the dimensional homogeneity of Equation (11).

The nondimensional form of the constitutive Equation (11) is

$$ \tau(z,t) = \sigma^{1-\alpha}\mu(z)^{C}\mathcal{D}_{t}^{1-\alpha}\frac{\partial u(z,t)}{\partial z},\ 0 < \alpha \leq 1, \tag{13} $$

where $\sigma = \frac{V_0\sigma_0}{d}$.

The differential operator in Equation (13) can be written in the following equivalent form:

$$ {}^{C}\mathcal{D}_{t}^{\alpha}\varphi(z,t) = \int_0^t \frac{(t-s)^{-\alpha}}{\Gamma(1-\alpha)}\frac{\partial\varphi(z,s)}{\partial s}ds,\ \ 0 < \alpha < 1, t > 0. \tag{14} $$

Let us recall that the integral fractional operator is defined by

$$ I_t^{\alpha}\varphi(z,t) = \frac{t^{\alpha-1}}{\Gamma(\alpha)} * \varphi(z,t) = \frac{1}{\Gamma(\alpha)}\int_0^t (t-s)^{\alpha-1}\varphi(z,s)ds,\ \alpha > 0,\ t > 0. \tag{15} $$

The Laplace transforms of convolutions (13) and (15) are

$$ \begin{aligned} &L\{{}^{C}\mathcal{D}_{t}^{\alpha}\varphi(z,t)\}(q) = q^{\alpha}L\{\varphi(z,t)\} - q^{\alpha-1}\varphi(z,0),\ 0 < \alpha \leq 1, \\ &L\{I_t^{\alpha}\varphi(z,t)\}(q) = q^{-\alpha}L\{\varphi(z,t)\},\ \alpha > 0, \end{aligned} \tag{16} $$

where $L\{\varphi(z,t)\} = \int_0^{\infty}\varphi(z,t)\exp(-qt)dt = \widehat{\varphi}(z,q)$ is the Laplace transform of the function $\varphi(z,t)$, and q is the Laplace parameter.

Let us note that for $\alpha = 0$ and $\varphi(z,0) = 0$, the derivative defined by Equation (14) represents the function itself. Therefore, in the case of $\alpha = 1$, the generalized constitutive Equation (13) reduces to the ordinary constitutive Equation $(10)_2$.

Using relations (13)–(16), it is easy to show that the following properties are true:

$$ \begin{aligned} &I_t^{\alpha}\left({}^{C}\mathcal{D}_{t}^{\alpha}\varphi(z,t)\right) = \varphi(z,t) - \varphi(z,0), \\ &I_t^{1-\alpha}\left(\frac{\partial\varphi(z,t)}{\partial t}\right) = {}^{C}\mathcal{D}_{t}^{\alpha}\varphi(z,t). \end{aligned} \tag{17} $$

By using (13), the constitutive Equation (12) can be written in the following equivalent form:

$$ \tau(z,t) = \frac{\sigma^{1-\alpha}}{\Gamma(\alpha)}\mu(z)\int_0^t (t-s)^{\alpha-1}\frac{\partial^2 u(z,s)}{\partial z\partial s}ds,\ 0 < \alpha \leq 1. \tag{18} $$

The constitutive equation considered in this article describes a process in which the history of the velocity gradient in the interval (0, t) influences the stress state from the moment t.

The first to consider a constitutive equation in which the stress is influenced by the history of velocity was Gerasimov [19] and he studied viscoelastic flows between two plates. An interesting discussion about the equation proposed by Gerasimov is made by Rogosin and Mainardi (see [20], Equations (10) and (11)).

On the other hand, fractional equations similar to the one proposed by us in this article can be found in articles that analyze processes by anomalous diffusion (for example [21], Equations (10.205), (10.209)).

Equation (18) clearly highlights the difference between the ordinary fluid model and the generalized model. In the ordinary model, the shear stress values at a fixed time t are given by the values of the velocity gradient, whereas in the generalized model, the shear stress values are determined not only by the velocity gradient but also by its history. The power memory kernel damps the values of the velocity gradient up to time t.

3. Solutions to the Problem

3.1. Solution of the Fractional Model

In this section, we will determine the solution of Equations $(10)_1$ and (12), along with the initial and boundary conditions $(10)_3$ and $(10)_4$.

By inserting (12) into Equation $(10)_1$, we obtain the fractional differential equation

$$Re\frac{\partial u(z,t)}{\partial t} = \frac{\partial}{\partial z}\left(\mu(z)^C\mathcal{D}_t^{1-\alpha}\frac{\partial u(z,t)}{\partial z}\right). \tag{19}$$

Using relation (17), Equation (19) is written in the following equivalent form:

$$Re^C\mathcal{D}_t^{\alpha}u(z,t) = \frac{\partial}{\partial z}\left(\mu(z)\frac{\partial u(z,t)}{\partial z}\right). \tag{20}$$

Applying the Laplace transform to Equation (20) and using formula (15), we obtain that the Laplace transform of the velocity field $u(z,t)$ is the solution of the differential equation

$$\mu(z)\frac{\partial^2\widehat{u}(z,q)}{\partial z^2} + \frac{d\mu(z)}{dz}\frac{\partial\widehat{u}(z,q)}{\partial z} + a(q,\alpha)Re\widehat{u}(r,q) = 0 \tag{21}$$

where $\widehat{u}(z,q)$ is the Laplace transform of the function $u(z,t)$, and $a(q,\alpha) = -q^{\alpha}\sigma^{\alpha-1}$.

In addition, the Laplace transform $\widehat{u}(z,q)$ has to satisfy the boundary conditions

$$\widehat{u}(0,q) = \widehat{f}_0(q),\ \widehat{u}(1,q) = \widehat{f}_1(q). \tag{22}$$

By introducing the function $\mu(z)$ given by Equation (11) into Equation (21), we find the equation for $\widehat{u}(z,q)$:

$$[\beta(1-z)+1]^n\frac{\partial^2\widehat{u}(z,q)}{\partial z^2} - \beta n[\beta(1-z)+1]^{n-1}\frac{\partial\widehat{u}(z,q)}{\partial z} + a(q,\alpha)Re\widehat{u}(z,q) = 0. \tag{23}$$

By inserting the function $\widehat{u}(z,q) = [\beta(1-z)+1]^{\frac{1-n}{2}}\widehat{U}(z,q)$, Equation (23) becomes

$$\begin{gathered}[\beta(1-z)+1]^2\frac{\partial^2\widehat{U}(z,q)}{\partial z^2} - \beta[\beta(1-z)+1]\frac{\partial\widehat{U}(z,q)}{\partial z} + \\ \left[a(q,\alpha)Re[\beta(1-z)+1]^{2-n} - \left(\frac{\beta(n-1)}{2}\right)^2\right]\widehat{U}(z,q) = 0.\end{gathered} \tag{24}$$

3.1.1. The Case of $n \neq 2$

Using the new variable ζ, defined as

$$\zeta = \frac{2\sqrt{a(q,\alpha)Re}}{\beta(2-n)}[\beta(1-z)+1]^{\frac{2-n}{2}} \tag{25}$$

and noting $\widehat{V}(\zeta,q) = \widehat{U}(\zeta^{-1}(z),q)$, Equation (24) becomes

$$\zeta^2\frac{\partial^2\widehat{V}(\zeta,q)}{\partial\zeta^2} + \zeta\frac{\partial\widehat{V}(\zeta,q)}{\partial\zeta} + \left[\zeta^2 - \left(\frac{n-1}{2-n}\right)^2\right]\widehat{V}(\zeta,q) = 0, \tag{26}$$

which is a Bessel equation. The general solution of Equation (26) is given by

$$\widehat{V}(\zeta,q) = A(q)J_v(\zeta) + B(q)Y_v(\zeta), \tag{27}$$

where

$$v = \frac{n-1}{2-n} \tag{28}$$

and $A(q)$, $B(q)$ are integration constants determined from the boundary conditions.

Using (25) and (27), we obtain the Laplace transform of the fluid velocity as

$$\begin{aligned}\widehat{u}(z,q) = [\beta(1-z)+1]^{\frac{1-n}{2}}\Big\{A(q)J_v\Big(b_n(q,\alpha)[\beta(1-z)+1]^{\frac{2-n}{2}}\Big) + \\ B(q)Y_v\Big(b_n(q,\alpha)[\beta(1-z)+1]^{\frac{2-n}{2}}\Big)\Big\},\end{aligned} \tag{29}$$

where

$$b_n(q,\alpha) = \frac{2\sqrt{a(q,\alpha)Re}}{\beta(2-n)} \tag{30}$$

By imposing the boundary conditions (19), the following expressions for the functions $A(q)$ and $B(q)$ are obtained:

$$\begin{aligned} A(q) &= \frac{\widehat{f}_0(q)(\beta+1)^{\frac{n-1}{2}}Y_v(b_n(q,\alpha)) - \widehat{f}_1(q)Y_v(\beta_n b_n(q,\alpha))}{J_v(\beta_n b_n(q,\alpha))Y_v(b_n(q,\alpha)) - J_v(b_n(q,\alpha))Y_v(\beta_n b_n(q,\alpha))}, \\ B(q) &= \frac{-\widehat{f}_0(q)(\beta+1)^{\frac{n-1}{2}}J_v(b_n(q,\alpha)) + \widehat{f}_1(q)J_v(\beta_n b_n(q,\alpha))}{J_v(\beta_n b_n(q,\alpha))Y_v(b_n(q,\alpha)) - J_v(b_n(q,\alpha))Y_v(\beta_n b_n(q,\alpha))}, \; \beta_n = (\beta+1)^{\frac{2-n}{2}}. \end{aligned} \tag{31}$$

To determine the inverse Laplace transform of function (29), we will use the residue theorem in complex analysis. First, using the relations in (31), we write function (29) in the following equivalent form:

$$\begin{aligned} &\widehat{u}(z,q) = h(z)g_n(z)(\beta+1)^{\frac{n-1}{2}}\widehat{f}_0(q)\times \\ &\frac{Y_v(b_n(q,\alpha))J_v(b_n(q,\alpha)g_n(z)) - J_v(b_n(q,\alpha))Y_v(b_n(q,\alpha)g_n(z))}{J_v(\beta_n b_n(q,\alpha))Y_v(b_n(q,\alpha)) - J_v(b_n(q,\alpha))Y_v(\beta_n b_n(q,\alpha))} + \\ &h(z)g_n(z)\widehat{f}_1(q)\times \\ &\frac{J_v(\beta_n b_n(q,\alpha))Y_v(b_n(q,\alpha)g_n(z)) - J_v(b_n(q,\alpha)g_n(z))Y_v(\beta_n b_n(q,\alpha))}{J_v(\beta_n b_n(q,\alpha))Y_v(b_n(q,\alpha)) - J_v(b_n(q,\alpha))Y_v(\beta_n b_n(q,\alpha))}, \end{aligned} \tag{32}$$

where

$$h(z) = [\beta(1-z)+1]^{-1/2}, \; g_n(z) = [\beta(1-z)+1]^{\frac{2-n}{2}}. \tag{33}$$

For each fixed n, $n \neq 2$, we use r_{nk}, $k = 1, 2, \ldots$, to denote the positive roots of the transcendental equation

$$J_v(\beta_n\, r)Y_v(r) - J_v(r))Y_v(\beta_n\, r) = 0. \tag{34}$$

For each fixed value of the index n, we denote by $f_n(r)$ the function defined by $f_n(r) = J_v(\beta_n r)Y_v(r) - J_v(r)Y_v(\beta_n r)$. The $r_{nk}, k = 1, 2, \ldots$ positive roots of this function are determined using the "$root(f_n(r), r, x_{nk}, y_{nk})$" subroutine in the MathCAD 15 software package. In the previous relation (x_{nk}, y_{nk}) is the interval that separates the root r_{nk}.

The poles of the functions

$$\begin{aligned}\widehat{F}_1(z,q) &= \frac{Y_v(b_n(q,\alpha))J_v(b_n(q,\alpha)g_n(z)) - J_v(b_n(q,\alpha))Y_v(b_n(q,\alpha)g_n(z))}{J_v(\beta_n b_n(q,\alpha))Y_v(b_n(q,\alpha)) - J_v(b_n(q,\alpha))Y_v(\beta_n b_n(q,\alpha))} = \frac{\widehat{P}_1(z,q)}{\widehat{A}_0(q)},\\ \widehat{F}_2(z,q) &= \frac{J_v(\beta_n b_n(q,\alpha))Y_v(b_n(q,\alpha)g_n(z)) - J_v(b_n(q,\alpha)g_n(z))Y_v(\beta_n b_n(q,\alpha))}{J_v(\beta_n b_n(q,\alpha))Y_v(b_n(q,\alpha)) - J_v(b_n(q,\alpha))Y_v(\beta_n b_n(q,\alpha))} = \frac{\widehat{P}_2(z,q)}{\widehat{A}_0(q)},\end{aligned} \tag{35}$$

are given by

$$q^{\alpha} = -\frac{\beta^2(2-n)^2 r_{nk}^2}{4Re\sigma^{\alpha-1}}, k = 1, 2, \ldots \tag{36}$$

namely

$$q_{nk} = \left(-\frac{\beta^2(2-n)^2 r_{nk}^2}{4Re\sigma^{\alpha-1}}\right)^{\frac{1}{\alpha}}, k = 1, 2, \ldots \tag{37}$$

The residues of the functions $\widehat{F}_1(z,q)$ and $\widehat{F}_2(z,q)$ in the pole q_{nk}, $k = 1, 2, \ldots$, are given by

$$Res\left(\widehat{F}_j(z,q); q = q_{nk}\right) = \frac{\widehat{P}_j(z,q)}{\frac{d\widehat{A}_0(q)}{dq}} \exp(qt)\Bigg|_{q=q_{nk}}, j = 0, 1;\ k = 1, 2, \ldots \tag{38}$$

By using the formulas [22,23]

$$\begin{aligned}&J_{v-1}(z) - J_{v+1}(z) = 2J_v{}'(z),\ Y_{v-1}(z) - Y_{v+1}(z) = 2Y_v{}'(z),\\ &J_{v-1}(z) + J_{v+1}(z) = \tfrac{2v}{z}J_v(z),\ Y_{v-1}(z) + Y_{v+1}(z) = \tfrac{2}{z}Y_v(z),\ z \neq 0,\\ &J_v(z)Y_{v+1}(z) - J_{v+1}(z)Y_v(z) = \tfrac{-2}{\pi z},\ z \neq 0,\end{aligned} \tag{39}$$

we obtain

$$\frac{d\widehat{A}_0(q)}{dq}\Bigg|_{q=q_{nk}} = \frac{\alpha}{\pi q_{nk}} \frac{(J_v(\beta_n r_{nk}))^2 - (J_v(r_{nk}))^2}{J_v(\beta_n r_{nk})J_v(r_{nk})} \tag{40}$$

The calculations necessary to obtain relation (40) are presented in detail in Appendix A. Therefore,

$$\begin{aligned}Res(\widehat{F}_1(z,q); q = q_{nk}) &= \tfrac{\pi q_{nk}}{\alpha} \tfrac{J_v(\beta_n r_{nk})J_v(r_{nk})\exp(q_{nk}t)}{(J_v(\beta_n r_{nk}))^2 - (J_v(r_{nk}))^2} \times\\ &[Y_v(r_{nk})J_v(r_{nk}g_n(z)) - J_v(r_{nk})Y_v(r_{nk}g_n(z))],\\ Res(\widehat{F}_2(z,q); q = q_{nk}) &= \tfrac{\pi q_{nk}}{\alpha} \tfrac{J_v(\beta_n r_{nk})J_v(r_{nk})\exp(q_{nk}t)}{(J_v(\beta_n r_{nk}))^2 - (J_v(r_{nk}))^2} \times\\ &[J_v(\beta_n r_{nk})Y_v(r_{nk}g_n(z)) - J_v(r_{nk}g_n(z))Y_v(\beta_n r_{nk})].\end{aligned} \tag{41}$$

The inverse Laplace transform of function (32) is given by

$$
\begin{aligned}
u(z,t) = h(z)g_n(z)(\beta+1)^{\frac{n-1}{2}} \sum_{k=1}^{\infty} \frac{\pi q_{nk}}{\alpha} \frac{J_v(\beta_n r_{nk})J_v(r_{nk})f_0(t) * \exp(q_{nk}t)}{(J_v(\beta_n r_{nk}))^2 - (J_v(r_{nk}))^2} \times \\
[Y_v(r_{nk})J_v(r_{nk}g_n(z)) - J_v(r_{nk})Y_v(r_{nk}g_n(z))] + \\
h(z)g_n(z) \sum_{k=1}^{\infty} \frac{\pi q_{nk}}{\alpha} \frac{J_v(\beta_n r_{nk})J_v(r_{nk})f_1(t) * \exp(q_{nk}t)}{(J_v(\beta_n r_{nk}))^2 - (J_v(r_{nk}))^2} \times \\
[J_v(\beta_n r_{nk})Y_v(r_{nk}g_n(z)) - J_v(r_{nk}g_n(z))Y_v(\beta_n r_{nk})].
\end{aligned}
\tag{42}
$$

In the above equation, the notation " $*$ " denotes the convolution operator, namely $\varphi(t) * \psi(t) = \int_0^t \varphi(t-\tau)\psi(\tau)d\tau$.

In the following, we also present a numerical algorithm for determining the values of function (29) in the real domain. Based on the algorithm formulated by Stehfest [24], the values of the inverse Laplace transform of the function $\widehat{u}(z,q)$ are given by the relation

$$
u(z,t) \cong \frac{\ln(2)}{t} \sum_{j=1}^{2p} (-1)^{j+p} \sum_{i=\left[\frac{j+1}{2}\right]}^{\min(j,p)} \frac{i^p (2i)!}{(p-i)!i!(i-1)!(j-1)!(2i-j)!} \widehat{u}\left(z, j\frac{\ln(2)}{t}\right) \tag{43}
$$

where p is a strictly positive integer number, $\min(j,p) = \frac{1}{2}(j+p-|j-p|)$, and $[x]$ denotes the integer part of the real number x.

The values of the $u(z,t)$ function determined with expressions (42) and (43) were used to draw the curves in Figure 1. Very good agreement is observed between the values obtained with the two expressions of velocity $u(z,t)$.

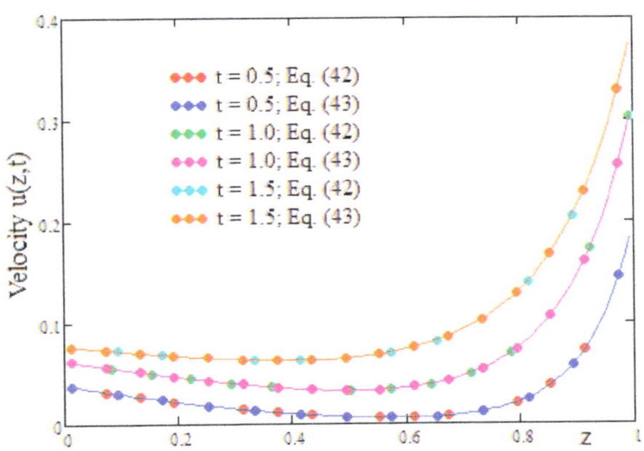

Figure 1. Coincidence of velocity profiles given by Equations (42) and (43) for $n = 3/2$, $\alpha = 1$, $\beta = 5$, Re $= 5$ and $f_0(t) = 0.1(1 - e^{-t})$, $f_1(t) = 0.5(1 - e^{-t})$.

3.1.2. The Case of $n = 2$

For $n = 2$, Equation (20) becomes

$$
[\beta(1-z)+1]^2 \frac{\partial^2 \widehat{u}(z,q)}{\partial z^2} - 2\beta[\beta(1-z)+1]\frac{\partial \widehat{u}(z,q)}{\partial z} + a(q,\alpha)Re\,\widehat{u}(z,q) = 0. \tag{44}
$$

By replacing the variable z with the new variable ξ, defined as

$$\xi = \ln(\beta(1-z)+1), \tag{45}$$

Equation (44) can be written as a differential equation with constant coefficients, namely

$$\frac{\partial^2 \widehat{V}(\xi,q)}{\partial \xi^2} + \frac{\partial \widehat{V}(\xi,q)}{\partial \xi} + \frac{a(q,\alpha)Re}{\beta^2}\widehat{V}(\xi,q) = 0, \tag{46}$$

where $\widehat{V}(\xi,q) = \widehat{u}(\beta^{-1}(\beta+1-\exp(\xi)),q)$.

Integrating Equation (46) and returning to the initial variable, we obtain the general solution of Equation (44), given by

$$\widehat{u}(z,q) = [\beta(1-z)+1]^{-1/2}\left\{C_1(q)[\beta(1-z)+1]^{\varphi(q,\alpha)} + C_2(q)[\beta(1-z)+1]^{-\varphi(q,\alpha)}\right\}, \tag{47}$$

where

$$\varphi(q,\alpha) = \frac{1}{2\beta}\sqrt{\beta^2 - 4a(q,\alpha)Re}. \tag{48}$$

By imposing boundary conditions (19), we find the following integration constants:

$$\begin{aligned} C_1(q,\alpha) &= \frac{\widehat{f}_0(q)(\beta+1)^{\frac{1}{2}} - \widehat{f}_1(q)(\beta+1)^{-\varphi(q,\alpha)}}{(\beta+1)^{\varphi(q,\alpha)} - (\beta+1)^{-\varphi(q,\alpha)}}, \\ C_2(q,\alpha) &= \frac{-\widehat{f}_0(q)(\beta+1)^{\frac{1}{2}} + \widehat{f}_1(q)(\beta+1)^{\varphi(q,\alpha)}}{(\beta+1)^{\varphi(q,\alpha)} - (\beta+1)^{-\varphi(q,\alpha)}}. \end{aligned} \tag{49}$$

Even though the inverse Laplace transform of function (47) could be obtained with the methods of complex analysis, its form is too complicated to be useful for numerical simulations. For this reason, we prefer to perform numerical simulations in this case using the algorithm given by Equation (43).

4. The Particular Case of Ordinary Fluids (The Fractional Parameter $\alpha = 1$)

In this section, we will customize the solutions obtained in the previous section so that we can compare the solutions presented in this article with other previously published solutions for similar problems.

When the α fractional parameter is equal to 1, the generalized constitutive Equation (12) reduces to the ordinary one $(10)_2$. Therefore, our solution (42) becomes

$$\begin{aligned} u(z,t) = {} & \frac{\pi\beta^2(2-n)^2}{4Re}h(z)g_n(z)(\beta+1)^{\frac{n-1}{2}}\sum_{k=1}^{\infty} r_{nk}^2 \frac{J_v(\beta_n r_{nk})J_v(r_{nk})f_0(t) * \exp(q_{nk}t)}{(J_v(r_{nk}))^2 - (J_v(\beta_n r_{nk}))^2} \times \\ & [Y_v(r_{nk})J_v(r_{nk}g_n(z)) - J_v(r_{nk})Y_v(r_{nk}g_n(z))] + \\ & \frac{\pi\beta^2(2-n)^2}{4Re}h(z)g_n(z)\sum_{k=1}^{\infty} r_{nk}^2 \frac{J_v(\beta_n r_{nk})J_v(r_{nk})f_1(t) * \exp(q_{nk}t)}{(J_v(r_{nk}))^2 - (J_v(\beta_n r_{nk}))^2} \times \\ & [J_v(\beta_n r_{nk})Y_v(r_{nk}g_n(z)) - J_v(r_{nk}g_n(z))Y_v(\beta_n r_{nk})], \\ q_{nk} = {} & -\frac{\beta^2(2-n)^2 r_{nk}^2}{4Re}. \end{aligned} \tag{50}$$

The solution given by Equation (50) is equivalent to that obtained by Rajagopal et al. (see [1], Equation (27)).

If $n = 2$, our solution given by Equation (47) is equivalent to those given by Rajagopal et al. (see Equation (30) from [1]) and Fetecau and Agop (see Equations (41) and (42) from [24]).

If the fluid viscosity depends linearly on the pressure, for $n = 1$, our solution given by Equation (50) reduces to that obtained by Fetecau and Bridges (see Equation (37) from [25]).

The curves in Figure 2 were drawn to highlight the equivalence of the solution given by Equation (37) in reference [25] to our solution given by Equation (50) for $n = 1$.

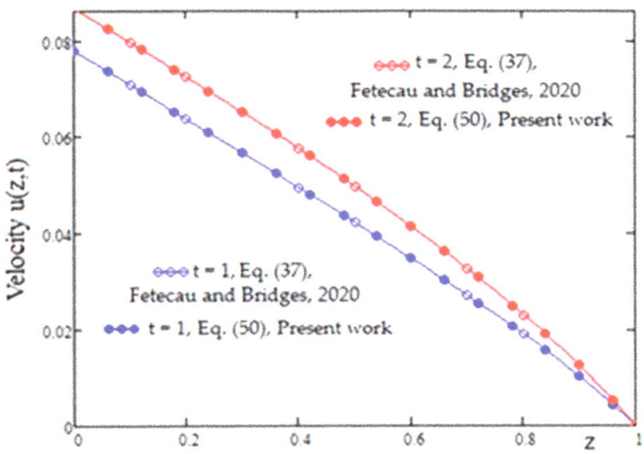

Figure 2. Profiles of the velocity given by Equation (37) in [25] and Equation (50) in the present paper for $n = 1$, $\beta = 2$, $\text{Re} = 5$ and $f_0(t) = 0.1(1 - e^{-t})$, $f_1(t) = 0$.

Let us also specify that if the viscosity depends on the pressure according to the power law with the index $n = 4/3$, then our solution (50) becomes equivalent to that given by Equation (27) in reference [26].

5. Numerical Results and Discussion

In this article, we study the flows of a fluid in a domain determined by two parallel plates extended to infinity under the assumption that the fluid's viscosity depends on pressure as a power function. The plates translate in their planes with time-dependent velocities, and the fluid does not slip on the two plates. A novelty of this article is that we consider a fluid model whose rheological equation includes the shear stress memory phenomenon. The constitutive equation is formulated using the Caputo fractional derivative and has the property that when the α fractional parameter is equal to 1, it reduces to the well-known equation of Newtonian fluids.

Using appropriate transforms of the variable, we showed that for the power function index $n \neq 2$, the differential equation determining the flow velocity is equivalent to a Bessel equation in the Laplace domain. The fluid velocity in the real domain was determined using both analytical methods from complex analysis and the Stehfest algorithm for the numerical inversion of Laplace transforms.

The numerical simulations and graphical representations aimed to highlight the effects of the fractional parameter on fluid behavior. Comparing the results corresponding to the values $0 < \alpha < 1$ with those corresponding to the case $\alpha = 1$ highlights the significant differences between the two rheologies.

Figure 3a,b show contour plots of the velocity u(z,t) when $z \in [0, 1]$ and $t \in [0, 2.5]$ for two values of the fractional parameter α, namely, $\alpha = 0.3$ and $\alpha = 1$. From these two figures, essential differences can be observed in the fluid motion modeled with and without the memory formalism. First, the areas corresponding to the maximum velocity (orange color) are significantly different in the two cases. This happens because the kernel of the fractional derivative damps the velocity gradient.

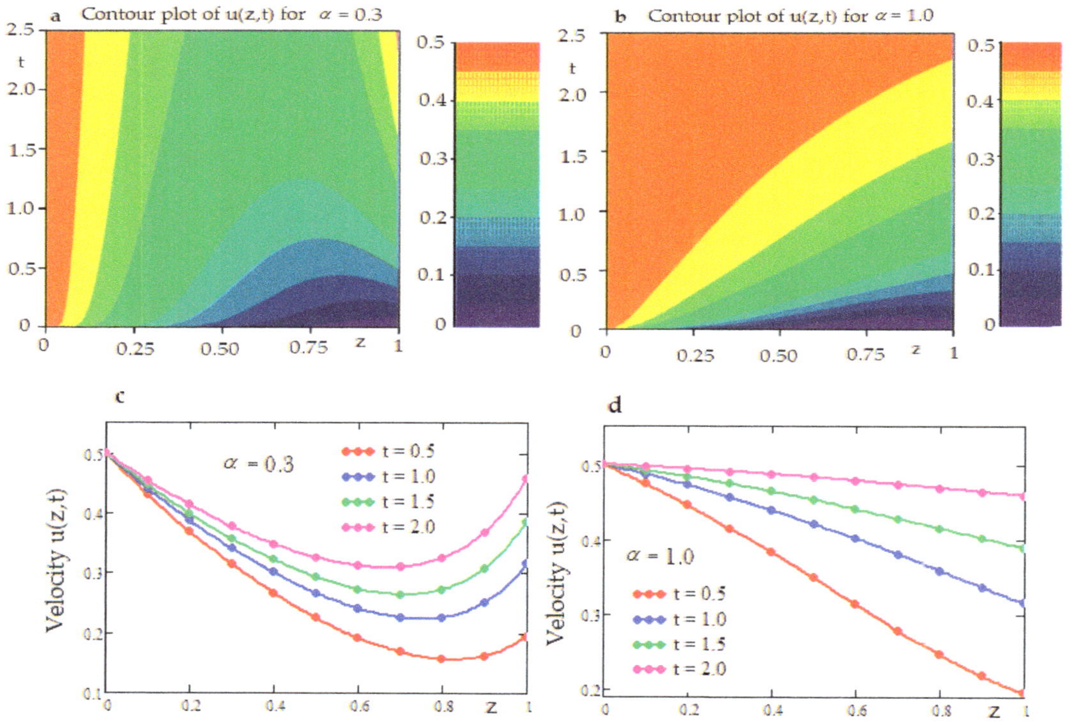

Figure 3. Contour plot and profiles of velocity $u(z,t)$ for $n = 3/2$, $\beta = 2$, $\mathrm{Re} = 5$, $f_0(t) = 0.5$, $f_1(t) = 0.5(1 - e^{-t})$, $\alpha = 0.3, \sigma = 0.2$, as well as $\alpha = 1$. (**a**) Contour plot of the velocity u(z,t) for $\alpha = 0.3$; (**b**) Contour plot of the velocity u(z,t) for $\alpha = 1.0$; (**c**) Velocity profiles for $\alpha = 0.3$; (**d**) Velocity profiles for $\alpha = 1.0$.

Let us mention that the velocities of the two plates considered in our analysis tend to become equal for large values of time t, and therefore, the smoothing of the fluid velocity in the time domain will be achieved. This is evident in Figure 3b. For $t > 2.2$, the fluid velocity is the same at any position in the channel. This smoothing of flow velocity values is delayed by the memory effects introduced by fractional rheology, as seen in Figure 3a.

Figure 3c,d show the velocity profiles $u(z,t)$ at different times for the fractional parameter values $\alpha = 0.3$ and $\alpha = 1$. The curves in these figures show the same properties illustrated by Figure 3a,b. For example, in Figure 3d, the curve corresponding to the time value $t = 2$ is almost parallel to the horizontal axis, while the corresponding curve in Figure 3c does not have this property. The curves in Figure 3d show an attenuation of the fluid velocity compared to those in Figure 3c.

Contour plots and velocity profiles $u(z,t)$ for $z \in [0,1]$, $\alpha \in [0,1]$, and two time t values are shown in Figure 4a–d. As expected, the fluid located in the area close to the plate in the $z = 1$ plane moves very slowly because the velocity of this plate has small values for small time t values. These figures highlight the damping of the fluid motion due to the memory effect.

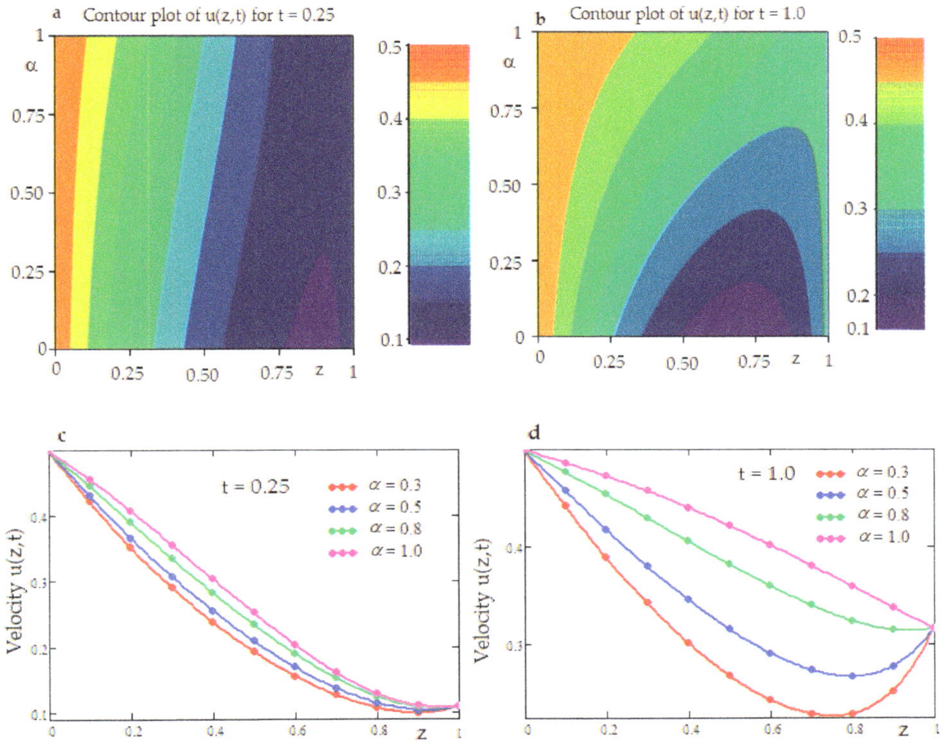

Figure 4. Contour plot and profiles of velocity $u(z,t)$ for $n = 3/2$, $\beta = 2$, Re $= 5$, $f_0(t) = 0.5$, $f_1(t) = 0.5(1 - e^{-t})$, $t = 0.25, \sigma = 0.2$ as well as $t = 1$. (**a**) Contour plot of the velocity u(z,t) for $t = 0.25$; (**b**) Contour plot of the velocity u(z,t) for $t = 1.0$; (**c**) Velocity profiles for $t = 0.25$; (**d**) Velocity profiles for $t = 1.0$.

The curves in Figure 5 were drawn in order to highlight the influence of the β pressure parameter on the fluid velocity. The curves were drawn for the fractional parameter $\alpha = 0.5$ and for three values of time t and of the pressure parameter $\alpha = 0.5$. It can be observed that for the analyzed case, the velocity values increase with the pressure parameter β.

The influence of the power-law index of viscosity on fluid motion is highlighted by the curves in Figure 6. These curves were constructed for two values of the fractional parameter α, namely, $\alpha = 0.3$ and $\alpha = 1$, and for two values of time t, $t = 0.5$ and $t = 0.75$. Increasing the values of the parameter n causes an increase in the values of the fluid velocity for both the fluid with fractional rheology and the Newtonian fluid. As we have seen in the previous figures, the fluid with fractional rheology moves more slowly than the Newtonian fluid. This is because the velocity gradient is damped by the fractional derivative kernel.

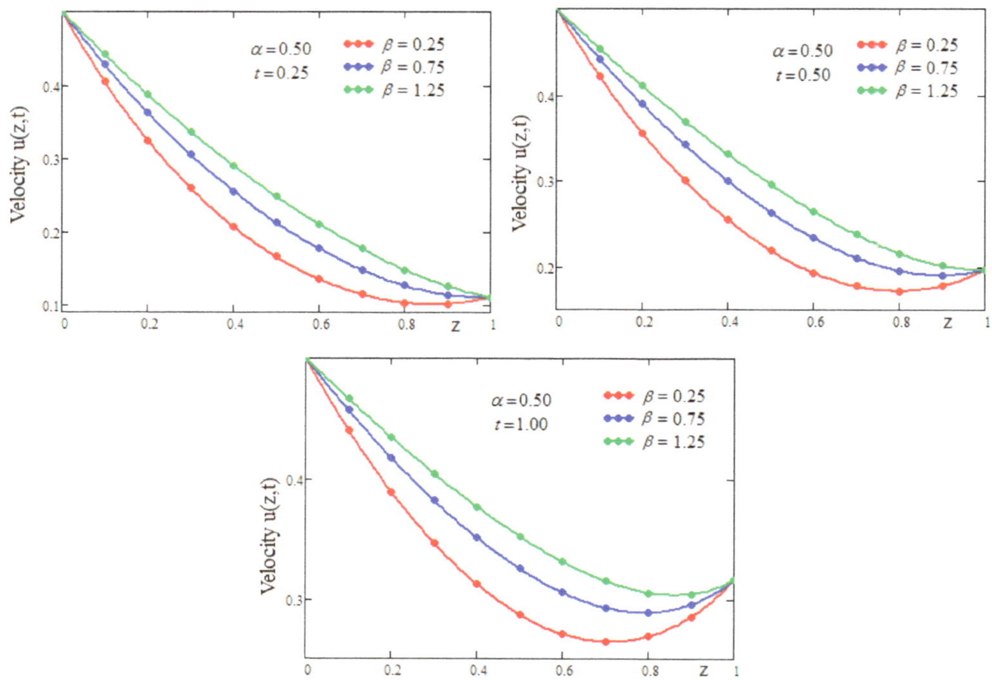

Figure 5. Influence of the β parameter on the fluid velocity for $n = 3/2$, $\alpha = 0.5$, $\text{Re} = 5$, $f_0(t) = 0.5$, $f_1(t) = 0.5(1 - e^{-t})$ and for different values of time t.

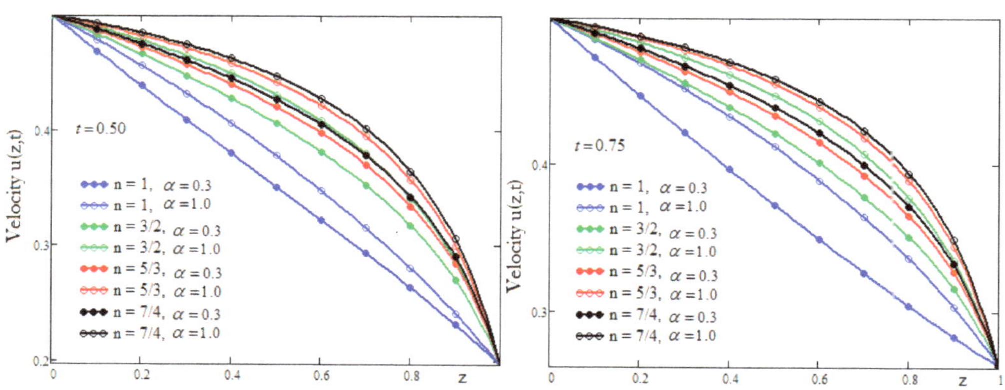

Figure 6. The influence of the n parameter on the fluid velocity for $\beta = 6$, $\text{Re} = 5$, $f_0(t) = 0.5$, $f_1(t) = 0.5(1 - e^{-t})$.

6. Conclusions

This article presents an analytical study of the flow of a fluid with pressure-dependent viscosity in the form of a power law in a rectangular domain using a constitutive equation based on Caputo fractional derivatives.

The mathematical model studied in this paper includes the memory phenomenon in the fluid's behavior.

The analytical solution for the fluid's dimensionless velocity was determined in the general case for the coefficient characterizing the pressure dependence of viscosity.

By particularizing our solution, we were able to compare it with previously published solutions for a Newtonian fluid.

The fluid with fractional rheology moves more slowly than the Newtonian fluid. This is because in the considered rheological model, the kernel of the fractional derivative plays an essential role in damping the velocity gradient.

Author Contributions: Conceptualization, D.V. and C.F.; methodology, D.V. and C.F.; software, D.V. and Z.I.; validation, D.V., C.F. and Z.I.; formal analysis, D.V.; investigation, D.V., C.F. and Z.I.; resources, D.V. and Z.I.; data curation, D.V., C.F. and Z.I.; writing—original draft preparation, D.V. and Z.I.; writing—review and editing, D.V., Z.I. and C.F.; visualization, D.V. and Z.I.; supervision, D.V., C.F. and Z.I.; project administration, D.V. All authors have read and agreed to the published version of the manuscript.

Funding: This research received no external funding.

Data Availability Statement: The original contributions presented in this study are included in the article. Further inquiries can be directed to the corresponding author.

Conflicts of Interest: The authors declare no conflicts of interest.

Appendix A

Using the definition of function $\widehat{A}_0(q)$ and first two relation (39), we obtain

$$\left.\frac{d\widehat{A}_0(q)}{dq}\right|_{q=q_{nk}} = \frac{\alpha\beta_n b_n(q,\alpha)}{4q}\{[J_{\nu-1}(\beta_n b_n(q,\alpha))Y_\nu(b_n(q,\alpha)) - J_\nu(b_n(q,\alpha))Y_{\nu-1}(\beta_n b_n(q,\alpha))] -$$
$$[J_{\nu+1}(\beta_n b_n(q,\alpha))Y_\nu(b_n(q,\alpha)) - J_\nu(b_n(q,\alpha))Y_{\nu+1}(\beta_n b_n(q,\alpha))]\}_{q=q_{nk}} +$$
$$\frac{\alpha b_n(q,\alpha)}{4q}\{[J_\nu(\beta_n b_n(q,\alpha))Y_{\nu-1}(b_n(q,\alpha)) - J_{\nu-1}(b_n(q,\alpha))Y_\nu(\beta_n b_n(q,\alpha))] -$$
$$[J_\nu(\beta_n b_n(q,\alpha))Y_{\nu+1}(b_n(q,\alpha)) - J_{\nu+1}(b_n(q,\alpha))Y_\nu(\beta_n b_n(q,\alpha))]\}_{q=q_{nk}}$$

A direct calculation based on the second and third series of relations (39) and on relation (34) leads to the equality

$$\begin{aligned}\left.\frac{d\widehat{A}_0(q)}{dq}\right|_{q=q_{nk}} &= \left.\frac{\alpha\beta_n b_n(q,\alpha)}{4q}\frac{-4J_\nu(b_n(q,\alpha))}{\pi\beta_n b_n(q,\alpha)J_\nu(\beta_n b_n(q,\alpha))}\right|_{q=q_{nk}} + \\ &\left.\frac{\alpha b_n(q,\alpha)}{4q}\frac{4J_\nu(\beta_n b_n(q,\alpha))}{\pi b_n(q,\alpha)J_\nu(b_n(q,\alpha))}\right|_{q=q_{nk}} = \\ &\left.\frac{\alpha}{\pi q}\frac{J_\nu^2(\beta_n b_n(q,\alpha)) - J_\nu^2((q,\alpha))}{J_\nu(\beta_n b_n(q,\alpha))J_\nu(b_n(q,\alpha))}\right|_{q=q_{nk}}\end{aligned} \tag{A1}$$

References

1. Rajagopal, K.R.; Saccomandi, G.; Vergori, L. Unsteady flows of fluids with pressure dependent viscosity. *J. Math. Anal. Appl.* **2013**, *404*, 362–372. [CrossRef]
2. Jones Parry, E.; Tabor, D. Pressure dependence of the shear modulus of various polymers. *J. Mater. Sci.* **1974**, *9*, 289–292. [CrossRef]
3. Kannan, K.; Rajagopal, K.R. Flows of fluids with pressure dependent viscosities between rotating parallel plates. In *New Trends in Mathematical Physics*; Fergola, P., Gentile, M., Eds.; World Scientific: Singapore, 2005.
4. Alharbi, S.O.; Alderson, T.L.; Hamdan, M.H. Riabouchinsky flow of a pressure-dependent viscosity fluid in porous media. *Asian J. Appl. Sci.* **2016**, *4*, 637–651.
5. Vasudevaiah, M.; Rajagopal, K.R. On fully developed flows of fluids with a pressure dependent viscosity in a pipe. *Appl. Math.* **2005**, *50*, 341–353. [CrossRef]
6. Bulicek, M.; Majdoub, M.; Malek, J. Unsteady flows of fluids with pressure dependent viscosity in unbounded domains. *Nonlinear Anal. Real World Appl.* **2010**, *11*, 3968–3983. [CrossRef]

7. Chen, X.; Jian, Y.; Xie, Z. Electrokinetic flow of fluids with pressure dependent viscosity in a nanotube. *Phys. Fluids.* **2021**, *33*, 122002. [CrossRef]
8. Calusi, B.; Palade, L.I. Modeling of a fluid with pressure-dependent viscosity in Hele-Shaw flow. *Modelling* **2024**, *5*, 1490–1504. [CrossRef]
9. Housiadas, K.D. Internal viscoelastic flows for fluids with exponential type pressure-dependent viscosity and relaxation time. *J. Rheol.* **2015**, *59*, 769–791. [CrossRef]
10. Mainardi, F. *Fractional Calculus and Waves in Linear Viscoelasticity: An Introduction to Mathematical Models*; World Scientific: Singapore, 2010. [CrossRef]
11. Hristov, J. New perspectives of the Lambert-Widder transform: Singular non-local operators with exponential memory. *Progr. Fract. Differ. Appl.* **2025**, *11*, 547–584. [CrossRef]
12. Hristov, J. Constitutive fractional modeling. In *Mathematical Modeling: Principle and Theory*; Dutta, H., Ed.; AMS Series Contemporary Mathematics; AMS Publication: Providence, RI, USA, 2023; Volume 786, pp. 37–140. [CrossRef]
13. Garra, R.; Polito, F. Fractional calculus modelling for unsteady unidirectional flow of incompressible fluids with time-dependent viscosity. *Commun. Nonlin. Sci. Numer. Simul.* **2012**, *17*, 5073–5078. [CrossRef]
14. Shah, N.A.; Chung, J.D.; Vieru, D.; Fetecau, C. Unsteady flows of Maxwell fluids with shear rate memory and pressure-dependent viscosity in a rectangular channel. *Chaos Solitons Fractals* **2021**, *148*, 111078. [CrossRef]
15. Mainardi, F.; Spada, G. Creep, relaxation and viscosity properties for basic fractional models in rheology. *Eur. Phys. J. Special Topics* **2011**, *193*, 133–160. [CrossRef]
16. Liu, Y.; Jiang, M. Magnetohydrodynamic analysis and fast calculation for fractional Maxwell fluid with adjusted dynamic viscosity. *Magnetochemistry* **2024**, *10*, 72. [CrossRef]
17. Kilbas, A.A.; Srivastava, H.M.; Trujillo, J.J. Theory and Applications of Fractional Differential Equations. *North Holl. Math. Stud.* **2006**, *204*, 1–523.
18. Sikora, B. Remarks on the Caputo fractional derivative. *MINUT* **2023**, *5*, 76–84.
19. Gerasimov, A. Generalization of linear laws of deformation and its application to problems with internal friction. *Prikl. Math. I Mekhanika* **1948**, *12*, 251–260. (In Russian)
20. Rogosin, S.; Mainardi, F. George William Scott Blair-the pioneer of fractional calculus in rheology. *Comm. Appl. Ind. Math.* **2014**, *6*, e681. [CrossRef]
21. Hristov, J. Derivatives with non-singular kernels from the Caputo-Fabrizio definition and beyond: Appraising analysis with emphasis on diffusion models. In *Frontiers in Fractional Calculus*; Bhalekar, S., Ed.; Bentham Science Publishers: Oak Park, IL, USA, 2017; Volume I, pp. 270–342. [CrossRef]
22. Watson, G.N. *A Treatise on the Theory of Bessel Functions*, 2nd ed.; Cambridge University Press: Cambridge, UK, 1966.
23. Andrews, L.C. *Special Functions of Mathematics for Engineers*, 2nd ed.; McGrawHill: New York, NY, USA, 1992; pp. 237–284.
24. Fetecau, C.; Agop, M. Exact solutions for oscillating motions of some fluids power-law dependence of viscosity on the pressure. *Ann. Acad. Rom. Sci. Ser. Math. Appl.* **2020**, *12*, 295–311. [CrossRef]
25. Fetecau, C.; Bridges, C. Analytical solutions for some unsteady flows of fluids with linear dependence of viscosity on the pressure. *Inverse Probl. Sci. Eng.* **2020**, *29*, 378–395. [CrossRef]
26. Fetecau, C.; Vieru, D. Exact solutions for unsteady motion between parallel plates of some fluids with power-law dependence of viscosity on the pressure. *Appl. Eng. Sci.* **2020**, *1*, 100003. [CrossRef]

mathematics

MDPI

Article

Mathematical Modeling of Light-Powered Self-Adhesion of Peeling Strips via Abrupt Transition

Dali Ge [1,2,*], Shenshen Wei [1] and Yanli Hu [1]

[1] School of Civil Engineering, Anhui Jianzhu University, Hefei 230601, China; ssWay318@stu.ahjzu.edu.cn (S.W.); 23201010201@stu.ahjzu.edu.cn (Y.H.)

[2] CAS Key Laboratory of Mechanical Behavior and Design of Materials, Department of Modern Mechanics, University of Science and Technology of China, Hefei 230026, China

* Correspondence: dalige@ahjzu.edu.cn

Abstract

Self-oscillating systems convert steady external stimuli into sustained motion, enabling diverse applications in robotics, energy absorption, optics, and logic. Inspired by the adhesion–detachment behavior of climbing plants, we propose a novel light-powered self-adhesion oscillator comprising an elastic strip–substrate structure and a weight suspended by a photo-responsive liquid crystal elastomer fiber. By integrating a nonlinear beam deformation model with Dugdale's cohesive model, we develop a nonlinear dynamic framework to describe the self-adhesion behavior of the elastic strip. Quasi-static analysis reveals two distinct operating modes: a static mode and a self-adhesion mode. Under constant light exposure, the liquid crystal elastomer fiber undergoes light-induced contraction, increasing peeling force and triggering a sudden transition from adhesion-on to adhesion-off. Upon entering the adhesion-off state, the fiber recovers its contraction, leading to a sharp return to the adhesion-on state. This cycle sustains a four-stage oscillation: gradual peeling, abrupt adhesion-off, gradual adhering, and abrupt adhesion-on. Furthermore, we identify the critical conditions for initiating self-adhesion and demonstrate effective control over the oscillation period. The system exhibits key advantages including amplitude controllable oscillation, widely tunable frequency, well-defined motion trajectories, and structural simplicity. These characteristics suggest promising potential for applications in self-healing adhesion systems, rescue devices, military engineering, and beyond.

Keywords: interface cohesive; self-oscillation; liquid crystal elastomers; optically responsive; adhesion–detachment mechanism

MSC: 74G05; 74-10; 74F05; 93B52

1. Introduction

Self-sustained oscillations represent a class of persistent, rhythmic dynamics that arise in active matter or engineered structures, powered by a steady external energy source [1–3]. These systems operate without requiring alternating stimuli or discrete triggering signals, depending primarily on continuous power input and built-in regulatory feedback loops [3,4]. Such autonomous operation exhibits inherent stability and often structural simplicity, with the oscillation frequency largely governed by the system's intrinsic parameters rather than the characteristics of the external energy supply [2,3]. Owing to these attributes, self-sustained oscillators are highly promising for a range of technologies including autonomous robotics [5–9], energy dissipators [10–13], matter transport platforms [14], photonic devices [15], and logic gate implementations [16,17].

Considerable research has been directed toward achieving self-sustained oscillations using a range of stimuli-responsive materials, such as thermally sensitive polymers [5,18], hydrogels [19,20], and liquid crystal elastomers (LCEs) [21–27], among others. By building upon these materials, a wide spectrum of self-oscillatory behaviors has been successfully realized. These include bending [28–30], rolling [31], vibrating [32–35], twisting [36,37], expansion and contraction [38–40], swinging [41–44], rocking [45], wobbling [46], tapping [47], toppling [48], ejecting [49], striking [50], Huygens-type synchronization [51], and even hybrid multi-mode motions [52–55]. A fundamental aspect of these rhythmic behaviors is that they often originate from intrinsic nonlinear feedback mechanisms within the material systems. Representative examples include self-shadowing [15,56,57], which enables periodic modulation of stimulus exposure; non-uniform environmental fields with spatial gradients in stimulus intensity [58–61]; and self-regulated field effects involving dynamically controlled energy release cycles or pathways [62,63]. These designed nonlinearities effectively transform a constant external energy supply into continuous periodic motion.

From the perspective of dynamic behavioral characteristics, self-sustained motion exhibits three primary patterns: bifurcation-driven motion around a unique static equilibrium point [29,32], snap-through motion involving transitions between multiple steady states [16,17], and steady-state motion with zero-energy modes [63]. Among these, bistable systems, which utilize their natural bistable characteristics to induce non-equilibrium dynamics, have gained considerable interest in the study of self-sustained oscillations [16,17,64–67]. These systems feature two stable states separated by an energy barrier, which must be overcome for a transition to occur. During the transition, the system may momentarily exhibit instability before settling into the new stable state. Leveraging bistable systems for self-sustained motion offers advantages, including enhanced amplitude regulation due to clearly defined stable states, well-characterized motion profiles governed by transition pathways, and the ability to maintain the system in either an 'on' or 'off' state. Current research explores various bistable structures for oscillation generation, such as elastic membranes undergoing snap-through between concave and convex states under constant pressure [16,17], pH-responsive hydrogels that oscillate between swollen-buckled and complementary configurations [66], bilayer shallow shells shifting between stable equilibrium states under illumination [67], and bistable systems performing complex sequential logic operations through controlled transitions [17].

Indeed, building a self-sustaining system with bistable properties is a complex task, as there are few structural configurations capable of displaying distinct energy barriers, and inducing transitions between these states proves difficult. To address this, nature provides ingenious models where biological systems accomplish effective state transitions through advanced structural or mechanical processes. One such example is climbing plants, such as Boston ivy and common ivy, which use specialized tendrils to attach themselves to rigid surfaces. Under external forces, such as wind, these tendrils may temporarily detach, but upon force reduction, they may reattach [68,69], as illustrated in Figure 1. Inspired by the dynamic adhesion-detachment behavior found in nature, we propose a novel light-powered self-adhesion oscillator consisting of an elastic strip–substrate structure and a weight suspended by a photo-responsive LCE fiber. By introducing a baffle, the peeling strip is prevented from excessive separation, creating two energy barriers between the adhesion-on and adhesion-off states. Under constant light exposure, the contraction of the LCE fiber increases the peeling force that acts on the strip, prompting a rapid transition from the adhesion-on state to the adhesion-off state. In the adhesion-off state, the fiber's length recovery reduces the peeling force, leading to a swift return to the adhesion-on state.

The unexpected self-adhesion cycles, caused by imperfections in the strip detached from the substrate, are reminiscent of the behavior observed in imperfect electronic circuits [70]. This dynamic behavior is also akin to stick-slip systems with hysteresis and magnetic oscillators [71,72]. Additionally, when subjected to external disturbances or considering the dynamics of weight, this self-adhesion oscillator may exhibit chaotic oscillatory behavior or undergo dynamic bifurcations [73–76].

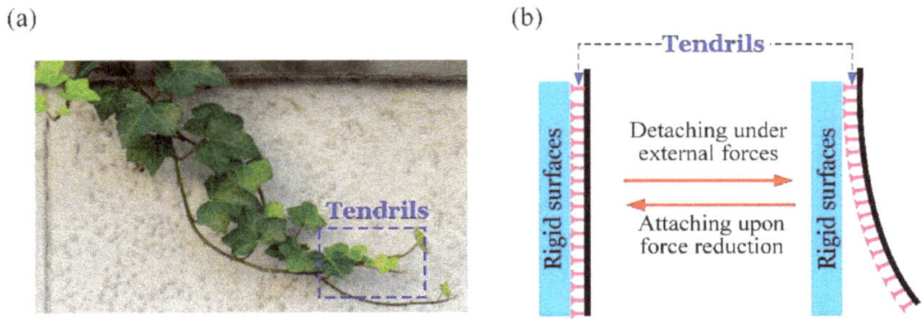

Figure 1. Switchable adhesion between tendrils and rigid surfaces. (**a**) Climbing plants with tendrils. (**b**) Switchable adhesion.

Through quasi-static analysis, we establish a comprehensive dynamic framework to describe the self-adhesion behavior of the elastic strip, and identify two operating modes: static and self-adhesion. This alternating cycle facilitates the self-sustaining oscillation of the system. Thanks to the advantages of mathematical modeling [77], the critical conditions for initiating self-adhesion and controlling the strategy of the oscillation period are explicitly derived. The system offers advantages such as well-defined reversible motion trajectories, broad tunability of the oscillation period, and structural simplicity. We anticipate that this study will encourage the creation of innovative self-sustaining motion patterns and provide foundational insights for applications in self-healing adhesives, search and rescue operations, and military technologies.

The organization of this paper is outlined as follows. Section 2 develops a theoretical model of the light-powered self-adhesion oscillator, combining a nonlinear beam deformation formulation with Dugdale's cohesive zone model. Section 3 analyzes the two motion modes exhibited by the oscillator under steady illumination and elucidates the detailed mechanics of the self-adhesion process. Section 4 establishes the critical conditions required to initiate self-sustained adhesion. Section 5 discusses the influence of key system parameters on the oscillation cycle. Finally, Section 6 concludes the paper with a summary of findings.

2. Theoretical Framework and Governing Equations

This section establishes a theoretical model for a self-adhesion oscillator under constant illumination, including the photo-induced self-adhesion oscillator dynamics, elastic thin-strip peeling behavior, transitions between the adhesion-on and adhesion-off states, and nondimensionalization.

2.1. Model of Photo-Induced Self-Adhesion Oscillator

The structural model of the light-powered self-adhesion oscillator comprises a long strip with thickness h, adhered to a rigid substrate at its top surface, as shown in Figure 2a. A baffle is positioned below the strip at distance b from its right end. A liquid reservoir is positioned beneath the strip, where the liquid surface is at a distance of L_0 from the strip. A suspended weight with length L is attached to the strip's right end via a nematic LCE fiber.

In the reference state, the stress-free LCE fiber has initial length L_0 and uniform alignment of LC mesogens along its axis. For the case where the mass density of the weight exceeds that of the liquid, the weight is submerged in the underlying liquid. It is well-known that under light exposure, photothermal heating progressively increases the temperature of the nematic LCE fiber, leading to a nematic-to-isotropic phase transition, which induces axial contraction. This contraction is fully reversible upon cooling [23–25,78].

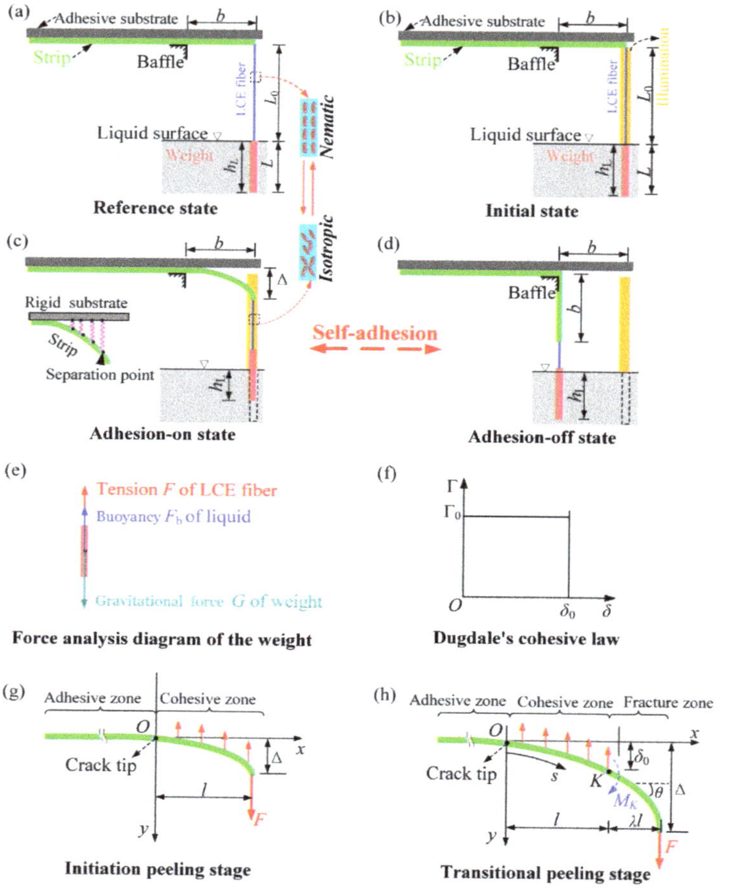

Figure 2. Schematic of the light-powered self-adhesion oscillator: (**a**) reference state; (**b**) initial state; (**c**) adhesion-on state; (**d**) adhesion-off state; (**e**) force analysis diagram of the weight; (**f**) Dugdale's cohesive law; (**g**) initial peeling stage; (**h**) transition peeling stage. Under steady illumination, the peeling strip via abrupt transition displays periodic self-adhesion behavior.

Upon release of the weight, the gravitational force induces the tension of LCE fiber, generating a peeling force on the elastic strip. This peeling force is counteracted by the adhesive force of the substrate, thereby maintaining the strip in an almost fully bonded adhesion-on state. In the initial state, a steady light illuminates a narrow zone near the central plane of the LCE fiber, leaving the rest in darkness, as shown in Figure 2b. Since the LCE fiber in the illuminated zone, contraction along its length occurs. As a result, the weight gradually rises above the liquid surface, leading to a corresponding decrease in buoyancy, thereby increasing the tension of the LCE fiber and the peeling force on the strip. This initiates a gradual separation at the strip-substrate interface, marking the transition toward an adhesion-off state, as shown in Figure 2c. With further contraction of the LCE fiber and an increase in the peeling force on the strip, sudden detachment from the substrate may occur. However, peeling ceases at the baffle position (Figure 2d), marking the adhesion-off state. In this state, the weight submerges deeper, abruptly increasing buoyancy while the LCE fiber moves into the dark zone. Subsequent relaxation of the LCE fiber in darkness further increases submersion depth and buoyancy. This elevated buoyancy reduces both LCE fiber's tension and peeling force, enabling strip reattachment to the substrate due to adhesion—thus re-establishing the adhesion-on state. Accordingly, the LCE fiber moves back to the illuminated zone. Thus, periodic oscillations of the LCE fiber between illumination zones and darkness drive cyclical transitions of the strip between adhesion-on and adhesion-off states, as shown in Figure 2c,d.

During the self-adhesive oscillation of the strip, its right end experiences peeling force F equivalent to the tension of the LCE fiber. For simplicity, the gravity of the LCE fiber is neglected, allowing F to be determined through force analysis on the weight as depicted in Figure 2e. The weight is subjected to three forces: the tension F of LCE fiber, the gravitational force G of weight, and the buoyant force F_b from the liquid. Using a quasi-static analysis method, the peeling force F is determined by the following equation:

$$F = G - F_b, \tag{1}$$

where gravitational force $G = \rho g L$ (ρ is the mass per unit length of weight; g is gravitational acceleration), and buoyant force $F_b = \rho_L g h_L$ (ρ_L denotes the buoyancy coefficient, and h_L is the submerged length of the weight in liquid). Geometrical analysis yields the weight's submerged length h_L through the expression:

$$h_L = L + \Delta - \Delta L_0, \tag{2}$$

in which Δ represents the vertical peeling displacement of the strip, and ΔL_0 is the contraction length of the LCE fiber. It is worth noting that for LCE fiber subjected to both light exposure and tensile loading from a weight, the elastic deformation caused by the tensile force results in a smaller actual shrinkage compared to the deformation caused by photothermal shrinkage alone. However, this discrepancy can be compensated by increasing the actual photothermal shrinkage. Furthermore, if the elastic stiffness of the LCE fiber is sufficiently high, the elastic deformation becomes negligible. For simplicity, this work considers only the photothermal shrinkage of the LCE fiber. Thus, the contraction length of the LCE fiber is calculated as

$$\Delta L_0 = \varepsilon(t) L_0, \tag{3}$$

where $\varepsilon(t)$ denotes the photothermal contraction in the LCE fiber.

Combining Equations (2) and (3), Equation (1) can be rewritten as

$$F = \rho g L - \rho_L g L - \rho_L g \Delta + \rho_L g L_0 \varepsilon(t). \tag{4}$$

It is worth noting that the weight's submerged length must satisfy the condition $0 \le h_L \le L$. When $h_L < 0$, the peeling force F is equal to the gravitational force of the weight, i.e., $F = G$. When $h_L > L$, the peeling force F is determined by the following expression:

$$F = \rho g L - \rho_L g L. \tag{5}$$

Clearly, the peeling force must satisfy $\rho g L - \rho_L g L \le F \le \rho g L$.

As observed from Equation (4), during the adhesion-on state between the strip and substrate, continuous illumination elevates the photothermal contraction of LCE fiber, gradually increasing peeling force F. When F reaches the critical detachment force F_{on} of adhesion-on ($F = F_{\text{on}}$), the system suddenly transitions from adhesion-on to adhesion-off. Conversely, in the adhesion-off state, when peeling force F decreases to the critical attachment force F_{off} of adhesion-off ($F = F_{\text{off}}$), the system suddenly reverts to adhesion-on. Consequently, F_{on} and F_{off} govern the adhesive state transitions between the strip and substrate, which will be calculated subsequently.

2.2. Critical Conditions of Adhesion-On and Adhesion-Off

Progressive interface separation occurs with increasing detachment force. Typically, peeling of an elastic strip from a rigid substrate involves three stages: Initial peeling stage where force increases with displacement until reaching maximum, Transitional peeling stage where force decreases with further displacement [79–82], and Steady-state peeling stage governed by Kendall's model where force remains constant [80–83]. We define the maximum detachment force at the initial-to-transition stage transition as the critical detachment force F_{on}. Conversely during steady-state peeling, reduced detachment force may initiate rapid strip reattachment; thus, we define this steady-state detachment force as the critical attachment force F_{off}.

To compute the critical detachment force, schematics of the initial and transitional peeling stages are presented in Figure 2g,h, respectively. The light-induced contraction and recovery rates of LCE materials are closely related to their thickness. Specifically, the photothermal relaxation process involves a gradual decrease in temperature, resulting in a slow recovery of LCE deformation. Consequently, the strip undergoes a progressive detachment from the initial adhesion-on state to the critical adhesion-on state. Once the detachment force reaches the critical detachment force F_{on} in the adhesion-on state, rapid detachment of the strip may occur. Similarly, the strip undergoes a progressive reattachment from the initial adhesion-off state to the critical adhesion-off state. Once the detachment force reaches the critical attachment force F_{off} in the adhesion-off state, rapid reattachment of the strip may occur. Therefore, a quasi-static detachment force is applied vertically at the right end of the strip in both the adhesion-on and adhesion-off states. During peeling, the strip-substrate interface gradually separates ahead of the peeling front, forming a cohesive zone described by a constant-stress Dugdale cohesive law [84,85] (Figure 2f). Interfacial failure is determined by normal interface separation. According to this cohesive law, interfacial traction Γ and interfacial separation δ relate as follows:

$$\Gamma = \begin{cases} 0, \ \delta = 0 \\ \Gamma_0, \ 0 < \delta \leq \delta_0 \\ 0, \ \delta > \delta_0 \end{cases}, \tag{6}$$

where Γ_0 represents the interfacial strength and δ_0 denotes the critical interfacial separation, at which the interface will completely fail. For constant-stress cohesive law, interface toughness integrates as:

$$G_c = \int_0^{\delta_0} \Gamma \mathrm{d}\delta = \Gamma_0 \delta_0. \tag{7}$$

During the transitional peeling stage, the strip comprises three distinct regions [82,83] (Figure 2h): (1) Left of the interface crack tip exhibiting perfect substrate adhesion; (2) An adjacent cohesive zone of length l at the interface obeying constant-stress cohesive law with uniformly distributed stress; and (3) A remaining interface failure region of length λl devoid of traction. For the peeling strip, a rectangular coordinate system (x, y) describes deformation, with origin O positioned at the interface crack tip and following crack propagation. With a small deformation assumption for the cohesive zone [86], the governing equation of an infinitesimal beam-element is approximately represented as:

$$\frac{d^2y}{dx^2} = \frac{M}{E^*I}, \ 0 \le x \le l, \tag{8}$$

variable y denotes strip's cohesive zone deflection (i.e., interfacial separation), where M is for the strip, and equivalent elastic modulus $E^* = E/(1-v^2)$ with E and v being Young's modulus and Poisson's ratio, respectively.

The bending moment M in Equation (8) can be expressed as

$$M = \begin{cases} F(l + \lambda l - x) - \frac{1}{2}\Gamma_0 (l-x)^2, & 0 < x \le l \\ F(l + \lambda l - x), & l < x \le l + \lambda \end{cases} . \tag{9}$$

For the strip adhered to a rigid substrate (as shown in Figure 2g,h), the strip-substrate interface experiences point contact at the crack tip [82,87], resulting in the following boundary conditions:

$$M(x)|_{x=0} = 0, \cdot \left.\frac{dy}{dx}\right|_{x=0} = 0 \text{ and } y|_{x=0} = 0. \tag{10}$$

Therefore, the cohesive zone length can be obtained

$$F = \frac{\Gamma_0 l}{2(1+\lambda)}, \tag{11}$$

and the cohesive zone deflection can be obtained as follows:

$$y = \frac{1+2\lambda}{12(1+\lambda)E^*I}\Gamma_0 l x^3 - \frac{1}{24E^*I}\Gamma_0 x^4, 0 \le x \le l. \tag{12}$$

From Equation (11), it is evident that the cohesive zone length l depends on both F and λ. Consider the following conditions,

$$y|_{x=l} = \begin{cases} \Delta, & \lambda = 0 \\ \delta_0, & \lambda > 0 \end{cases}, \tag{13}$$

yields to

$$l = \begin{cases} \left(24E^*I\frac{\Delta}{\Gamma_0}\right)^{\frac{1}{4}}, & \lambda = 0 \\ \left(24E^*I\frac{(1+\lambda)\delta_0}{(1+3\lambda)\Gamma_0}\right)^{\frac{1}{4}}, & \lambda > 0 \end{cases} \tag{14}$$

Subsequently, the detachment force F can be determined using Equation (11) as follows:

$$F = \begin{cases} \left(\frac{3E^*I{\Gamma_0}^3}{2}\Delta\right)^{\frac{1}{4}}, & 0 < \Delta \le \delta_0 \ (\lambda = 0) \\ \left(\frac{3E^*I{\Gamma_0}^3}{2(1+\lambda)^3(1+3\lambda)}\delta_0\right)^{\frac{1}{4}}, & \Delta > \delta_0 \ (\lambda > 0) \end{cases} . \tag{15}$$

From Equation (15), Figure 2g,h, it can be observed that during the initial peeling stage, where $0 < \Delta \le \delta_0$ and $\lambda = 0$, the peeling displacement Δ increases monotonically as the detachment force F rises. Once the detachment force F reaches its peak, the transitional peeling stage begins, characterized by $\Delta > \delta_0$ and $\lambda > 0$, where the peeling displacement continues to increase and the length λl of the interfacial failure zone increases [79–81]. Meanwhile, the bending moment M_K ($M_K = F\lambda l$) at the cohesive-fracture interface K increases with the length λl of the failure zone (as shown in Figure 2h), until the peeling angle reaches 90° [80,81]. Eventually, the peeling behavior enters a steady state [81,82].

During the steady-state peeling stage, the peeling displacement Δ increases, while both the length λl and the elastic bending moment M_K remain constant [80]. Therefore, detachment force maximization occurs at $\Delta = \delta_0$ and $\lambda = 0$, and critical detachment force F_{on} can be derived from Equation (15) as:

$$F_{on} = \left(\frac{3E^* I \Gamma_0{}^3 \delta_0}{2}\right)^{\frac{1}{4}}. \tag{16}$$

By substituting Equation (7), Equation (16) can be rewritten as

$$F_{on} = \left(\frac{3E^* I G_c \Gamma_0{}^2}{2}\right)^{\frac{1}{4}}. \tag{17}$$

and the maximum value of the cohesive zone length can be obtained from Equation (14) as:

$$l_{max} = \frac{2}{\Gamma_0}\left(\frac{3E^* I G_c \Gamma_0{}^2}{2}\right)^{\frac{1}{4}}. \tag{18}$$

In the adhesion-on state, as illumination continuously heats the LCE, detachment force F gradually increases until reaching the critical detachment force F_{on}. At this transition point where $F = F_{on}$, the photothermal contraction defines the adhesion-on threshold ε_{on}. When $\varepsilon(t) \geq \varepsilon_{on}$, the strip detaches abruptly from the substrate, causing the system to switch from the adhesion-on to adhesion-off state while the LCE fiber translocates to the dark zone. Notably, this occurs when the strip's vertical peeling displacement satisfies $\Delta = \delta_0$. Solving Equations (5) and (17) yields ε_{on} as:

$$\varepsilon_{on} = \frac{1}{\rho_L L_0}\left[\left(\frac{3E^* I G_c \Gamma_0{}^2}{2}\right)^{\frac{1}{4}} + \rho_L g(L+\delta_0) - \rho g L\right]. \tag{19}$$

It is worth mentioning that several typical constitutive relations of the cohesive zone have been proposed [79]. Generally, deriving explicit solutions for the maximum detachment force F_{on} and the maximum cohesive zone length l_{max} during the initial-to-transition stage is difficult. However, analytical solutions for F_{on} and l_{max} can been obtained for the special cases of Dugdale's constant-stress model and the type I triangular traction-separation law. Considering that the curve shape of the traction-separation relation has a relatively minor impact on interface characterization compared with strength and toughness parameters [79,80], this study employs the Dugdale's cohesive law. For other cohesive zone models (e.g., triangular or exponential forms), the maximum detachment force F_{on} shows a slight decrease [81], but it does not physically change the transition from the adhesion-on state to the adhesion-off state.

For this 90° detachment force in adhesion-off state, variables l, λ and F will remain constant [77,80]. According to the classical Kendall's model [78,82], steady-state detachment force equals interface toughness. Therefore, the critical attachment force F_{on} can be rewritten as:

$$F_{off} = G_c. \tag{20}$$

In the adhesion-off state, the detachment force F persistent reduces due to the LCE cooling in darkness. At this transition point where $F = F_{off}$, the corresponding photothermal contraction defines the adhesion-off threshold ε_{off}. When $\varepsilon(t) \leq \varepsilon_{off}$, the system switches from the adhesion-off state to adhesion-on state, while the LCE fiber moves into the illuminated zone and becomes re-exposed to light. Notably, the vertical peeling displacement Δ at this stage results from the combined action of detachment force and the baffle constraint. For analytical simplicity, Δ is fixed at distance b between the baffle and strip's right end in the reference state ($\Delta = b$). Solving Equations (5) and (17) determines ε_{off} as follows:

$$\varepsilon_{\text{off}} = \frac{1}{\rho_{\text{L}} L_0}[G_c + \rho_{\text{L}} g(L+b) - \rho g L]. \tag{21}$$

2.3. Duration of the Self-Adhesion

The self-adhesion process of the strip is governed by changes in photothermal contraction. This section focuses on the dynamic model of photothermal contraction $\varepsilon(t)$ in the LCE fiber. To simplify, it is assumed that the photothermal contraction is linearly dependent on the temperature difference $T(t)$ in the LCE fiber, i.e.,

$$\varepsilon(t) = CT(t), \tag{22}$$

where C is the photothermal contraction coefficient of the photothermal-responsive LCE material.

Given the fiber's negligible radius, the temperature across the LCE fiber can be considered uniform. Through photothermal conversion, the fiber transforms light illumination into thermal energy at rate q (light intensity). Concurrent heat exchange with the environment exhibits heat flux linearly proportional to $T(t)$. Under illumination, $T(t)$ is governed by:

$$\frac{\mathrm{d}T(t)}{\mathrm{d}t} = \frac{q - kT}{\rho_c}. \tag{23}$$

where k denotes heat transfer coefficient and ρ_c specific heat capacity. Crucially, $T_{\text{Lim}} = q/k$ represents the maximum attainable temperature difference, while $\tau = \rho_c/k$ characterizes the photothermal fiber-environment heat exchange timescale. Larger τ values prolong attainment of T_{Lim}. Thus, Equation (23) is rewritten as follows:

$$\frac{\mathrm{d}T(t)}{\mathrm{d}t} = \frac{T_{\text{Lim}} - T(t)}{\tau}. \tag{24}$$

The temperature difference $T(t)$ can be obtained by solving Equation (24) as:

$$T(t) = T_{\text{Lim}} + (T_0 - T_{\text{Lim}})\exp\left(-\frac{t}{\tau}\right), \tag{25}$$

where T_0 is the temperature difference at the initial moment of exposed to light.

In this work, the LCE fiber alternates between illumination zone and darkness zone. In Case I, where the LCE fiber transitions from the darkness zone to the illumination zone with a transient temperature difference $T_0 = T_{\text{dark}}$, Equation (25) can be simplified to:

$$T(t) = T_{\text{Lim}} + (T_{\text{dark}} - T_{\text{Lim}})\exp\left(-\frac{t_1}{\tau}\right). \tag{26}$$

where t_1 is the duration of exposed to light.

Considering that the instantaneous photothermal contraction for the activation adhesion-on satisfies $\varepsilon = \varepsilon_{\text{off}}$, the transient temperature difference T_{dark} can be derived from Equation (21) and expressed as:

$$T_{\text{dark}} = \frac{1}{C\rho_{\text{L}} L_0}(G_c + \rho_{\text{L}} g(L+b) - \rho g L). \tag{27}$$

The adhesion-off phase is activated when $\varepsilon(t) = \varepsilon_{on}$. Following this, the transient temperature difference T_{illum} for the abrupt transition from adhesion-on to adhesion-off can be derived from Equation (19) and expressed as:

$$T_{illum} = \frac{1}{C\rho_L L_0}\left(\left(\frac{3E^* I G_c {\Gamma_0}^2}{2}\right)^{\frac{1}{4}} + \rho_L g\left(L + \frac{G_c}{\Gamma_0}\right) - \rho g L\right). \quad (28)$$

Therefore, by combining Equations (27) and (28) and setting $T(t) = T_{illum}$ into Equation (26), the solution of t_1 is the total duration t_{on} for adhesion-on state. Thus, t_{on} can be obtained as follows:

$$t_{on} = \tau \ln\left(\frac{T_{Lim} - \frac{1}{C\rho_L L_0}(G_c + \rho_L g(L+b) - \rho g L)}{T_{Lim} - \frac{1}{C\rho_L L_0}\left(\left(\frac{3E^* I G_c}{2}\right)^{\frac{1}{4}} + \rho_L g\left(L + \frac{G_c}{\Gamma_0}\right) - \rho g L\right)}\right). \quad (29)$$

In Case II, where the LCE fiber transitions from the illumination zone to darkness zone. with a transient temperature difference $T_0 = T_{illum}$. Setting $T_{Lim} = 0$, Equation (26) can be simplified to:

$$T(t) = T_{illum} \exp\left(-\frac{t_2}{\tau}\right), \quad (30)$$

where t_2 is the duration of darkness. The adhesion-on phase is activated when $\varepsilon(t) = \varepsilon_{off}$. Therefore, by setting Equation (27) that $T(t) = T_{dark}$ into Equation (30), the solution of t_2 is the total duration t_{off} for adhesion-off state. Thus, t_{off} can be obtained as follows:

$$t_{off} = \tau \ln\left(\frac{\left(\frac{3E^* I G_c {\Gamma_0}^2}{2}\right)^{\frac{1}{4}} + \rho_L g\left(L + \frac{G_c}{\Gamma_0}\right) - \rho g L}{G_c + \rho_L g(L+b) - \rho g L}\right). \quad (31)$$

It is worth mentioning that Equations (25) and (26), respectively, govern the temperature difference evolution of the LCE fiber in the adhesion-on and adhesion-off states. These two distinct evolution behaviors are the underlying cause of the hysteresis effect in the self-adhesion system. When exposed to external disturbances or influenced by the dynamics of weight, this self-adhesion oscillator could display chaotic oscillations or experience dynamic bifurcations.

2.4. Nondimensionalization

For analytical simplification, the following dimensionless quantities are defined: $\overline{t} = t/\tau$, $\overline{t}_{on} = t_{on}/\tau$, $\overline{t}_{off} = t_{off}/\tau$, $\overline{L} = L/h$, $\overline{L}_0 = L_0/h$, $\overline{b} = b/h$, $\overline{\Gamma}_0 = \Gamma_0/(\rho g)$, $\overline{G}_c = G_c/(\rho g h)$, $\overline{E} = E^*/(\rho g)$, $\overline{\rho}_L = \rho_L/\rho$, $\overline{C} = CT_{Lim}$, $\overline{\Delta} = \Delta/h$, $\overline{h}_L = h_L/h$, $\overline{T} = T/T_{Lim}$, $\overline{F} = F/(\rho g h)$, $\overline{F}_{on} = F_{on}/(\rho g h)$ and $\overline{F}_{off} = F_{off}/(\rho g h)$. During the self-adhesion, the dimensionless buoyant force $\overline{F}$ in Equation (5) is re-expressed as

$$\overline{F} = \overline{L} - \overline{\rho}_L(\overline{L} + \overline{\Delta}) + \overline{\rho}_L \overline{L}_0 \varepsilon(\overline{t}), \quad (32)$$

and the dimensionless weight's submerged length $\overline{h}_L$ is

$$\overline{h}_L(\overline{t}) = \overline{L} + \overline{\Delta} - \overline{L}_0 \varepsilon(\overline{t}). \quad (33)$$

The dimensionless vertical peeling displacement $\overline{\Delta}$ under the adhesion-on state in Equation (15) satisfies:

$$\overline{\Delta} = \frac{8\overline{F}^4}{\overline{E}\overline{\Gamma}_0{}^3}, \tag{34}$$

under the adhesion-off state is

$$\overline{\Delta} = \overline{b}, \tag{35}$$

Crucially, the dimensionless submerged length $\overline{h}_{\mathrm{L}}$ must satisfy $0 \leq h_{\mathrm{L}} \leq \overline{L}$, while the dimensionless detachment force $\overline{F}$ is constrained by $(1 - \overline{\rho}_{\mathrm{L}})\overline{L} \leq \overline{F} \leq \overline{L}$.

From Equations (17) and (20), the dimensionless critical detachment force $\overline{F}_{\mathrm{on}}$ and the critical attachment force $\overline{F}_{\mathrm{off}}$ can be given as

$$\overline{F}_{\mathrm{on}} = \left(\frac{\overline{E}\overline{G}_c\overline{\Gamma}_0{}^2}{8}\right)^{\frac{1}{4}}, \tag{36}$$

and

$$\overline{F}_{\mathrm{off}} = \overline{G}_c. \tag{37}$$

From Equations (19) and (21), the critical photothermal contraction of adhesion-on $\varepsilon_{\mathrm{on}}$ and adhesion-off $\varepsilon_{\mathrm{off}}$ are expressed as:

$$\varepsilon_{\mathrm{on}} = \frac{1}{\overline{L}_0\overline{\rho}_{\mathrm{L}}}\left[\left(\frac{\overline{E}\overline{G}_c\overline{\Gamma}_0{}^2}{8}\right)^{\frac{1}{4}} + \overline{\rho}_{\mathrm{L}}\left(\overline{L} + \frac{\overline{G}_c}{\overline{\Gamma}_0}\right) - \overline{L}\right], \tag{38}$$

and

$$\varepsilon_{\mathrm{off}} = \frac{1}{\overline{L}_0\overline{\rho}_{\mathrm{L}}}\left(\overline{G}_c + \overline{\rho}_{\mathrm{L}}\left(\overline{L} + \overline{b}\right) - \overline{L}\right), \text{ respectively.} \tag{39}$$

From Equations (29) and (31), the dimensionless durations $\overline{t}_{\mathrm{on}}$ and $\overline{t}_{\mathrm{off}}$ are expressed as:

$$\overline{t}_{\mathrm{on}} = \ln\left(\frac{1 - \frac{1}{\overline{C}\overline{\rho}_{\mathrm{L}}\overline{L}_0}\left(\overline{G}_c + \overline{\rho}_{\mathrm{L}}\left(\overline{L} + \overline{b}\right) - \overline{L}\right)}{1 - \frac{1}{\overline{C}\overline{\rho}_{\mathrm{L}}\overline{L}_0}\left(\left(\frac{\overline{E}\overline{G}_c\overline{\Gamma}_0{}^2}{8}\right)^{\frac{1}{4}} + \overline{\rho}_{\mathrm{L}}\left(\overline{L} + \frac{\overline{G}}{\overline{\Gamma}_0}\right) - \overline{L}\right)}\right), \tag{40}$$

and

$$\overline{t}_{\mathrm{off}} = \ln\left(\frac{\left(\frac{\overline{E}\overline{G}_c\overline{\Gamma}_0{}^2}{8}\right)^{\frac{1}{4}} + \overline{\rho}_{\mathrm{L}}\left(\overline{L} + \frac{\overline{G}_c}{\overline{\Gamma}_0}\right) - \overline{L}}{\overline{G}_c + \overline{\rho}_{\mathrm{L}}\left(\overline{L} + \overline{b}\right) - \overline{L}}\right), \text{ respectively.} \tag{41}$$

The photothermal contraction in Equation (22) is rewritten as:

$$\varepsilon(\overline{t}) = \overline{C}\overline{T}(\overline{t}), \tag{42}$$

From Equation (24), the dimensionless photothermal temperature difference $\overline{T}(\overline{t})$ for adhesion-on state evolves as follows:

$$\frac{\mathrm{d}\overline{T}(\overline{t})}{\mathrm{d}\overline{t}} = 1 - \overline{T}(\overline{t}). \tag{43}$$

Notably, the maximum attainable temperature difference T_{Lim} is zero for the adhesion-off state. Therefore, the evolution of $\overline{T}(\overline{t})$ for the adhesion-off state is given by:

$$\frac{\mathrm{d}\overline{T}(\overline{t})}{\mathrm{d}\overline{t}} = -\overline{T}(\overline{t}). \tag{44}$$

Under the small deformation assumption for the cohesive zone, the dynamics of the self-adhesion oscillator, which operates in both adhesion-on and adhesion-off states, are described explicitly by Equations (32)–(44). For a specified temperature difference $\overline{T}_{\mathrm{i}}$ at a given time $\overline{t}_{\mathrm{i}}$, the current photothermal contraction $\varepsilon_{\mathrm{Li}}$ of the LCE fiber can be calculated using Equation (41), and the state of the strip is determined using Equations (38) and (39). Subsequently, the temperature difference $\overline{T}_{\mathrm{i+1}}$ at a particular time $\overline{t}_{\mathrm{i+1}}$ can be determined from Equations (43) and (44). Therefore, the dynamics of the self-adhesion oscillator can be derived through iterative computations using the provided parameters: $\overline{C}$, $\overline{\Gamma}_0$, $\overline{G}_c$, $\overline{L}_0$, $\overline{L}$, $\overline{b}$, $\overline{E}$ and $\overline{\rho}_{\mathrm{L}}$.

2.5. Verification by Numerical Solutions

In this section, the accurate peeling model solution is provided to validate the analytical solutions based on the small deformation assumption. The operation of the self-adhesion oscillator results from multiphysics coupling, which includes the adhesion between the strip and substrate, the photothermal contraction and recovery of LCE fiber, the buoyancy of the weight in liquids, and the boundary effects of the baffle. Among these, the peeling process of the strip under the influence of photothermal contraction in LCE fibers is crucial to the study. Therefore, we have incorporated a numerical solution based on an accurate peeling model to examine the effect of photothermal contraction on strip peeling and compared it with the original analytical solution based on the small deformation assumption. To describe the deformation of the strip, a curvilinear coordinate system (s,θ) is introduced, with its origin O located at the interface crack tip and following the direction of crack propagation, as illustrated in Figure 2h. The relationship between the rectangular coordinate system (x,y) and the curvilinear coordinate system (s,θ) can be expressed as follows:

$$\frac{\mathrm{d}\overline{s}}{\mathrm{d}\overline{x}} = \frac{1}{\cos\theta}, \tag{45}$$

$$\frac{\mathrm{d}\overline{y}}{\mathrm{d}\overline{x}} = \tan\theta. \tag{46}$$

where $\overline{s} = s/h$, $\overline{x} = x/h$ and $\overline{y} = y/h$. Considering only the contribution of the bending moment M, the precise governing equation for the strip in relation to M can be expressed as

$$\frac{\mathrm{d}\theta}{\mathrm{d}s} = \frac{M(x)}{E^* I}. \tag{47}$$

Defining $\overline{M} = M/(\rho g h^2)$ and inserting Equation (45), Equation (47) can be rewritten as

$$\frac{\mathrm{d}\theta}{\mathrm{d}\overline{s}} = \frac{12\overline{M}(x)}{\overline{E}\cos\theta}. \tag{48}$$

From Equation (9), the dimensionless elastic bending moment in cohesive zone can be expressed as

$$\overline{M}(\overline{x}) = \overline{F}\left(\overline{l} - \overline{x}\right) - \frac{1}{2}\overline{\Gamma}_0\left(\overline{l} - \overline{x}\right)^2,\ 0 < \overline{x} \le \overline{l}. \tag{49}$$

The end-separation $\overline{\Delta}$ at the strip terminus and the y-axis coordinate can be obtained by solving the following equations:

$$\overline{\Delta} = \int_{0}^{(1+\lambda)\overline{l}} \tan\theta \mathrm{d}\overline{x}. \tag{50}$$

$$\overline{y} = \int_{0}^{\overline{x}} \tan\theta \mathrm{d}\overline{x}. \tag{51}$$

Let $\lambda = 0$, the cohesive zone deflection described in Equation (12), based on the small deformation assumption, can be rewritten as

$$\overline{y} = \frac{2\overline{F}}{\overline{E}}\overline{x}^3 - \frac{\overline{\Gamma}_0}{2\overline{E}}\overline{x}^4, 0 \le \overline{x} \le \frac{2\overline{F}}{\overline{\Gamma}_0}. \tag{52}$$

As shown in Equation (32), the detachment force $\overline{F}$ of the strip depends on both the end-separation $\overline{\Delta}$ and photothermal contraction ε. Meanwhile, $\overline{\Delta}$ in Equation (50) is determined by the solutions of the differential Equations (45)–(47), which involve the unknown parameters $\overline{F}$ and l. Deriving analytical solutions for such a system proves challenging. By incorporating the boundary conditions from Equation (10), numerical methods are employed to derive the results. With the given parameters $\overline{G}_c = 0.6$, $\overline{\Gamma}_0 = 0.8$, $\overline{L}_0 = 20$, $\overline{L} = 5$, $\overline{E} = 1950$ and $\overline{\rho}_{\mathrm{L}} = 0.9$, both analytical and numerical solutions are visualized in Figure 3. Importantly, the analytical solution for the cohesive zone's deflection can be obtained from Equation (52), and the end-separation $\overline{\Delta}$ is derived by solving Equations (34) and (36) simultaneously. As shown in Figure 3a, under the adhesion-on state, part of the strip shows detachment deflection. As the photothermal contraction ε increases gradually, the strip progressively detaches from the substrate, and the end-separation $\overline{\Delta}$ enlarges, as demonstrated in Figure 3b. A comparison between the analytical solutions (derived under the small deformation hypothesis) and the numerical solutions of the precise peeling model reveals a satisfactory level of consistency in the results. However, explicit analytical solutions are more suitable for investigating the dynamics of self-adhesion oscillators. As a result, all subsequent calculations are based on the analytical solutions.

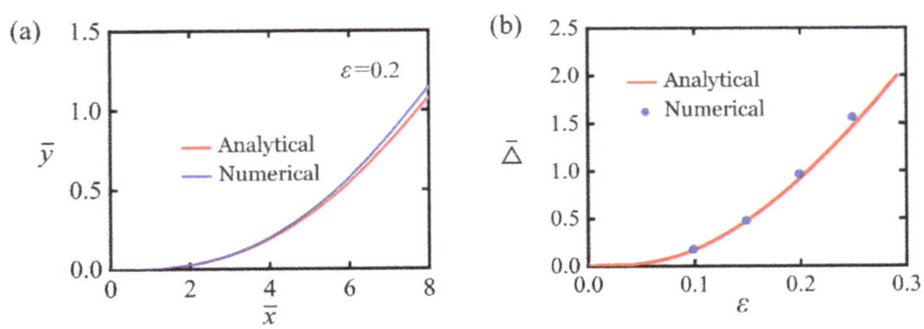

Figure 3. The comparison between analytical solutions and numerical solutions. (**a**) Strip profile for $\varepsilon = 0.2$. (**b**) Variation of $\overline{\Delta}$ with ε. The comparison of the analytical and numerical solutions shows good agreement.

3. Two Motion Modes and Mechanism of Self-Adhesion

This section explores two distinct motion modes of light-powered self-adhesion oscillator—the static mode and the self-adhesion mode—and provides a mechanistic analysis of the self-adhesion phenomenon.

3.1. Two Motion Modes

Equations (32) to (44) govern transitions between adhesion-off and adhesion-on states in the self-adhesion oscillator. To investigate self-adhesion behavior, we establish baseline dimensionless parameters from experimental data [79,82,86,88–95]. Table 1 summarizes typical material properties and geometric parameters, with corresponding dimensionless quantities provided in Table 2. These parameter values are subsequently employed to analyze self-peeling dynamics under steady illumination. It is worth noting that the adhesion parameters between the elastic strip and the adhesive substrate can vary significantly depending on factors such as the molecular type of the selected strip material, the smoothness of the substrate, or the potential use of additional adhesives. Experimental investigations can flexibly adjust these parameters as needed. Additionally, the use of dimensionless system parameters in the model enhances its scalability and broadens its applicability in terms of both material properties and geometric parameters.

Table 1. Material properties and geometric parameters.

Parameter	Definition	Value	Units
L_0	LCE fiber's initial length	0~50	mm
L	Weight's length	0~50	mm
b	Distance of the baffle	0~5	mm
h	Thickness of thin strip	0~5	mm
ρ_L	Buoyancy coefficient	0~0.1	kg/mm^2
ρ	Weight's mass per unit length	0~0.1	kg/mm^2
E	Young's modulus of thin strip	0~50	Mpa
v	Poisson's ratio of thin strip	0.5	
α	Photothermal contraction coefficient	0~0.003	/K
τ	Thermal relaxation time	0~0.1	s
T_{Lim}	Maximum attainable temperature difference	0~200	K
g	Gravitational acceleration	10	m/s^2
Γ_0	Interfacial strength	0~1	Mpa
G_c	Interface toughness	0~10	mJ/mm^2

Table 2. Dimensionless parameters.

Parameter	$\overline{C}$	$\overline{G}_c$	$\overline{\Gamma}_0$	$\overline{L}_0$	$\overline{L}$	$\overline{b}$	$\overline{E}$	$\overline{\rho}_L$
Value	0~0.5	0~2	0~5	0~100	0~50	0~10	0~10,000	0~1

Figure 4 illustrates the dynamic temporal evolution of the light-powered self-adhesion in peeling strip under two distinct motion modes, with specific dimensionless photothermal contraction coefficients $\overline{C}$, interfacial strength $\overline{\Gamma}_0$, and distance $\overline{b}$ of the baffle $\overline{b}$. Characteristic parameters include: $\overline{G}_c = 0.6$, $\overline{L}_0 = 20$, $\overline{L} = 5$, $\overline{E} = 1950$ and $\overline{\rho}_L = 0.9$. Yellow shading indicates illumination zones. For certain values of $\overline{C} = 0.1$, $\overline{\Gamma}_0 = 0.8$ and $\overline{b} = 4$, the weight's submerged length $\overline{h}_L$ consistently decreases in a smooth, monotonic manner toward stabilization. Meanwhile, the strip's vertical peeling displacement $\overline{\Delta}$ reaches a stable equilibrium, remaining in a persistent adhesion-on state, this represents the static mode (Figure 4a,b). In contrast, for other values of $\overline{C} = 0.3$, $\overline{\Gamma}_0 = 0.8$ and $\overline{b} = 4$, weight's submerged length $\overline{h}_L$ first gradually decreases, then suddenly increases, before slowly rising toward a balanced value.

The strip's vertical peeling displacement $\overline{\Delta}$ initially shows a gradual increase, followed by a sharp jump, and finally stabilizes, indicating that the strip eventually rests in the adhesion-off state. This motion mode also falls under the category of a static mode (Figure 4c,d). For further combinations of $\overline{C} = 0.3$, $\overline{\Gamma}_0 = 0.8$ and $\overline{b} = 2$, weight's submerged length $\overline{h}_L$ undergoes phase-locked alternations: a controlled gradual decline → a sharp, abrupt surge → a modulated decline → and a final, sharp drop. The strip's vertical peeling displacement $\overline{\Delta}$ experiences a pronounced cyclic progression: a subtle, gradual increase → a sudden, accelerated surge → a sustained steady-state → followed by a rapid, sharp decline. These autonomous periodic oscillations represent continuous, reversible transitions between adhesion-on and adhesion-off states under constant steady illumination, defining the self-adhesion mode (Figure 4e,f). It is worth noting that Figure 3 presents the theoretical predictions based on Equations (32) to (44). Certain factors in real-world scenarios, which are not considered in the theoretical model, may have a quantitative, rather than qualitative, impact on the results.

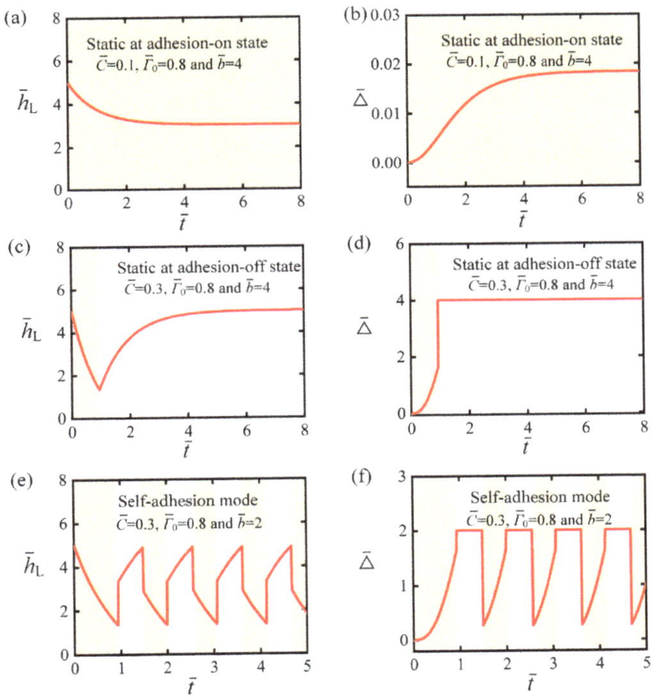

Figure 4. Temporal evolution of the self-adhesion oscillator under two distinct motion modes. Temporal evolution of (**a**) $\overline{h}_L$ and (**b**) $\overline{\Delta}$ for $\overline{C} = 0.1$, $\overline{\Gamma}_0 = 0.8$ and $\overline{b} = 4$. Temporal evolution of (**c**) $\overline{h}_L$ and (**d**) $\overline{\Delta}$ for $\overline{C} = 0.3$, $\overline{\Gamma}_0 = 0.8$ and $\overline{b} = 4$. Temporal evolution of (**e**) $\overline{h}_L$ and (**f**) $\overline{\Delta}$ for $\overline{C} = 0.3$, $\overline{\Gamma}_0 = 0.8$ and $\overline{b} = 2$. Under steady illumination, the self-adhesion oscillator displays two distinct dynamic responses: a static mode and a self-adhesion mode. Yellow shading indicates illumination zones.

It is worth mentioning that energy conversion efficiency is a key indicator of self-oscillating systems. In this work, the energy conversion efficiency can be simply estimated by the ratio of the maximum gravitational potential energy V_p gained by the weight to the light energy E_{Light}. To calculate the light energy within one cycle, the illuminated area is taken as covering the LCE fiber, where the minimum illumination width can be roughly equal to the cross-sectional thickness h_0 of the LCE fiber. Thus, the optical energy released by the light source in one cycle is $E_{\text{Light}} = qh_0L_0(t_{\text{on}} + t_{\text{off}})$, and the increment of the weight's gravitational potential energy is $V_p = \rho g L(L - h_L)$. Consequently, the energy conversion efficiency can be expressed as

$$\eta = \frac{\rho g L(L - h_L)}{q h_0 L_0 (t_{on} + t_{off})} \times 100\%, \tag{53}$$

Referring to the typical values of the self-adhesive system: $h = 5$ mm, $L_0 = 100$ mm, $L = 25$ mm, $h_0 = 1$ mm, $\rho = 0.11$kg/m, $g = 10$ m/s^2, $\tau = 0.1$ s and $q = 10$kW/m^2 and the typical cases in Figure 4e,f, the energy conversion efficiency is estimated to be approximately 1%. However, in real-world scenarios, due to the inability to precisely control the illuminated area, the energy conversion efficiency is lower than the calculated result. Therefore, the light-powered self-adhesion oscillator may not be suitable for scenarios requiring high energy transfer efficiency.

3.2. Mechanism of Self-Adhesion

Previous analysis identified two distinct motion modes for the light-powered self-adhesion of peeling strip: static mode and self-adhesion mode. This section examines the self-adhesion mechanism through typical parameter calculations. Figure 5a displays the temporal evolution of the fiber's photothermal contraction $\varepsilon(\bar{t})$, which exhibits periodic variation under conditions corresponding to Figure 4e,f. Yellow shading indicates illumination zones. When $\varepsilon(\bar{t}) < \varepsilon_{on}$, the LCE remains illuminated while the strip maintains adhesion-on state with the substrate; $\varepsilon(\bar{t})$ evolves continuously from point①to②as detachment force $\bar{F}(\bar{t})$ (Figure 5b) and vertical peeling displacement $\bar{\Delta}$ (Figure 5c) synchronously complete①→② evolution. When $\varepsilon(\bar{t})$ reaches ε_{on}, adhesion-on-to-off transition occurs: $\bar{\Delta}$ abruptly surges ②→③while $\bar{F}(\bar{t})$ drops sharply②→③, displacing the LCE fiber from illumination. Subsequently, $\varepsilon(\bar{t})$ decreases from③→④with corresponding changes in $\bar{F}(\bar{t})$ and $\bar{\Delta}$ (Figure 5b,c). At $\varepsilon(\bar{t}) = \varepsilon_{off}$, the strip re-adhesion initiates: $\bar{\Delta}$ plunges steeply④→①while the LCE fiber re-enters illumination. The clockwise limit cycle (trajectory①→②→③→④→①) confirms periodic self-adhesion under steady illumination (Figure 5d). Figure 6 shows snapshots of the peeling strip during one cycle of self-adhesion. The results indicate that the peeling strip undergoes an abrupt transition between the adhesion-on and adhesion-off states, with the LCE fiber switching between the illuminated and dark zones. The self-adhesion oscillator exhibits periodic self-adhesion behavior.

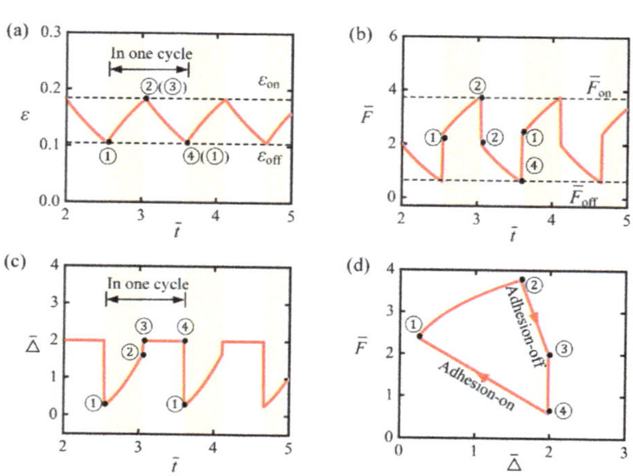

Figure 5. Mechanism of the light-powered self-adhesion in peeling strip. Temporal evolution of **(a)** $\bar{T}(\bar{t})$, **(b)** $\bar{\Delta}$ and **(c)** $\bar{F}(\bar{t})$. **(d)** Limit cycle between $\bar{\Delta}$ and $\bar{F}(\bar{t})$. These factors collectively demonstrate

the self-adhesion dynamics driven by periodic exposure to constant light, coupled with abrupt transitions between the adhesion-on and adhesion-off states. Yellow shading indicates illumination zones.

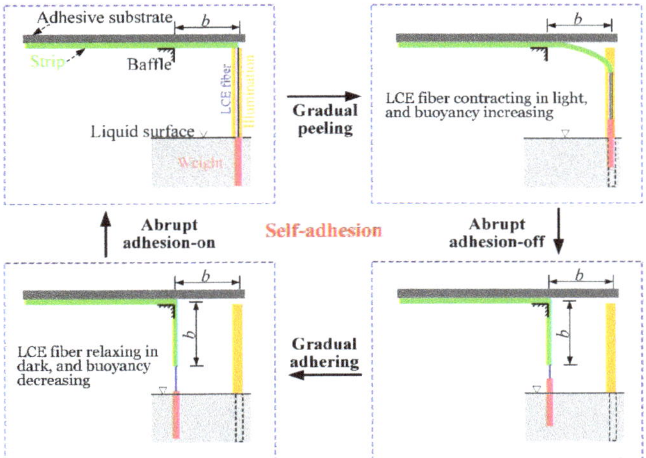

Figure 6. Snapshots of the light-powered self-adhesion oscillator during one cycle of self-adhesion. This cyclic process sustains a four-stage oscillation: gradual peeling, abrupt adhesion-off, gradual adhering, and abrupt adhesion-on.

4. Regulating the Transition Between Adhesion-On and Adhesion-Off States

To better understand the system's dynamic behavior, it is essential to examine how system parameters affect the transition between adhesion-on and adhesion-off states.

4.1. Transition from Adhesion-On to Adhesion-Off

In the adhesion-on state, the LCE fiber is continuously heated and contracted, resulting in an increasing detachment force. From Equation (38), it is evident that the critical photothermal contraction threshold ε_{on} is influenced by six parameters: $\overline{\Gamma}_0$, $\overline{G}_c$, $\overline{E}$, $\overline{\rho}_{\text{L}}$, $\overline{L}_0$ and $\overline{L}$. If the photothermal contraction exceeds the critical threshold, the transition from adhesion-on to adhesion-off can be triggered.

Figure 7 systematically explores parametric variations in $\overline{\Gamma}_0$, $\overline{G}_c$, $\overline{E}$, $\overline{\rho}_{\text{L}}$, $\overline{L}_0$ and $\overline{L}$ on the photothermal contraction threshold ε_{on} required to trigger adhesion-on to adhesion-off transitions. Figure 7a demonstrates the influence of interfacial strength $\overline{\Gamma}_0$ under fixed parameters $\overline{G}_c = 0.6$, $\overline{L}_0 = 20$, $\overline{L} = 5$, $\overline{b} = 2$, $\overline{E} = 1950$ and $\overline{\rho}_{\text{L}} = 0.9$. Results indicate that for interfacial strength $\overline{\Gamma}_0 < 0.73$, the transition from the adhesion-on state to the adhesion-off state cannot be triggered, as the separation between the strip and the substrate has not reached the critical separation distance. As $\overline{\Gamma}_0$ increases, ε_{on} grows monotonically because enhanced adhesion necessitates greater photothermal contraction to: (i) reduce submerged length of the weight and (ii) increase detachment force $\overline{F}$ to the critical detachment force $\overline{F}_{\text{on}}$, thereby enabling state transition from adhesion-on to adhesion-off. At $\overline{\Gamma}_0 \geq 1.83$, this mechanism fails—after full emergence of the weight from the liquid, detachment force plateaus and further $\overline{\Gamma}_0$ increases prevent transitions, locking the system in static mode. Notably, the variation in interface toughness $\overline{G}_c$ with respect to critical contraction threshold ε_{on} follows the same trend as that of interfacial strength $\overline{\Gamma}_0$, as shown in Figure 7b. This similarity arises because both parameters are characteristic of the adhesive strength between the strip and the substrate.

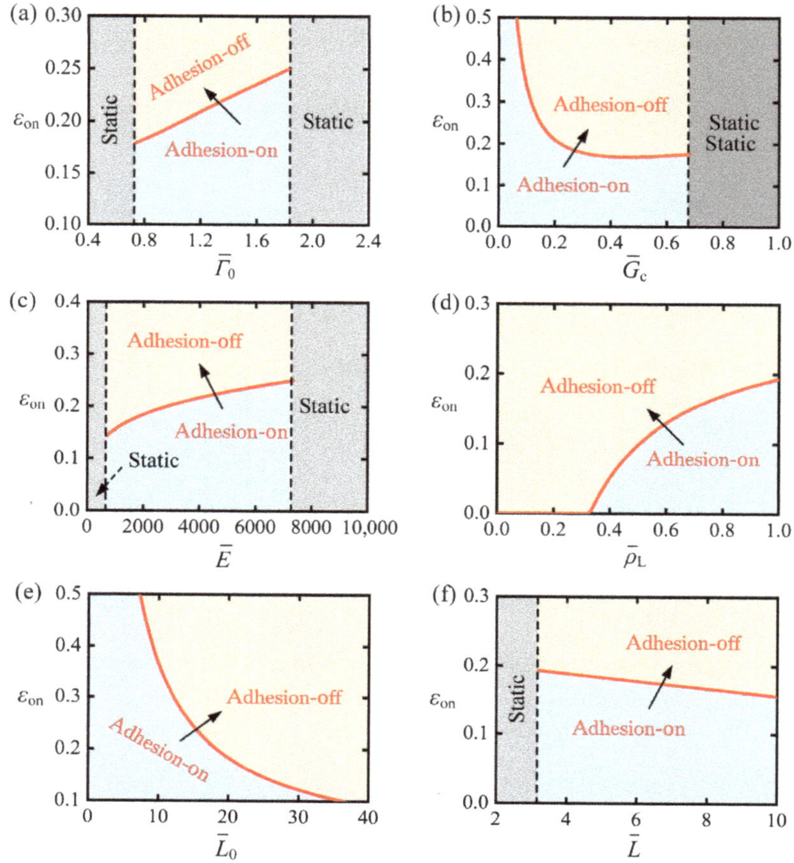

Figure 7. Effect of parameters on the photothermal contraction threshold ε_{on}. (**a**) $\overline{\Gamma}_0$ versus ε_{on}, (**b**) $\overline{G}_c$ versus ε_{on}, (**c**) $\overline{E}$ versus ε_{on}, (**d**) $\overline{\rho}_L$ versus ε_{on}, (**e**) $\overline{L}_0$ versus ε_{on}, (**f**) $\overline{L}$ versus ε_{on}. Analysis reveals ε_{on} increases monotonically with $\overline{\Gamma}_0$, $\overline{G}_c$, $\overline{E}$ and $\overline{\rho}_L$, while decreasing monotonically with $\overline{L}_0$ and $\overline{L}$. Arrow indicates transition from adhesion-on to adhesion-off.

Figure 7c demonstrates the effect of bending stiffness $\overline{E}$ on the photothermal contraction threshold ε_{on} under fixed parameters $\overline{\Gamma}_0 = 0.8$, $\overline{G}_c = 0.6$, $\overline{L}_0 = 20$, $\overline{L} = 5$, $\overline{b} = 2$ and $\overline{\rho}_L = 0.9$. Result indicates that for bending stiffness $\overline{E} < 690$, the transition from the adhesion-on state to the adhesion-off state cannot be triggered, as the separation between the strip and the substrate has not reached the critical separation distance. When $\overline{E} \geq 690$, it exhibits that ε_{on} monotonically increases with increasing $\overline{E}$, as heightened deformation resistance necessitates greater detachment force to induce strip bending sufficient to achieve the critical interfacial separation required for adhesion failure and transition from adhesion-on to adhesion-off state. When $\overline{E} > 7333$, the weight fully emerges from the liquid with maximum detachment force $\overline{F} = \overline{L}$, yet detachment remains unattainable, preventing adhesion state transitions and resulting in permanent static-mode operation.

Figure 7d illustrates the effect of the buoyancy coefficient $\overline{\rho}_L$ on the photothermal contraction threshold ε_{on} under fixed parameters $\overline{\Gamma}_0 = 0.8$, $\overline{G}_c = 0.6$, $\overline{L}_0 = 20$, $\overline{L} = 5$, $\overline{b} = 2$ and $\overline{E} = 1950$. From the figure, it can be observed that when $\overline{\rho}_L \leq 0.324$, $\varepsilon_{on} = 0$. This phenomenon can be explained as follows: for smaller buoyancy coefficients, the minimum detachment force when the weight is fully immersed in the liquid exceeds the critical detachment force $\overline{F}_{\text{on}}$. As a result, regardless of whether the LCE fiber contracts, the transition from the adhesion-on to the adhesion-off state can be triggered. Subsequently, ε_{on} increases monotonically with the increase in $\overline{\rho}_{\text{L}}$. This is because, as the buoyancy coefficient $\overline{\rho}_{\text{L}}$ increases, the buoyant force acting on the weight in the liquid also increases, necessitating a greater contraction of the LCE fiber to lift the weight from the liquid, thereby enhancing the detachment force.

Figure 7e illustrates the effect of the initial length $\overline{L}_0$ of the LCE fiber on the photothermal contraction threshold ε_{on}, with fixed parameters $\overline{\Gamma}_0 = 0.8$, $\overline{G}_c = 0.6$, $\overline{L} = 5$, $\overline{b} = 2$, $\overline{E} = 1950$ and $\overline{\rho}_{\text{L}} = 0.9$. From the figure, it can be observed that as $\overline{L}_0$ increases, ε_{on} decreases monotonically. This is because, in the given strip-substrate system, the critical detachment force $\overline{F}_{\text{on}}$ remains constant. As a result, the total contraction $\Delta\overline{L}_0$ required to trigger the transition from the adhesion-on to the adhesion-off state is fixed. Thereby, increasing $\overline{L}_0$ reduces the demand for the LCE contraction rate, as only the product of the two values needs to meet the total contraction threshold for the transition from adhesion-on to adhesion-off.

Figure 7f demonstrates how weight length $\overline{L}$ influences the photothermal contraction threshold ε_{on}, with fixed parameters $\overline{\Gamma}_0 = 0.8$, $\overline{G}_c = 0.6$, $\overline{L}_0 = 20$, $\overline{b} = 2$, $\overline{E} = 1950$ and $\overline{\rho}_{\text{L}} = 0.9$. For $\overline{L} < 3.24$, the system operates in static mode. This is because a small $\overline{L}$ means that the weight exerts a smaller gravitational force. When the detachment force equals the gravitational force of the weight, it is still less than the critical detachment force $\overline{F}_{\text{on}}$, preventing the transition from the adhesion-on to the adhesion-off state from being triggered. When $\overline{L} \geq 3.24$, ε_{on} decreases monotonically with increasing $\overline{L}$. This inverse relationship arises because constant $\overline{F}_{\text{on}}$ in the strip-substrate system entails that greater gravitational force proportionally amplifies detachment force $\overline{F}$, thereby diminishing the requisite contraction magnitude to achieve critical interfacial separation and activate state switching.

4.2. Transitions from Adhesion-Off to Adhesion-On

In the adhesion-on state, the LCE fiber undergoes continuous cooling and recovery contraction, leading to an increase in the detachment force. According to Equation (39), the critical photothermal contraction threshold ε_{off} is influenced by six parameters: $\overline{\Gamma}_0$, $\overline{G}_c$, $\overline{b}$, $\overline{\rho}_{\text{L}}$, $\overline{L}_0$ and $\overline{L}$. If the photothermal contraction falls below this critical threshold, the system will transition from the adhesion-off to the adhesion-on state.

Figure 8 provides a systematic analysis of how variations in the parameters $\overline{\Gamma}_0$, $\overline{G}_c$, $\overline{E}$, $\overline{\rho}_{\text{L}}$, $\overline{L}_0$ and $\overline{L}$ affect the photothermal contraction threshold ε_{off} required to initiate the transition from adhesion-off to adhesion-on. Figure 8a illustrates the effect of interfacial strength $\overline{\Gamma}_0$ under fixed parameters $\overline{G}_c = 0.6$, $\overline{L}_0 = 20$, $\overline{L} = 5$, $\overline{b} = 2$, $\overline{E} = 1950$ and $\overline{\rho}_{\text{L}} = 0.9$. The results show that the system remains in a static mode for $\overline{\Gamma}_0 < 0.12$. This is because a small $\overline{\Gamma}_0$ implies a weak adhesive force between the strip and the substrate. Even when the LCE fiber fully recovers its contraction, the minimum detachment force still exceeds the critical attachment force $\overline{F}_{\text{off}}$, preventing the system from transitioning from the adhesion-off state to the adhesion-on state. As $\overline{\Gamma}_0$ increases, the photothermal contraction threshold ε_{off} also rises. This is because stronger interfacial strength results in a more robust adhesive force between the strip and the substrate, which in turn increases the $\overline{F}_{\text{off}}$, enabling the LCE strip to transition from adhesion-off to adhesion-on under higher photothermal contraction conditions. It is worth noting that the change in interface toughness $\overline{G}_c$ with respect to the critical contraction threshold ε_{off} follows a similar trend to that of interfacial strength $\overline{\Gamma}_0$, as depicted in Figure 8b. This similarity is due to both parameters being indicative of the adhesive strength between the strip and the substrate.

Figure 8c shows the impact of baffle distance $\overline{b}$ on the photothermal contraction threshold ε_{off} under fixed parameters: $\overline{\Gamma}_0 = 0.8$, $\overline{G}_c = 0.6$, $\overline{L}_0 = 20$, $\overline{L} = 5$, $\overline{E} = 1950$ and $\overline{\rho}_{\text{L}} = 0.9$. The results reveal that the threshold ε_{off} increases monotonically with the baffle distance $\overline{b}$. This trend occurs because an increase in baffle distance $\overline{b}$ corresponds to a longer detachment length of the strip, allowing a greater portion of the weight to immerse in the liquid. As a result, the LCE fiber can achieve the required reduction in contraction recovery, which reduces the detachment force to the critical attachment force. This, in turn, increases the photothermal contraction threshold ε_{off}, enabling the transition from the adhesion-off state back to the adhesion-on state.

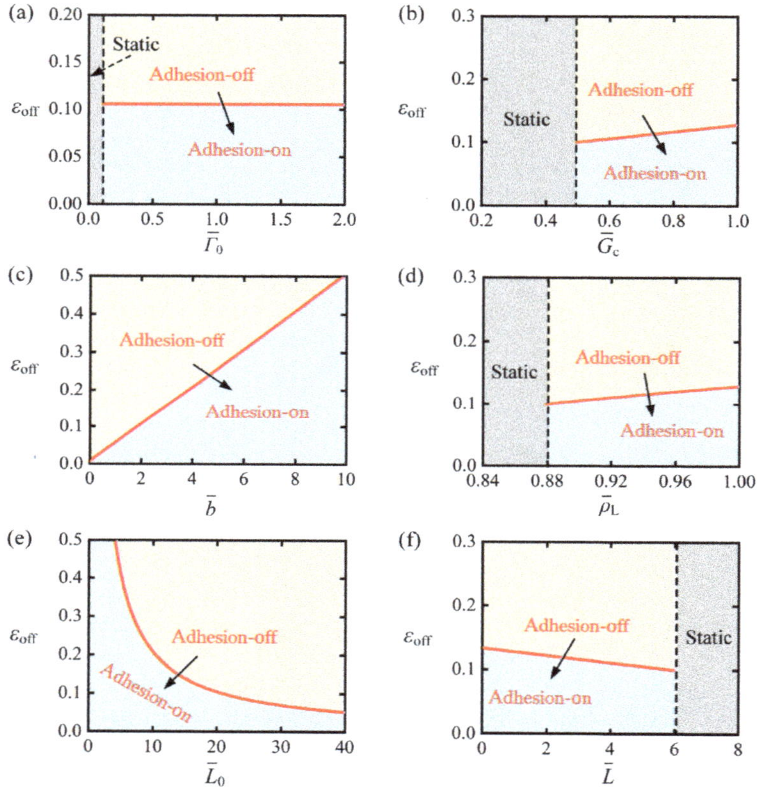

Figure 8. Effect of parameters on the photothermal contraction threshold ε_{off}. (**a**) $\overline{\Gamma}_0$ versus ε_{off}, (**b**) $\overline{G}_c$ versus ε_{off}, (**c**) $\overline{b}$ versus ε_{off}, (**d**) $\overline{\rho}_{\text{L}}$ versus ε_{off}, (**e**) $\overline{L}_0$ versus ε_{off}, (**f**) $\overline{L}$ versus ε_{off}. Analysis reveals ε_{off} increases monotonically with $\overline{\Gamma}_0$, $\overline{G}_c$, $\overline{b}$ and $\overline{\rho}_{\text{L}}$, while decreasing monotonically with $\overline{L}_0$ and $\overline{L}$. Arrow indicates transition from adhesion-off to adhesion-on.

Figure 8d demonstrates the influence of the buoyancy coefficient $\overline{\rho}_{\text{L}}$ on the photothermal contraction threshold ε_{off} under the following fixed parameters: $\overline{\Gamma}_0 = 0.8$, $\overline{G}_c = 0.6$, $\overline{L}_0 = 20$, $\overline{L} = 5$, $\overline{b} = 2$, $\overline{E} = 1950$ and $\overline{\rho}_{\text{L}} = 0.9$. The results reveal that when $\overline{\rho}_{\text{L}} \leq 0.88$, the system maintains a static state. For lower buoyancy coefficients, complete recovery of photothermal contraction causes the minimum detachment force $\overline{F}$, however the minimum detachment force still exceeds the critical attachment force $\overline{F}_{\text{off}}$, preventing transition to the adhesion-on state. When $\overline{\rho}_{\text{L}} > 0.88$, as $\overline{\rho}_{\text{L}}$ increases, ε_{off} shows a corresponding increase. This behavior occurs because at higher buoyancy coefficients $\overline{\rho}_{\text{L}}$, the LCE fiber experiences a more significant reduction in detachment force when recovering the same contraction magnitude. Consequently, the system can maintain larger photothermal contractions while allowing the detachment force to decrease below the critical attachment force $\overline{F}_{\text{off}}$.

Figure 8e demonstrates the relationship between the initial length $\overline{L}_0$ of the LCE fiber and the photothermal contraction threshold ε_{off} under constant parameters: $\overline{\Gamma}_0 = 0.8$, $\overline{G}_c = 0.6$, $\overline{L} = 5$, $\overline{b} = 2$, $\overline{E} = 1950$ and $\overline{\rho}_{\text{L}} = 0.9$. The results exhibit a monotonic decrease in ε_{off} with increasing $\overline{L}_0$, which arises from the system's fixed critical attachment force $\overline{F}_{\text{off}}$ and constant total contraction requirement $\Delta\overline{L}_0$ for state transition in the strip-substrate configuration. Consequently, longer initial fiber lengths require proportionally smaller photothermal contractions to reduce the detachment force to the critical threshold $\overline{F}_{\text{off}}$, as the absolute contraction $\Delta\overline{L}_0$ needed to achieve the adhesion state transition remains unchanged in this system. This inverse proportionality between $\overline{L}_0$ and ε_{off} directly results from the constant critical force condition and fixed displacement requirement governing the interfacial adhesion behavior.

Figure 8f demonstrates the influence of weight length $\overline{L}$ on the photothermal contraction threshold ε_{off} under fixed parameters: $\overline{\Gamma}_0 = 0.8$, $\overline{G}_c = 0.6$, $\overline{L}_0 = 20$, $\overline{b} = 2$, $\overline{E} = 1950$ and $\overline{\rho}_{\text{L}} = 0.9$. The results reveal that ε_{off} decreases monotonically as weight length $\overline{L}$ increases, due to the greater gravitational force exerted by the larger weight, which generates stronger detachment forces on the strip. As a result, the LCE fiber needs to recover more contraction to submerge the weight into the liquid and reduce the detachment force. When $\overline{L}$ exceeds 6, the system enters a static mode. This happens because, for sufficiently heavy weights, the detachment force remains above the critical attachment force $\overline{F}_{\text{off}}$ even after complete photothermal contraction recovery, thus preventing the transition from the adhesion-off to adhesion-on state.

5. Regulation of the Self-Adhesion Period

Next, the self-adhesion period is studied. One cycle of self-adhesion consists of four stages: gradual peeling, abrupt adhesion-off, gradual adhering, and abrupt adhesion-on. Given the negligible duration of the abrupt transition between detachment and attachment relative to the overall cycle period, the self-peeling period $\overline{t}_{\text{p}} = \overline{t}_{\text{on}} + \overline{t}_{\text{off}}$ is defined as the total duration of the adhesion-on and adhesion-off states. By explicitly solving Equations (40) and (41), the self-peeling period can be determined. It is worth noting that, in practical scenarios, the inertia of the strip may reduce the durations of both the adhesion-on and adhesion-off states. Furthermore, the abrupt durations of adhesion-off and adhesion-on are not exactly zero, which may result in a quantitative difference between the self-peeling period in real-world situations and the calculated results in this study. For simplicity, this work only considers the impact of the durations of the adhesion-on and adhesion-off states.

It is evident that the self-peeling period depends on dimensionless parameters such as $\overline{\Gamma}_0$, $\overline{G}_c$, $\overline{E}$, $\overline{\rho}_{\text{L}}$, $\overline{C}$, $\overline{L}_0$, $\overline{L}$ and $\overline{b}$. Notably, $\overline{\Gamma}_0$, $\overline{G}_c$ and $\overline{E}$ represent the adhesion characteristics between the strip and the substrate, while $\overline{\rho}_{\text{L}}$ captures the buoyancy properties of the liquid. Therefore, $\overline{\Gamma}_0$, $\overline{G}_c$, $\overline{E}$ and $\overline{\rho}_{\text{L}}$ are classified as material properties. In contrast, $\overline{C}$, $\overline{L}_0$, $\overline{L}$ and $\overline{b}$ reflect the geometric properties of the system, specifically its length characteristics, and are categorized as geometric parameters. It is worth noting that although $\overline{C}$ represents the deformability of the LCE material, it always acts in conjunction with $\overline{L}_0$, primarily influencing the change in the length of the LCE fiber. Thus, $\overline{C}$ is classified under geometric parameters. The following discussion explores how the self-peeling period varies with the material properties and geometric parameters. It is worth mentioning that Equations (40) and (41) demonstrate that the self-adhesion period is determined by the coupling of system parameters. To focus on qualitatively analyzing the variation in the self-adhesion period, this work examines the effect of individual parameter changes on it.

5.1. Regulation of the Self-Adhesion Period by Material Properties

Figure 9 systematically examines parametric dependence of self-adhesion period $\bar{t}_p$ on material characteristics: $\overline{\Gamma}_0$, $\overline{G}_c$, $\overline{E}$ and $\bar{\rho}_L$. Figure 9a presents the relationship between the self-adhesion period $\bar{t}_p$ and interfacial strength $\overline{\Gamma}_0$ under fixed parameters: $\overline{G}_c = 0.6$, $\overline{E} = 1950$, $\bar{\rho}_L = 0.9$, $\overline{C} = 0.3$, $\overline{L}_0 = 20$, $\overline{L} = 5$ and $\bar{b} = 2$. The system exhibits two distinct behavioral regimes based on $\overline{\Gamma}_0$ values. For $\overline{\Gamma}_0 < 0.73$ or $\overline{\Gamma}_0 > 1.83$, the system remains in static mode. For too small interfacial strength, the LCE fiber requires minimal or no contraction to transition from the adhesion-on to adhesion-off state, after which insufficient interfacial adhesion prevents recovery to the adhesion-on state. Conversely, for too large interfacial strength, even with the maximum photothermal contraction of the LCE fiber, the detachment force remains below the critical detachment threshold, thus maintaining a permanent adhesion-on state. When $0.73 \le \overline{\Gamma}_0 \le 1.83$, the system demonstrates self-adhesion behavior with a monotonically increasing period as $\overline{\Gamma}_0$ increases. This trend results from enhanced interfacial adhesion requiring greater photothermal contraction to generate sufficient detachment force for state transition, thereby prolonging both the transition duration and overall self-adhesion cycle period. Notably, the effect of interface toughness $\overline{G}_c$ on self-adhesion period follows similar trends to $\overline{\Gamma}_0$, as both parameters reflect interfacial adhesion strength, as shown in Figure 9b, where $10.73 \le \overline{\Gamma}_0 \le 1.83$. the system demonstrates self-adhesion behavior with a monotonically increasing period as $\overline{\Gamma}_0$ increases for $0.5 \le \overline{G}_c \le 0.68$.

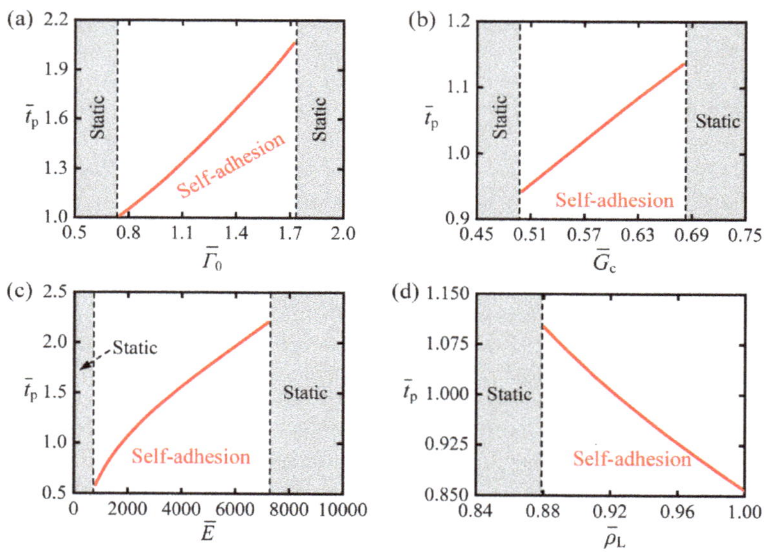

Figure 9. Parametric dependence of self-adhesion period $\bar{t}_p$ on material characteristics: (**a**) interfacial strength $\overline{\Gamma}_0$, (**b**) interface toughness $\overline{G}_c$, (**c**) bending stiffness $\overline{E}$, and (**d**) buoyancy coefficient $\bar{\rho}_L$. Analysis reveals $\bar{t}_p$ monotonically elevates with increasing $\overline{\Gamma}_0$, $\bar{\delta}_0$, and $\overline{E}$, while exhibiting inverse proportionality to $\bar{\rho}_L$.

Figure 9c illustrates the variation in self-adhesion period $\bar{t}_p$ under different bending stiffness $\overline{E}$ with fixed parameters: $\overline{\Gamma}_0 = 1.2$, $\overline{G}_c = 0.6$, $\bar{\rho}_L = 0.9$, $\overline{C} = 0.3$, $\overline{L}_0 = 20$, $\overline{L} = 5$ and $\bar{b} = 2$. The system exhibits two distinct regimes: a static mode when $\overline{E} < 650$ or $\overline{E} > 7333$, and a self-adhesion mode within the range $650 \le \overline{E} \le 7333$. In the self-adhesion mode, the self-adhesion period $\bar{t}_p$ increases monotonically as $\overline{E}$ increases. This behavior can be explained through the interfacial adhesion mechanics: The critical detachment force $\overline{F}_{on}$

increases with $\overline{E}$, requiring greater critical contraction ε_{on} for the adhesion-on to adhesion-off transition. Consequently, the LCE fiber needs more time to reduce the contraction strain from ε_{on} to the critical value ε_{off} for the reverse transition. These combined effects result in the observed prolongation of the self-adhesion period with increasing $\overline{E}$.

Figure 9d demonstrates the dependence of the self-adhesion period $\overline{t}_{\text{p}}$ on the buoyancy coefficient $\overline{\rho}_{\text{L}}$ under fixed parameters: $\overline{\Gamma}_0 = 1.2$, $\overline{G}_c = 0.6$, $\overline{E} = 1950$, $\overline{C} = 0.3$, $\overline{L}_0 = 20$, $\overline{L} = 5$ and $\overline{b} = 2$. The system exhibits three distinct behavioral regimes based on $\overline{\rho}_{\text{L}}$ values. For $\overline{\rho}_{\text{L}} < 0.88$, the system remains in static mode. For too small $\overline{\rho}_{\text{L}}$, the detachment force in the adhesion-off state remains above the critical attachment force $\overline{F}_{\text{on}}$, inhibiting the transition back to adhesion-on state. When $\overline{\rho}_{\text{L}} \geq 0.88$, the system exhibits self-adhesion behavior with a monotonically decreasing period as $\overline{\rho}_{\text{L}}$ increases. This trend arises because larger $\overline{\rho}_{\text{L}}$ values amplify buoyancy variations during the weight's immersion depth changes, thereby reducing both the heating and cooling durations required for the LCE fiber to complete one self-adhesion cycle.

5.2. Regulation of the Self-Adhesion Period by Geometric Parameters

Figure 10 provides a systematic analysis of how the self-adhesion period $\overline{t}_{\text{p}}$ depends on geometric characteristics: photothermal contraction coefficient $\overline{C}$, LCE fiber's initial length $\overline{L}_0$, weight's length $\overline{L}$ and baffle distance $\overline{b}$. Figure 10a presents the relationship between the self-adhesion period $\overline{t}_{\text{p}}$ and photothermal contraction coefficient $\overline{C}$ under fixed parameters: $\overline{\Gamma}_0 = 1.2$, $\overline{G}_c = 0.6$, $\overline{E} = 1950$, $\overline{\rho}_{\text{L}} = 0.9$, $\overline{L}_0 = 20$, $\overline{L} = 5$ and $\overline{b} = 2$. The system exhibits two distinct behavioral regimes based on the photothermal contraction coefficient values $\overline{C}$. For $\overline{C} < 0.185$, the system remains in static mode. This occurs because, for too small $\overline{C}$, even with the maximum photothermal contraction of the LCE fiber, the detachment force remains below the critical detachment threshold, maintaining a permanent adhesion-on state. When $\overline{C} \geq 0.185$, the system exhibits self-adhesion behavior with a period $\overline{t}_{\text{p}}$ that monotonically decreases as the contraction coefficient $\overline{C}$ increases. This trend is due to larger photothermal contraction, meaning the LCE fiber can reach the critical contraction threshold ε_{on} more quickly, reducing the time spent in the illuminated region. The recovery time in the dark zone, governed by the transition from the critical contraction threshold ε_{on} to ε_{off}, is independent of the contraction coefficient. Therefore, the self-adhesion period $\overline{t}_{\text{p}}$ decreases monotonically with an increase in the contraction coefficient $\overline{C}$. It is noteworthy that the initial length $\overline{L}_0$ of the LCE fiber influences the fiber's contraction and recovery in a manner similar to the photothermal contraction coefficient. As a result, the effect of $\overline{L}_0$ on $\overline{t}_{\text{p}}$ follows the same trend as $\overline{C}$, as shown in Figure 10b, where the critical initial length that triggers the phase transition between the static mode and the self-adhesion mode is approximately.

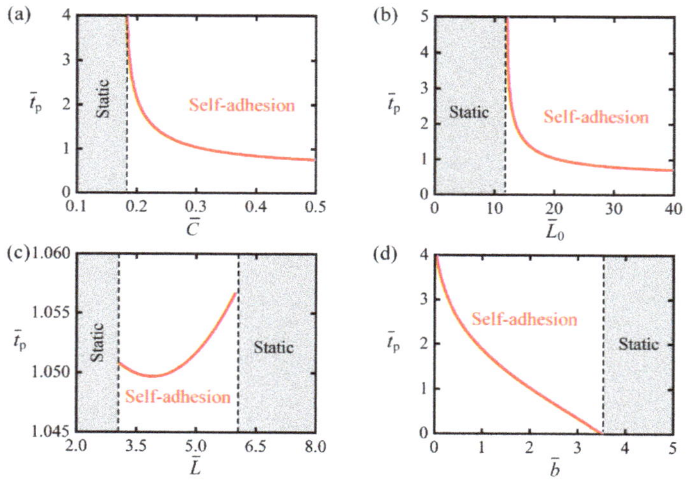

Figure 10. Parametric dependence of self-adhesion period $\bar{t}_p$ on geometric parameters: (**a**) photothermal contraction coefficient $\bar{C}$, (**b**) LCE fiber's initial length $\bar{L}_0$, (**c**) weight's length $\bar{L}$, and (**d**) baffle distance $\bar{b}$. Analysis demonstrates a monotonic decrease in $\bar{t}_p$ with increasing $\bar{C}$, $\bar{L}_0$, and $\bar{b}$, while it decreases first and then increases as $\bar{L}$ increases.

Figure 10c illustrates the variation in the self-adhesion period $\bar{t}_p$ with respect to the weight length $\bar{L}$, while keeping the parameters $\bar{\Gamma}_0 = 1.2$, $\bar{G}_c = 0.6$, $\bar{\rho}_L = 0.9$, $\bar{C} = 0.3$, $\bar{L}_0 = 20$, $\bar{E} = 1950$ and $\bar{b} = 2$ fixed. The system exhibits two distinct regimes: a static mode when $\bar{L} < 3.1$ or $\bar{L} > 6$, and a self-adhesion mode within the range $3.1 \leq \bar{L} \leq 6$. In the self-adhesion mode, the self-adhesion period $\bar{t}_p$ decreases first and then increases as $\bar{L}$ increases. This is because, as $\bar{L}$ increases, LCE fiber requires less time $\bar{t}_{on}$ to complete the desired contraction under illumination but more time $\bar{t}_{off}$ to restore contraction in the dark state. Since the self-adhesion period is the sum of durations $\bar{t}_{on}$ and $\bar{t}_{off}$, this results in non-monotonic changes with increasing $\bar{L}$.

Figure 10d shows how the self-adhesion period $\bar{t}_p$ varies with the baffle distance $\bar{b}$ under fixed parameters: $\bar{\Gamma}_0 = 1.2$, $\bar{G}_c = 0.6$, $\bar{E} = 1950$, $\bar{\rho}_L = 0.9$, $\bar{C} = 0.3$, $\bar{L}_0 = 20$ and $\bar{L} = 5$. The system exhibits two distinct regimes depending on the baffle distance $\bar{b}$ values. The results indicate that in scenarios with $b > 3.53$, the system remains in static mode. This is because, for excessively large $\bar{b}$ values, when the system transitions from the adhesion-on state to the adhesion-off state, the detachment force reaches the attachment threshold and immediately switches back to the adhesion-on state. As a result, the LCE is unable to cool down and absorb light energy again, which prevents the system from maintaining periodic motion. When $b \leq 3.53$, the system shows self-adhesion behavior, with the period $\bar{t}_p$ decreasing monotonically as the baffle distance $\bar{b}$ increases. This behavior occurs because larger baffle distances cause a further reduction in the detachment force during the transition from adhesion-on to adhesion-off, which in turn leads to shorter cooling times for the LCE fibers. Consequently, the system can switch more rapidly back to the adhesion-on state, thereby reducing the self-adhesion period.

6. Conclusions

In nature, the tendrils of climbing plants can detach temporarily under external forces and reattach when the force diminishes. Inspired by this dynamic adhesion-detachment mechanism, we introduce a novel light-powered self-adhesion oscillator, comprising an elastic strip–substrate system and a weight suspended by a photo-responsive LCE fiber. By integrating a nonlinear beam deformation model with Dugdale's cohesive law, we develop a dynamic framework to model the self-adhesion behavior of the elastic strip. Quasi-static analysis identifies two distinct operational modes: static and self-adhesion. With continuous light exposure, the contraction of the LCE fiber increases the detachment force on the strip, triggering a rapid transition from the adhesion-on to adhesion-off state. In the adhesion-off state, the fiber's recovery reduces the detachment force, swiftly returning the system to the adhesion-on state.

Furthermore, the critical conditions for initiating self-adhesion and controlling the strategy of the oscillation period are explicitly derived. The self-adhesion behavior is governed by several essential parameters, including the interfacial strength $\overline{\Gamma}_0$, interface toughness $\overline{G}_c$, bending stiffness $\overline{E}$, buoyancy coefficient $\overline{\rho}_{\mathrm{L}}$, the contraction coefficient $\overline{C}$, initial length $\overline{L}_0$, weight's length $\overline{L}$, and baffle distance $\overline{b}$. Parameter analysis indicates that the self-adhesion period $\overline{t}_{\mathrm{p}}$ increases monotonically with $\overline{\Gamma}_0$, $\overline{G}_c$, and $\overline{E}$, while it decreases with $\overline{\rho}_{\mathrm{L}}$, $\overline{C}$, $\overline{L}_0$, and $\overline{b}$; additionally, $\overline{t}_{\mathrm{p}}$ decreases first and then increases as $\overline{L}$ increases. Notably, in real-world settings, unavoidable factors—including the elastic deformation of LCE fibers, boundary effects of baffles on strip delamination, and damping of heavy objects in liquids—lead to quantitative (rather than qualitative) discrepancies between theoretical calculations and real-world results.

The self-adhesion system offers advantages such as well-defined reversible motion trajectories, precise control over the performance of the self-adhesion oscillator and structural simplicity. To advance this research, the next stage should focus on experimentally validating the self-adhesion phenomenon and exploring practical applications. However, several limitations currently hinder system optimization and targeted deployment: adhesive fatigue between the strip and substrate, the slow thermal relaxation rate of LCE fiber, and low energy conversion efficiency of the system. Despite these challenges, we anticipate that this work will lay foundational insights for future applications, such as self-healing adhesives, search and rescue operations, and military technologies.

Author Contributions: Conceptualization, D.G.; Methodology, D.G.; Validation, S.W.; Data curation, Y.H.; Writing—original draft, S.W.; Writing—review and editing, D.G.; Supervision, D.G. All authors have read and agreed to the published version of the manuscript.

Funding: This research was funded by Anhui Provincial Natural Science Foundation (2208085Y01), Anhui Provincial Natural Science Foundation (2008085QA23), National Natural Science Foundation of China (12172001) and University Natural Science Research Project of Anhui Province (KJ2020A0449).

Data Availability Statement: No new data were created or analyzed in this study.

Acknowledgments: The authors acknowledge the financial support from Anhui Provincial Natural Science Foundation.

Conflicts of Interest: The authors declare no conflicts of interest.

References

1. Li, J.J.; Mou, L.L.; Liu, Z.F.; Zhou, X.; Chen, Y.S. Oscillating light engine realized by photothermal solvent evaporation. *Nat. Commun.* **2022**, *13*, 5621. [CrossRef]
2. Alipanah, Z.; Zakerhamidi, M.S.; Ranjkesh, A. Light-fueled self-oscillation of liquid crystal polymer network: Effect of photostabilizers. *J. Appl. Polym. Sci.* **2024**, *141*, e54923. [CrossRef]
3. Wang, J.C.; Song, T.F.; Zhang, Y.H.; Liu, J.G.; Yu, M.M.; Yu, H.F. Light-driven autonomous self-oscillation of a liquid-crystalline polymer bimorph actuator. *J. Mater. Chem. C* **2021**, *9*, 12573–12580. [CrossRef]
4. Zhao, J.; Zhang, Z.R.; Sun, X.D.; Zuo, W.; Li, K. Multi-modal self-sustained motions of a silicone oil paper disc on a surface driven by hot steam. *Chaos Soliton Fract.* **2025**, *191*, 115898. [CrossRef]
5. Yan, Z.; Wang, Y.L.; Bian, M.X.; Wang, M.; Zhou, X.; Yin, S.G.; Qin, W.J.; Liu, Z.F. Transformable thin-film robots capable of crawling, rolling, and oscillation. *Appl. Mater. Today* **2022**, *28*, 101514. [CrossRef]

6. Li, Z.W.; Myung, N.V.; Yin, Y.D. Light-powered soft steam engines for self-adaptive oscillation and biomimetic swimming. *Sci. Rob.* **2021**, *6*, eabi4523. [CrossRef]
7. Lv, X.D.; Wang, W.Z.; Clancy, A.J.; Yu, H.F. High-speed, heavy-load, and direction-controllable photothermal pneumatic floating robot. *ACS Appl. Mater. Interfaces* **2021**, *13*, 23030–23037. [CrossRef]
8. Guo, K.X.; Yang, X.H.; Zhou, C.; Li, C. Self-regulated reversal deformation and locomotion of structurally homogenous hydrogels subjected to constant light illumination. *Nat. Commun.* **2024**, *15*, 1694. [CrossRef]
9. Fu, L.; Zhao, W.Q.; Ma, J.Y.; Yang, M.Y.; Liu, X.M.; Zhang, L.; Chen, Y. A humidity-powered soft robot with fast rolling locomotion. *Research* **2022**, *2022*, 9832901. [CrossRef]
10. Wang, Q.; Wu, Z.; Li, J.; Guo, J.B.; Yin, M.Z. Spontaneous and continuous actuators driven by fluctuations in ambient humidity for energy-harvesting applications. *ACS Appl. Mater. Interfaces* **2022**, *14*, 38972–38980. [CrossRef]
11. Ge, D.L.; Bao, B.; Chen, H.M.; Li, K. A liquid crystal elastomer-based generator using light-powered self-oscillations. *Chaos Soliton Fract.* **2025**, *199*, 116690. [CrossRef]
12. Chang, L.F.; Wang, D.P.; Huang, Z.S.; Wang, C.F.; Torop, J.; Li, B.; Wang, Y.J.; Hu, Y.; Aabloo, A. A versatile ionomer-based soft actuator with multi-stimulus responses, self-sustainable locomotion, and photoelectric conversion. *Adv. Funct. Mater.* **2023**, *33*, 2212341. [CrossRef]
13. Yang, L.L.; Chang, L.F.; Hu, Y.; Huang, M.J.; Ji, Q.X.; Lu, P.; Liu, J.Q.; Chen, W.; Wu, Y.C. An autonomous soft actuator with light-driven self-sustained wavelike oscillation for phototactic self-locomotion and power generation. *Adv. Funct. Mater.* **2020**, *30*, 1908842. [CrossRef]
14. Zhai, F.; Feng, Y.Y.; Li, Z.Y.; Xie, Y.X.; Ge, J.; Wang, H.; Qiu, W.; Feng, W. 4D-printed untethered self-propelling soft robot with tactile perception: Rolling, racing, and exploring. *Matter* **2021**, *4*, 3313–3326. [CrossRef]
15. Liu, J.Q.; Xu, L.L.; Ji, Q.X.; Chang, L.F.; Hu, Y.; Peng, Q.Y.; He, X.D. A MXene-based light-driven actuator and motor with self-sustained oscillation for versatile applications. *Adv. Funct. Mater.* **2024**, *34*, 2310955. [CrossRef]
16. Preston, D.J.; Rothemund, P.; Jiang, H.J.; Nemitz, M.P.; Rawson, J.; Suo, Z.G.; Whitesides, G.M. Digital logic for soft devices. *Proc. Nat. Acad. Sci. USA* **2019**, *116*, 7750–7759. [CrossRef] [PubMed]
17. Helou, C.E.; Hyatt, L.P.; Buskohl, P.R.; Harne, R.L. Intelligent electroactive material systems with self-adaptive mechanical memory and sequential logic. *Proc. Nat. Acad. Sci. USA* **2024**, *121*, e2317340121. [CrossRef] [PubMed]
18. Ge, F.J.; Zhao, Y. A new function for thermal phase transition-based polymer actuators: Autonomous motion on a surface of constant temperature. *Chem. Sci.* **2017**, *8*, 6307–6312. [CrossRef]
19. Zhu, Q.L.; Liu, W.X.; Khoruzhenko, O.; Breu, J.; Bai, H.Y.; Hong, W.; Zheng, Q.; Wu, Z.L. Animating hydrogel knotbots with topology-invoked self-regulation. *Nat. Commun.* **2024**, *14*, 300. [CrossRef]
20. Zhu, Q.L.; Liu, W.X.; Khoruzhenko, O.; Breu, J.; Bai, H.Y.; Hong, W.; Zheng, Q.; Wu, Z.L. Closed twisted hydrogel ribbons with self-sustained motions under static light irradiation. *Adv. Mater.* **2024**, *36*, 2314152. [CrossRef]
21. Bai, C.; Kang, J.; Wang, Y.Q. Kirigami-Inspired Light-Responsive Conical Spiral Actuators with Large Contraction Ratio Using Liquid Crystal Elastomer Fiber. *ACS Appl. Mater.* **2025**, *17*, 14488–14498. [CrossRef] [PubMed]
22. Bai, C.; Kang, J.; Wang, Y.Q. Light-induced wrinkling in annulus anisotropic liquid crystal elastomer films. *Phys. Rev. E* **2025**, *111*, 015421. [CrossRef]
23. Yang, H.X.; Yin, X.F.; Zhang, C.; Chen, B.H.; Sun, P.; Xu, Y. Weaving liquid crystal elastomer fiber actuators for multifunctional soft robotics. *Sci. Adv.* **2025**, *11*, eads3058. [CrossRef]
24. Wang, L.Q.; Wei, Z.X.; Xu, Z.T.; Yu, Q.M.; Wu, Z.L.; Wang, Z.J.; Qian, J.; Xiao, R. Shape morphing of 3D printed liquid crystal elastomer structures with precuts. *ACS Appl. Polym. Mater.* **2023**, *5*, 7477–7484. [CrossRef]
25. Yang, H.X.; Zhang, C.; Chen, B.H.; Wang, Z.J.; Xu, Y.; Xiao, R. Bioinspired design of stimuli-responsive artificial muscles with multiple actuation modes. *Smart Mater. Struct.* **2023**, *32*, 085023. [CrossRef]
26. Kang, W.D.; Cheng, Q.; Liu, C.Y.; Wang, Z.J.; Li, D.F.; Liang, X.D. A constitutive model of monodomain liquid crystal elastomers with the thermal-mechanical-nematic order coupling. *J. Mech. Phys. Solids* **2025**, *196*, 105995. [CrossRef]
27. Wang, Y.; Yin, R.; Jin, L.S.; Liu, M.Z.; Gao, Y.H.; Raney, J.; Yang, S. 3D-printed photoresponsive liquid crystal elastomer composites for free-form actuation. *Adv. Funct. Mater.* **2023**, *33*, 2210614. [CrossRef]
28. Zheng, R.; Ma, L.L.; Feng, W.; Pan, J.T.; Wang, Z.Y.; Chen, Z.X.; Zhang, Y.H.; Li, C.Y.; Chen, P.; Bisoyi, H.K.; et al. Autonomous self-sustained liquid crystal actuators enabling active photonic applications. *Adv. Funct. Mater.* **2023**, *33*, 2301142. [CrossRef]
29. Ren, L.Q.; He, Y.L.; Wang, B.F.; Xu, J.Y.; Wu, Q.; Wang, Z.G.; Li, W.X.; Ren, L.; Zhou, X.L.; Liu, Q.P.; et al. 4D printed self-sustained soft crawling machines fueled by constant thermal field. *Adv. Funct. Mater.* **2024**, *34*, 2400161. [CrossRef]
30. Mao, T.H.; Liu, Z.Y.; Guo, X.X.; Wang, Z.F.; Liu, J.J.; Wang, T.; Geng, S.B.; Chen, Y.; Cheng, P.; Zhang, Z.J. Engineering covalent organic frameworks with polyethylene glycol as self-sustained humidity-responsive actuators. *Angew. Chem.* **2023**, *135*, e202216318. [CrossRef]
31. Wu, H.Y.; Ge, D.L.; Qiu, Y.L.; Li, K.; Xu, P.B. Mechanics of light-fueled bidirectional self-rolling in a liquid crystal elastomer rod on a track. *Chaos Solitons Fractals* **2025**, *191*, 115901. [CrossRef]

32. Wu, H.; Lou, J.; Dai, Y.; Zhang, B.; Li, K. Multi-scale analysis of the self-vibration of a liquid crystal elastomer fiber-spring system exposed to constant-gradient light. *J. Zhejiang Univ. Sci. A* **2025**, *26*, 652–665. [CrossRef]
33. Zhao, Y.S.; Liu, Z.X.; Shi, P.J.; Chen, C.; Alsaid, Y.; Yan, Y.C.; He, X.M. Antagonistic-contracting high-power photo-oscillators for multifunctional actuations. *Nat. Mater.* **2025**, *24*, 116–124. [CrossRef] [PubMed]
34. Xiang, F.; Lou, J.; Wang, J.; Chuang, K.C.; Wu, H.M.; Huang, Z.L. A self-excited bistable oscillator with a light-powered liquid crystal elastomer. *Int. J. Mech. Sci.* **2024**, *271*, 109124.
35. Ge, D.L.; Bao, W.; Li, K.; Liang, H.Y. Self-oscillation-driven locomotion in a liquid crystal elastomer-based robot under constant illumination. *Commun. Nonlinear Sci. Numer. Simul.* **2025**, *145*, 108706. [CrossRef]
36. Hu, Z.M.; Li, Y.L.; Lv, J.A. Phototunable self-oscillating system driven by a self-winding fifiber actuator. *Nat. Commun.* **2021**, *12*, 3211. [CrossRef] [PubMed]
37. Zhou, N.Z.; Wang, M.; Huang, S.; Liu, Z.Y.; Yang, H. Multimodal self-sustainable autonomous locomotions of light-driven seifert ribbon actuators based on liquid crystal elastomers. *Angew. Chem. Int. Ed.* **2023**, *62*, e202304081.
38. Sun, X.; Zhou, K.; Xu, P.B. Chaotic self-beating of left ventricle modeled by liquid crystal elastomer. *Thin Walled Struct.* **2024**, *205*, 112540. [CrossRef]
39. Zeng, H.; Lahikainen, M.; Liu, L.; Ahmed, Z.; Wani, O.M.; Wang, M.; Yang, H.; Priimagi, A. Light-fuelled freestyle self-oscillators. *Nat. Commun.* **2019**, *10*, 5057. [CrossRef]
40. Huang, C.Y.; Yang, F.; Li, K.; Dai, Y.T.; Yu, Y. Modeling and analysis of self-sustaining oscillation behavior of liquid crystal elastomer fiber/baffle system under stable full-field illumination. *Chaos Solitons Fractals* **2025**, *194*, 116259. [CrossRef]
41. Xu, P.B.; Zhou, K.; Sun, X.; Li, K. Self-sustainable chaotic dynamics of a liquid crystal elastomer pendulum in radial linear temperature fields. *Commun. Nonlinear Sci. Numer. Simul.* **2025**, *152*, 109338. [CrossRef]
42. Sun, X.; Zhou, K.; Chen, Y.Q.; Gao, J.F.; Xu, P.B. Self-oscillation chaotic motion of a liquid crystal elastomer pendulum under gradient-stabilized illumination. *Chaos Soliton Fract.* **2025**, *193*, 116128. [CrossRef]
43. Zhao, J.; Wang, X.C.; Qiu, Y.L.; Chen, H.B.; Li, K. Light-powered self-swing of a bistable magnetic pendulum utilizing liquid crystal elastomer fibers. *Chaos Solitons Fractals* **2025**, *198*, 116565. [CrossRef]
44. Bai, C.P.; Kang, J.T.; Wang, Y.Q. Light-induced motion of three-dimensional pendulum with liquid crystal elastomeric fiber. *Int. J. Mech. Sci.* **2024**, *266*, 108911. [CrossRef]
45. Jayoti, D.; Peeketi, A.R.; Kumbhar, P.Y.; Swaminathan, N.; Annabattula, R.K. Geometry controlled oscillations in liquid crystal polymer films triggered by thermal feedback. *ACS Appl. Mater.* **2023**, *15*, 18362–18371. [CrossRef]
46. Yu, Y.; Huang, C.Y.; Liu, C.Y.; Wang, Z.J.; Ma, H.H.; Xu, P.B. Heat-driven self-wobbling of a liquid crystal elastomer double-wheel linkage. *Thin Wall Struct.* **2025**, *217*, 113829. [CrossRef]
47. Yu, Y.; Dai, Z.; Li, T.Y.; Wang, Z.J.; Ma, H.H.; Li, K. Self-tapping of a liquid crystal elastomer thin beam above a hot plate. *Chaos Soliton Fract.* **2025**, *199*, 116904. [CrossRef]
48. Dai, Y.T.; Jiang, X.Y.; Wang, K.X.; Li, K. A phototunable self-oscillatory bistable seesaw via liquid crystal elastomer fibers. *Chaos Soliton Fract.* **2025**, *200*, 117041. [CrossRef]
49. Zhang, Z.Z.; Qiu, Y.L.; Li, K. Light-fueled self-ejecting liquid crystal elastomer launcher inspired by lizard tail autotomy. *Chaos Solitons Fractals* **2025**, *194*, 116256. [CrossRef]
50. Qiu, Y.L.; Li, K. Light-powered self-striking liquid crystal elastomer hammers inspired by mantis shrimp. *Commun. Nonlinear Sci. Numer. Simul.* **2025**, *146*, 108802. [CrossRef]
51. Vantomme, G.; Elands, L.C.M.; Gelebart, A.H.; Meijer, E.W.; Pogromsky, A.Y.; Nijmeijer, H.; Broer, D.J. Coupled liquid crystalline oscillators in Huygens' synchrony. *Nat. Mater.* **2021**, *20*, 1702–1706. [CrossRef]
52. Qi, F.J.; Li, Y.B.; Hong, Y.Y.; Zhao, Y.; Qing, H.T.; Yin, J. Defected twisted ring topology for autonomous periodic flip-spin-orbit soft robot. *Proc. Natl. Acad. Sci. USA* **2024**, *121*, e2312680121. [CrossRef] [PubMed]
53. Zhao, Y.; Hong, Y.Y.; Qi, F.J.; Chi, Y.D.; Su, H.; Yin, J. Self-sustained snapping drives autonomous dancing and motion in free-standing wavy rings. *Adv. Mater.* **2023**, *35*, 2207372. [CrossRef] [PubMed]
54. Zhou, X.R.; Chen, G.C.; Jin, B.J.; Feng, H.J.; Chen, Z.K.; Fang, M.Q.; Yang, B.; Xiao, R.; Xie, T.; Zheng, N. Multimodal autonomous locomotion of liquid crystal elastomer soft robot. *Adv. Sci.* **2024**, *11*, 2402358. [CrossRef]
55. Kim, D.S.; Lee, Y.J.; Kim, Y.B.; Wang, Y.C.; Yang, S. Autonomous, untethered gait-like synchronization of lobed loops made from liquid crystal elastomer fibers via spontaneous snap-through. *Sci. Adv.* **2023**, *9*, eadh5107. [CrossRef]
56. Pilz da Cunha, M.; Peeketi, A.R.; Ramgopal, A.; Annabattula, P.B.K.; Schenning, P.A.P.H.J. Light-driven continual oscillatory rocking of a polymer film. *ChemistryOpen* **2020**, *9*, 1149–1152. [CrossRef] [PubMed]
57. Lv, X.D.; Yu, M.M.; Wang, W.Z.; Yu, H.F. Photothermal pneumatic wheel with high loadbearing capacity. *Compos. Commun.* **2021**, *24*, 100651. [CrossRef]
58. Li, J.J.; Zhang, G.H.; Cui, Z.P.; Bao, L.L.; Xia, Z.G.; Liu, Z.F.; Zhou, X. High performance and multifunction moisture-driven Yin-Yang-interface actuators derived from polyacrylamide hydrogel. *Small* **2023**, *19*, 2303228. [CrossRef]

59. Ge, Y.H.; Cao, R.; Ye, S.J.; Chen, Z.; Zhu, Z.F.; Tu, Y.F.; Ge, D.T.; Yang, X.M. Bio-inspired homogeneous graphene oxide actuator driven by moisture gradients. *Chem. Commun.* **2018**, *54*, 3126–3129. [CrossRef]
60. Che, X.P.; Wang, T.; Zhang, B.L.; Zhai, Z.Z.; Chen, Y.J.; Pei, D.F.; Ge, A.L.; Li, M.J.; Li, C.X. Two-dimensionally nano-capsulating liquid metal for self-sintering and self-oscillating bimorph composites with persistent energy-harvest property. *Adv. Funct. Mater.* **2024**, *34*, 2307830. [CrossRef]
61. Wei, S.Z.; Ghosh, T.K. Moisture-driven cellulose actuators with directional motion and programmable shapes. *Adv. Intell. Syst.* **2024**, *6*, 2300638. [CrossRef]
62. Zhang, H.; Zeng, H.; Eklund, A.; Guo, H.S.; Priimagi Ikkala, O. Feedback-controlled hydrogels with homeostatic oscillations and dissipative signal transduction. *Nat. Nano Technol.* **2022**, *17*, 1303–1310. [CrossRef]
63. Baumann, A.; Sánchez-Ferrer, A.; Jacomine, L.; Martinoty, P.; Le Houerou, V.; Ziebert, F.; Kulić, I.M. Motorizing fibres with geometric zero-energy modes. *Nat. Mater.* **2018**, *17*, 523–527. [CrossRef]
64. Rothemund, P.; Ainla, A.; Belding, L.; Preston, D.J.; Kurihara, S.; Suo, Z.G.; Whitesides, G.M. A soft, bistable valve for autonomous control of soft actuators. *Sci. Rob.* **2018**, *3*, eaar7986. [CrossRef]
65. Zhang, Z.Z.; Jiang, X.Y.; Qiu, Y.L.; Li, K. Stepwise self-oscillation of a photo-oscillator via time delay. *Int. J. Mech. Sci.* **2025**, *288*, 110046. [CrossRef]
66. Hua, M.T.; Kim, C.; Du, Y.J.; Wu, D.; Bai, R.B.; He, X.M. Swaying gel: Chemo-mechanical self-oscillation based on dynamic buckling. *Matter* **2021**, *4*, 1029–1041. [CrossRef]
67. Ge, D.L.; Li, K. Pulsating self-snapping of a liquid crystal elastomer bilayer spherical shell under steady illumination. *Int. J. Mech. Sci.* **2022**, *233*, 107646. [CrossRef]
68. Frederike, K.; Stefanie, S.; Holger, F.B.; Svenja, K.; Marc, T.; Thomas, S. Biomechanics of tendrils and adhesive pads of the climbing passion flower Passiflora discophora. *J. Exp. Bot.* **2022**, *73*, 1190–1203.
69. Burris, J.N.; Lenaghan, S.C.; Stewart, C.N., Jr. Climbing plants: Attachment adaptations and bioinspired innovations. *Plant Cell Rep.* **2018**, *37*, 565–574. [CrossRef]
70. Bucolo, M.; Buscarino, A.; Famoso, C.; Fortuna, L.; Gagliano, S. Imperfections in integrated devices allow the emergence of unexpected strange attractors in electronic circuits. *IEEE Access* **2021**, *9*, 29573–29583. [CrossRef]
71. Wiggins, S. *Nonlinear Differential Equations and Dynamical Systems*; Springer: Berlin/Heidelberg, Germany, 1990.
72. Arnold, V.I. *Geometrical Methods in the Theory of Ordinary Differential Equations*; Springer: Berlin/Heidelberg, Germany, 1983.
73. Buyadzhi, V.V.; Glushkov, A.V.; Khetselius, O.Y.; Bunyakova, Y.Y.; Florko, T.A.; Agayar, E.V.; Solyanikova, E.P. An effective chaos-geometric computational approach to analysis and prediction of evolutionary dynamics of the environmental systems: Atmospheric pollution dynamics. *J. Phys.* **2017**, *905*, 012036. [CrossRef]
74. Glushkov, A.V.; Khetselius, O.Y.; Brusentseva, S.V.; Duborez, A.V. Modeling chaotic dynamics of complex systems with using chaos theory, geometric attractors, and quantum neural networks. *Proc. Int. Geom. Cent.* **2014**, *7*, 87–94.
75. Pecora, L.M.; Carroll, T.L. Synchronization in chaotic systems. *Phys. Rev. Lett.* **1990**, *64*, 821. [CrossRef]
76. Zarei, A.; Tavakoli, S. Design and control of a multi-wing dissipative chaotic system. *Int. J. Dynam. Control* **2018**, *6*, 140–153. [CrossRef]
77. Hakeem, E.; Jawad, S.; Ali, A.H.; Kallel, M.; Neamah, H.A. How mathematical models might predict desertification from global warming and dust pollutants. *Methodsx* **2025**, *14*, 103259. [CrossRef] [PubMed]
78. Wang, Y.C.; Dang, A.L.; Zhang, Z.F.; Yin, R.; Gao, Y.C.; Feng, L.; Yang, S. Repeatable and reprogrammable shape morphing from photoresponsive gold nanorod/liquid crystal elastomers. *Adv. Mater.* **2020**, *32*, 2004270. [CrossRef]
79. Yin, H.B.; Liang, L.H.; Wei, Y.G.; Peng, Z.L.; Chen, S.H. Determination of the interface properties in an elastic film/substrate system. *Int. J. Solids Struct.* **2020**, *191–192*, 473–485. [CrossRef]
80. Peng, Z.L.; Yin, H.B.; Yao, Y.; Chen, S.H. Effect of thin-film length on the peeling behavior of film-substrate interfaces. *Phys. Rev. E* **2019**, *100*, 032804. [CrossRef] [PubMed]
81. Yin, H.B.; Chen, S.H.; Liang, L.H.; Peng, Z.L.; Wei, Y.G. Quantitative prediction of the whole peeling process of an elastic film on a rigid substrate. *J. Appl. Mech.* **2018**, *85*, 091004. [CrossRef]
82. Zhao, H.; Wei, Y. Determination of interface properties between micron-thick metal film and ceramic substrate using peel test. *Int. J. Fract.* **2007**, *144*, 103–112. [CrossRef]
83. Kendall, K. The shapes of peeling solid films. *J. Adhes.* **1973**, *5*, 105–117. [CrossRef]
84. Williams, J.G.; Hadavinia, H. Analytical solutions for cohesive zone models. *J. Mech. Phys. Solids* **2002**, *50*, 809–825. [CrossRef]
85. Tvergaard, V.; Hutchinson, J.W. The relation between crack growth resistance and fracture process parameters in elastic-plastic solids. *J. Mech. Phys. Solids* **1992**, *40*, 1377–1397. [CrossRef]
86. Yin, H.B.; Peng, Z.L.; Yao, Y.; Chen, S.H.; Gao, H.J. A general solution to the maximum detachment force in thin film peeling. *Int. J. Solids Struct.* **2022**, *242*, 111546. [CrossRef]
87. Kendall, K. Thin-film peeling: The elastic term. *J. Phys. D Appl. Phys.* **1975**, *8*, 1449–1452. [CrossRef]

88. Wei, L.; Yang, Z.Q. The integration of sensing and actuating based on a simple design fiber actuator towards intelligent soft robots. *Adv. Mater. Technol.* **2022**, *7*, 2101260.
89. Xu, Z.; Chen, Y.; Zhu, L.; Ge, Q.; Wu, Z.L.; Qu, S.; Xiao, R. Tailored helix morphing of 3D-printed liquid crystal elastomer bilayers. *Cell Rep. Phys. Sci.* **2025**, *6*, 102835. [CrossRef]
90. Zhu, L.; He, M.; Chen, B.; Qian, J.; Xiao, R. Inflation of a polydomain nematic elastomeric membrane. *J. Mech. Phys. Solids* **2025**, *198*, 106075. [CrossRef]
91. He, Q.G.; Yin, R.; Hua, Y.C.; Jiao, W.J.; Mo, C.Y.; Shu, H.; Raney, J.R. A modular strategy for distributed, embodied control of electronics-free soft robots. *Sci. Adv.* **2023**, *9*, eade9247. [CrossRef]
92. Sun, J.H.; Wang, Y.P.; Liao, W.; Yang, Z.Q. Ultrafast, high-contractile electrothermal-driven liquid crystal elastomer fibers towards artificial muscles. *Small* **2021**, *17*, 2103700. [CrossRef]
93. Poulard, C.; Restagno, F.; Raphael, W.; Léger, L. Mechanical tuning of adhesion through micro-patterning of elastic surfaces. *Soft Matter* **2011**, *7*, 2543–2551. [CrossRef]
94. Peng, Z.L.; Wang, C.; Chen, L.; Chen, S.H. Peeling behavior of a viscoelastic thin-film on a rigid substrate. *Int. J. Solids Struct* **2014**, *51*, 4596–46032008. [CrossRef]
95. Garg, R.; Datla, N.V. Peeling of heterogeneous thin films: Effect of bending stiffness, adhesion energy, and level of heterogeneity. *J. Adhes.* **2019**, *95*, 169–186. [CrossRef]

MDPI AG
Grosspeteranlage 5
4052 Basel
Switzerland
Tel.: +41 61 683 77 34

Mathematics Editorial Office
E-mail: mathematics@mdpi.com
www.mdpi.com/journal/mathematics

www.ingramcontent.com/pod-product-compliance
Lightning Source LLC
Chambersburg PA
CBHW061601210926
51850CB00009B/2179
9783725875184